The Legacy of
Robert Higgs

Advanced Studies in Political Economy

Series Editors: Virgil Henry Storr
and Stefanie Haeffele

The Advanced Studies in Political Economy series consists of republished as well as newly commissioned work that seeks to understand the underpinnings of a free society through the foundations of the Austrian, Virginia, and Bloomington schools of political economy. Through this series, the Mercatus Center at George Mason University aims to further the exploration of and discussion on the dynamics of social change by making this research available to students and scholars.

Nona Martin Storr, Emily Chamlee-Wright, and Virgil Henry Storr,
  How We Came Back: Voices from Post-Katrina New Orleans
Don Lavoie, *Rivalry and Central Planning: The Socialist Calculation Debate Reconsidered*
Don Lavoie, *National Economic Planning: What Is Left?*
Peter J. Boettke, Stefanie Haeffele, and Virgil Henry Storr, eds.,
  Mainline Economics: Six Nobel Lectures in the Tradition of Adam Smith
Matthew D. Mitchell and Peter J. Boettke, *Applied Mainline Economics: Bridging the Gap between Theory and Public Policy*
Jack High, ed., *Humane Economics: Essays in Honor of Don Lavoie*
Edward Stringham, ed., *Anarchy, State and Public Choice*
Peter J. Boettke and David L. Prychitko, eds., *The Market Process: Essays in Contemporary Austrian Economics*
Richard E. Wagner, *To Promote the General Welfare: Market Processes vs. Political Transfers*
Donald J. Boudreaux and Roger Meiners, eds., *The Legacy of Bruce Yandle*
Peter J. Boettke and Alain Marciano, eds., *The Soul of Classical Political Economy: James M. Buchanan from the Archives*
Peter J. Boettke, *The Struggle for a Better World*
Peter J. Boettke and Christopher J. Coyne, eds., *The Legacy of Richard E. Wagner*
Christopher J. Coyne, ed., *The Legacy of Robert Higgs*

The Legacy of Robert Higgs

Edited by
Christopher J. Coyne

MERCATUS CENTER
George Mason University
Arlington, Virginia

About the Mercatus Center

The Mercatus Center at George Mason University is the world's premier university source for market-oriented ideas—bridging the gap between academic ideas and real-world problems.

A university-based research center, the Mercatus Center advances knowledge about how markets work to improve people's lives by training graduate students, conducting research, and applying economics to offer solutions to society's most pressing problems.

Our mission is to generate knowledge and understanding of the institutions that affect the freedom to prosper, and to find sustainable solutions that overcome the barriers preventing individuals from living free, prosperous, and peaceful lives.

Founded in 1980, the Mercatus Center is located on George Mason University's Arlington and Fairfax campuses.

© 2024 by the Mercatus Center at George Mason University.

All rights reserved. Printed in the United States of America.

978-1-942951-44-5 (hardcover)
978-1-942951-45-2 (paper)
978-1-942951-46-9 (electronic)

Mercatus Center at George Mason University
3434 Washington Blvd., 4th Floor
Arlington, VA 22201
www.mercatus.org
703-993-4930

Cover design: Jessica Hogenson, Cantelon Design
Editorial and production: Westchester Publishing Services
Library of Congress Cataloging-in-Publication data are available for this publication.

Contents

Figures

Tables

About Robert Higgs

Robert Higgs is a retired senior fellow in political economy at the Independent Institute and founding editor and former at-large editor of *The Independent Review*. He received his PhD in economics from Johns Hopkins University in 1968 and has taught at the University of Washington, Lafayette College, Seattle University, and Prague University of Economics and Business. He has been a visiting scholar at Oxford University and Stanford University, as well as at George Mason University, where he was F. A. Hayek Distinguished Visiting Professor (2015–2016) with the F. A. Hayek Program for Advanced Study in Philosophy, Politics, and Economics at the Mercatus Center at George Mason University. He has also been a fellow at the Hoover Institution and the National Science Foundation.

In addition to more than 100 journal articles and reviews, Higgs is the author of many books including *Crisis and Leviathan*; *Delusions of Power*; *Depression, War, and Cold War*; *Neither Liberty nor Safety*; *Resurgence of the Warfare State*; *Against Leviathan*; *The Transformation of the American Economy, 1865–1914*; and *Competition and Coercion*. He has edited several books, including *Emergence of the Modern Political Economy* and *Arms, Politics, and the Economy*, and co-edited *The Challenge of Liberty* and *Opposing the Crusader State*. His popular articles have appeared in the *Wall Street Journal*, *Los Angeles Times*, *Chicago Tribune*, *San Francisco Examiner*, and *San Francisco Chronicle*; and he has appeared on NPR, NBC, ABC, C-SPAN, CBN, CNBC, and international networks.

His awards include the Premio Juan de Mariana, Alexis de Tocqueville Award, Gary Schlarbaum Award for Lifetime Defense of Liberty, Thomas Szasz Award for Outstanding Contributions to the Cause of Civil Liberties, Lysander Spooner Award for Advancing the Literature of Liberty, Friedrich von Wieser Memorial Prize for Excellence in Economic Education, Murray N. Rothbard Medal of Freedom, and Templeton Honor Rolls Award on Education in a Free Society.

The Legacy of Robert Higgs

Christopher J. Coyne

T his volume honors the academic legacy of Robert (Bob) Higgs, a prolific economist who made numerous scholarly contributions during
his career.[1] The purpose of this introduction is to provide personal and
professional background on Bob and an overview of the chapters that follow.

PERSONAL BIOGRAPHY

Bob Higgs was born on February 1, 1944, in Okemah, Oklahoma, to William Jess
and Doris Geraldine Higgs. His older brother, William Victor Higgs, was born
in 1935. In 1944, Bob's family relocated to Hillsboro, Oregon, so that his father
could work as a ship welder in the Kaiser shipyard in the Portland area (north of
Hillsboro). They remained in Oregon until the end of the war in 1945, when the
Higgs family returned to Oklahoma. In 1951, the Higgs family relocated to a rural
area of California (west of Fresno), and over the following years they lived in, or
near, several California locations, including Madera, Dos Palos, and Firebaugh.
Bob's father and brother found work as tractor drivers and, in the summer of
1958, Bob began his first hourly employment, working as a ranch irrigator.

Writing about his parents' influence on him, Bob noted that

> I didn't need any commandment to honor my father and mother. It never
> occurred to me to do otherwise, in view of the examples they set. My
> father belonged to a generation in which a father generally did not play
> the role of pal to his kids. Although I never doubted that he loved me, he
> occupied a different, somewhat elevated stratum. So, as I matured, I auto-
> matically came to respect him, at the same time that I loved him. I appre-
> ciated that his own understanding of his chief duty in life was to support
> his family, which he invariably did, even during the Great Depression,
> when finding work was a difficult task. He was not the kind of man to go on
> the dole. Indeed, I doubt that he ever gave any thought to that possibility,

I would like to thank Samuel Branthoover, Amy Crockett, Jeremiah Ludwig, and John Temming
for useful comments and suggestions.

even when people all around him were eagerly accepting some sort of relief. (Higgs 2009a)

Writing about his mother, Bob noted, "As I have reflected on my relationship with her, I have come to believe that in an extremely important regard she influenced me in exactly the same way that my dad influenced me—which is to say, she gave me an appreciation of the joy of working, and of doing one's work readily and well, rather than grudgingly and carelessly" (Higgs 2011).

In 1961, at the age of 17, Bob left home and was sworn into the U.S. Coast Guard as a cadet at Alameda, California, before reporting to the U.S. Coast Guard Academy in New London, Connecticut. Although he only remained at the academy for a year, his time there had an important impact on his thinking— an impact that can be seen in his later writings on the nature of the state and its warmaking. Reflecting on his brief time in the Coast Guard Academy in a 2015 interview, Bob noted the following:

> When I was 17, I went to the US Coast Guard Academy in New London, Connecticut and that was a very rigorous place especially in those days. There was constant harassment and physical and psychological pressure being put on people constantly. So the idea was to drive away or break people who couldn't take the pressure. There was a kind of method in the madness.
>
> But one of the things I learned there is that in a situation like that where there are superiors and inferiors in a chain of command, some of the superiors will abuse their power and I think that is an insight that stuck with me from then on for the rest of my life.
>
> You give people power, even petty power, at your peril and there are people who enjoy abusing those who can be abused. I think that sensibility was important to me as my political thinking developed, which happened during the 1960s. I didn't fancy myself a libertarian. If anything, when I was in college, I thought of myself as a new leftist, which wasn't all bad. I was always opposed to the Vietnam War even when most Americans didn't know it was happening.
>
> So that was a big influence on me too because that taught me that the government is capable of routinely committing horrible crimes for years on end for the slightest political motives. (Burrus and Powell 2015, timestamp 1:30–3:13)

After leaving the U.S. Coast Guard Academy, Bob transferred to San Francisco State College, where he graduated in 1965 with a BA in economics, receiving the award for the most outstanding student in economics.

Following his graduation, Bob spent a year in the PhD program at the University of California at Santa Barbara before transferring to Johns Hopkins University in the fall of 1966. He defended his dissertation, "Location Theory and the Growth of Cities in the Western Prairie Region, 1870–1900," in the spring of 1968 under the guidance of H. Louis Stetler III and Edwin S. Mills, the co-chairmen of his dissertation committee. The other members of his committee were George Heberton Evans and Alfred Chandler, the well-known business historian who was a member of Hopkins's history department. Reflecting on his time in graduate school at Johns Hopkins, Bob noted that "I shall always be grateful to the faculty there who took a chance on a young man from a third-rate college and tolerated him so graciously during the time he spent with them" (Higgs 2018). Indeed, his time at Hopkins set the stage for the prolific professional career that would follow.

PROFESSIONAL BIOGRAPHY

Early Career

In the summer of 1968, Bob moved to Seattle, where he began his first academic job as a member of the Department of Economics at the University of Washington. Bob was recruited by future Nobel laureate Douglass North, the chairman of the department of economics, and joined a department that included Yoram Barzel, Steven Cheung, and Donald Gordon as faculty members. This collection of scholars were known for their work in institutional economics, economic history, and transaction-cost economics.

From the earliest days of his career, Bob's scholarly productivity was extremely impressive. In 1971, Bob published his first book, *The Transformation of the American Economy, 1865–1914: An Essay in Interpretation*. The purpose of the book was to provide an accessible exploration of the evolution of the American economy from the end of the Civil War to the beginning of World War I. In his review of the book in the *Journal of Economic History*, William Hartley (1972) noted that "It brings to the reader the result of research on various questions in United States economic history much more quickly than would be possible through the traditional text book approach. . . . It thus becomes a rather flexible teaching tool. This book will be a welcome addition to the libraries of American economic historians" (981).

In 1977, Bob published his second book, *Competition and Coercion: Blacks in the American Economy, 1865–1914*. In this important book, Bob argued that economic competition played a key role in insulating Blacks from racial political coercion that remained after the ratification of the 13th Amendment in 1865. Bob's treatment is nuanced in that it fully appreciated the brutal legacy of slavery and the prevalence of discrimination and coercion against Blacks. His point was that competition via mobility provided some means for Blacks to avoid the full brunt of this coercion while, in the process, providing them a way to increase their incomes, literacy, and ownership of property. "The black man's most effective response to persecution was simply to flee, an action that could succeed after 1865 on a scale impossible under the slave regime" (Higgs 1977, 61). In a 2015 interview, Bob highlighted a central insight of this book: "[Economic] competition is the salvation of oppressed people, and that can be seen in any case. Pick your ethnic group and you see the same phenomena operating" (Burress and Powell 2015, timestamp 11:18—11:34).

Competition and Coercion was positively reviewed in a number of academic journals. In his review in the Journal of Economic Literature, for instance, Keith Aufhauser concluded that "the book is thorough and innovative in many ways. It is likely to encourage still more innovations and, perhaps, a boom in post-emancipation studies" (1978, 598).

Although I have focused on his books, a review of Bob's overall scholarly output (see the appendix in this volume) during the 1970s is extremely impressive. He published numerous academic journal articles on a range of topics in outlets such as the American Economic Review, Explorations in Economic History, the Journal of Economic History, the Journal of Political Economy, and The Review of Economics and Statistics. As a result of his scholarly productivity, Bob was promoted to associate professor with tenure in 1972, and to full professor in 1978. He would remain at the University of Washington until 1983, when he moved to Lafayette College after accepting a chaired professorship—the William E. Simon Professor of Political Economy.

Crisis and Leviathan

It was during his time at Lafayette College that Bob published his most well-known book, Crisis and Leviathan: Critical Episodes in the Growth of American Government, in 1987. Through a detailed analysis of the ideological change caused by the Progressive Era and the US government's actions during the two World Wars and the Great Depression, Bob showed how governments can grow in the wake of crises. I will highlight three of the book's numerous contributions.

First, Bob's analytical approach emphasized that the overall size of government cannot be captured through standard aggregate metrics of scale, such as budget size or number of employees. Instead, the overall size of government requires an appreciation of the scope, or range of government powers. After all, it is possible that a government, or an agency within a government, with a relatively small budget can possess a significant range (i.e., scope) of powers that perversely affects the well-being and rights of citizens. The scope aspects of government power aren't obvious from measures of scale and can only be uncovered through careful historical analysis of government activity.

Second, Bob offered a framework—the ratchet effect framework—for understanding the overall growth of government. At the core of his framework is the Crisis Hypothesis, which holds that "under certain conditions national emergencies call forth extensions of government control over or outright replacement of the market economy" because "national emergencies markedly increase both the demand for and the supply of governmental controls" (Higgs 1987, 17). Bob's ratchet effect model consists of five stages.

The first stage is "Pre-Crisis Normality," which reflects the growth of government that would occur absent the crisis. The second stage, "Expansion," introduces a crisis that increases the overall size (scale and scope) of government. This expansion occurs because citizens call upon government to "do something" in response to the crisis. During stage three, "Maturity," the crisis-induced increase in the overall size of government reaches its peak, followed by stage four, "Retrenchment," where government's size decreases from its peak in stage three. The final stage, "Post-Crisis Normality," represents the government's growth path in the wake of the crisis. The important point is that the post-crisis growth of government is higher than the counterfactual growth path captured in the first stage (the government growth that would have occurred without the crisis). The retrenchment of government leads to a reduction from the crisis peak, but not a full return to pre-crisis normality. This gap between pre- and post-crisis normality represents the ratchet effect.

Third, Bob's framework incorporated and emphasized the importance of ideology, which he defined as "a somewhat coherent, rather comprehensive belief system about social relations" (1987, 37), as central to the growth of government in response to crisis. Ideology matters in two ways. First, a certain ideology sets the stage for government expansion in response to a crisis. Recall that the second stage ("Expansion") is the result of the public calling on government to "do something" to address this crisis. This requires a certain ideology—a belief system and expectations about the appropriate role of government in society—in order for the expansion to occur. Second, the government response to the crisis itself can influence citizen ideology regarding the role of government in the present and future in society through three channels.

For one, the reversal of some crisis-related policies provides a sense of government rollback in the wake of the crisis; this can assuage the fear that government responses undermine all freedoms (1987, 71–72). Further, the government's crisis response creates an opportunity for some people to benefit, and these people will look on the new sociopolitical order in a favorable manner (1987, 72). Finally, crisis politics result in "occasions for the improvement of command-and-control mechanisms, which renders them less obnoxious" to the general public (1987, 73). Expansions in government become normalized such that behaviors that would have been unacceptable pre-crisis now become the "new normal," with a certain segment of the population (the young and unborn) entirely unfamiliar with how things were prior to the crisis.

In order to show how ideology and crisis interact, Bob analyzed the Progressive Era as a turning point in the ideology of the American elite. Discussing the implications of this period, he concluded that "the dominant ideology of political and economic elites had now become one that not only tolerated a greatly expanded role for government in economic decision-making; it positively insisted on such activism" (1987, 121–22). This ideological shift set the stage for government growth in subsequent crises—World War I, the Great Depression, and World War II.

Crisis and Leviathan had a significant impact on scholars interested in economic history and government growth. Hugh Rockoff (1988) concluded his review of the book in *The Economic History Review* by noting that "my admiration for this book is immense. It is elegantly written, brilliantly argued, and based on massive research. It will be a model for the next generation of economic historians as they integrate the techniques of the old and the new economic history" (666).

The Independent Review

Bob left Lafayette College in 1989, moving to Seattle University, where he would remain until 1994, when he joined the Independent Institute, a think tank founded by David Theroux in 1986. At the Independent Institute, Bob held the position of research director (1994–97) and then senior fellow in political economy (1994–2017, after which he became retired senior fellow in political economy). In 1996, David and Bob launched *The Independent Review* with Bob as the founding editor (Theroux 2013). Here is how Bob described the aims and scope of the journal in his Editor's Welcome, which appeared in the first issue:

> Writing that would interest only economists or only philosophers or only historians—indeed work that would interest only the practitioners of any academically defined scientific or humanistic specialty—will not appear

in this journal. Rather, I intend to feature writing that crosses the bound-aries of a variety of disciplines, including all the social sciences, philoso-phy, history, law, and related fields. . . . The main purpose here is not to develop a particular discipline but to advance the reader's understanding of the multifaceted reality to which the term "political economy" refers.

Highly formal and technically challenging work will not appear in *TIR*. Heavily mathematical forms of exposition have become *de rigueur* in economics and increasingly in political science. Other fields, such as philosophy, have their own ways of excluding strangers from the con-versation. Good arguments can be made for these expositional conven-tions. But whatever the merits of esoteric forms of communication in the various disciplines, my aims as editor dictate that the common language of this journal, as a rule, must be English. I intend to reject the work of writers who cannot express their ideas clearly. Those who write with vigor, wit, and flair will be received with open arms. (Higgs 1996, 5)

Bob delivered on his promise. He served as the sole editor of the journal for seventeen years (in 2013 he became founding editor and editor at large), edit-ing 66 issues consisting of over 900 articles. During this time he created an intellectual space for scholars from a diverse set of fields and perspectives to analyze the most pressing issues in political economy. The content of the jour-nal is rigorous yet accessible to a wide and diverse readership.

The Myth of Wartime Prosperity and Regime Uncertainty

Over the course of the 1990s, Bob published numerous academic and popular articles. Three of his academic papers on the topics of the Great Depression and World War II deserve special mention.[2] The first, "Wartime Prosperity? A Reassessment of the U.S. Economy in the 1940s" (Higgs 1992), overturned the conventional view that World War II resulted in "war prosperity" that improved the well-being of private citizens. Bob countered the orthodox story by reconsidering employment, output, and real consumption data in the United States in light of economic theory.

According to standard measures, unemployment fell during the war. Bob showed that this decrease in unemployment was a result of increased employ-ment in the military sector. However, from an economic standpoint these two lines of employment are not the same. Private employment produces value-added consumer goods through peaceful and voluntary social cooperation. "But military 'jobs' differed categorically. Often they entailed substantial risks of death, dismemberment, and other physical and psychological injuries.

Military service yielded little pay under harsh conditions and, like it or not, lasted for the duration of the war. Sustained involvement in combat drove many men insane" (1992, 43). And we must not forget, Bob reminds us, that a significant portion (10 million of the 16 million) of those who served in the armed forces during the war were conscripted. The result, Bob concluded, was that "the 'prosperous' condition of the labor force was spurious: Official unemployment was virtually nonexistent, but four-tenths of the total labor force was not being used to produce consumer goods or capital comparable of yielding consumer goods in the future" (1992, 44).

While unemployment was falling during the war, output, measured by gross national product (GNP), was increasing. This increase in output is typically taken as evidence of prosperity due to the US government's war activities. Bob made the important point that not all output is the same. Output that is value-added from the perspective of private consumers is fundamentally different from output that satisfies the plans of military decision makers. Here Bob was making an elementary, but often overlooked and misunderstood, point about the very nature of economic decision-making under alternative institutional arrangements.

> Economics is not a science of hammers and nails, of production or consumption in the raw; it is the science of choice, and therefore of values. Valuation is inherent in all national income accounting. In a command economy, the fundamental accounting difficulty is that the authorities suppress and replace the only genuinely meaningful manifestation of people's valuations, namely, free market prices. (1992, 49)

Because governments are bureaucratic entities, they do not rely on profit and loss to gauge performance. One implication is that government spending on military goods and services is solely a measure of monetary outlays, or accounting costs. This is especially the case during major wars, such as World War I and World War II, where the competitive price system was largely displaced by government control of economic activity (1992, 49).

In a subsequent paper, "Wartime Socialization of Investment: A Reassessment of U.S. Capital Formation in the 1940s," Bob built on this point through an analysis of capital investment in the US economy during World War II (Higgs 2004). He made the important distinction between capital formation resulting from private entrepreneurs and capital formation resulting from government planners. The former, reflected by private property, prices, and profit and loss, reflects the subjective valuations of private economic actors.

The latter reflects the valuations of government planners rather than private consumers. A narrow focus on aggregate statistics overlooks this important distinction and the distortionary, welfare-reducing effects of wartime government planning.

This suggests that removing military expenditures from aggregate output measures is a better indicator of output that improves consumer well-being. In his "Wartime Prosperity?" paper, Bob removed the US government's military expenditures from GNP. After doing so, he found that GNP actually *decreased* during the 1942–44 period, which stands in direct contrast to the conventional story of wartime prosperity (Higgs 1992, 44–46).

Regarding personal consumption, Bob emphasized that appropriate adjustments need to be made for wartime inflation, which reduces consumers' purchasing power, and hence their well-being. After adjusting to deflate personal consumption spending per capita, he concluded that "real consumption per capita reached a prewar peak in 1941 that was nearly 9 percent above the 1939 level; it declined by more than 6 percent during 1941–43 and rose during 1943–45; still, even in 1945, it had not recovered to the 1941 level (1992, 52). Moreover, he made the important point that consumer well-being was reduced in many other ways during the war. "To get available goods," he noted, "millions of people had to move, many of them long distances, to centers of war production" (1992, 52). This is in addition to having to work harder and under more dangerous work conditions while dealing with the welfare-reducing consequences of government-imposed price controls and rationing mandates (1992, 53).

Summing up the main implications of his analysis, Bob concluded that "the war *itself* did not get the economy out of the Depression. The war economy produced neither a 'carnival of consumption' nor an investment boom, however successfully it overwhelmed the nation's enemies with bombs, shells, and bullets" (1992, 8, emphasis in original).

In a subsequent paper, "Regime Uncertainty: Why the Great Depression Lasted So Long and Why Prosperity Resumed after the War" (1997), Bob connected his prior paper on the myth of wartime prosperity to a reconsideration of the duration of the Great Depression. In his 1997 paper, he offered insight into the "Great Duration," which lasted for 12 years following the "Great Contraction" (1929–33). In Bob's telling, the Great Duration can be explained by the failure of private investment to recover after collapsing during the Great Contraction. But what explains the failure of private investment to recover?

To answer this question, Bob introduced the concept of "regime uncertainty," by which he meant that businesspeople are "distressed that investors' private property rights in their capital and the income it yields will be attenuated further by government action" (1997, 568). Bob documents how during the 1933–40 period, the Roosevelt administration and Congress introduced an array of laws that threatened private property rights. "The many menacing New Deal measures, especially those from 1935 onward, gave businesspeople and investors good reason to fear that the market economy might not survive in anything like its traditional form and that even more drastic developments, perhaps even some kind of collectivist dictatorship, could not be ruled out entirely" (1997, 571).

To provide evidence for his thesis regarding the role of regime uncertainty, Bob draws on public polling data for the 1939–41 period regarding business and public perceptions and expectations. This evidence suggests that "a majority of the general public believed the Roosevelt administration's stance vis-à-vis business was delaying recovery, and they expected government control of business to increase over the next decade, which presumably would further impede recovery" (1997, 577). Another piece of evidence are the yields on corporate bonds, which provide insight into the risk premium required by investors on long-term investments. From this Bob concluded that "investors' confidence in their ability to appropriate the longer-term interest payments and principal repayments promised by the country's most secure corporation plummeted between early 1934 and early 1936. Confidence remained at an extremely depressed level from 1936 through the first quarter of 1941" (1997, 584).

Bob's analysis provided a novel theoretical contribution—the idea of "regime uncertainty"—and empirical evidence to support the thesis that the New Deal prolonged the Great Depression. In doing so, he also provided insight into the "Great Escape." It wasn't World War II that got the US economy out of the Great Depression, but instead a change in the expectations of private investors regarding government policy toward private property. "In 1945 and 1946, with Roosevelt dead, the New Deal in retreat, and most of the wartime controls being removed, investors came out in force. . . . The government no longer seemed to possess the terrifying potential that businesspeople had perceived before the war. For investors, the nightmare was over. For the economy, once more, prosperity was possible" (1997, 586).

The Post-9/11 Warfare State

In the wake of the September 11, 2001, attacks, the US government launched a transnational "war on terror." Bob wrote numerous articles (both academic and popular) applying his prior work on crisis and the growth of government to the US government's war efforts. These writings were published in three books: *Resurgence of the Warfare State: The Crisis since 9/11* (2005), *Neither Liberty nor Safety: Fear, Ideology, and the Growth of Government* (2007), and *Delusions of Power: New Explorations of the State, War, and Economy* (2012).

Across these books, Bob provided a political economy analysis of a range of topics including, but not limited to, the war on terror and growth of government as per the logic of the ratchet effect, the ineffectiveness of federalized airport security, the political economy of the military-industrial-congressional complex and the run-up to the Iraq war, and the human costs of war in terms of harms to innocent civilians. When considered together, the insights from these books can be summarized in 10 themes.

First, US political leaders framed their "war on terror" as a new kind of war. However, government war-making activities pose a potential threat to the very liberties they purport to protect as per the logic of the ratchet effect. From this standpoint, the war on terror was not unique, but rather business as usual as it pertains to the relationship between war and the growth of government.

Second, proponents of expansions in the national-security state leveraged fear to garner public support for their actions. There is an incentive for policymakers to engage in threat inflation to stoke fear in order to secure more resources and power. Social scientists and analysts tend to neglect the role of threat inflation in their study of national-security policy.

Third, advocates for a larger security state often rely on crude aggregate statistics—for example, government spending as a percentage of GDP, number of employees—which fail to capture the true scope of government involvement in social and economic life. These aggregate statistics may offer some insight into the scale of government, but they fail to capture the range, or scope, of government actions and their effect on citizen well-being.

Fourth, the war on terror was the latest iteration of Congress abdicating its constitutional responsibilities to serve as a check on the war-making powers of the executive. The result was an entrenchment and extension of the imperial presidency.

Fifth, the Founding Fathers were overly optimistic about the feasibility of a sustainable limited government. Theory and historical evidence suggest that government will expand through time, even in the presence of constitutional constraints. This reality opens the door to consider alternative political arrangements, including those that do not rely on the existence of a centralized, coercive state.

Sixth, in America, starting in the early 1900s, ideological changes coupled with several major national emergencies changed the relationship between citizens and the state and fostered the creation of a variety of private and public political special interests. These groups, best illustrated by the military-industrial-congressional complex, seek to advance their own narrow interests under the guise of pursuing the "national interest."

Seventh, war and taxes go hand in hand. War-related taxes can be explicit direct taxes, or they can be hidden taxes in the form of inflation. New taxes and methods of collection (e.g., income-tax withholding) tend to be sticky and remain in the wake of wars.

Eighth, the Department of Defense (DoD) has failed to satisfy basic financial accounting practices and to meet federal laws that require all executive agencies of the federal government to successfully pass a financial audit. All the while, the DoD requested, and received, increasing amounts of funding. These increases in funding were provided in response to the failure of the national-security state to protect Americans from the September 11 attacks.

Ninth, changes in ideology and the growth of government (especially in the military sector) led to a structural transformation of the American economic system toward "military-economic fascism." This system is defined by private ownership over the means of production but with an emphasis on national collectivism around the "national interest," which is placed on a pedestal over individual rights. This shift undermines the dynamism of the competitive market economy while expanding the reach of government in private economic life.

Tenth, the widespread faith in foreign policy "experts" is mis-founded and dangerous. Supposed experts suffer from severe epistemic limitations and perverse incentives. Moreover, the selection mechanisms in US political institutions often result in power being granted to people who are cruel, incompetent, and vainglorious. The concentration of power in the hands of such people poses a severe danger to the life and liberty of millions of people around the world.

OVERVIEW OF THE VOLUME

The chapters in this volume explore the key contributions of Bob's scholarly oeuvre. Authors were asked to discuss the main ideas of Bob's scholarship related to their chapter topic, as well as the contemporary relevance of these ideas. The result is a collection of papers that demonstrates a wide-ranging research program full of opportunities for future research on an array of pressing issues.

Art Carden (chapter 1) explores how Bob's scholarship, from the early 1970s through the mid-1980s, changed how we understand American racial history, labor history, and institutional history. He notes that Bob's work influenced how people thought about a range of issues—labor market discrimination, the effect of the boll weevil on the Southern economy, and African American economic agency—through his emphasis on commercial economic agency and competition.

Jayme Lemke (chapter 2) continues the discussion of Bob's work on the role of state power and the oppression of certain groups of people. She discusses three themes in Bob's work to understand the nature, function, and persistence of discriminatory institutional environments. First, because institutional environments are comprised of both publicly and privately organized rules, understanding discriminatory institutions requires appreciating the interaction between public discriminatory law and private discriminatory social norms. Second, because institutions are defined, in part, by the competitive landscape within which they exist, both market and political competition are important for understanding the nature of discriminatory oppression. Third, ideology plays an important role in shaping and maintaining racially discriminatory policies and practices.

Robert Whaples (chapter 3) focuses on the topic of inequality. He identifies four concerns typically associated with inequality—objections to differences in status, objections to a mismatch between outcomes and merit, concerns about fairness, and the possibility that inequality causes other problems that threaten the fabric of society. Whaples discusses Higgs's scholarship on inequality, including his critiques of official inequality statistics, and then examines modern income levels in comparison to the distribution of income among all human beings who have ever lived. He closes by discussing the important connection between inequality and virtue.

Next, Vincent Geloso (chapter 4) discusses what he calls "coercion bias" in economic measurement. He begins by noting that in standard economic models, government's coercive powers are assumed to be used in a productive manner—for example, state power is used to extract taxes to finance the production of value-added public goods. In these cases, both measured output and well-being will increase. Geloso notes, however, that when government engages in harmful coercion—for example, enslavement or repression—output (measured by national accounts data) will overstate well-being, hence the coercion bias in measurement. To illustrate the relevance of coercion bias, Geloso reconsiders debates over the economic consequences of slavery in the United States during the antebellum period, and debates regarding the role of economic freedom in stimulating economic growth.

Donald Boudreaux (chapter 5) makes the important distinction between "regime uncertainty" and "market uncertainty." He draws on Bob's work on the duration of the Great Depression and regime uncertainty—the expectation by private investors that their private property rights in capital and income will be weakened through government policy. Boudreaux uses this as an entry point to compare regime uncertainty to market uncertainty—the uncertainty inherent in purely private markets. From the perspective of one economic school of thought—the equilibrium-always economists most often associated with the Chicago school—the economic efficiency of markets is complete, meaning market uncertainty is a nonissue, and can only be undermined by government interventions and regime uncertainty. In contrast, those working in the Austrian tradition place economic uncertainty at the center of their theory of the market process. Boudreaux discusses how market institutions, in contrast to political institutions, create an environment conducive to economic actors navigating a world of uncertainty in welfare-improving ways.

The next five chapters deal with Bob's work on the ratchet effect, ideology, and government growth. Abigail Hall (chapter 6) discusses the various theories of government growth and situates Bob's work on the ratchet effect within this literature. She discusses several common misunderstandings of the ratchet effect framework, recent scholarship employing the framework, and avenues for future research.

Anthony Gregory (chapter 7) reminds us that Bob's work on government growth is not a mechanical story of inevitability, but rather a nuanced analysis of the interaction of ideology and various structures through time. The ratchet effect is not an immutable law of nature, but rather one mechanism through which government expands in some cases but not others. Gregory notes that appreciating the qualitative and nuanced dimensions of state power and ideology can aid in constructing more sophisticated historical narratives regarding the transformation of the American government.

Next, Sarah Burns (chapter 8) applies the ratchet effect framework to the war powers of the executive branch of the US federal government. She explores the historical ideological and structural shifts that, through time, led to the concentration of war powers in the hands of US presidents. A key part of her analysis is identifying how Congress and the federal courts enabled this concentration.

Jonathan Newman (chapter 9) applies the logic of the ratchet effect to government control of money and banking with four applications. First, he considers government control over money and banking as one instance of an expansion in the scope of government power. Second, he discusses how fiat inflation and debt monetization allow the government to conceal the true costs of government actions during a crisis. Third, he highlights how the government's use of inflation to conceal costs in one crisis can lead to subsequent crises. Fourth, he explores how inflation can lead to psychological and cultural changes that further encourage the public's acceptance of government interventions.

In the subsequent chapter (chapter 10), Laurie Calhoun draws on the insights from *Crisis and Leviathan* to analyze the US government's response to the COVID-19 pandemic. In doing so, she highlights how Bob's framework for analyzing crises extends beyond war and economic depression to other cases, such as public health emergencies.

The next three chapters analyze the political economy of the military sector. Nathan Goodman (chapter 11) explores the rise of the military-industrial complex (MIC) in the United States in light of the ratchet effect framework. He also discusses how the rise of the MIC has contributed to a broader militarization of society, including domestic security and law enforcement. Next, Christopher Coyne and Yuliya Yatsyshina (chapter 12) engage Bob's scholarship on the nature, operation, and perverse effects of the military sector. They explore the unique nature of the military system to understand its overarching structure and features. They then discuss the incentives facing private and public participants and the harmful economic effects, both immediate and long term, of the military system. Thomas Duncan (chapter 13) discusses the origins, operation, and ongoing costs of the permanent war economy. In doing so, he sheds light on how a large defense sector necessarily affects and reshapes the private economy.

Next, Raymond March (chapter 14) discusses Bob's often overlooked scholarly contributions to health economics. These contributions include the role of decision-making under uncertainty by healthcare consumers, comparative institutional analysis of healthcare, regulatory standards for medical device quality, and the growth of federal health agencies such as the Food and Drug Administration (FDA). Importantly, March emphasizes that Bob's work in this area has relevance for contemporary health policy.

The last two chapters explore issues in political philosophy. Taking inspiration from Bob's work on the philosophical foundations of the state, Tate Fegley (chapter 15) considers whether, *if* men were governed by an angelic state, all problems of governance would then be solved. He argues that even if government was run by angels, the state would still face the economic calculation problem, making the results no better, and likely worse, than if these functions were instead left to angelic entrepreneurs operating in a free market. He also argues that a state that is open to control by non-angels will not be governed by angels for long, if at all. Finally, Edward Stringham and Spencer Brown (chapter 16) explore two paths toward anarcho-pacifism. They discuss how some 19th-century Christians, such as Leo Tolstoy, and modern (20th- and 21st-century) laissez-faire economists, such as Bob, reach similar anarcho-pacifist conclusions despite starting with different assumptions and world-views. Together, these chapters invite readers to think about the normative foundations of the state and of a free society of dignified equals.

The appendix includes a selection of writings from across Bob's career. In addition to capturing the breadth of Bob's career, it will serve as an important reference for readers wishing to engage with Bob's scholarly writings.

CONCLUSION

In putting this volume together, I had two goals. First, I wanted to provide a resource for readers not yet familiar with the scope of Bob's scholarship and contributions. Second, for those already familiar with Bob's research, I wanted to provide an opportunity to celebrate his legacy. At the same time, I wanted to avoid being purely backward-looking because that would neglect the fact that Bob's research program is far from complete and offers numerous entry points to study the most pressing issues in the world today. Issues of oppression and repression, of market competition as a way of empowering ordinary people, of public policy and regime uncertainty, of healthcare policy, of the costs and consequences of war and the warfare state, and of the philosophical founda-tions of a free society remain as relevant today as when Bob wrote about them. My hope is that the engagement with Bob's work in this volume will inspire readers to continue his work through refinement, application, and extension.

In closing, I would like to express my own personal appreciation for Bob. His work has been, and continues to be, a major intellectual influence on my own thinking and research. Although I have never formally taken a class from Bob, I consider him to be a teacher and mentor. My first contact with Bob was in 2002, when I presented a paper as a first-year graduate student at the Mises Institute's 2002 Austrian Scholars Conference. Bob reached out to me after the conference and asked if I would be interested in submitting the paper I presented to *The Independent Review*. After I submitted the paper, Bob worked with me to improve the paper's content and style; the result was my first academic journal publication. This experience was an enormous confidence booster for a first-year graduate student. Bob and I have kept in touch ever since.

I see my own research on the political economy of war, foreign intervention, and peace as building directly on Bob's scholarship on these issues. In 2013, I had the honor of taking over the coeditorship of *The Independent Review* (along with Robert Whaples and Michael Munger). In that role, I do my best to continue to advance Bob's vision for the journal as laid out in his "Editor's Welcome" discussed earlier. During the 2015–16 academic year, Bob was the inaugural F. A. Hayek Distinguished Visiting Professor with the F. A. Hayek Program for Advanced Study in Philosophy, Politics, and Economics at the Mercatus Center at George Mason University. He spent time with us at GMU, meeting with faculty and graduate students to discuss their research and giving several seminars based on his scholarship.[3] It is a privilege to know Bob Higgs and to honor his legacy—a legacy that will live on.

NOTES

1. A Festschrift honoring Bob was published in 2007 (Fishback 2007). While the papers in that volume were inspired by Bob's work, they did not systematically engage his full body of scholarship; this volume aims to fill this gap.

2. These and related articles were published together in *Depression, War, and Cold War: Studies in Political Economy* (2006), with the subsequent paperback edition titled *Depression, War, and Cold War: Challenging the Myths of Conflict and Prosperity* (2009b).

3. I also had the opportunity to interview Bob about his career and work. These videos, which are available through the Mercatus Center (https://www.mercatus.org/hayekprogram/economic -insights/mercatus-original-videos/research-program-robert-higgs-intellectual & https://www .mercatus.org/hayekprogram/economic-insights/mercatus-original-videos/research-program -robert-higgs-austrian), provide additional insight into Bob's work and life in his own words.

REFERENCES

Aufhauser, Keith. 1978. "'Competition and Coercion: Blacks in the American Economy, 1865–1914' by Robert Higgs." *Journal of Economic Literature* 16 (2): 597–98.

Burrus, Trevor, and Aaron Ross Powell. 2015. "Taking a Stand with Robert Higgs." Free Thoughts Podcast, Episode 109, November 20. Audio, 63:03. https://www.libertarianism.org/media /free-thoughts/taking-stand.

Fishback, Price (ed.). 2007. *Government and the American Economy: A New History*. Chicago: University of Chicago Press.

Hartley, William B. 1972. "The Transformation of the American Economy, 1865–1914: An Essay in Interpretation by Robert Higgs." *Journal of Economic History* 32 (4): 980–81.

Higgs, Robert. 1971. *The Transformation of the American Economy, 1865–1914: An Essay in Interpretation*. New York: John Wiley and Sons.

———. 1977. *Competition and Coercion: Blacks in the American Economy, 1865–1914*. New York: Cambridge University Press.

———. 1987. *Crisis and Leviathan: Critical Episodes in the Growth of American Government*. New York: Oxford University Press.

———. 1992. "Wartime Prosperity? A Reassessment of the U.S. Economy in the 1940s." *Journal of Economic History* 52 (1): 41–60.

———. 1996. "Editor's Welcome." *Independent Review* 1 (1): 5–7.

———. 1997. "Regime Uncertainty: Why the Great Depression Lasted So Long and Why Prosperity Resumed after the War." *Independent Review* 1 (4): 561–90.

———. 2004. "Wartime Socialization of Investment: A Reassessment of U.S. Capital Formation in the 1940s." *Journal of Economic History* 64 (2): 500–520.

———. 2005. *Resurgence of the Warfare State: The Crisis since 9/11.* Oakland, CA: Independent Institute.

———. 2006. *Depression, War, and Cold War: Studies in Political Economy.* New York: Oxford University Press.

———. 2007. *Neither Liberty nor Safety: Fear, Ideology, and the Growth of Government.* Oakland, CA: Independent Institute.

———. 2009a. "William Jess Higgs (March 21, 1909–October 15, 1977)." *The Beacon,* March 21. https://blog.independent.org/2009/03/21/william-jess-higgs-march-21-1909-october-15-1977/.

———. 2009b. *Depression, War, and Cold War: Challenging the Myths of Conflict and Prosperity.* Oakland, CA: Independent Institute.

———. 2011. "Work in Progress: A Boy and His Mom." *The Beacon,* April 2. https://blog.independent.org/2011/04/02/work-in-progress-a-boy-and-his-mom/.

———. 2012. *Delusions of Power: New Explorations of the State, War, and Economy.* Oakland, CA: Independent Institute.

———. 2018. "Johns Hopkins University: Launching Pad for My Fifty Years as a Professional Economist." *The Beacon,* May 22. https://blog.independent.org/2018/05/22/johns-hopkins-university-launching-pad-for-my-fifty-years-as-a-professional-economist/.

Rockoff, Hugh. 1988. "Review of 'Crisis and Leviathan: Critical Episodes in the Growth of American Government by Robert Higgs.'" *Economic History Review* 41 (4): 665–66.

Theroux, David J. 2013. "Robert Higgs: A Personal and Professional Appreciation." *Independent Review* 18 (2): 279–85.

Chapter 1

Competition, Coercion, and African American Economic Progress in the Work of Robert Higgs

Art Carden

> Robert Higgs is one of a few economists who have departed from the traditional preoccupation of what the whites did to blacks to inquire in addition what blacks did for themselves and what the economy did for them. His findings, generally speaking, stand in marked contrast to the traditional picture.
>
> —C. Vann Woodward (1978, 194)

According to legend, Julius Caesar wept before a statue of Alexander the Great because, by the time he was Caesar's age, he had conquered the world. Caesar was sure he would never measure up. For the ambitious (and insecure) scholar, reading the early work of the economic historian Robert Higgs might evoke a similar feeling. Higgs had a productive, distinguished career as a scholar that would have been the envy of almost any observer—and that's just including what he did before publishing his classic *Crisis and Leviathan* at the age of 43 in 1987. Higgs's work on the economic history of the American South and African American economic achievement, most of which he did in the 1970s and early 1980s, stands out and still holds up more than four and a half decades later.

Higgs's training as an economist meant he wasn't an economic *historian*, but it didn't mean he was merely an *economic* historian. He was an *economic historian*, italicized all the way through, with scholarly output scattered across both disciplines' journals. Higgs is just as at home in the *Journal of American History* or *Agricultural History* as in the *Journal of Political Economy* and the *American Economic Review*. He was part of the generation of so-called New

---

Parts of this paper are adapted from Carden (2021).

Economic Historians who explored the rough paths broken by Douglass C. North, Robert W. Fogel, and others (Higgs 2016). They turned these paths into highways using neoclassical economic theory to formulate testable hypotheses, which they tested by combining historical data with state-of-the-art econometric techniques. They became known as "cliometricians," a portmanteau of "econometrician" and Clio, the Greek muse of history.

In the 1970s, Higgs published two books that paid special attention to the period between the end of the Civil War and the outbreak of World War I. His first book, *The Transformation of the American Economy, 1865–1914* (Higgs [1971] 2011), offered a concise cliometric assessment and revision of what we knew about the period between Robert E. Lee's surrender at Appomattox and the booming Guns of August 1914. Higgs's second book, *Competition and Coercion: Blacks in the American Economy, 1865–1914* (Higgs 1977a), focused more specifically on the Black experience during the first half-century following slavery's abolition. It remains a distinguished contribution to African American economic, political, social, and cultural history.

This chapter explores how Higgs changed how we understand American racial history, labor history, and institutional history from the early 1970s through the middle of the 1980s. Like other economic historians of his era, Higgs upended much of what everybody "knew" about labor market discrimination, the boll weevil's effect on the Southern economy, African American economic agency, and other issues. In contrast to histories that emphasized political action and agency, Higgs explored how African Americans exercised commercial agency in the ordinary business of life.

To Higgs, African Americans from Reconstruction through the early 1900s were not just subjects that were acted upon—though they were, and violently. They were historical actors who made noteworthy economic gains wherever they were allowed to compete in free markets and where others were required to compete for their services. Increased African American literacy, income, and wealth were not part of political planners' designs or achievements. They were unintended (but welcome) consequences of a decentralized social process: free market exchange. Higgs developed these insights by devising and testing specified hypotheses with carefully collected data.

Later in his career, Higgs would be reborn as a Misesian and disavow "hypothesis testing" in economic history. As he put it in the preface to his 2011 edition,

> I no longer stand by the book's methodological pronouncements or by much of what it represents as "modern economic theory." Yet, I do not

want to apologize too much. A great deal of the economic analysis still seems sound to me; after all, in the area known as applied microeconomics, the neoclassicals and the Austrians hold similar views in regard to their basic understanding of how many actions and events are interrelated. (Higgs [1971] 2011, vi)

This is not to say he rejected quantification, of course, writing, "If one views the econometric findings not as a means of making inferences in testing hypotheses, but simply as descriptive statistics, one may make valuable use of such findings in writing economic history" (Higgs [1971] 2011, vi). Useful they were and are: even if we dispense with the language of hypothesis testing, Higgs's analysis painted a very different—and dare I say hopeful—picture of the economic history of race in America.

THE NEW ECONOMIC HISTORY AND THE CLIOMETRIC REVOLUTION

> The history of all hitherto existing society is the history of class struggles.
>
> —*Karl Marx and Friedrich Engels (1848)*

During the middle of the 20th century, a small intellectual revolution overturned many beliefs people had developed by viewing history through Marxian glasses. The New Economic Historians maintained that the history of all hitherto existing societies was *not* the history of class struggles but the history of social phenomena emerging from individual choices. In 1993, Robert W. Fogel of the University of Chicago and Douglass C. North of Washington University in Saint Louis were awarded the Sveriges Riksbank Prize in Economic Sciences in Memory of Alfred Nobel "for having renewed research in economic history by applying economic theory and quantitative methods to explain economic and institutional change." The Johns Hopkins University–trained Higgs, who was North's colleague at the University of Washington through the 1970s and who might have been Fogel's colleague at the University of Chicago had they not hired Deirdre McCloskey from Harvard University (who went on to have a notable career of her own), was an important contributor to this revived tradition.

Higgs recognized that facts are marvelous things that do not "speak for themselves." They speak for and against different theories and, in Higgs's hands, show that there is much more to history than class struggle. The cliometricians did more than compile statistical facts. They shifted focus away from power, domination, and politics and brought decentralized, competitive processes on both the supply and the demand sides of markets for land, labor, crops, and capital to the fore.

As Higgs defines it, "A theory is a logically consistent set of assumptions and implications. It provides a means of relating facts to one another, of organizing and interpreting them so that they make sense" (Higgs [1971] 2011, 6). He would go on to show that the facts are at odds with the treatment of Southern history as the history of class struggle (Higgs 1977a, xii). His respect for W. E. B. Du Bois notwithstanding, Higgs described his *Black Reconstruction in America* as "an unsuccessful attempt to force the facts into a Marxist mold" (Higgs 1977a, 185). Higgs and other cliometricians argued that the appropriate economic framework for historical analysis is neoclassical, not Marxian.

For example, Higgs agrees with many other economists that a wage gap *per se* is insufficient evidence that the gap is itself the product of discrimination. Following Becker (1971), he also works to be precise about what he means by "discrimination." A 12-year-old Black male who earns less than a 35-year-old white male is not necessarily a victim of discrimination because most of the gap is likely explained by differences in education and experience. "Discrimination" happens when someone earns less than another person who is alike in every relevant respect except for a morally arbitrary characteristic unrelated to productivity, like race. Throughout his work, Higgs would find evidence that otherwise-identical Black and white workers earned the same wages.

Economic theory imposes discipline on thinking and writing, and statistical tests helped scholars identify the theories with the most explanatory power. Higgs was quick to point this out in books he reviewed for economics and history journals. His and R. M. Hartwell's 1971 review of David Landes's classic *The Unbound Prometheus* expressed disappointment that Landes had not used his massive collection of information to develop and test hypotheses (Hartwell and Higgs 1971).

In a review of a book titled *Railroads and the Granger Laws*, he wrote that "the principal defect of the book is the low level of its economic analysis" (Higgs 1972b, 552). Further, he argued that the slipshod use of economic theory and method made for an incoherent and self-contradictory analysis, noting that the author "never makes up his mind about the source of this discrimination, ascribing it here to competition, there to monopoly; at one point (p. 151), he refers to the 'worst abuses of railway competition' and a paragraph later to 'railroads and their monopolistic practices'" (Higgs 1972b, 553). It calls to mind policy debates about fierce competition between technology and retail monopolies.

Higgs rejects an approach to history that conflates passing legislation with achieving social outcomes. Furthermore, he guarded against the *post hoc ergo propter hoc* fallacy: just because event B happened after event A does not mean A caused B. Many other things could have caused B, or it could have been the product of trends preceding A. The histories of occupational safety and child labor provide useful examples. It's true that workplace safety improved with the adoption of stringent safety regulations and that child labor fell as it was outlawed or regulated, but workplaces were already getting safer, and child labor was already falling because of competition and rising general prosperity. Armed with modern neoclassical economic theory, statistical techniques, and ever-improving computing power, Higgs explored the effects of competition and coercion on African American economic life in slavery's aftermath.

COMPETITION, COERCION, AND AFRICAN AMERICAN ECONOMIC PROGRESS, 1865–1914

Through the 1970s, Higgs published a series of studies reevaluating African American economic history in the late 19th and early 20th centuries. Emancipation meant freedom, but freedom entered into with essentially no assets and in a world ruled by people to whom the notion that the freedmen had rights white people were bound to respect was still novel. Public discrimination worked against Black economic advancement (e.g., Higgs 1982, 736). Political disfranchisement meant governments were largely unresponsive to the freedmen's wants, public support for schooling was practically nonexistent, and legal institutions could not be counted upon to protect Black rights to their persons and property. Higgs documented a half-century of African American economic achievement in the face of the strong headwinds of ignorance, oppression, and political ignorance. He explains how their commercial agency worked to the freed slaves' benefit. Higgs argued that their access to competitive markets rather than the state's coercive machinery explained their rapid ascent.

Higgs's work has important implications. Emphasizing political history at the expense of commercial history leads to mistaken conclusions about the course of human events. Higgs casts serious doubt on Marxian interpretations of history by showing that the history of African Americans in the American economy in the decades after emancipation is *not* the history of class struggle as much as it is the history of the complex interplay between cooperation, competition, and coercion—with competition frequently working against "class interests." What might advance "class interest" via coordinated action by a cartel of monopolists or monopsonists in a one-shot game is self-defeating when people compete in repeated games. As Reid (1973, 110) explained, "The Black Codes' stern penalties for 'vagrancy' and 'enticing' and recurrent attempts to organize planter cartels were insufficient to stifle the upward pressure on wages."

The freedmen were widely and roundly abused and faced ubiquitous political discrimination. However, the need to attract and retain workers and customers restrained people's cupidity. Under slavery, masters did not have to count slaves' foregone leisure among their costs or have strong incentives to consider their slaves as anything more than chattel (Higgs 1977a, 40). Emancipation did not mean the freedmen could be perfectly safe and secure in their persons and property. It did, however, unleash the forces of competition to their benefit. Market forces stepped in and provided protection where political institutions failed. Higgs quotes an Arkansas planter: "The constant demand for their labor affords them the amplest protection" (Higgs 1977a, 76).

Higgs's work speaks against two interpretations of racial history, specifically racism and political determinism. Racists like George Fitzhugh argued that legal compulsion was necessary to get Blacks to work and to avoid their becoming financial burdens on whites. However, Black labor force participation was higher than white labor force participation, which flatly contradicts racist convictions about the freedmen's fitness for participation in free commercial society (Higgs 1977a, 7, 41).

Higgs's analysis also implies that political achievement matters less than previously thought (Higgs 1979b, 492). While he argues that political discrimination explains slower Black economic progress because it meant Black schooling was limited and Black property rights were poorly protected, "he fairly notes that this explanation seems to conflict with the economic record of Japanese Americans" (Reid 1977, 1341). Higgs explored the Japanese experience in greater detail in papers published after *Competition and Coercion* and found that legal restrictions like the 1913 California Alien Land Law were "immediately, openly, and widely evaded" (Higgs 1978, 216). Having a law on the books does not accomplish much if the law is easy to evade. When competition is allowed at least some room to operate, people can make considerable progress despite political, cultural, and social institutions dedicated to preventing it—exactly what the freedmen did with their newfound (but limited) economic freedom.

Competition against Discrimination

Higgs's work on wage discrimination in postbellum Southern agriculture applied the methods of the New Economic History to a question with an "obvious" answer. In asking whether or not Southern farmers discriminated, he began with Becker's (1971) theory of discrimination and then examined available data to see if they showed white employers exercising a "taste for discrimination" by systematically underpaying Black workers, and if they showed white employees exercising a "taste for discrimination" by commanding a wage premium for working in an integrated environment. Higgs specified models with testable implications, collected previously neglected data from old government reports and other sources, and then used state-of-the-art statistical techniques to test the hypotheses. He found that white and Black workers earned comparable wages for comparable work, and it appeared that racist farmers were not, at the margin, willing to sacrifice material well-being to satisfy any "taste for discrimination" they might have had (Higgs 1972a). Furthermore, piece rates in cotton picking and coal mining were the same regardless of race (Higgs 1989, 19).

Southern employers could discriminate legally. Many wanted to and were encouraged to; however, whether they could discriminate effectively is a question about the incentives they faced in Southern labor markets (Higgs 1977a, 1977b, 1989). Following Becker's (1971) analysis, Higgs asked whether Black workers were systematically paid less than comparable white workers for the same work (Higgs 1977a, 8ff). He answers that they were not. If whites had a "taste for discrimination" for which their labor commanded a wage premium, it was extremely weak (Higgs 1977a, 8–9). Moreover, "equal payment within a given occupation was the most common practice," and commercial discrimination was weaker and harder to identify than political discrimination (Higgs 1977b, 239, 244). His conclusions were consistent with what he had found in a 1971 paper in the *Journal of Economic History* about immigrants, where he wrote that "the evidence is quite convincing that at least some American employers preferred wealth to the pleasures of discrimination" (Higgs 1971, 436). The free market did not eliminate discrimination but punished it (Higgs 1972a; see also the exchange in Roberts and Higgs 1975).

Competition and coercion worked at cross purposes (Higgs 1973, 169). Where competition was allowed to operate, it undermined planters' allegedly unified class interests, as few were willing to sacrifice the profits they could earn by hiring away a competitor's underpaid workers. As Ray Stannard Baker put it (quoted in Higgs 1977a, 118), "One of the most significant things I saw in the South—and I saw it everywhere—was the way in which the white people were torn between their feeling of race prejudice and their downright economic needs." At the polling place, Southern whites' "feeling of race prejudice" won, but in the marketplace, their prejudice yielded to "their downright economic needs."

People might have been racists, but they weren't racist enough to put their money where their mouths were. It was a topic to which Higgs devoted considerable attention through the 1970s. In 1971, he identified "(1) the existence of the slave system and (2) the abolition of that system through destructive civil war and haphazard emancipation" as the sources of persistent Southern poverty (Higgs [1971] 2011, 114). Even in the face of formidable political obstacles, African Americans between 1865 and 1914 made economic progress that was nothing short of remarkable.

Land, Skills, and Wealth

The freedmen started with next to nothing. Landless emancipation left the freedmen with nothing to sell but their labor power and "caused organizational chaos in the economic life of the South that had permanently harmful consequences" (Higgs [1971] 2011, 18). Later, Higgs wrote, "All that emancipation gave the blacks was, in short, themselves" (Higgs 1977a, 118). They were also almost all illiterate and unskilled: "To become a skilled farmer required instruction, example, and most of all experience. In 1865, relatively few blacks could independently manage a farm successfully" (Higgs 1977a, 121). They lacked the education and experience to be successful farmers once their chains were broken. While a brief efflorescence of Black political power meant higher tax collections and more spending on schooling (Logan 2020), they were politically impotent after Reconstruction ended.

These impediments did not stop them, and many freedmen surmounted seemingly insurmountable obstacles. Landless emancipation accounted for "a substantial part of the racial difference in farm size as late as 1910" (Higgs 1973, 166), but progress was remarkable. Higgs expanded on his 1970s work in the 1980s, when he studied Black property accumulation, finding that "during the half-century following emancipation the Georgia freedmen and their descendants—and other southern blacks as well—rapidly accumulated wealth" (Higgs 1982, 735).[1] Home ownership rates moved steadily upward, and even after the Great Depression African Americans still owned almost a quarter of the homes they occupied (Higgs 1989, 14). They made substantial gains in literacy within a single generation after emancipation (Higgs 1977a, 120). Slavery affected family structures and increased single motherhood, but this effect was dying out by 1900 (Miller 2018). In his studies of Japanese immigrants in California, Higgs (1978, 1979b) explained that initial conditions did not seem to matter as much as was previously thought. Even with nothing to sell but their labor power and legal institutions arrayed against them, Japanese immigrants in the early 20th century—and the freedmen in the late 19th century—accumulated property at an impressive pace.

This is not to say the freedmen would not have been better off had they been compensated for their time in chains and granted land. Miller (2011) argues that former slaves in the Cherokee nation who had been emancipated with land were better off, and she further estimates that they faced a smaller racial wealth gap. Collins, Holtkamp, and Wanamaker (2022) argue that Black land ownership meant higher home ownership and literacy rates. Racial inequality would have been lower (Miller 2020). Nonetheless, Higgs argues that 40 acres and a mule would have likely had a "modest" effect on African American living standards after two generations (Higgs 1977a, 93).

Slavery, Sharecropping, and the Boll Weevil

How do we explain the causes and effects of share tenancy? As Higgs (1977a, 45) writes, "Many writers seem to believe that share tenancy was a method of race control imposed on helpless blacks by all-powerful whites, but the evidence is almost entirely inconsistent with such an interpretation." It does not appear that "sharecropping replaced slavery" or that it was used as a means of race control.

Was sharecropping inefficient? Adam Smith thought sharecropping provided inefficient incentives, but the answer lies in the structure of property rights (Cheung 1968, 1120). Reid (1973, 112) explains that contemporary racist observers thought "the supposed ignorance and sloth of Negro labor not directly supervised by whites" meant sharecropping would be less efficient than other forms of agricultural tenure. Finally, many historians believed sharecropping was a form of social control imposed on Black farmers by their landlords and creditors.

In a series of papers, Higgs evaluated these popular hypotheses. Sharecropping is better understood as the result of competitive, rather than coercive, processes. Sharecropping, he argued, did not emerge because planters and landlords had the power to exploit farmers and trap them in debt peonage (cf. Fishback 1989). Their alleged cotton "overproduction" was not because creditors demanded a cash crop but most likely an exercise of their comparative advantages given limited skills in the decades following emancipation (Higgs 1977a, 77). Citing work by Jennifer Roback, Higgs (1989, 22) argues that "most well-documented cases of genuine peonage, for example, appear actually to have been kidnapping or enslavement abetted by local legal authorities." Higgs argues that a cycle of perpetual debt was not inherent in sharecropping or the crop-lien system, and people could (and did) switch landlords regularly (Higgs 1977a, 74; Fishback 1989). It was instead the product of weak legal protections for Black farmers (Higgs 1977a, 57).

Building on Cheung (1968) and Reid (1973) in particular, Higgs tells a different story where agricultural land tenure emerged and evolved in response to transaction costs. Sharecropping, economists argued, emerged as an "understandable market response" to the vagaries of the postbellum agricultural marketplace and was not a system of exploitation foisted upon the powerless by the powerful (Reid 1973). Economists argued that it is a mistake to consider agricultural contracting in terms of imposition rather than cooperation. While Reid (1973,126; 1976, 575) disputes Cheung's argument that sharecropping emerged to share risk efficiently (Cheung 1968), he nonetheless explained how sharecropping benefited landlords *and* sharecroppers. As he put it, "*The central feature of a sharecropping contract is the continuing interest of both landlord and tenant in the efficiency of agricultural production*" (Reid 1973, 126, emphasis in original). Different contracts embodied different risk-sharing arrangements (Higgs 1973; Alston and Higgs 1982).

Even Adam Smith was skeptical of sharecropping as he believed it weakened people's incentives to produce (Reid 1976, 549ff). In contrast to the thesis that sharecropping was inefficient insofar as the share owed to the landlord acted like a tax and therefore reduced croppers' incentives to produce, sharecropping made it possible to get more output out of inputs that would have produced less under alternative institutions (Reid 1976, 576). Landlords and tenants may not have worked for one another's benefit deliberately, but self-interest and competition pushed them to find mutually advantageous arrangements.[2]

A landlord's time, energy, and attention were all scarce. Sharecropping economized the monitoring costs necessary with wage labor (Higgs 1974, 469). Importantly, landlords had managerial expertise many of their tenants lacked (Reid 1977, 406). As Reid (1973, 126) explains in an analysis of sharecropping contracts, "The sharecropping landlord supplied managerial expertise as well as land to his tenants." Sharecropping made it easier for landlords and tenants to take advantage of gains from the division of knowledge and from the division of labor.

To see sharecropping as an exercise of power by one party—the landlord— is an error. It is better considered an exchange—a contract (Reid 1973, 1976, 1977). Sharecropping, wage labor, and fixed rent tenure emerged in response to competitive economic forces rather than noncompetitive economic power. As Higgs wrote in a review of Donald L. Winters's *Farmers without Farms:*

Agricultural Tenancy in Nineteenth-Century Iowa, "Historians henceforth must accept farm tenancy as what it was, a useful and productive institution" (Higgs 1979a, 1169). Using county-level data, Garrett and Xu (2003) lend further empirical support to this proposition.

What about the effect of the boll weevil? While it perhaps induced better public health and educational innovation (Clay, Schmick, and Troesken 2019; Baker, Blanchette, and Eriksson 2020), it may not have been the decisive force in the Great Migration—the mass movement of African Americans from the rural South to the North and West—as had been thought previously. Higgs's work on the relationship between the boll weevil, the Great Migration, and cotton cultivation is a useful example of his scholarship answering and re-answering old historical questions. He argued that traditional emphasis on the boll weevil as a "push" factor in the Great Migration is overstated. Many people left the weevil-less Carolinas, and Texas had net population gains even though it battled the boll weevil from 1892 onward. Furthermore, as Higgs argues, farmers adapted: "As farmers learned how to alter their methods of production to reduce weevil damage—before 1920 mainly by early planting and heavy fertilization, afterwards by these plus the application of calcium arsenate—they generally abandoned their hasty attempts to diversify and returned to their traditional specialization in cotton" (Higgs 1976, 344–45).

In Higgs's ([1971] 2011) analysis, competition and market forces have considerable power to explain the transformation of the American economy between 1865 and 1914. The freed slaves left bondage and entered a world arrayed against their freedom. Would more government intervention have been to their benefit? Higgs believes not, and his work exploring ideology and economic outcomes helps us understand why.

Higgs argued that African American economic progress would have been more rapid were it not for oppressive political institutions. The institutions, in turn, were the product of political opportunism and racist ideology. Formally, many explicit rules attenuated Black property rights. Informally, Blacks were expected to master and practice "race etiquette" (Alston 1986). Racism could manifest itself on different margins. Higgs argued that insufficient enforcement of Blacks' recognized rights mattered more than explicitly racist legislation (Higgs 1977a, 10; see also Prentice, Konya, and Prentice 2019). The laws did not provide equal protection in theory, but more importantly, law enforcement did not provide equal protection in practice (Carden 2009; Carden and Coyne 2013). This meant lower risk-adjusted returns on investments in physical and human capital (Higgs 1977a, 11–12). Citing Williams (2011) and Friedman

(1962), Wright (2022) explains that illiberal institutions are the friends of racism and discrimination while liberal institutions are their enemies. Political competition, Higgs argued, "worked in support of discrimination rather than in opposition to it" (Higgs 1989, 25).

CONCLUSION: POLITICS, THE ECONOMY, AND ECONOMIC AGENCY

> He strives for a balanced treatment and will probably be rewarded by attacks from both sides.
>
> —C. Vann Woodward (1978, 195)

It bears repeating that Higgs did not deny the oppression that occurred after emancipation and persisted into the 20th century. Rather, he documented how the freedmen and their descendants made substantial gains even in a political environment containing many elements explicitly designed to stop them. These gains were considerable. Why weren't they greater?

Higgs blames political discrimination rather than commercial discrimination, writing, "Discrimination *outside* the market sector had an important influence in determining the opportunities open to blacks *inside* the market sector" (Higgs 1977a, 9). When the freedmen had access to the ballot and political office, their outcomes improved (Logan 2020). Especially after Reconstruction, Southern legal institutions ranged between oppressive and unreliable. As Higgs writes, "To appeal to the law was to seek the enemy's stronghold," and "such salvation as the black man found, he found in the private sector" (Higgs 1977a, 132, 133). He did not find it there because the people were necessarily kinder, more moral, or more racially enlightened. Many voted for the very politicians and policies responsible for persistent Black poverty. As Higgs explains, however, when faced with an explicit trade-off between indulging one's taste for discrimination and making money, they frequently chose the money. African American economic progress in land ownership, home ownership, wealth accumulation, income, literacy, and many other areas was not the consciously designed outcome of articulated policies crafted to achieve noble moral goals. It was the systemic outcome of competitive social and commercial processes.[3] These insights remain among Robert Higgs's enduring contributions.

NOTES

1. See also Higgs (1984) for replies to comments on his 1982 paper.

2. In a different context, Higgs's analysis of Coasian bargains in the Coeur d'Alene mining district shows how people have found ways to cooperate despite high transaction costs (Higgs 2012).

3. On the relationship between intentional and systemic political causation, see Sowell (1980, 2007).

REFERENCES

Alston, Lee J. 1986. "Race Etiquette in the South: The Role of Tenancy." *Research in Economic History* 10: 199–211.

Alston, Lee J., and Robert Higgs. 1982. "Contractual Mix in Southern Agriculture since the Civil War: Facts, Hypotheses, and Tests." *Journal of Economic History* 42 (2): 327–53.

Baker, Ricard B., John Blanchette, and Katherine Eriksson. 2020. "Long-Run Impacts of Agricultural Shocks on Educational Attainment: Evidence from the Boll Weevil." *Journal of Economic History* 80 (1): 136–74.

Becker, Gary. 1971. *The Economics of Discrimination*, 2nd ed. Chicago: University of Chicago Press.

Carden, Art. 2009. "Inputs and Institutions as Conservative Elements." *Review of Austrian Economics* 22 (1): 1–19.

———. 2021. "Robert Higgs: A Birthday Appreciation." American Institute for Economic Research, February 1. https://www.aier.org/article/robert-higgs-a-birthday-appreciation/.

Carden, Art, and Christopher J. Coyne. 2013. "The Political Economy of the Reconstruction Era's Race Riots." *Public Choice* 157: 57–71.

Cheung, Steven N. S. 1968. "Private Property Rights and Sharecropping." *Journal of Political Economy* 76 (6): 1107–22.

Clay, Karen, Ethan Schmick, and Werner Troesken. 2019. "The Rise and Fall of Pellagra in the American South." *Journal of Economic History* 79 (1): 32–62.

Collins, William J., Nicholas C. Holtkamp, and Marianne H. Wanamaker. 2022. "Black Americans' Landholdings and Economic Mobility after Emancipation: New Evidence on the Significance of 40 Acres." NBER Working Paper 29858.

Fishback, Price V. 1989. "Debt Peonage in Postbellum Georgia." *Explorations in Economic History* 26 (2): 219–36.

Friedman, Milton. 1962. *Capitalism and Freedom*. Chicago: University of Chicago Press.

Garrett, Martin A., and Zhenhui Xu. 2003. "The Efficiency of Sharecropping: Evidence from the Postbellum South." *Southern Economic Journal* 69 (3): 578–95.

Hartwell, R. M., and Robert Higgs. 1971. "Review: Good Old Economic History." *American Historical Review* 76 (2): 467–74.

Higgs, Robert. 1971. "Race, Skills, and Earnings: American Immigrants in 1909." *Journal of Economic History* 31 (2): 420–28.

———. (1971). 2011. *The Transformation of the American Economy, 1865–1914*. Auburn, AL: Ludwig von Mises Institute.

———. 1972a. "Did Southern Farmers Discriminate?" *Agricultural History* 46 (2): 325–28.

———. 1972b. "Review of *Railroads and the Granger Laws*, by George H. Miller." *Agricultural History* 46 (4): 552–53.

———. 1973. "Race, Tenure, and Resource Allocation in Southern Agriculture, 1910." *Journal of Economic History* 33 (1): 149–69.

———. 1974. "Patterns of Farm Rental in the Georgia Cotton Belt, 1880–1900." *Journal of Economic History* 34 (2): 468–82.

———. 1976. "The Boll Weevil, the Cotton Economy, and Black Migration, 1910–1930." *Agricultural History* 50 (2): 335–50.

———. 1977a. *Competition and Coercion: Blacks in the American Economy, 1865–1914.* Chicago: University of Chicago Press.

———. 1977b. "Firm-Specific Evidence on Racial Wage Differentials and Workforce Segregation." *American Economic Review* 67 (2): 236–45.

———. 1978. "Landless by Law: Japanese Immigrants in California Agriculture to 1941." *Journal of Economic History* 38 (1): 205–25.

———. 1979a. "Review of *Farmers without Farms: Agricultural Tenancy in Nineteenth-Century Iowa*, by Donald L. Winters." *American Historical Review* 84 (4): 1169.

———. 1979b. "The Wealth of Japanese Tenant Farmers in California, 1909." *Agricultural History* 53 (2): 488–93.

———. 1982. "Accumulation of Property by Southern Blacks before World War I." *American Economic Review* 72 (4): 725–37.

———. 1984. "Accumulation of Property by Southern Blacks before World War I: Reply." *American Economic Review* 74 (4): 777–81.

———. 1989. "Black Progress and the Persistence of Racial Economic Inequalities, 1865–1940." In *The Question of Discrimination: Racial Inequality in the U.S. Labor Market*, edited by Steven Shulman and William Darity Jr., 9–31. Middletown, CT: Wesleyan University Press.

———. 2012. "Coasian Contracts in the Coeur d'Alene Mining District." *Independent Review* 17 (2): 239–52.

———. 2016. "Douglass C. North: Trailblazer." *Independent Review* 21 (1): 139–42.

Logan, Trevon D. 2020. "Do Black Politicians Matter? Evidence from Reconstruction." *Journal of Economic History* 80 (1): 1–37.

Marx, Karl, and Friedrich Engels. 1848. "Manifesto of the Communist Party." https://www.marxists.org/archive/marx/works/1848/communist-manifesto/ch01.htm#007.

Miller, Melinda C. 2011. "Land and Racial Wealth Inequality." *American Economic Review* 101 (3): 371–76.

———. 2018. "Destroyed by Slavery? Slavery and African American Family Formation following Emancipation." *Demography* 55 (5): 1587–1609.

———. 2020. "'The Righteous and Reasonable Ambition to Become a Landholder': Land and Racial Inequality in the Postbellum South." *Review of Economics and Statistics* 102 (2): 381–94.

Prentice, Khayen, Laszlo Konya, and David Prentice. 2019. "Was the African American Great Migration Delayed by Outlawing Emigrant Agents?" *Essays in Economic and Business History* 37 (1): 43–75.

Reid, Joseph D. 1973. "Sharecropping as an Understandable Market Response: The Post-Bellum South." *Journal of Economic History* 33 (1):106–30.

———. 1976. "Sharecropping and Agricultural Uncertainty." *Economic Development and Cultural Change* 24 (3): 549–76.

———. 1977. "The Theory of Share Tenancy Revisited—Again." *Journal of Political Economy* 85 (2): 403–7.

Roberts, Charles A., and Robert Higgs. 1975. "Did Southern Farmers Discriminate? An Exchange." *Agricultural History* 49 (2): 441–47.

Sowell, Thomas. 1980. *Knowledge and Decisions*. New York: Basic Books.

———. 2007. *A Conflict of Visions: Ideological Origins of Political Struggles*. New York: Basic Books.

Williams, Walter. 2011. *Race and Economics: How Much Can Be Blamed on Discrimination?* Stanford, CA: Hoover Institution Press.

Woodward, C. Vann. 1978. "Review of *Competition and Coercion: Blacks in the American Economy, 1865–1914*, by Robert Higgs." *Agricultural History* 52 (1): 194–95.

Wright, Walker. 2022. "Illiberal Economic Institutions and Racial Intolerance in the United States." *Economic Affairs* 42: 307–26.

Chapter 2

The Origins and Persistence
of Discriminatory Institutions
and Ideologies

Jayme S. Lemke

R obert Higgs has contributed extensively to a variety of important questions in political economy. I do not dare aspire to address all of them
in this chapter. Instead, I will focus on Higgs's work on the role of
state power in the oppression of particular social groups. This is most evident in Higgs's research on Black workers in the American economy in the
half-century after emancipation (e.g., Higgs 1972, 1976a, 1976b, 1977a, 1977b,
1982, 1984). However, related themes—including the significance of ideology, the dynamic interplay between social norms and political action, and
the nature of governmental power—recur throughout his work (e.g., Higgs
1991, 2007, 2008, [1987] 2012). Writings throughout Higgs's career suggest a
variety of ways that economic reasoning and careful historical study can help
us to understand the nature of oppression, when and how that oppression can
come to target particular groups, and how those targeted groups may recover
from oppression in spite of continued socio-ideological and political barriers.

In the next section, I will offer a brief overview of Higgs's work and
method, focusing on their connection to questions of discrimination and discriminatory rule systems in order to provide context for the subsequent discussion. I will then draw out three themes from Higgs's work that can be applied
to better understand the nature of discriminatory institutional environments.
First, an institutional environment is comprised of both publicly and privately
organized rule schema that are interconnected rather than existing in isolation. As such, understanding a discriminatory institutional environment
requires understanding the interaction between public discriminatory law and
private discriminatory social norms. Second, institutions are defined in part
by the alternative institutional arrangements that either do or could coexist.

Thank you to Chris Coyne and Mikayla Novak for their thoughtfulness and helpful suggestions.

The competitive landscape—both in the sense of competition within markets and competition between governance regimes—is critical to understanding the nature of discriminatory oppression and how it might abate or become further entrenched. Third, Higgs offers several important hypotheses about ideology and race, including how racist ideologies might develop, how they contribute to shaping the landscape of market opportunity, and how they can alter political incentives in ways that encourage the implementation of racially motivated laws.

In the final section, I will offer some potential directions for future scholarship. Public choice and institutional frameworks have been greatly underutilized in the study of questions of discriminatory ideologies and policies, and Robert Higgs's work suggests numerous ways to remedy that unfortunate deficiency.

HIGGS'S METHOD AND ITS RELEVANCE TO QUESTIONS OF DISCRIMINATION

Statistics and Narrative in Economic History

In *Competition and Coercion: Blacks in the American Economy 1865–1914*, Robert Higgs (1977a) turned his attention to a critically important set of questions about the relationship between economic competition and the race-based coercion that deprived Black Americans of so many opportunities, economic and otherwise. This book was written in the early 1970s, and as such, there has been a great deal of advancement in the study of BIPOC (Black, Indigenous, and people of color) communities in the decades since. However, the book and related journal articles are organized around sound economic logic. Particularly given how few advancements have been made in race studies by public choice and institutional economists since—with notable exceptions, including Grynaviski and Munger (2017), Levy and Peart (2020), Magness (2020), Novak (2018, 2021), Roback (1986), Sowell (1977), and Williams (1982)—Higgs provides an invaluable jumping-off point for further analysis.

In his earliest books, Higgs uses neoclassical economic theory to interpret demographic and other statistical data on changing standards of living in the United States (Higgs [1971] 2011, 1977a). His 1971 book *The Transformation of the American Economy, 1865–1914* considers the economy *in general*, operating primarily on the level of statistical aggregates. Even when Higgs is considering more institutional questions, such as the contributions of medicine or incorporation law to economic growth, much of the discussion is general rather than focused on variation between groups. One of the limitations of such an approach is that focusing on the aggregate is not as neutral of a position as it might sound. Who is the aggregate person, and if we could identify them, would their experiences help us understand the social and economic reality of the time? Particularly in this case, where the recordkeepers of the time were significantly more thorough in their recording of white male landowner's experiences than anyone else's, the "aggregate" person's experiences may bear very little resemblance to the lives lived by large swathes of the population.[1]

Higgs ([1971] 2011) does pose some questions about race and inequality, but the hypotheses he begins to develop about the economic experiences of formerly enslaved Black Americans and how they differed from those of the white population are only fully fleshed out in his subsequent book, *Competition and Coercion: Blacks in the American Economy, 1865–1914*. For instance, Higgs ([1971] 2011, 120) notes that "whether the rate of growth of black incomes exceeded the rate of growth of white incomes, however, remains open to conjecture." This is a question he will go on to address more explicitly in Higgs (1977a), suggesting that the later book may have been intended to bring additional complexity into the earlier, more general analysis.

A tool Higgs used frequently in his early work was demographic analysis (e.g., Higgs 1976b, 1977a, 24–36). However, he does not merely present the data. Even in his more statistically oriented earlier works, he is clear from the outset that there can be no meaningful interpretation without theory, and that failing to specify the theory at hand will generate only confusion (Higgs [1971] 2011, 6). Rather, demographic data is analyzed through an economic lens to identify possible implications, and then those implications are put to empirical test through what would now be identified as the analytic narrative approach to economic history (Boettke, Coyne, and Leeson 2013; Koyama 2018). This method draws on as wide a range of historical sources as possible—including but not limited to census data, newspapers, biographical and autobiographical accounts, and secondary sources—in order to construct a plausible account of the behavioral logic underlying commonly observed historical patterns. One of the advantages of incorporating multiple methods within a political economy framework is that it enables use of a logical framework without requiring the analyst to deliberately ignore the complexities of social reality (Boettke, Palagashvili, and Lemke 2013; Lemke and Kroencke 2020). As Higgs (1977a, 118) put it, "The present objective is to incorporate as much genuine complexity as possible within an intelligible interpretation."

The use of multiple methods enables Higgs to address theoretical questions that are best understood in the context of empirical realities that are not reducible to statistical aggregates. For instance, Higgs asks, what can we infer from the demographic observation that geographic mobility among the Black population was significantly more limited in the 50 years following emancipation than many expected? Why did so many Black Americans stay in the South rather than fleeing to the North and West, away from former slavers? Was it "a lack of many genuinely superior opportunities outside the South, ignorance of opportunities that did exist, or obstacles of cost or coercion" (Higgs 1977a, 30)? Neither demographic data nor economic theory alone can resolve this question.

However, drawing on historical sources can show that Black Americans did move, and that some even moved to the North or to popular frontier destinations such as Kansas, suggesting that they were aware of alternative options. As such, ignorance cannot be the explanation. Instead, firsthand accounts suggest that the wage differential was simply not enough to justify the high cost of relocation, particularly in light of the fact that Black migrants to Northern cities would often be competing for low-wage jobs with large immigrant populations (Higgs 1977a, 30–32). This analysis demonstrates the efficacy of a multiple methods approach in the social sciences (Poteete, Janssen, and Ostrom 2010).

Although Higgs would continue to be an exemplar of identifying what can be learned from data while remaining acutely aware of its limitations (Higgs [1971] 2011), his methodological priorities would change over time. In particular, he became skeptical of the use of econometrics as a tool of causal inference, and more interested in the process-oriented, subjectivist approach of Austrian economists such as Ludwig von Mises and F. A. Hayek. However, he writes in the introduction to one of his early books, "Even in regard to the econometrics on which I relied for the first fifteen or twenty years of my career, I have come to believe that not all of my work (and others' work along similar lines) was for naught. . . . If one views the econometric findings not as a means of making inferences in testing hypotheses, but simply as descriptive statistics, one may make valuable use of such findings in writing economic history" (Higgs [1971] 2011, vi). And a good descriptive understanding of history is vitally important: "There is no good substitute for knowing, quite literally, what we are talking about. One must, then, study history; one must comprehend the great variety of acting and interacting individuals whose actions compose our subject and the diverse and changing institutions that condition the actors' choices" (Higgs [1971] 2011, 33).

Can Economics Be Used to Understand Difference and Discrimination?

The existence of the book *Competition and Coercion* is itself all the evidence really needed to show that Higgs believed economics can be used to understand difference and discrimination. The key question explored in Higgs (1977a) is whether Black Americans benefited from the economic development that occurred in the United States during the Reconstruction era (Higgs 1977a, 95–117). Data from the time period is limited and biased toward containing information about the relatively small number of Black Americans who lived in Northern cities, despite the fact that the majority of Black Americans continued to live in the rural South for long after emancipation. Taking into account the deficiencies of the data, Higgs is unwilling to make too declarative a statement, but he concludes that although "the blacks of 1900 remained poor in some absolute sense or poor relative to the whites," "the likelihood that over a third of a century [1867–1900] black incomes advanced more rapidly than white incomes is a matter of great significance" (Higgs 1977a, 102). In short, Black Americans had some success in "catching up" to white Americans despite the many barriers they faced in being able to fully access the market.

In another example of Higgs's use of multiple methods, he draws upon both available statistics and first-person accounts in order to evaluate changes in living standards. One interesting bit of nontraditional and nonquantitative evidence that speaks to the increase in living standards for Black Americans is the extent to which white Americans began to criticize them for lavish spending. Higgs quotes one farmer who complained that his Black tenant farmers were wasting money on "illustrated Bibles, patent nostrums, hair straighteners, skin bleaches, pistols, sewing machines, organs, pianos, and clocks" (Higgs 1977a, 104). Interestingly, this set of goods raises an important point about the role of expectations and beliefs, concepts to be addressed in greater detail in this chapter's next section. Most Black farmers had very limited discretionary income at this time. That they would use what little income they had left after the purchase of necessities to buy hair straighteners and skin bleaches speaks to the extent that Black Americans felt they had to invest in appearing more culturally and physically similar to white Americans in order to accomplish their objectives.

By turning his attention to how institutions and outcomes differed according to racial identity, Higgs was also able to contribute to an important debate about the compensation received by the freedmen in the decades following emancipation (Higgs 1972, 1975, 1977a, 1977b, 1978b). Higgs's main conclusion from this branch of research is that "ever since emancipation the main thrust of racial economic discrimination in America has been not the payment of lower wages to blacks than to productively identical whites, but rather a variety of measures that have had the effect of keeping the productivity of black labor low" (Higgs 1977b, 243). Even in the 1870s, in the immediate aftermath of slavery, "in many jobs the workers received the same pay regardless of race"

(Higgs 1977a, 60). There were some jobs where this was not the case, where workers filled out time cards that specified one rate for a Black worker and another, higher rate for a white worker (Higgs 1977a, 87). However, disparities were more often due to exclusion from particular occupations, exclusion from unions that had successfully commanded a higher wage, or to a belief that Black Americans were not suited to particular jobs than to discriminatory practices within jobs (Higgs 1977a, 86–69).

One clarification worth making is that in his study of difference and discrimination, Higgs follows in the tradition of Austrian economics and of the political theory of James Buchanan in observing that neither societies nor governments, or any other organized groups, have a singular shared welfare function (Buchanan 1959; Vaughn [1995] 2021). Instead, there is great disagreement between and within governments and all other organizational types. The processes through which those disagreements are resolved often explain quite a bit about observed outcomes. For instance, in the context of government, Higgs observes in 1991 that "there are more than 80,000 separate governments, more than 60,000 with the power to tax. . . . Supposing that the government operates as if it were a single decision maker cannot take us far toward a realistic understanding of modern government or its growth" (Higgs 1991, 11). Neither the size of the government nor the diversity in the preferences of its agents have changed since that time.

As such, Higgs is both interested in group phenomenon and clear about the fact that he does not consider *groups* to be *classes* if the term "class" is used to refer to "an overriding agreement on objectives and a unity of action among the individuals who comprise the class" (Higgs 1977a, 130). Disagreements among members of groups are common and can contribute significantly to variation in experiences across the membership. Higgs offers this as a plausible explanation for why white planters mostly failed in their attempts to restrict the wages of Black tenant farmers (Higgs 1977a, 130). Cartels are extraordinarily difficult to maintain without the use of coercion when each member of the cartel stands to gain so significantly by being the one to raise wages and therefore attract the most productive tenants to their property. The benefits to the cartel of employing coercion under such circumstances may explain the increasing effort over time to build discrimination explicitly into legal institutions rather than relying on private enforcement, eventually culminating in the Jim Crow system of laws: "The whole panoply of segregation ordinances constituted a well-enforced exclusion of blacks from an array of consumption opportunities on racial grounds alone; and these restrictions had the full weight of the law and its enforcement machinery to support them" (Higgs 1977a, 132). This question of the relationship between ideological and legal discrimination will be returned to in the next section.

USING THE IDEAS OF ROBERT HIGGS TO UNDERSTAND IDEOLOGICAL AND POLITICAL DISCRIMINATION

Interaction between Economic, Social, and Political Institutions

Robert Higgs's work highlights the importance of not considering one type of institutional environment in isolation. Instead, different institutional spheres often interact with others at critical junctures. It is a narrow view indeed to attempt to understand markets without recognizing the political rules that bound them, or to attempt to understand political institutions without recognizing how they are shaped by beliefs and ideologies. Further, Higgs's approach to institutions seems to appreciate their complexity, recognizing that rules and their enforcement is not the exclusive purview of public organizations. Rather, public and private practices operate in tandem to define the law as it is experienced by those it governs. In the context of the Reconstruction era, Higgs describes "a reign of 'private' lawlessness, intimidation, and violence that had pervasive effects" that began with personal choices but were bolstered by "the public sector's complicity in these actions" (Higgs 1977a, 10). He discusses this phenomenon both in the context of racism against Blacks and in the context of private and legally mandated discrimination against Japanese Americans in the first half of the 20th century (Higgs 1978a).

Law was used to oppress Black Americans in the 19th and 20th centuries in an extraordinary variety of ways even after emancipation. Disenfranchisement, differential public investment, and explicitly racialized law gathered strength in the time period between 1865 and 1914 (Higgs 1977a, 123–24). Further, "A more pervasive influence than the written law was the actual day-to-day enforcement of the law—or the lack of it—by white officers. Especially in the rural South the sheriff, his deputies, and the local judge normally awaited the behest of influential whites" (Higgs 1977a, 124). Even when the *de jure* (i.e., legally recognized) letter of the law is the same, if *de facto* (i.e., in practice) enforcement varies in a predictable way along group lines, then one group is effectively living in a different institutional environment than the other (Lemke 2015). In the case of Black Americans during the time period Higgs studies, the institutional differences experienced by different racial groups were stark.

However, when it came to the oppression and control of Black Americans, members of the state were often more than happy to share their monopoly on violence with a variety of private actors. The clearest examples of this phenomenon were the privately organized death sentences white citizens took upon themselves to arrange. Between 1882 and 1915, some 3,000 Black Americans died from lynching or being otherwise tortured and executed by white mobs (Higgs 1977a, 90). A mostly less violent but still important example of privately exercised coercion were the labor unions that fought against the employment of Black Americans, "on occasion by violent means" but also by striking or threatening to strike against the hiring of black workers (Higgs 1977a, 86).

Another way Higgs accounts for the interconnectedness of public and private is by investigating the way that culture and beliefs impacted *both* market and political institutions. He argues that the particularly strong "taste for discrimination" among the white Southern population during the slavery, Reconstruction, and Jim Crow eras led to both "'private' coercion and persecution" and public discrimination. This public discrimination was significantly exacerbated by the fact that "governmental officials were privileged to occupy positions from which discrimination might be exercised at little or no cost to them" (Higgs 1977a, 11). As such, private and public actors worked in tandem to restrict access to public schools and obfuscate legal routes to protect property rights, significantly curtailing the economic progress of Black Americans.

The interplay between private and public can also be seen in Higgs's analysis of the Alien Land Law of 1913 (Higgs 1978a, 214–21). The motivation behind the law was anti-Asian racism combined with the economic tensions that emerged when Japanese farmers proved to be effective economic competitors. This created the perfect storm for passage of legislation explicitly designed to "limit their presence by curtailing their privileges which they may enjoy here; for they will not come in large numbers and long abide with us if they may not acquire land" (State Attorney General U. S. Webb quoted in Higgs 1978a, 215).

Higgs's (1977a, 9–10) explanation for why discrimination against Blacks persisted in the American South despite the fact that it was costly to both victims and perpetrators is also one that hinges on recognizing the interplay between public and private rule. His argument is twofold. First, Higgs argues that the logic of the Beckerian model (Becker 1971) that describes economic competition as a vehicle through which costly discrimination is likely to be limited is sound. However, Becker's theory is only applicable to environments of robust market competition. In the American South, Black Americans were explicitly denied access to markets, both politically through Jim Crow and other segregationist laws and culturally by white Americans who were not prepared to invite Black Americans into their communities and workplaces.

Freedmen and other Black Americans made significant gains in wealth, income, and opportunity, but their efforts were also regularly frustrated by political and economic processes that favored the white and the educated. Illiterate Black tenant farmers could not audit the books for themselves and faced greater obstacles in even knowing their legal rights, let alone exercising them. As such, "many were genuinely robbed," and without recourse other than spreading the word that a particular planter was a cheat and best avoided (Higgs 1977a, 53). Higgs sums up the situation: "That competition did moderate the extent to which the blacks were cheated is beyond question; that some cheating persisted despite competitive pressures is equally beyond doubt. The ignorance of many blacks and their exclusion from the equal protection of the law created opportunities for cheating too numerous and easily exploited to be demolished completely by competitive forces" (Higgs 1977a, 54).

The second part of Higgs's argument questions the applicability of the Beckerian model to instances where discrimination is as violent and intense as it was in the American South. Beliefs about the inherent inferiority and inhumanity of those born with darker skin, developed during the era of chattel slavery and consistently reinforced through the Reconstruction era, persisted into the Jim Crow era and beyond:

> To say that American slavery was a system of carefully justified racial discrimination is to utter the obvious, but an important and not-so-obvious implication is that under slavery racial discrimination acquired a value that transcended the economic gains it made possible for the master class. Long before 1865 the whites had acquired what Gary Becker has called a "taste for discrimination," and that taste, being a fundamental part of their views about proper social life, was certain to persist long after the institution that nurtured it had disappeared. (Higgs 1977a, 8)

If a group of people are so far gone that they are unwilling to even imagine the humanity of a fellow human being, it is unlikely that a higher cost of labor or higher cost of goods will change their mind. In the perception of those individuals, to accept Black Americans as equals would be to violate their fundamental ideas about right and wrong, which in Higgs's analysis were shaped to a great degree by their participation in the institution of slavery in the first place. Slavers had sacrificed their liberality and could not now bring it back without admitting to the most grievous wrongdoing. Their taste for discrimination was simply too deeply embedded.

The Role of Market Competition and Political Competition

Higgs considers competition in all its manifestations to be a critically impor-tant component of understanding what kinds of opportunities are available and the extent to which individuals will be able to take advantage of them. External governments and groups can have an enormous impact on the dynamics within a group. Higgs discusses this in the context of how foreign relations have impacted the growth of government (Higgs 1991, 18). Another way Higgs investigates the role of external dynamics is in his investigation of how the economic opportunities available in the Northern United States and along the 19th-century frontier impacted the economic well-being of the Black workers who primarily lived in the Southern United States (Higgs 1976a, 1976b, 1977a, 1978b, 1982). But you don't need to look outside the country or even outside the region to understand the importance of options and competi-tive forces, whether economic, political, or ideological. Even the choice to quit one landlord and rent from another was an important competitive force and a discipline that discouraged white landlords from dealing dishonestly with Black tenant farmers (Higgs 1977a, 48–54).

This is why, despite his concerns about the limitations of the Becker model in the case of Black Americans during Reconstruction, Higgs still emphasizes the role markets played in enabling improvements in the economic situation of recently emancipated Black Americans. Southern planters went to great efforts to try to compensate freedmen as little as possible, even going so far as attempting collusion among themselves in order to keep wages down (Higgs 1977a, 46–48). Yet, those same planters also desperately needed labor, and quickly. Consequently, they often had no choice but to offer higher wages and better terms than they might have hoped.

Higgs (1977a, 48–49) quotes one planter who describes sending out hiring agents who would spend "day after day" riding around making job offers to freedmen. According to the planter, these efforts were frustrated more often than not by the fact that the freedmen already had better job offers or had good reason to expect a better offer would be coming soon. Higgs finds these personal accounts reflected in the data: "Whereas many laborers had received only one-tenth or one-eights of the crop (plus food, clothing, and shelter) in 1865, such small fractions were unknown in later years. . . . By the 1870s, ten-ants who provided only labor normally received one-half of the crops plus a cabin, fuel, and garden plot" (Higgs 1977a, 49).

These forces of competition were met with both legal and extralegal efforts to limit competitive market forces and the attendant gains to Black farm laborers.

For instance, Southern states enacted anti-enticement laws to discourage other white planters from attempting to hire freedmen who had a preexisting labor contract, regardless of how much better the newly offered alternative might be (Higgs 1977a, 75). There is some question over how well enforced these laws were, but they are certainly an example of an attempt by the state to prevent Blacks from participating freely in market processes.

On the private and occasionally extralegal side, white farmers in Mississippi formed "whitecap organizations" to discourage freedmen from renting their own land rather than accepting employment or sharecropping deals on white plantations. These whitecappers "issued warnings, burned homes, beat blacks, and fired shots into houses" (Higgs 1977a, 76). This strategy was effective at discouraging Black farmers from renting within the community, but ineffective at encouraging those who had been attacked from working for their attackers. Instead, those who were attacked by whitecappers often left the area entirely. Although in this case, the law eventually sided against the whitecappers, in cases of conflict the *de facto* law often sided with white landlords rather than Black tenants. Higgs offers as example an 1890 case in Lowndes County, Alabama, where a white landlord threatened to shoot a Black tenant for not following work orders. The Black tenant shot first and was lynched for defending himself and his wife (Higgs 1977a, 76).

The Alien Land Law of 1913 is a particularly interesting case of anticompetitive agitation as it illustrates how legislation can be designed in a way that appears on the surface to have general implications, when in actuality the legislation very intentionally targets one specific group of people:

> On its face it appeared only to define certain property rights of "all aliens eligible to citizenship under the laws of the United States." It provided, however, that "all aliens other than those" could enjoy only such property rights as "prescribed by any treaty now existing between the government of the United States and the nation or country of which such alien is a citizen or subject"; the single exception was that aliens ineligible for citizenship could "lease lands in this state for agricultural purposes for a term not exceeding three years." As the Japanese were legally ineligible for naturalization, and as the treaty of 1911 between Japan and the United States gave the Japanese no explicit rights to own or lease agricultural land in the United States, and as the Chinese had long been denied the privilege of immigration, the act in effect applied only to the Japanese. (Higgs 1978a, 215)

The laws were not entirely effective at keeping away Japanese competitors, as there were many ways that mutually beneficial exchanges could be made between aspiring Japanese farmers and individuals with names and backgrounds that would not trigger suspicion on the part of the court (Higgs 1978a, 220–21). This provides yet another historical example of the difficulty of maintaining racial discrimination in the presence of adequately tempting profit opportunities.

However, as Higgs observes, this case also illustrates the fact that market opportunity is not enough to stop a government determined to oppress. Despite the success for a time of the questionably legal market arrangements between white and Japanese farmers, the Japanese American population was greatly diminished by the Alien Exclusion Act of 1924. Those who remained were subject to horrible crimes on the part of the US government when they were imprisoned in concentration camps during World War II simply for their apparent Japanese ancestry: "In the hysteria of 1942–1945 the immigrant generation lost practically everything it had so arduously accumulated. Emerging from the concentration camps in 1945, the aging immigrants were too old to start anew. Their children, much younger and more vigorous, with excellent educations, would make extraordinary economic progress in the postwar era. But their great gains should blind no one to the vast losses of their parents, losses for which only token restitution was ever made" (Higgs 1978a, 224). The great efforts by both private and public actors to minimize the force of competition are themselves a testament to how effectively competition stood to enable changes that white planters and anti-Black racists found undesirable.

Choice between political jurisdictions can be another important form of competition. For instance, one debated question in the study of Black history is why the "Great Migration," in which roughly 1.3 million Black Americans moved from the South to Northern cities between 1916 and 1929, happened when it did and not earlier (Higgs 1976a, 335). Why did freedmen and their descendants wait so long after emancipation to move to wealthier areas where they would be less likely to experience racial violence? Why did the forces of political competition not pull more Black Americans away from the South? Higgs's analysis finds that industrial employment opportunities were an important and "sufficient" reason for the mass relocations (1976a, 350). Whether differences in law didn't have more of an effect because physical survival was too pressing a concern or because Black Americans did not perceive the covert racism of the North to be preferable to the overt racism of the South is hard to say. But once again, the importance of recognizing the interaction between political and economic institutions is clear.

Higgs's analysis speaks to the extent that being able to move between governing regimes—whether those of formal governments or of private law—can be a more effective means of protecting one's rights than turning to legal authorities. This was particularly true for Black Americans in the Reconstruction and Jim Crow eras, when turning to law often meant turning to their former or current oppressors:

> From plantation to plantation, from countryside to city, from east to west the freedmen moved, establishing a precedent that would prove invaluable in keeping their freedom more than a mere legality. The Southern whites, with the legal machinery they increasingly and eventually completely controlled, sought to suppress this mobility. Through laws against vagrancy and the enticement of employees or tenants under contract, through statutes placing prohibitive taxes on emigrant labor agents and making certain indebtedness subject to criminal rather than civil prosecution, and through extralegal threats and intimidation the whites attempted to keep the black laborers and tenants in place. (Higgs 1977a, 119)

Competition between institutional regimes can also take the form of people simply refusing to participate—a phenomenon that falls under the category of activities Albert Hirschman (1972) termed "exit." One of the difficult decisions members of an oppressed group will face is the determination of when to fight for inclusion and acceptance from their current or former oppressors, and when to create their own communities, businesses, and spaces (Novak 2021). W. E. B. Du Bois called the latter the "group economy" (quoted in Higgs 1977a, 90), an idea captured pithily by Daymond John in 1992 when he founded the clothing brand FUBU: "for us, by us."[2] The fact that open markets contain within them opportunities to refuse to patronize existing sellers or work for existing employers is an important piece in understanding how it is that competition could be a force against discrimination.

Ideology and the Role of Beliefs

Another important direction Higgs's work points us in is the study of the role of ideology (including but far from limited to Higgs 2007, 2008, [1971] 2011, and [1987] 2012). For Higgs, recognizing the role of ideology in shaping action is not contrary to the use of economic logic. Rather, "ideology can be understood as consistent with rather than the antithesis of rational action. . . . The quest to determine econometrically whether ideology mattered in determining a certain set of political actions, seeks to answer a non-question. Of course it matters. It always matters, because people cannot even think about political questions, much less undertake political actions, without an ideology" (Higgs

[1971] 2011, 23). Higgs ([1971] 2011, 23) quotes Mises's statement on the matter, situating his own argument once again in the context of the Austrian tradition: "What a man considers his interest is the result of his ideas. . . . Free men do not act in accordance with their interests. They act in accordance with what they believe furthers their interests."

This discussion of ideology is vitally important to understanding some of the more important questions and paradoxes in American political history. How could a country premised so openly and proudly on the ideals of freedom and justice for all have turned such a blind eye to the many ways that Blacks, Indigenous populations, women, and immigrants were denied rights throughout the 19th century and into the 20th (Lavoie [1985] 2016)? The fact that people could have been treated so differently based on matters that to us seem as superficial as how they looked, the language they used, or where they were born speaks to the power of ideology:

> Ideologies are belief systems about social relations. Chief among their dimensions is the cognitive: ideologies structure and give meaning to a person's perceptions of social life. They also place affective weight on those apperceptions, designating some things good or right, other things bad or wrong. They also point toward a justifiable political program and open up the potential for solidarity with likeminded comrades. Such solidarity serves as an important means of establishing and maintaining a social identity; it helps to determine people's psychologically essential conceptions of who they are. (Higgs [1971] 2011, 24)

Connecting ideology to identity suggests not only that ideology is an important input into political decision-making, but also that to ask people to change their ideology will often be to ask them to be rule-breakers and to bear the costs associated with breaking the social rules in effect in their families and communities. In other words, our ideologies can become enforced through our identities. Change will be costly, and will only be likely to occur within environments that make continued ideological compliance more costly than change.

The issue of identity raises the question of how discrimination based on observable external characteristics differs from other kinds of discrimination. Higgs (1977a, 3–9) presents a counterfactual of what the economic experience of freed slaves would have been if "freedmen" appeared to be white rather than Black. The core of the argument is that although the disadvantages of having lived under enslavement would have been significant, it would have likely taken only a generation or two for the descendants of the slavers and the descendants of the enslaved to become virtually indistinguishable. However, the fact that only Blacks were enslaved in the United States meant that free Black Americans would continue to be viewed through the lens of the beliefs about inherent inferiority and other justifications for enslavement for many, many generations to come.

For example, enslavement was often justified by the false belief that Blacks were less mature and less capable of caring for themselves than their white neighbors. A Mississippi newspaper editorial opined, "The child is already born who will behold the last negro in the State of Mississippi. With no one to provide for the aged and the young, the sick and the helpless incompetent to provide for themselves, and brought unprepared into competition with the superior intelligence, tact, and muscle of free white labor, they must surely and speedily perish" (quoted in Higgs 1977a, 14).

Another false belief developed under the institution of slavery was that Black "freedmen" would only work if coercively compelled:

> Southern whites had misled themselves with uncritical inductive reasoning. . . . So thoroughly had the whites confused black behavior with slave behavior, it was difficult for them to realize that under slavery—property rights being what they were—avoiding the lash was the slave's only incentive aside from petty gifts and occasional time off that the master might arbitrarily bestow. The freedman, endowed with property rights over his own labor services, responded quickly to the prospect of a pecuniary return. (Higgs 1977a, 38)

It seems so painfully obvious from a modern-day vantage point that any enslaved person would resist the master's work that one wonders how those "Southern whites" ever convinced themselves that race had anything to do with it. Such is the nature of human belief systems.

One of the fundamental lessons of institutional economics—perhaps *the* fundamental lesson—is that individuals will respond to the rules of the systems they are embedded within. Southern whites were consistently rewarded, not only through ill-gotten economic gains but also by their peers and by political agents for acting as if slavery was an essential and morally justifiable practice (see Grynaviski and Munger [2017]). This widespread belief system, reinforced daily and connected to race by virtue of the fact that the US government permitted the enslavement of Blacks but not of whites, persisted through generations. This phenomenon illustrates how beliefs about entire groups of people can carry their own momentum, becoming mutually reinforcing through both peer effects (holders of the belief assuring each other of its veracity) and the discouragement of change. For example, those who believe a particular group is inherently lazy will be less likely to hire a member of that group. In turn, knowing how an application will likely be received will discourage members of the group believed to be lazy from applying for the job in the first place, thus reinforcing the shared belief further regardless of its empirical veracity or inevitability.

Another poignant illustration of the practical importance of ideology is in the way the institutional environment faced by Black Americans "required careful behavior from the black man. He must not attempt too much; he must not argue his own case too strongly; he must at all times assent to the white man's judgment and opinion; he must scrupulously observe the racial etiquette; above all he must never appear 'uppity,' for his life itself would thereby be endangered. In short, he must stay 'in his place'" (Higgs 1977a, 125). An institutional environment structured around the idea of keeping a group of people in their place is not one that can reasonably be expected to coexist with creativity and progress. Rather, these social and cultural constraints, especially where reinforced by formal law or law enforcement practices, served as a significant discouragement to market activity. Higgs continues,

> Not only did all this take its toll in manhood and self-respect but it had important economic consequences. A farm owner might have to forego acquiring a good farm near the main road or the white church in favor of a poorer farm near the swamp or up on a distant hillside. A laborer must simply concede the earnings fraudulently withheld by a dishonest employer. To argue only added personal risk to pecuniary loss; one could only move on and hope for better treatment elsewhere. Similarly, a tenant with a grievance against his landlord was well advised to keep quiet, lest he find himself of the chain gang, the victim of a trumped-up charge, a phoney trial, and a harsh sentence. (Higgs 1977a, 125)

Higgs asks whether these "discriminatory constraints" might have an adverse impact on "motivation, attitudes, and ambition" in addition to their primary effect of blocking or increasing the cost of some opportunity (Higgs 1977a, 128). After all, "few men will persist in knocking on a door that is usually slammed in their faces" (Higgs 1977a, 129). Questions about the magnitude and distribution of this kind of discouragement are extraordinarily difficult to answer, but it is almost certain that expectation shapes action: "For the black man the future was always more uncertain than for the white man. . . . To swim in the sea of a dynamic and highly competitive economic system was difficult enough without the weight of racial discrimination for-ever pulling downward" (Higgs 1977a, 13). An individual who expects to face a higher than usual risk that they will be shut out of the labor market will be less likely to invest in education, move to an area with better job opportuni-ties, or work hard accumulating property that could be taken from them either through discriminatory policy or an angry mob with torches.

The experiences of Black Americans in the labor force illustrate the poten-tial for long-run consequences if a person's market opportunities are limited for even a short time. A former slave

> could build a slave shanty; he could construct a rough sugar hogshead and resole a shoe; in exceptional cases he could do even careful and inge-nious work in certain lines; but as a rule he knew little of the niceties of modern carpentry or iron-working, he knew practically nothing of mills and machinery, very little about railroads . . . and if he was ignorant, who was to teach him? Certainly not his white fellow workmen, for they were his bitterest opponents because of strong race-prejudice and because of the fact that the Negro works for low wages. (W. E. B. Du Bois, quoted in Higgs 1977a, 84–85)

The combination of lack of access to markets and enduring prejudice even once access to markets was opened to Black Americans (albeit incompletely) created a situation that would delay progress for freedmen. If the sons of car-penters are more likely to become carpenters, and the sons of lawyers more likely to become lawyers, then this dynamic could have a discouraging effect for generations of freedmen. Our ideas and beliefs about ourselves and our lives can have a powerful, enduring impact.

DIRECTIONS FOR FURTHER RESEARCH

In analyzing processes of political and ideological change, Higgs's scholarship raises a variety of important questions relevant for understanding discrimina-tory institutions and the circumstances under which they might be changed. In his critique of "magical" theorizing, he encourages us to not be satisfied simply with identifying a pattern. Instead, understanding requires us to push further, searching for an explanation of the process through which the pattern is generated: "Just because a course of action is 'necessary' in some systemic sense for the successful operation of an economy does not ensure that anyone has a personal incentive to work toward fulfilling the requirement. . . . Who did what to make it happen? And why did these actors find it in their interest to take such actions?" (Higgs 1991, 10). There are several areas of inquiry that could be addressed productively by taking such an approach.

First, the frameworks developed in the fields of public choice and constitutional political economy can be used to devise possible institutional alternatives to be proposed to the public, in the spirit of James Buchanan's (1964) encouragement to be an input into democratic rather than authoritarian processes. For example, one particularly interesting argument Higgs presents in *Competition and Coercion* is that a more thorough and effective land grant program would have created a significantly different institutional environment, potentially leading to a very different series of relationships between Black and white Americans during the Reconstruction era (Higgs 1977a, 79–80). If Black farmers owned their own land, they would not have been made vulnerable by the need to trust the white landowners who may not have been managing the books fairly. Perhaps white planters would have gotten less used to cheating Black laborers, and Black workers would have gotten less used to being cheated. How much more trust could have been built under this alternative paradigm? A similar approach can be taken to understanding how political, social, and economic institutions impact beliefs, expectations, and opportunities for different groups today.

A second insight from Higgs that can be usefully applied to understanding whether or not a particular group will become a target for oppression is that, unlike in simple market models where the identities of individuals buying and exchanging do not matter much, individual personalities can have a significant impact on the activities of governments: "In politics one person can make a difference—not that very many can or do, but the potential exists when the right person and the right occasion conjoin" (Higgs 1991, 15). Coercive discrimination, whether public or private, has an ideological basis that can change greatly over time (Vaughn [1994] 2021). Deirdre McCloskey (2019, 134) notes that cultural values are far from fixed and can change relatively rapidly in response to changes in rhetoric, ideology, or policy. As such, there is ample room for case studies of ideological entrepreneurs and investigation into the circumstances that foster ideological entrepreneurship. Further, this research direction is important not only for understanding the rights and welfare of oppressed persons—though that would certainly be sufficient justification. As heterodox institutional economists including Bateman (2019) and McCloskey (2010, 2016) have noted, discriminatory ideologies that prevent people from contributing their best to the world impoverish *everybody*. Exclusion is as bad for our material well-being as it is for our souls.

A third research direction would be to use the tools of public choice and institutional economics to study how it is that people define group boundaries and come to identify as individuals who must follow one set of rules rather than another. Higgs (1977a, 1) quotes W. E. B. Du Bois on what it meant to be Black in his time: "The black man is a person who must ride 'Jim Crow' in Georgia." This definition seems intended to emphasize the role that social rule systems and our beliefs about them play in shaping how we see ourselves and how we are seen by others. Although the Black man and woman in Georgia had little choice but to comply with their prescribed identity, this implies that racial boundaries and popularly accepted definitions of what it means to be a *something* are determined in part through the exercise of political authority and are thus changeable. This could have important implications for understanding of modern xenophobia and racism, tensions in areas of high immigration, and LGBTQ rights. In pursuing this research, public choice and new institutional scholars may find it particularly fruitful to connect to the growing strand of literature in "stratification economics," which seeks to understand the interaction of defined, overlapping social groups (Darity, Hamilton, and Stewart 2015, Davis 2019). Although the methods are different, many of the questions are the same, thereby creating an opportunity for productive scholarship across subfields that are currently mostly isolated.

Answering questions like these is not a trivial matter; it is a question of what kind of society our children and grandchildren will inhabit. Higgs (1977a) notes that a thoughtful observer might wonder how freedmen were able to accomplish so very much in the decades after emancipation despite seemingly being discouraged at every turn. In the words of Frederick Douglass, we may "marvel that they have, under the circumstances, done so well" (quoted in Higgs 1977a, 134). Similarly, one might ask what more could have been accomplished if Black Americans had been invited to participate in "that aggressive pushing behavior for which economically successful Americans have been justly famous" rather than having to take "a circuitous route to his achievement" (Higgs 1977a, 125). How might the world look different today if Black Americans had not been made to take the long way around? What contributions have been missed, might there be more social trust, and how would our political institutions look if so many of them had not been developed within a discriminatory institutional environment?

These are counterfactuals that can never be conclusively answered. However, in addressing more carefully questions about our own institutions and their potential for discrimination and the obfuscation of opportunity, we may be able to avoid being confronted with more such painful questions in the future.

NOTES

1. Pils and Schoenegger (2021) offer an interesting extension of this argument in their discussion of standpoint epistemology and how it may be more directly relevant than is commonly realized to questions in new institutional economics and Austrian economics about how knowledge is shared, aggregated, and interpreted.

2. Tim Ferris, "The Making of FUBU—An Interview with Daymond John," *Tim Ferriss* (blog), April 7, 2011, https://tim.blog/2011/04/07/fubu-daymond-john/.

REFERENCES

Bateman, Victoria. 2019. *The Sex Factor: How Women Made the West Rich*. New York: John Wiley and Sons.

Becker, Gary S. 1971. *The Economics of Discrimination*, 2nd ed. Economic Research Studies. Chicago: University of Chicago Press.

Boettke, Peter J., Christopher J. Coyne, and Peter T. Leeson. 2013. "Comparative Historical Political Economy." *Journal of Institutional Economics* 9 (3): 285–301.

Boettke, Peter, Liya Palagashvili, and Jayme Lemke. 2013. "Riding in Cars with Boys: Elinor Ostrom's Adventures with the Police." *Journal of Institutional Economics* 9 (4): 407–25.

Buchanan, James M. 1959. "Positive Economics, Welfare Economics, and Political Economy." *Journal of Law and Economics* 2 (October): 124–38.

———. 1964. "What Should Economists Do?" *Southern Economic Journal* 30 (3): 213–22.

Darity, William A., Darrick Hamilton, and James B. Stewart. 2015. "A Tour de Force in Understanding Intergroup Inequality: An Introduction to Stratification Economics." *Review of Black Political Economy* 42 (1–2): 1–6.

Davis, John B. 2019. "Stratification Economics as an Economics of Exclusion." *Journal of Economics, Race, and Policy* 2 (3): 163–72.

Grynaviski, Jeffrey D., and Michael C. Munger. 2017. "Reconstructing Racism: Transforming Racial Hierarchy from 'Necessary Evil' into 'Positive Good.'" *Social Philosophy and Policy* 34 (1): 144–63.

Higgs, Robert. (1971) 2011. *The Transformation of the American Economy, 1865-1914: An Essay in Interpretation*. Auburn, AL: Ludwig von Mises Institute.

———. 1972. "Did Southern Farmers Discriminate?" *Agricultural History* 46: 325–28.

———. 1975. "Did Southern Farmers Discriminate? Interpretive Problems and Further Evidence." *Agricultural History* 49 (2): 441–47.

———. 1976a. "The Boll Weevil, the Cotton Economy, and Black Migration, 1910–1930." *Agricultural History* 50 (2): 335–50.

———. 1976b. "Participation of Blacks and Immigrants in the American Merchant Class, 1890–1910: Some Demographic Relations." *Explorations in Economic History* 13 (2): 153–64.

———. 1977a. *Competition and Coercion: Blacks in the American Economy, 1865-1914*. New York: Cambridge University Press.

———. 1977b. "Firm-Specific Evidence on Racial Wage Differentials and Workforce Segregation." *American Economic Review* 67 (2): 236–45.

———. 1978a. "Landless by Law: Japanese Immigrants in California Agriculture to 1941." *Journal of Economic History* 38 (1): 205–25.

———. 1978b. "Racial Wage Differentials in Agriculture: Evidence from North Carolina in 1887." *Agricultural History* 52 (2): 308–11.

———. 1982. "Accumulation of Property by Southern Blacks before World War I." *American Economic Review* 72 (4): 725–37.

———. 1984. "Accumulation of Property by Southern Blacks before World War I: Reply." *American Economic Review* 74 (4): 777–81.

———. (1987) 2012. *Crisis and Leviathan: Critical Episodes in the Growth of American Government.* Oakland, CA: Independent Institute.

———. 1991. "Eighteen Problematic Propositions in the Analysis of the Growth of Government." *Review of Austrian Economics* 5 (1): 3–40.

———. 2007. *Neither Liberty nor Safety: Fear, Ideology, and the Growth of Government.* Oakland, CA: Independent Institute.

———. 2008. "The Complex Course of Ideological Change." *American Journal of Economics and Sociology* 67 (4): 547–65.

Hirschman, Albert O. 1972. *Exit, Voice, and Loyalty.* Cambridge, MA: Harvard University Press.

Koyama, Mark. 2018. "Analytic Narratives." In *An Economist's Guide to Economic History,* edited by Matthias Blum and Christopher L. Colvin, 371–78. London: Palgrave Macmillan.

Lavoie, Don. 2016 [1985]. *National Economic Planning: What Is Left?* Arlington, VA: Mercatus Center at George Mason University.

Lemke, Jayme S. 2015. "An Austrian Approach to Class Structure." In *New Thinking in Austrian Political Economy,* edited by Christopher J. Coyne and Virgil Henry Storr, 167–92. Bingley, UK: Emerald Group.

Lemke, Jayme, and John Kroencke. 2020. "Methodological Confusions and the Science Wars in Economics." *Review of Austrian Economics* 33 (1): 87–106.

Levy, David M., and Sandra J. Peart. 2020. *Towards an Economics of Natural Equals: A Documentary History of the Early Virginia School.* Cambridge: Cambridge University Press.

Magness, Phillip W. 2020. "The Anti-Discriminatory Tradition in Virginia School Public Choice Theory." *Public Choice* 183 (3): 417–41.

McCloskey, Deirdre Nansen. 2010. *The Bourgeois Virtues: Ethics for an Age of Commerce.* Chicago: University of Chicago Press.

———. 2016. "Max U versus Humanomics: A Critique of Neo-Institutionalism." *Journal of Institutional Economics* 12 (1): 1–27.

———. 2019. *Why Liberalism Works: How True Liberal Values Produce a Freer, More Equal, Prosperous World for All.* New Haven, CT: Yale University Press.

Novak, Mikayla. 2018. *Inequality: An Entangled Political Economy Perspective.* New York: Springer.

———. 2021. *Freedom in Contention: Social Movements and Liberal Political Economy.* Lanham, MD: Rowman and Littlefield.

Pils, Raimund, and Philipp Schoenegger. 2021. "On the Epistemological Similarities of Market Liberalism and Standpoint Theory." *Episteme* (May): 1–21.

Poteete, Amy R., Marco A. Janssen, and Elinor Ostrom. 2010. *Working Together: Collective Action, the Commons, and Multiple Methods in Practice.* Princeton, NJ: Princeton University Press.

Roback, Jennifer. 1986. "The Political Economy of Segregation: The Case of Segregated Streetcars." *Journal of Economic History* 46 (4): 893–917.

Sowell, Thomas. 1977. *Race and Economics.* London: Longman.

Vaughn, Karen I. (1994) 2021. "Can Democratic Society Reform Itself? The Limits of Constructive Change." In *Essays on Austrian Economics and Political Economy.* Edited by Karen I. Vaughn. Fairfax, VA: Mercatus Center at George Mason University.

———. [1995] 2021. "Should There Be an Austrian Welfare Economics?" In *Essays on Austrian Economics and Political Economy.* Edited by Karen I. Vaughn. Fairfax, VA: Mercatus Center at George Mason University.

Williams, Walter Edward. 1982. *The State against Blacks.* New York: New Press.

Chapter 3

Reconsidering Inequality
Limitations and Opportunities
Robert Whaples

> Is more economic inequality better? For most American intellectuals, the answer is obvious. The question itself would strike them as either frivolous or callously reactionary. For the typical intellectual . . . it is clear that more economic equality is better.
>
> I disagree. In doing so, I am not claiming that more economic equality is necessarily worse. I simply insist that the societal distribution of income or wealth itself, whatever it might happen to be, is morally neutral; neither an increase nor a decrease in the degree of inequality has any unambiguous moral meaning. Everything hinges on *why* the distribution changes
>
> —Higgs (2004, 3), emphasis in the original

Concern about economic and social inequality, especially in the political arena but also among scholars, has grown strongly in the past half-century, becoming a core focus in recent years. A recent Gallup poll reports that only 36 percent of American adults are satisfied with the way wealth is distributed (American Enterprise Institute 2021, 10). Another indication is the Google Ngram in figure 3.1, which shows surging references to both "economic inequality" and "social inequality."

I begin this chapter by considering *why* people care about social and economic inequality, concluding that objections to it often encompass four concerns: objections to differences in status, objections to a mismatch between outcomes and merit, concerns about fairness, and the specter that inequality itself causes other problems, especially the abuse of power and conflicts that tear apart the fabric of society. I then consider what economists have contributed to our understanding of inequality and follow that with a consideration of Robert Higgs's important scholarship on inequality. After that, I broaden beyond the usual focus on inequality in annual income within a country to

Figure 3.1. Ngram for "social inequality" and "economic inequality," 1950–2019

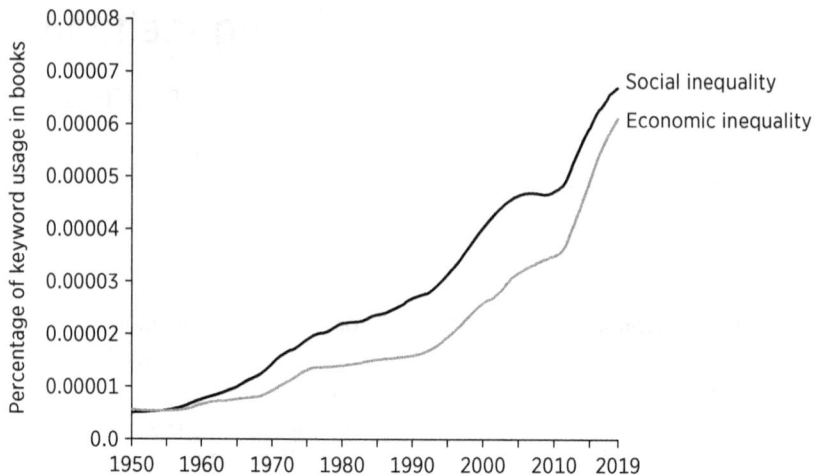

Source: https://books.google.com/ngrams.

examine modern income levels in comparison to the distribution of income among *all* the human beings who have ever lived; the Gini coefficient of income among all people who have ever lived—and who will live in the future; and inequality of life expectancy when counting *all* lives, not just those that appear in conventional statistics. The final section pushes further by considering inequality in something everyone deems to be important—virtue—examining measures of inequality in net tax contributions to the common good, blood donations, and religious attendance.

WHY PEOPLE CARE ABOUT INEQUALITY

Concern about economic and social inequality has grown strongly in the past few decades, perhaps because official measures of income and wealth inequality have trended upward.

But why do people care about inequality? For example, why should we care that some people have more (or less) income, wealth, or anything else than other people, especially when they have more than we do? Perhaps we shouldn't care (or shouldn't care very much). Perhaps we should.[1]

One reason we care is that worries about status seem to be innate—we simply cannot avoid them even if we should, some argue. By one account, every sentient creature cares about status. It's hardwired. Jordan Peterson (2018) observes that when a dominant lobster is badly defeated, "its brain basically dissolves" before it grows a new subordinate's brain "more appropriate to its new, lowly position" (2018, 7). Evolutionary biologists believe that this dominance hierarchy has been around for half a billion years: "We were struggling for position before we had skin, or hands, or lungs, or bones" (2018, 14). "There is an unspeakably primordial calculator, deep within you, at the very foundation of your brain, far below your thoughts and feelings. It monitors exactly where you are positioned in society" (2018, 15).

Another account related to the origin of concern about status puts it this way: "Abel was a keeper of sheep, and Cain a tiller of the ground. In the course of time Cain brought to the Lord an offering of the fruit of the ground, and Abel brought of the firstlings of his flock and of their fat portions. And the Lord had regard for Abel and his offering, but for Cain and his offering he had no regard. So Cain was very angry, and his countenance fell" (Genesis 4:2–5 [RSV]). Seeing that his status was lower, Cain slew Abel.

If relative status is the root cause of worries about inequality—and it seems to be for many people—then worrying about it may be a losing game at the level of an entire society. If one person's relative status rises, someone else's must fall by definition. *Should* status matter to us so much? Should human beings share the worldview of lobsters? Does pulling someone else down (or killing him) to gain status add value for society as a whole and really make us better off? Concern about relative status, per se, seems to root concern about inequality in envy, one of the seven deadly sins.

A second cause of concern about inequality arises when it emerges because those at the top do not deserve their good fortune and/or those at the bottom do not deserve their bad fortune.[2] Such inequality can violate our sense of justice even though no one has broken any rules. In this case the concern isn't so much about lack of equality, it's about *who* has high or low status. The concern doesn't arise when those with great wealth earn it by doing good for society—say by producing goods and services that we value highly. It arises when great wealth isn't "earned" but comes merely from an undeserved windfall or fortune of birth—say good parents, good genes, or good connections. Likewise, the concern could arise when those with low earning power at the bottom have played by the rules but have caught undeserved bad breaks—say bad health, random accidents, or lack of opportunity.

Hayek ([1976] 1982, 71) points out that economic life in a market economy is "wholly analogous to a game." There are rules, and people do better in the game if they develop the skills needed to play well—say by producing highly valued goods and services—but there's always an element of luck. Too much luck—good luck or bad luck—can make the game unappealing. However, the economic game isn't a zero-sum game, unlike poker or pinochle. It's a positive-sum game. The "losers" can do well. The "losers" can be lucky too—and (as I will expand upon below) in the modern world the losers have increasingly high standards of living, even if they are below those of the winners. In most card games, all the face cards are pretty valuable. But a pinochle deck removes every card below a nine, doubling up on the other cards. In this case, jacks and queens just don't rank very high and so aren't likely to be winners very often. Someone with mostly jacks and queens could be seen as a "loser." However, in the economic world, standards of living have risen so much that virtually no one lives at the level of a deuce, trey, or even an eight. In many ways, modern Americans live in a pinochle deck world. The rules of the economic game have given us plenty of jacks and queens, so middle-class people now have standards of living that in many ways (aside from relative status) are greater than most royalty of premodern times—and even the poor consume far more than most people have historically (as I will demonstrate below). The luck of this hand seems pretty appealing. Unless status is your central concern, why would you legitimately complain that someone else is even luckier than you?

Now the third reason people care about inequality. What if the people at the top don't deserve their success because they have cheated—they've stacked the deck (or worse)—and taken their winnings from others? Most would agree that the game isn't worthy if it is rigged so that cheaters win. The outcome must be changed, as the rule breakers must be penalized. Breaking the rules of society, or nature, or God is not to be tolerated.

This brings us to the fourth cause of concern about inequality—that it weakens society and degrades mankind. This can happen when those at the top—whether or not they cheated to get there—use their wealth to grasp power and use this power to give themselves unfair advantages over others and deprive others of their rights, or when those at the top see themselves as better than everyone else and are unconcerned about them, demeaning humanity—theirs and that of other people. This can also happen when those at the bottom react to their position by turning to violence, self-pity, or self-destruction and by putting in less effort to be good citizens, neighbors, and parents—harming themselves and those around them.[3] These consequences of inequality are a genuine concern, can wreck the economic game, and can lead to political movements that destabilize society.

Objections to inequality often boil down to these four concerns: objections to differences in status; objections to a mismatch of outcomes and merit; objections about cheating to obtain status; and objections that even when status differences aren't tied to luck or cheating, large differences in status can have negative spillover effects. Continuing the card playing analogy—which may be apt since calls for "new deals" are about a century old—these four concerns about inequality are approximately (1) I hate losing and/or seeing others whom I care about lose; (2) I hate it when people win mainly because they are lucky (unless I'm the lucky one?); (3) I hate it when cheaters (or other bad people) win; and (4) winners treat losers badly and/or losers act destructively when they lose. It's very difficult to solve the first problem as there are always relative "winners" and "losers"—unless we decide to stop playing the game. However, it is hard to avoid playing the economic game. Calls for redistribution clearly tap into this concern but are usually cloaked behind the other three concerns.

ECONOMISTS ON INEQUALITY

Neoclassical economics pays considerable attention to inequality because it pays considerable attention to income and wealth creation. Its core insight is that in competitive markets payments are tied to productivity. More precisely, the value of the marginal product of an input to production (say, labor) equals the demand for that input in a competitive market. Labor market income makes up the vast majority of income, so in general people's incomes are tied to how much they work and their wage rates. In competitive markets, wages and income will be higher when the demand for labor is higher—when the worker is more productive and/or produces things that are valued more by others. In addition, wages will be higher when the supply of labor is smaller—when there are fewer people with these (often hard to acquire and master) skills. This is the central approach of mainstream economics.[4]

Much of the neoclassical approach derives from the insights of Carl Menger and other Austrian economists, whose marginal thinking is at the core of modern economics. Menger ([1871] 1981, 108) argued that "man, with his needs and his command of the means to satisfy them, is himself the point at which human economic life both begins and ends." The central point is that the supply and demand for goods and factors of production, which determine the range of incomes in a society, aren't exogenous facts—they arise from the purposive behavior of people. And they are completely *subjective* in nature. "For Austrian economists, the subjective nature of human beings permeates all aspects of economics. . . . Evaluations of the desired ends, as well as the determination of the best means to achieve those ends, are uniquely subjective to the individual chooser" (Coyne and Boettke 2020, 7). This applies not only to benefits but also to costs, as "subjective opportunity cost is purely in the mind" (2020, 8).[5]

Building on this approach, Friedrich Hayek suggests that demands for redistribution and calls for social justice often stand on boggy ground. The general good may not be served by calls for equality and redistribution, because "in a free society the general good consists principally in the facilitation of the pursuit of unknown individual purposes" (Hayek, [1976] 1982, 1). We cannot generally know how to improve societal outcomes because we are not privy to the purposes other people see for themselves. Among members of a free society, "there will exist no agreement on the relative importance of their ends" ([1976] 1982, 3).

Moreover, the world is very complex, so it is difficult to know the full consequences of an action, especially at the societal level. Individuals act purposefully, but a society cannot act purposefully—and society-level outcomes are spontaneous orders that arise from people pursuing their own ends. By trial and error, individuals adopt the rules that serve them well. For example, trial and error shows that in pursuing gains from trade, both producers and consumers benefit. For this reason, a producer often benefits others most by simply producing products for profit. Indeed, "quite apart from the question of what he wants to do with his profits after he has earned them," the market producer "is led to benefit more people by aiming at the largest gain than he could if he concentrated on the satisfaction of the needs of known persons" ([1976] 1982, 145).[6] In Hayek's view, the merit of market economies isn't that they generate so much wealth (although they usually do, and this is generally a good thing). Wealth is a means to an end. Markets are useful because they incentivize people to cooperate—would-be enemies, those without common goals, learn that they can gain (each reaching his or her own private ends) by engaging with each other in the market.

A central contribution of Austrian economics is in saying to aspiring social planners and redistributionists: "Do not pretend that you know what you're doing. You are not omniscient. You cannot read people's minds. You do not know whether you will improve things. You would use force—taking away people's freedoms—to chase after a *mirage*." Hayek ([1976] 1982) aptly titled his book *The Mirage of Social Justice*. Planners simply lack the knowledge of what people value and how much they value each thing. While neoclassical economists often identify the "tradeoff between efficiency and equity" as the "big tradeoff" (e.g., Mankiw 2018, 242), Hayek emphasizes that the core tradeoff is between *freedom* and other valuable things: "Indeed, what will certainly be dead in the long run if we concentrate on immediate results is freedom" (Hayek [1976] 1982, 29). And enhancing freedom usually fixes economic problems. "Poverty is not a plumbing problem where economists are technical experts, the plumbers, who can fix the leaks and patch the holes. Poverty is a freedom problem" (Williamson 2020, 411). Austrian economists often point out that redistribution reduces the status of free people, who once cared for themselves—goading them to compete to be dependent on the government (i.e., others).

While neoclassical economists sometimes imply that inequality is a bad thing in and of itself—they are part of the class of intellectuals criticized by Higgs in the opening quote—and that the optimal Gini coefficient on income or wealth might be zero (smaller is better), Austrian economists cannot be accused of this. Hayek, for example, condoned a modicum of redistribution—a true safety net for the genuinely needy, such as orphans and disabled people, or spending on education—while pointing out the folly, danger, and immorality of forcible wholesale reductions in inequality. Murray Rothbard ([1974] 2000, 2) challenged the "beauty and goodness of the egalitarian ideal" itself, arguing that its ethical goal "violates the nature of man and/or the universe" ([1974] 2000, 5).

ROBERT HIGGS ON INEQUALITY

As the prefatory quote indicates, Robert Higgs argues that economic inequality is "morally neutral." He argues that "facts"—such as statistics estimating the percent of total income received by the lowest fifth of households or the percent of wealth held by the top 1 percent—are "virtually worthless" (Higgs 2004, 5). He criticizes these figures on empirical grounds—they are plagued by measurement issues, dissembling, miscalculations, and even purposeful omissions—but concludes that "even if these figures on the societal distribution of income were conceptually unambiguous and numerically precise, the question would remain: Is more equality better? And the answer would still be not necessarily" (2004, 5).

To demonstrate this, Higgs considers seven hypothetical scenarios— increased mortality transferring inheritances to the young, a loss of the ability to reproduce, forced labor, forced occupational mobility, increased robbery, mass abandonment of education and training, and forced underemployment. All of these would be "disasters" but would increase equality (2004, 6).[7] To decide whether increased or decreased inequality is a good thing or a bad thing, we have to know its causes. Higgs concludes that

> if we know that individual actions are just, that knowledge is all we need
> in order to make moral assessments. A supposedly deleterious change in
> the statistical measure of the societal distribution of income and wealth,

should it occur, is simply irrelevant. . . . Any changes in the aggregative
statistical profile brought about by . . . complex and variable individual
behavior are wholly uninformative for purposes of moral assessment.
In their simple-minded moral judgments about differences in societal
distributions, many intellectuals have committed astonishingly blatant
errors. They could have saved themselves from these blunders had they
kept their eyes focused on the only true economic and moral agent, the
individual human being. (Higgs 2004, 7)

Accordingly, Higgs is a determined foe of the welfare state, which often
crowns itself as a champion of fairness and equality. His essay "Nineteen
Neglected Consequences of Income Redistribution" (Higgs 2004, chapter 3)
starts with the negative material consequences of redistribution and concludes
with the moral and spiritual. The first neglected consequences include disin-
centives to work and invest in physical and human capital, which shrink the
economic pie, but he quickly moves to more noxious effects including forget-
ting how to help oneself, the development of a broader culture of dependency,
resentment among income recipients arising from differential treatment by the
state, resentment by taxpayers, the atrophy of self-help organizations, charity
withering away, growth of bureaucracy, rampant rent-seeking, the acceptance
of government expanding beyond its rightful bounds, and ultimately the
decline of liberty.

Ironically, in the full-fledged transfer society . . . hardly anyone is better
off as a result. . . . In the transfer society the general public is not only
poorer but less contented, less autonomous, more rancorous, and more
politicized. . . . Finally, one must recognize that, notwithstanding what
some regard as the institutionalization of compassion, the transfer society
quashes genuine virtue. Redistribution of income by government coercion
is a form of theft. Its supporters attempt to disguise its essential character
by claiming that democratic procedure give it legitimacy, but this justification is specious. Theft is theft whether it be carried out by one thief or
by 100 million thieves acting in concert. And it is impossible to found a
good society on the institutionalization of theft. (Higgs 2004, 28)[8]

His bottom line on any official measures of economic inequality, such as the
Gini coefficient, is that "it is hard to imagine another statistical artifact better
calculated to feed the fires of envy and political rapacity. Such information is
unnecessary for the conduct of a just government but well-nigh indispensable
for the operation of a predatory one" (Higgs 1998, 148).

While Higgs is deeply antagonistic to redistribution, he is a thorough-going champion of the oppressed and the underdog. This is especially obvious in works like *Competition and Coercion: Blacks in the American Economy, 1865–1914* (Higgs [1977] 1980).[9] The thesis of *Competition and Coercion*—a thesis that is ably supported—is that "competitive forces played an important part in protecting blacks from the racial coercion to which they were peculiarly vulnerable" ([1977] 1980, ix). Free markets were the "salvation" of free men ([1977] 1980, 37). Despite the fact that "real competition occurs in a context of incompletely enforced private property rights, substantial transaction costs, risks of various kinds, and limited information about market opportunities and resource costs—all subject to unexpected change from one day to the next" and that it "takes time, sometimes years, to exert profound effects," competition was the root cause of substantial Black economic progress in the decades after emancipation ([1977] 1980, xi). Competition overcame much (but not nearly enough) of the coercion that freedmen faced outside the market—especially violence by the state and its allowance of private lawlessness and intimation.

As Higgs repeatedly demonstrates, although landowners and employers hoped to give Blacks the lowest possible payments, their efforts were thwarted by two primary factors. Black workers, sharecroppers, renters, customers, and borrowers now had an exit option—they could look elsewhere if they didn't like the terms of an agreement—and white employers, landowners, retailers, and creditors found it impossible to form effective cartels. Because they desired to earn high profits, they bid against each other for workers and customers—and even found themselves selling land to Blacks. "Many contemporary observers recognized that intense competition for labor did more to enforce real freedom for the blacks than the military forces themselves" ([1977] 1980, 49). "The existence of nondiscriminatory opportunities itself grew out of the fraternal competition among the whites" ([1977] 1980, 130). Although the bargaining was often hard, it was effective. As previously noted, markets are useful because they incentivize people to cooperate—would-be enemies, those without common goals, learn that they can gain by engaging with each other in the market. While landowners, employers, and creditors competed with each other, they were *cooperating* with their Black workers, sharecroppers, renters, customers, and borrowers.

Higgs documents the resultant economic gains as thoroughly as possible—estimating that average Black incomes rose about 2.7 percent per year between 1867–68 and 1900—noticeably above the overall national increase of 2 percent ([1977] 1980, 102), demonstrating that Blacks were paid on par with white workers of equal skill (see, e.g., his table 4.2) and documenting the accumulation of property by Blacks.[10] He easily debunks claims that Blacks were enmeshed in debt peonage, for example, by quoting a contemporary who explained that "to allow the laborer to contract a large debt, is to tempt him to decamp without giving any notice of his intention to depart." "Once again," concludes Higgs, "the black man's mobility, the most precious jewel of emancipation, was his ultimate reliance in resisting oppression" ([1977] 1980, 59).

One lesson of this historical inquiry is that even in the face of innumerable hostile forces, the passage of time often erodes old inequalities. Racial inequality during this period was eroded by three primary factors—mobility (the ability to move to a new employer or a new location), the acquisition of education and skills, and the accumulation of property. As Higgs sees it, the first of these—the mainspring of competition—is of primary importance. Higgs uses forms of the word "competition" exactly 100 times in the 1980 edition of *Competition and Coercion*. Competition was undermined by coercion—a term he uses 82 times—although gradually winning the battle, one which was marked by many casualties.

No one should conclude that Higgs—who condemns coerced redistribution, argues that the level of inequality is morally neutral, and rejects the fixation on official measures of inequality—is unconcerned with inequality. In terms of the four reasons to be concerned about inequality that I outlined earlier—concerns about status per se, concerns about luck, concerns about fairness, and concerns about the spillover effects of inequality—Higgs clearly understands the last three of these, with the greatest emphasis on unfairness. In "Compassion—A Critical Factor for Attaining and Maintaining a Free Society" (Higgs and Higgs 2015), he makes a heartfelt call for individuals to voluntarily help overcome the suffering of their misfortunate neighbors: "We must recognize that regardless of the nature of the prevailing social order, many people are bound to be in trouble. Some are born with unalterable physical and mental defects and deficiencies. Others have lost limbs, physical capacities, or their sanity as a result of accidents or other damaging experiences. Some are children without parents or proper guardians or children suffering from parental neglect or abuse" (Higgs and Higgs 2015, 627). Here are the people who have "lost" the game due to bad luck or being cheated. Their problems cannot be wished away, and Higgs warns that if we are uncompassionate toward them, "an incentive arises for those tempted by evil to organize the poor and unfortunate politically as a menacing legion that threatens to wreak societal mayhem unless something is done to relieve their plight" (2015, 628). "So, in a sense, we serve our own interest by doing what we can to make compassion and voluntary succor an essential part of our efforts" to bring about a free society. However,

real compassion does not comport with such an ends-means calculation of compassion's desirability. Compassion . . . is itself a virtue rather
than merely a form of prudential, instrumental action. Its value lies in
our expression of something good that lies within the feasible bounds
of human action. Blessed are the merciful, Jesus taught, for they will be
shown mercy. . . . Nothing is gained by hardheartedness. . . . Nothing else
[than compassion] can get the job done. . . . In true compassionate charity, the giver as well as the recipient may be transformed for the better.
(2015, 628–29)

The final sentence of the previous quote suggests that Higgs disagrees with
an explicit assumption of textbook economics—the assumption that "more
is better" when it comes to material things.[11] This strong assumption could
and should be relaxed. Prophets and theologians have stressed throughout
history that more isn't necessarily better—*especially* when someone already
has enough or more than enough.[12] When this is true, focusing on material
inequality can be foolish. Suppose there are three men, each of whom weighs
1,000 pounds. The Gini coefficient for their weights is 0—they are all equal. In
another group the weights are 200, 300, and 400 pounds. They are less equal—
the Gini coefficient has jumped by 14.8 points—but they are probably better
off. In both cases, the level of inequality tells us little about society.

BROADENING HORIZONS—EXPANDING CONVENTIONAL MEASURES OF INEQUALITY IN INCOME AND LIFE EXPECTANCY

Robert Higgs's skepticism about the narrowness and inappropriateness
of most conventional measures of inequality suggests that we need to put
every measure of inequality into a broader context and broaden the range
of inequality measures we consider. The easier part is in broadening current
measures of social inequality—such as consumption, income, and wealth. The
harder part is in conceptualizing and especially in measuring more important
facets of social inequality. I will start with the easier task.

Higgs (2014) notes that income inequality is a "statistical artifact. . . . The
aggregate of the measure [such as the Gini coefficient] is arbitrary: why, for
example, should inequality be measured for the entire U.S. population rather
than for the population of the city or state in which one lives, the entire North
American population (including Mexico), the entire Western Hemisphere population, or indeed the entire world population?" Following Higgs, we should
keep on broadening. If all people are equally important, wouldn't the most

appropriate measure of inequality, such as an income distribution Gini coefficient or a measure of where today's poor fit in the overall distribution, be for *all people who have ever lived*? This would give a much truer picture of inequality for any particular measure—and perhaps dampen or remove the envy factor from our reactions to inequality measures.[13]

Branko Milanovic (2010) provides data showing where people in different income ventiles (twentieths of the distribution) in several countries fall within the world's income distribution. He finds that the income of the poorest 5 percent of Americans put them at the 68th percentile of the world's income distribution in 2010. Poor Americans are rather rich by the world's standards today. However, they are *far* richer in comparison to all the people who have ever lived. Inspired by Higgs's call to broaden inequality measures, in "Where Do the Poorest Americans Stand in the Income Distribution among All People Ever Born?" (Whaples 2022), I answered this question by comparing estimates from the US Census's Annual Social and Economic Supplement, data from Roser (n.d., using data from OECD 2014), and Maddison (2001) on the income distribution among historical populations, and population estimates from Kaneda and Haub (2020). The results are shown in table 3.1.

This suggests that the poorest 5 percent of Americans living today are at the 95th percentile among all the human beings who have ever lived. The historical poor might envy the material position of today's poor.

Using the same sources, it is possible to take a stab at estimating the Gini coefficient for income for everyone who has ever lived. I estimate this Gini coefficient to be 59.0. This is a crude estimate because estimates of incomes before the modern period are merely conjectures.[14] However, getting this number correct isn't my main purpose. My question is this: how is this all-time Gini coefficient for income likely to evolve in the future? Currently, there are about 135 million people born in the world each year (Ritchie 2019). At this rate,

Table 3.1. Position of poorest 5 percent of Americans among all people ever born

	Number of people	Percent above US bottom ventile	Number above US bottom ventile
Born before 1650	94.4 billion	1.9	1.8 billion
Born between 1650 and 1850	7.2 billion	2.8	0.2 billion
Born after 1850, no longer living	7.3 billion	20	1.46 billion
Now living	7.9 billion	32	2.53 billion
Total	116.8 billion		5.99 billion

Source: Author's calculations, based on data from US Census Annual Social and Economic Supplement, Roser (n.d., using data from OECD 2014), Maddison (2001), and Kaneda and Haub (2020).

it would take about 75 more years for the next 10 billion people to be born. Suppose that average real incomes continue to rise a bit over 2 percent per year, as they have in the past few decades (Our World in Data n.d.).[15] More specifically, let's assume that convergence continues, so that growth is faster for those with lower incomes and slower for those with higher income. (My calculations assume that growth at the bottom ventile is 3 percent per year, 2.9 percent for the second-lowest twentieth of the population and descending by 0.1 percent for each ventile until it reaches 1.1 percent for the top ventile.) If this trend continues, by the end of the century the incomes of the poorest group will be higher than today's median, and the total income of this group will approximately equal the incomes of everyone born before them. If this scenario plays out the Gini coefficient for income among all people who have ever lived will have approximately risen from 59.0 to 71.2. The point is that the all-time income distribution is likely to become substantially less equal as future generations are added because their incomes will be so much higher than those of people living in premodern times. As Higgs would argue, the rise in inequality in and of itself is morally neutral, but since the rise would largely be due to benign forces—past generations are not losing out because of the actions of those born after they die, actions such as improvements in technology and poorer nations adopting the successful institutions of richer nations—it would be difficult to see this rise in inequality as anything but a positive development. Unless disaster strikes, this rise in inequality is likely to continue for many centuries to come.

Samuel Peltzman's (2009) estimates of inequality in length of life are a valuable addition to measures of income and wealth inequality. Peltzman (2009, 178) shows that mortality inequality in the United States fell tremendously from 1852 to 2002, especially due to the near elimination of infant and childhood mortality, with the Gini coefficient falling from 47.6 to 10.8. He shows similar declines in Brazil, India, Japan, Russia, and Spain. His results could easily be generalized to look at the entire world as a single unit. Sadly, these official statistics omit a large fraction of deaths, which someone taking the broader point of view cannot overlook. The Centers for Disease Control (Murphy et al. 2018) reports 2,813,503 deaths in the United States in 2017. However, this omits deaths due to abortions, which totaled about 862,320, according to the Guttmacher Institute (2019). If these deaths are included, the Gini coefficient for length of life among those dying in 2017 rises from 10.5 to 31.4.

BROADENING HORIZONS—VIRTUE AND INEQUALITY

Although economists like Hayek ([1976] 1982, 109) sometimes argue that a free society has no "common hierarchy of particular ends," there is widespread agreement that living a life of virtue is man's most important end. Higgs (noted above) extols the virtue of compassion. Following this lead, here is a nonexhaustive list of virtues that almost everyone strives to attain and expects from others:

1. Don't lie, break promises, cheat, steal, or rip people off.

2. Don't use physical force or the threat of it or verbal harassment to get your way.

3. Take care of yourself: Support yourself if you are able-bodied and don't do things that will impair this ability. Don't be a sponge or parasite.

4. Take care of the people you are supposed to take care of—including your spouse, your children, and your aged parents (if they need help).

5. Don't be envious of other people's success and good fortune.

6. When you make mistakes, own up to them, learn from them, don't blame them on other people, and try to undo the damage from them.

7. Show gratitude—for all of creation, for the gifts your parents and ancestors have given you, and for all the blessings you've received in life.

8. Be genuinely kind, compassionate, and patient toward other people.

9. Show humility.

Many people would add a final virtue that encompasses and supplements the others (and that counters a presumption among many economists that most people try to free ride whenever they can):

10. Use your freedom to live life in general so that you give *more* than you get.

Many of the most important social inequalities are tied to these virtues. Are there ways to measure these kinds of inequality? Data certainly exist to estimate inequality in criminal activity. Likewise, data probably exist to estimate inequality in taking care of oneself and those one has a duty to take care of—for example, one might calculate inequality in the number of years in which minor children are supported by their biological parents.

Turning toward positive virtues, donating blood takes time and causes some discomfort but is a genuine way to help those in need. One might be able to calculate the Gini coefficient for blood donations. America's Blood Centers (2022) reports that among the 205 million Americans who are eligible, about 7.3 million donated a total of 10.9 million whole blood and apheresis red blood units and 2.4 million units of platelets during 2019. Among the whole blood donors, about 69 percent are repeat donors. This implies a Gini coefficient for blood donations of about 97.6, an extremely high number due to the fact that only about 3 percent of eligible individuals donate.[16]

One way to approach the last of the virtues listed is to calculate the amount of giving and taking when it comes to taxes and transfers. (This is certainly not the best way to measure giving versus taking, however, as taxes are coercive.) Data from the Congressional Budget Office (2020) on federal taxes and transfers for each income quintile in the United States for 2017 show that the bottom quintile received net transfers averaging $20,000, the second lowest quintile's net transfers averaged $15,500, and the middle quintile's net transfers averaged $6,300—in other words, the net taxes for these groups were all negative: –$20,000, –$15,500, and –$6,300.[17] The top two quintiles paid net taxes of $5,900 and $68,500. Gini coefficients can exceed 100 when some values are negative, as they are in this case. The Gini coefficient for this distribution of net federal taxes in 2017 in the United States was 243, according to these numbers. However, it is probably better to measure this inequality over the course of a lifetime. Alan Auerbach and Laurence Kotlikoff (2016) calculate average lifetime spending before and after taxes and benefits for individuals in their forties. Their calculations yield a Gini coefficient of 75 for net taxes paid.

Most people are religious. The world's major religions hold that the purpose of life—and highest virtue—is worshipping God.[18] A central aspect of worship is regularly attending services at a church, synagogue, mosque, temple, or other place of worship. Using data from National Survey of Families and Households (Sweet and Bumpass 1996), Dehejia, Deleire, and Luttmer (2007) estimate the number of times Americans attended religious services per year in 1996. Almost a quarter never attended, the median was 13, the 75th percentile was 50, while the 99th percentile was 189. These data, therefore, imply massive social inequality in this important aspect of human action. These yield a religious attendance Gini coefficient of 57.[19] However, it has probably grown substantially, as the share of Americans with "membership in houses of worship" fell below 50 percent for the first time ever in Gallup's eight-decade survey recently (Jones 2021).

CONCLUSION

The calculations in the two proceeding sections demonstrate that measures of inequality can be fruitfully pushed well beyond their traditional bounds. Money isn't the only important thing in life, so it would benefit us to carefully and critically examine measures of inequality beyond the merely economic. Robert Higgs reminds us that traditional measures of monetary inequality can provoke (and may be designed to inflame) envy, but these other measures may not suffer from this shortcoming—and might inspire emulation of virtuous behaviors.

Claudia Williamson (2020) reminds us that "what people believe are the facts of the social sciences, and norms, values, customs, [and] traditions shape these beliefs." Most people believe virtue is important, and most arrange their lives as if God matters. Economists and other social scientists have used their talents to help us understand how the economy and society work. Their insights may reveal even more if they were to broaden their horizons and expand their scope to consider the even more important and enduring ends of life.

NOTES

1. My questions are about inequality itself, not poverty, which may characterize all or none of those under consideration. Poverty is a separate issue, and the reasons to care about it are often different than the reasons to care about inequality, per se. The discussion will mainly concern the modern United States, where absolute poverty—for example, consumption below $2 or $3 per day—is almost nonexistent. This is not to imply that poverty cannot be a good thing. Leon Bloy ([1897] 1947, 118, 217) concludes that one should "not for a moment" hold "that poverty is degrading. It could not be, since it was the mantle of Jesus Christ. . . . The Saints who wedded Poverty from love of her, and begot many children by her, assure us that she is infinitely lovely." The protagonist of one of Thornton Wilder's best-selling novels (1934, 193) argues that "a poor person—even if he is a millionaire—is a person whose head's always full of anxious thoughts about money; and a rich person is a person whose head's not full of anxious thoughts about money."

2. Starmans, Sheskin, and Bloom (2017, 1) argue that "there is no evidence that people are bothered by economic inequality itself" and present evidence that "people prefer fair inequality over unfair equality."

3. Wilkinson and Pickett (2011) make this final argument, but their findings have been largely debunked by Snowdon (2011).

4. My discussion omits considerations of arguments made by prominent scholars like Piketty (2014) and Stiglitz (2012). Some argue that their perspective "has come to dominate public discourse about economic inequality" (Manish and Miller 2021, 7). Piketty advances the theory that inequality rises when the rate of return on capital exceeds the rate of growth of output and wages—which is most of the time—and purports to provide empirical evidence verifying this theory. His theory has been effectively criticized for its untenable assumptions (e.g., Krusell and Smith 2015; Rallo 2018), and his novel empirical evidence suffers from serious flaws that make the overall argument unsupportable (e.g., Magness 2021; McCloskey 2014).

Stiglitz argues that inequality is driven by the ability of the wealthy to write the economic rules of the game and choose referees who favor them. The theories I discuss below would not contest Stiglitz's broad point, but it is not clear how much major trends in inequality are driven by these forces.

5. As Ludwig von Mises (1998, 205–6) put it: "There are grades of intensity of the desire to attain a definite goal and this intensity determines the psychic profit which the successful action brings to the acting individual. But psychic quantities can only be felt. They are entirely personal, and there is no semantic means to express their intensity and to convey information about them to other people."

6. William Nordhaus (2004, 1, 22) estimates that only about 2.2 percent of the total present value of social returns to innovation are captured by innovators. "Most of the benefits of technological change are passed on to consumers rather than captured by producers."

7. He might have added war to this list, as wars often reduce economic inequality. See, for example, Scheidel (2018).

8. Higgs (1997) makes the point that "decent people, virtually by definition, do not seek to exercise political power over their fellows." This is a recurrent theme.

9. This point of view is also very clear in his scholarship on the experience of Japanese Americans on the West Coast in the first half of the 20th century (Higgs 1978). Although it is impossible to write economic history without looking at statistical aggregates, it is clear that Higgs's focus is people as people, not as numbers. For example, rather than titling his chapters in *Competition and Coercion* "Demographics Trends" and "How Markets Worked," his titles are "The *People*" and "The *People* at Work."

10. Higgs's general conclusion about rising relative income levels among Blacks—despite predominantly living in a region that increasingly lagged behind the rest of the nation—is corroborated by Margo's (2016) summary of the most recent findings almost four decades later.

11. In a survey (Whaples 2009) of professional economists that asked whether "economic growth in developed countries like the U.S. leads to greater levels of well-being," not a single person strongly disagreed, only 2 percent disagreed, and 89 percent either agreed or strongly agreed.

12. In *Aquinas and the Market: Toward a Humane Economy*, Mary Hirschfeld (2019) probes the shortcomings of the "more is better" assumption and the schools of economic thought that rely upon it. If the end of life is knowing and loving God, the "more [on earth] is better" assumption crumbles and economists' assumption of insatiability describes a warped humanity, because material things and experiences cannot satisfy; only God can. If material desires are insatiable, one will always be infinitely far away from fulfilling them. The economist observes that people's desires are insatiable and seems to say, "keep going!"—keep trying to get more. Theologians like Aquinas observe the same and say, "go somewhere else"—more here on earth will never satisfy. More here on earth may distract you from more in eternity. The desire for finite goods should properly be finite. The theological point of view sees the fundamental shortcoming in the "more is better" assumption—its covetousness. It sees the desire for endless economic growth as a reflection of man's fallen nature. The view that shapes the lives of most people is that we do not pursue perfection by economic maximization, but by becoming good and seeking the good. True happiness doesn't come from satisfying desires but by cultivating virtue. As Hirschfeld puts it (2019, 117), the painter doesn't improve a work of art by adding more and more paint, but by arranging things in beautiful harmony. Virtue isn't about having more things, but about using our things to achieve the good and the holy. When it comes to food, there is certainly a point when one can have too much. This is true for our bodies (avoiding obesity) and true for our souls (avoiding gluttony). One doesn't swallow an entire bottle of pills to improve one's health—instead, one takes the correct dosage. What holds for food, drink, and medicine holds for everything—for all goods and services taken together.

13. Surprisingly, Milanovic (2007, 112) dismisses this idea. "Suppose we combine all Japanese and all Maya of the fifteenth century and study their combined inequality. . . . This exercise is devoid of any meaning since the two groups have never interacted. It is only when a nation-state appears and people begin to view their co-citizens as their equals that conventional

studies of within-country inequality begin to make sense." If all men are viewed by God as brothers, Milanovic's argument fails.

14. In addition, this is probably an underestimate, as I have assumed no economic growth until after the start of the Industrial Revolution to keep the calculation tractable.

15. The data at Our World in Data (n.d.) indicate that the world's average real GDP per capita grew by 3.1 percent per year during the 1960s, 2 percent during the 1970s, 1.3 percent during the 1980s, 1.9 percent during the 1990s, 2.9 percent during the first decade of this century, and 1.8 percent from 2010 to 2018. This averages out to a bit over 2 percent per year.

16. I haven't found any sources that detail how many donations are made by repeat donors. In my estimates, I assume that there are 4.3 million one-time donors, 1 million two-time donors, 1 million three-time donors, and 1 million four-time donors among the 7.3 million reported donors. This adds up to 13.3 million donations, which is the actual total. This probably biases the Gini coefficient down a bit, as one can donate every eight weeks—up to six times per year—and many people do this. If those restricted from donating, for example due to health problems and factors that raise risks that blood is contaminated, are removed from the calculation, the Gini coefficient falls to about 95.7. For self-reported blood donation statistics from the National Health Interview Survey, see Patel et al. (2019).

17. My numbers come from Lincicome's (2020) figure 4, which relies on the CBO data.

18. About 82 percent of the world's population are Christian, Muslim, Hindu, Buddhist, or practice some other religion, according to the Pew Research Center (Hackett and McClendon 2017). More than half adhere to a monotheistic religion. Perhaps my sentence above could read "God or Gods."

19. Less detailed statistics from the Pew Research Center (2008, 154) suggest a similar Gini coefficient.

REFERENCES

American Enterprise Institute. 2021. "Capitalism under Consideration." *AEI Polling Report* 17 (8): 8–11.

America's Blood Centers. 2022. "U.S. Blood Donation: Statistics and Public Messaging Guide." https://americasblood.org/statistics_guide/.

Auerbach, Alan, and Laurence J. Kotlikoff. 2016. "We've Been Measuring Inequality Wrong: Here's the Real Story." *The Conversation*. https://theconversation.com/weve-been-measuring -inequality-wrong-heres-the-real-story-56179.

Bloy, Leon. (1897) 1947. *The Woman Who Was Poor*. New York: Sheed and Ward.

Congressional Budget Office. 2020. "Distribution of Household Income, 2017." https://www.cbo .gov/publication/56575.

Coyne, Christopher J., and Peter J. Boettke. 2020. *The Essential Austrian Economics*. Vancouver: Fraser Institute.

Dehejia, Rajeev, Thomas Deleire, and Erzo F. P. Luttmer. 2007. "Insuring Consumption and Happiness through Religious Organizations." *Journal of Public Economics* 91: 259–79.

Guttmacher Institute. 2019. "Induced Abortion in the United States." https://www.guttmacher.org /fact-sheet/induced-abortion-united-states.

Hackett, Conrad, and David McClendon. 2017. "Christians Remain World's Largest Religious Group, but They Are Declining in Europe." https://www.pewresearch.org/fact-tank/2017/04 /05/christians-remain-worlds-largest-religious-group-but-they-are-declining-in-europe/.

Hayek, Friedrich. (1976) 1982. *Law, Legislation, and Liberty: Volume 2: The Mirage of Social Justice*. London: Routledge and Kegan Paul.

Higgs, Robert. 1978. "Landless by Law: Japanese Immigrants in California Agriculture in 1941." *Journal of Economic History* 38 (1): 205–25.

———. (1977) 1980. *Competition and Coercion: Blacks and the American Economy, 1865–1914.* Chicago: University of Chicago Press.

———. 1997. "Public Choice and Political Leadership." *Independent Review* 1 (3): 465–68.

———. 1998. "Official Economic Statistics: The Emperor's Clothes Are Dirty." *Independent Review* 3 (1): 147–53.

———. 2004. *Against Leviathan: Government Power and a Free Society.* Oakland, CA: Independent Institute.

———. 2014. "Income Inequality Is a Statistical Artifact." *The Beacon.* https://blog.independent.org /2014/12/01/income-inequality-is-a-statistical-artifact/.

Higgs, Robert, and Elizabeth Bernard Higgs. 2015. "Compassion—a Critical Factor for Attaining and Maintaining a Free Society." *Independent Review* 19 (4): 627–30.

Hirschfeld, Mary L. 2019. *Aquinas and the Market: Toward a More Humane Economy.* Cambridge, MA: Harvard University Press.

Jones, Jeffrey M. 2021. "U.S. Church Membership Falls below Majority for First Time." Gallup News. https://news.gallup.com/poll/341963/church-membership-falls-below-majority-first-time.aspx.

Kaneda, Toshiko, and Carl Haub. 2020. "How Many People Have Ever Lived on Earth?" Population Research Bureau. https://www.prb.org/howmanypeoplehaveeverlivedonearth/.

Krusell, Per, and Anthony A. Smith Jr. 2015. "Is Piketty's 'Second Law of Capitalism' Fundamental?" *Journal of Political Economy* 123 (4): 725–48.

Lincicome, Scott. 2020. "The Reality of Incomes, Taxation and Redistribution in America." Cato at Liberty. https://www.cato.org/blog/reality-incomes-taxes-redistribution-america.

Maddison, Angus. 2001. *The World Economy: A Millennial Perspective.* Paris: OECD.

Magness, Phillip W. 2021. "The Economic History of Taxation and Inequality in the United States." In *Capitalism and Inequality: The Role of State and Market*, edited by G. P. Manish and Stephen C. Miller, 183–209. New York: Routledge.

Manish, G. P., and Stephen C. Miller. 2021. *Capitalism and Inequality: The Role of State and Market.* New York: Routledge.

Mankiw, N. Gregory. 2018. *Principles of Economics*, 8th ed. Boston: Cenage Learning.

Margo, Robert A. 2016. "Obama, Katrina, and the Persistence of Racial Inequality." *Journal of Economic History* 76 (2): 301–41.

McCloskey, D. N. 2014. "Measured, Unmeasured, Mismeasured and Unjustified Pessimism: A Review Essay of Thomas Piketty's *Capital in the Twenty-First Century*." *Erasmus Journal of Philosophy and Economics* 7 (2): 73–115.

Menger, Carl. (1871) 1981. *Principles of Economics.* New York: NYU Press.

Milanovic, Branko. 2007. "Why We All Care about Inequality (But Some of Us Are Loath to Admit It)." *Challenge* 50 (6): 109–20.

———. 2010. *The Haves and the Have Nots: A Brief and Idiosyncratic History of Global Inequality.* New York: Basic Books.

Mises, Ludwig von. 1998. *Human Action: A Treatise on Economics.* Auburn, AL: Ludwig von Mises Institute.

Murphy, Sherry L., Jiaquan Xu, Kenneth D. Kochanek, and Elizabeth Arias. 2018. "Mortality in the United States, 2017." *NCHS Data Brief* 328: 1–7.

Nordhaus, William. 2004. "Schumpeterian Profits in the American Economy: Theory and Measurement." NBER Working Paper 10433.

OECD. 2014. *How Was Life? Global Well-Being since 1820*. Edited by Jan Luiten van Zanden, Joerg Baten, Marco Mira d'Ercole, Auke Rijpma, and Marcel P. Timmer. Paris: OECD.

Our World in Data. n.d. "GDP per capita, 1820–2018." https://ourworldindata.org/grapher/gdp-per-capita-maddison-2020.

Patel, Eshan U., Evan M. Bloch, Mary K. Grabowski, Ruchika Goel, Parvez M. Lokhandwala, Patricia A. R. Brunker, Jodie L. White, Beth Shaz, Paul M. Ness, and Aaron A. R. Tobian. 2019. "Sociodemographic and Behavioral Characteristics Associated with Blood Donation in the United States: A Population-Based Study." *Transfusion* 59 (9): 2899–907.

Peltzman, Samuel. 2009. "Mortality Inequality." *Journal of Economic Perspectives* 23 (4): 175–90.

Peterson, Jordan. 2018. *12 Rules for Life: An Antidote to Chaos*. Toronto: Random House Canada.

Pew Research Center. 2008. "U.S. Religious Landscape Survey Religious Beliefs and Practices: Diverse and Politically Relevant." https://www.pewresearch.org/wp-content/uploads/sites/7/2008/06/report2-religious-landscape-study-full.pdf.

Piketty, Thomas. 2014. *Capital in the Twenty-First Century*. Cambridge, MA: Harvard University Press.

Rallo, Juan Ramon. 2018. "Some Fundamental Problems with Thomas Piketty's *Capital in the Twenty-First Century*." *Independent Review* 22 (4): 599–607.

Ritchie, Hannah. 2019. "Our World in Data. How Many People Die and How Many Are Born Each Year?" https://ourworldindata.org/births-and-deaths.

Roser, Max. n.d. "World Income Distribution, 1820 to 2000." Our World in Data. https://www.maxroser.com/roser/graphs/WorldIncomeDistribution1820to2000/WorldIncomeDistribution1820to2000.html.

Rothbard, Murray. (1974) 2000. *Egalitarianism as a Revolt against Nature and Other Essays*, 2nd ed. Auburn, AL: Ludwig von Mises Institute.

Scheidel, Walter. 2018. *The Great Leveler: Violence and the History of Inequality from the Stone Age to Twenty-First Century*. Princeton, NJ: Princeton University Press.

Snowdon, Christopher. 2011. *The Sprit Level Delusion: Fact-Checking the Left's New Theory of Everything*. London: Monday Books.

Starmans, Christina, Mark Sheskin, and Paul Bloom. 2017. "Why People Prefer Unequal Societies." *Nature Human Behaviour* 1: 1–7.

Stiglitz, Joseph. 2012. *The Price of Inequality*. New York: Norton.

Sweet, James A., and Larry L. Bumpass. 1996. "The National Survey of Families and Households—Waves 1 and 2: Data Description and Documentation." Center for Demography and Ecology. http://www.ssc.wisc.edu/nsfh/home.htm.

Whaples, Robert. 2009. "The Policy Views of American Economic Association Members: The Results of a New Survey." *Econ Journal Watch* 6 (3): 337–48.

———. 2022. "Where Do the Poorest Americans Stand in the Income Distribution among All People Ever Born?" *Independent Review* 27 (1): 155–59.

Wilder, Thornton. 1934. *Heaven's My Destination*. New York: Longmans, Green.

Wilkinson, Richard, and Kate Pickett. 2011. *The Spirit Level: Why Greater Equality Makes Societies Stronger*. London: Bloomsbury.

Williamson, Claudia R. 2020. "Are We Austrian Economists?" *Review of Austrian Economics* 33: 407–13.

Chapter 4

The Coercion Bias in Economic Measurement

Vincent Geloso

D oes coercion improve economic well-being? In terms of standard narratives in normative economics, someone can answer in the affirmative using positive rights-based models. In those models, the state's coercive powers are used to extract tax revenues that finance goods and services that markets would not provide (e.g., public goods such as national defense or flood controls, which are non-rivalrous and non-excludable, or the management of externalities). In this case, measured output and well-being should *both* increase.

What if rulers apply extreme coercion by enslaving their people, by introducing serfdom, or through some other coercive institutions? What I answer in this chapter is that *measured* output (i.e., measured by national accounts data) *overstates* well-being under extreme coercion. This creates what I call the "coercion bias"—which I name in honor of Robert Higgs, whose work made me realize its existence—that foils the meaning of economic measurements. I argue that this bias has important ramifications for both historical debates and modern policy debates. I illustrate that importance by considering debates of the economic consequences of slavery in the United States during the antebellum period and the debates over the role of economic freedom in stimulating economic growth.

THE COERCION BIAS

To understand what I mean by coercion bias, let us consider the case of wartime economic performance in United States between 1941 and 1945. Many historians (e.g., Rauchway 2015) argue that the war essentially ended the Great Depression—a claim that some economists (e.g., Eggertsson and Krugman 2012; Vernon 1994) have also made. In multiple works, Robert Higgs (1992,

I wish to thank Karl Skogstad, Livio di Matteo, Robert Higgs, and Christopher Coyne. I also thank Glenfiddich Single Malt for his ounces of inspirational help in the writing process. Any remaining errors are entirely our own.

1999, 2004, 2006) has questioned this narrative in a way *directly* relevant to how coercion reduces the meaningfulness of economic data.

Higgs questioned whether there had been improvements in living standards during World War II by raising a series of strong objections to the data frequently used. Some of these criticisms, such as the validity of the price indexes used in wartime when price controls existed, are widely accepted by economists. However, one of his criticisms has been mostly ignored. That criticism stated that the creation of a statistical aggregate of physical quantities into a monetary figure—which is estimating GDP or GNP—hinges on assumptions of free markets and strongly defined property rights that many economists fail to appreciate. The quantities consumed and produced, the choice of production techniques from the set of possible production plans, the types of goods produced, the quantity of leisure time to be taken, and so on, are all reflected in the prices that allow parties to freely exchange. If the state *forces* a vector of prices to apply, it will not be market clearing, and national accounts data will have a hard time reflecting the value of output. As, during the war, the American state disregarded the role of prices in determining allocation (Higgs 1992, 48) and opted for a command approach to meet the war needs (i.e., tanks, bullets, bombs, airplanes, cruisers, etc.), the meaning of the national accounts data is dubious according to Higgs. Simply put, in a command economy, the meaning of prices used to aggregate physical quantities into a statistical aggregate is dramatically dissipated. As such, one can be fooled by wartime data into believing that the war was a boon to well-being while it was actually a period of stagnating living standards.

To appreciate the importance of this point, consider the following illustration taken from Geloso and Pender (2022), who extend the work of Higgs to the Canadian case during World War II. Person i can produce a tank that a representative person j wishes to acquire. Person j has a maximum willingness to pay 1 ton of gold for the tank—a price that i finds too low. In this case, i produces other goods and there are no prices for tanks that are registered or observed for this good. The absence of the price reveals all the relevant economic information, and society was better off not producing the tank. However, if we tweak this scenario to introduce a ruler who seeks to invade a neighboring nation, this is no longer true. Taking by force a minimal share of the gold of all the j (he was a representative agent) in the economy, the ruler convinces i to produce the tank at a price above 1 ton of gold. This forcible reallocation of property rights creates noise in attempting to measure economic activity in ways that are synonymous to well-being. In national accounts, the tank's production reflects the marginal cost to i. However, this conveys *less* information than when no prices for the tank existed. The absence of price without coercion told us everything about the value of goods exchanged. With coercion, we must now estimate the cost of taxation to consumers and producers, the deadweight loss to taxation, the effect of production being reallocated to less valued uses. The introduction of coercion reduces the synonymity between national accounts and well-being.

In Higgs's work on the American economy during World War II, this loss of synonymity was considerable even though the coercion was milder than that of Germany during the war or to any other totalitarian regimes of the 20th century. Excluding military expenditures from total output allowed Higgs to focus exclusively on the well-being of American civilians and measure the amplitude of the problem.[1] In figure 4.1, I replicate his effort by expressing the corrected GNP figures as a share of the official GNP figures. As can be seen, the official figures misestimated living standards by as much as 40 percent at the height of the war. In the same figure, I also add the Canadian replication of Higgs's effort by Geloso and Pender (2022), where the same finding is made regarding the overstatement.

However, what happens with more extreme coercion? For example, what if the ruler forces i to produce the tank at no charge except subsistence payment and under threat of death? In that case, all that is seen by the statistician calculating economic activity is the "exchange" of whatever costs the ruler incurred to produce coercion. Yet, i is made worse off by being forced. This is in addition to the difficulties that materialized with the lesser case of coercion being used to tax all the j to obtain the amount to convince/force person i. Essentially, more coercion means a greater loss of synonymity between national accounts and well-being.

Figure 4.1. Corrected GNP measures (to exclude wartime production) as a share of official GNP measures, 1939–49

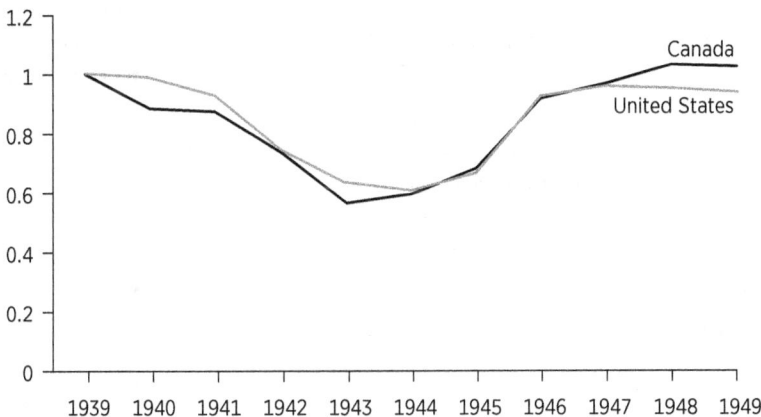

Source: US Bureau of Economic Analysis; Geloso and Pender (2022).

For our purposes, the tank in the example above can be replaced by *any* good that a ruler with coercive power wants produced and can produce using those powers. It can be the pyramids for the Egyptian pharaoh, the cotton for the American slave owner, the munitions from the prisoners of wars in a factory in WWII Germany, the nickel mined by gulag workers in the Soviet Union, or the clothing items manufactured by prison workers in the United States today. The use of coercive powers to force people to produce a given good entails that the utility-maximizing individual chooses between pain or death and producing a good at a pay rate that he would have refused if unco-erced. However, that good *is* measured in national accounts. Whatever "pay" is offered is the price at which GDP would be estimated at factor cost. Some industries may be smaller because they are unable to attract the coerced work-ers, and that will appear in GDP numbers. However, it will not appear *fully*. As Higgs efficiently summarized, "outside a more or less competitive equilibrium framework, the use of prices as weights in an aggregation of physical quantities loses its essential theoretical justification. All presumption that price equals marginal cost vanishes, and therefore no meaningful estimate of real national product is possible" (Higgs 1992, 48).

To better visualize this loss of synonymity, let us normalize to 1 the greatest level of economic freedom (i.e., the inverse of coercion). Let us also normal-ize to 1 the levels of output and well-being associated with a situation labeled "standard." I say "standard" to refer to the minimalist justification for state powers whereby the state has some coercive powers to finance the defined public goods that most often make it into textbook examples (e.g., lighthouses, national defenses) as well as the management of externalities.[2] Output can be taken as GDP as measured in national accounts. Well-being is defined as broadly defined living standards. Normally, we expect GDP to speak to living standards, with increases in one being synonymous with an increase in the other. However, the relation may be imperfect as GDP has many well-known flaws. As such, the object of interest here is the ratio of GDP to well-being. Under this standard justification, we can picture that *extra* coercion yields only deterioration in economic freedom (i.e., falling further away from 1, with 0 being extreme coercion—i.e., pure slavery). In turn, this extra reduction in economic freedom reduces GDP and well-being. If extra units of coercion reduce GDP in a proportional manner as well-being, the ratio of GDP to well-being remains unchanged regardless of the limitations inherent to GDP in speaking to well-being.

However, if coercion decays measured output at a slower pace than well-being, then the ratio is altered. This is what is illustrated in figures 4.2 and 4.3.

Figure 4.2. Physical output and well-being as function of coercion/economic freedom

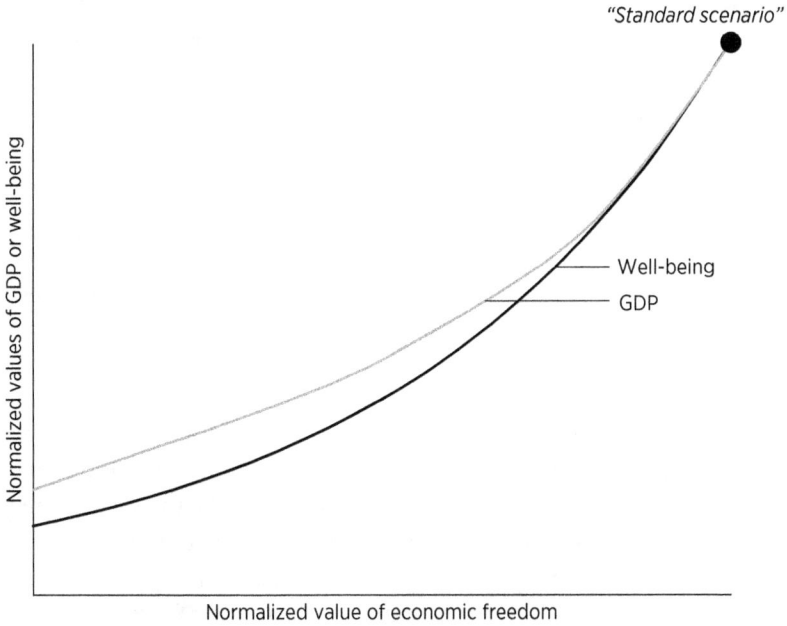

"Standard scenario"

Normalized values of GDP or well-being

Well-being

GDP

Normalized value of economic freedom

Figure 4.3. The coercion bias

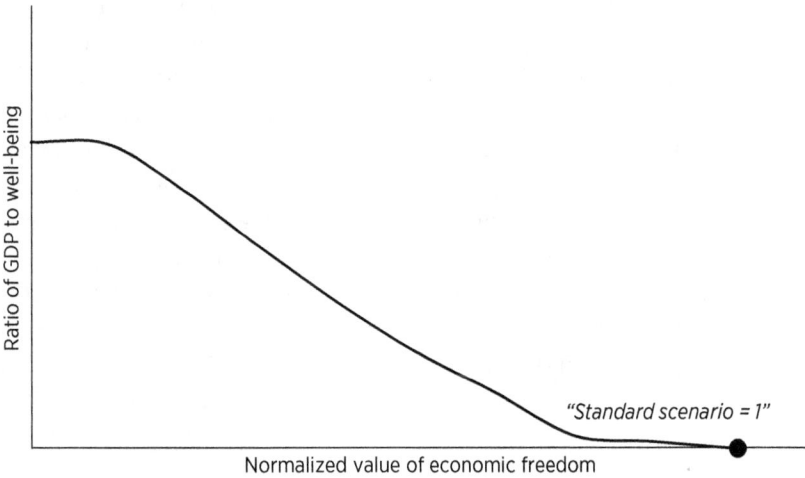

Ratio of GDP to well-being

"Standard scenario = 1"

Normalized value of economic freedom

In figure 4.2, the maximum value is the "standard scenario," and any increase in coercion means one moves leftwards on the economic freedom axis. As can be seen, when economic freedom decreases, well-being decreases faster than GDP. In that case, the biases of GDP in speaking to well-being increase as in figure 4.3. Essentially, the argument made by Higgs speaks very simply to the idea that greater coercion increases the problems of GDP in speaking to well-being.

THE COERCION BIAS AND AMERICAN ANTEBELLUM SLAVERY

The first illustration for the importance of coercion bias is tied to the debates on American antebellum slavery and southern economic growth during the period. In their *Time on the Cross*, Fogel and Engerman (1974) pointed out, using national accounts data produced by Richard Easterlin, that from 1840 to 1860, the southern slave states had enjoyed faster rates of economic growth than the North (even if they were poorer in level terms). This was one of the more contentious claims in that work, as it suggested that slavery was not a hindrance to economic growth.[3] The apparent lack of a negative relationship was seen by many as a repudiation of classical economics that slavery was naturally impoverishing and would produce societies that fail to develop economically.

One line of criticism is that the national accounts methods of Easterlin had some limitations. Some argue that the 1840 census—the source for the 1840 starting point—was heavily flawed (Gunderson 1973). Others argued that the endpoint—the census of 1860—was at the tail end of an unusually bountiful cotton harvest year (Cohn 1981). Some pointed out that it was necessary to correct for the shift of the South's population to the new slave states of Texas, Louisiana, and Arkansas (Hummel 2012). This is because these states had both higher *nominal* incomes and prices than other southern states. Averaging all nominal incomes without correcting for regional price differences led to a large overstatement of the income growth between 1840 and 1860. Others pointed to flawed estimates of some sectoral outputs that mattered more heavily in the northern states.[4] Others pointed to longer time windows that show a decline in the South's fortunes since the Revolutionary War (Lindert and Williamson 2016).

However, those criticisms obscure the important fact that output was probably overstated in the US South and that there was a bias *in favor* of finding a smaller gap between the southern states and the northern ones. The only persons to have realized this point were Fenoaltea (1984), Barzel (1977), Wright (2006), and Hummel (2012). And, with the exception of Hummel, they do not connect their findings to the economic growth debate. All four essentially argue that slavery was not a tax on output (i.e., expropriating slaves of the labor they produce). Rather, slavery was a tax on the leisure of slaves. Slave owners decided the amount of work done by slaves, which essentially means that they didn't have to convince them to forgo leisure by offering higher wages. They simply seized leisure away from them and overworked them. This is the coercion bias discussed here.

Consider the evidence advanced by Hummel (2012), which summarizes the historiography of the slavery debates superbly and in great technical details. Slaves received a minimal compensation in the form of food and shelter. The value of these in-kind payments—at market prices—was $30 to $60 in 1860 (Hummel 2012, 145, 193). This is essentially the "wage rate" they received (for lack of a better term). However, the hire rates for slaves between slave owners was between $103 and $367 (depending on the state and type of workers) (Hummel 2012, 345). These hire rates, because they were contracted between slave owners renting out workers between each other, best approximate the marginal product of labor of slaves. In other words, slaves would have needed to receive payment of between $103 and $171 to work the way (i.e., number of days adjusted for intensity during the day) they did. They only received $30 worth.[5] The gap between these amounts is the much-debated expropriation rate in the literature on slavery (Fogel and Engerman 1974, 153; Vedder 1975; Ransom and Sutch 2001).

The problem, as Hummel pointed out, is that this implicitly assumes the shape of the labor supply curve as being perfectly inelastic, as depicted in figure 4.4. In the figure, the slave owner decides the quantity of labor he desires (hence why it is inelastic). His rents as slave owner are equal to the gap between the marginal revenue product (point A) and the payment in-kind for subsistence made to the slave (point B) multiplied by the amount of work extracted. However, the proper counterfactual is an upward-sloping supply labor curve as—if free—slaves could have decided to refuse offers depending on the offered wage rates. In this case, figure 4.5 is more relevant. In a free labor market, slaves would have worked fewer days (the difference on the x-axis between points B and A). They would have also obtained extra payment equal to the y-axis difference between A and B. However, the expropriation now includes the extra payment (raising wages to point D) an employer would have had to make to encourage the same amount of labor as under slavery.

And this is where the coercion bias can be seen. The slave owner expropriated much more from slaves than is commonly appreciated by making them work more than they would have accepted freely. In figure 4.5, the x-axis difference

Figure 4.4. Illustrating expropriation under slavery

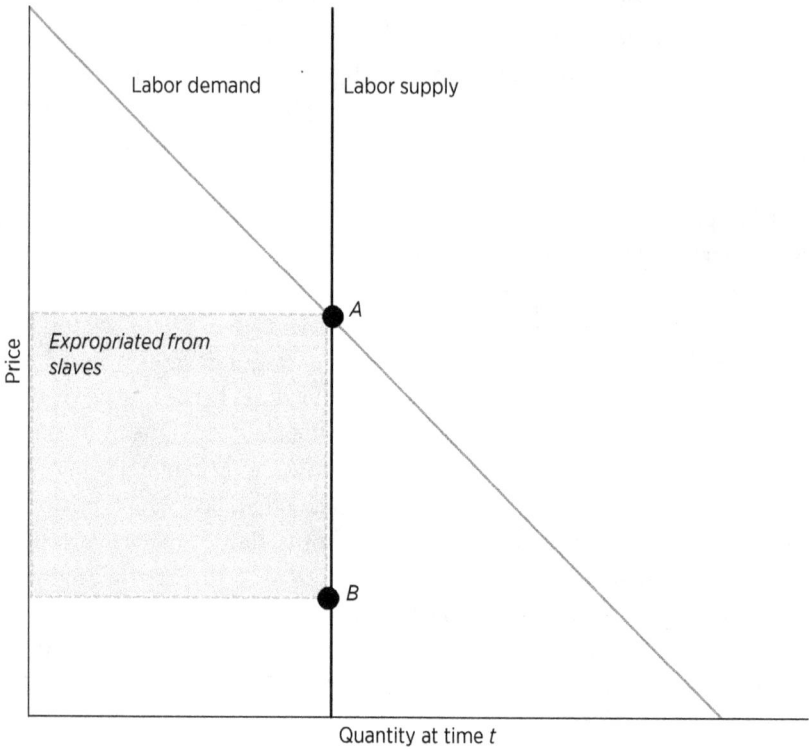

Quantity at time *t*

between A and C in labor used implies an overuse of labor to produce goods and services. Essentially, there is *inefficient* overproduction equal to the contribution of labor in production. The production of cotton by slaves is easy to measure through the censuses and the exports tables. As a result, measured production will appear greater—after all, more cotton was produced. The problem is that the *true* expropriation for slaves (the difference between B and D in figure 4.5 multiplied by the amount of labor worked) is largely unmeasurable. Indeed, with the data available, the best we could do is guesstimate using the logic in figure 4.3. Why "guesstimate"? Because the "free labor supply" curve has been coerced away. It forces us to propose counterfactuals based on hypotheses that may allow us to approximate the actual divorce between well-being and measured physical output (i.e., GDP) that was caused by coercion. This is a laborious effort that makes it hard to correct figures.

However, Hummel (2012) gives us an idea of the extent of overproduction under the logic of figure 4.5 as he attempted to produce a guesstimate of

Figure 4.5. A better illustration of expropriation under slavery

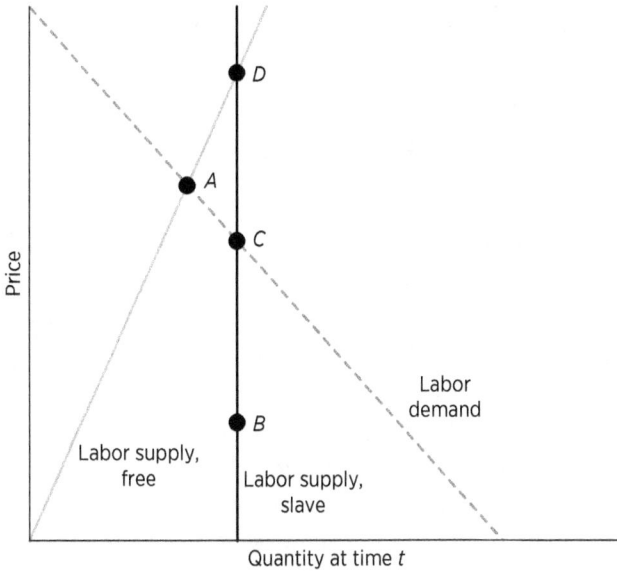

this inefficient overproduction. The range of values he estimated for the dead-weight loss of this overproduction was between $52 million and $190 million for the US South on net. This was equal to roughly 5 percent of the South's economy. In other words, this was the "coercion bias" in economic measurement. Economic historians were bound to find the southern slaves looking richer than they really were because of it. Moreover, Hummel pointed out (using other works by Robert Higgs, 1971 and 1977) that once slavery ended, incomes in the southern states fell. However, this was largely due to freed slaves working far fewer hours than before. The end of extreme coercion under slavery ended the divorce between income and actual well-being. The poverty of the South was thus plainly visible because the end of slavery also ended the coercion bias plaguing those who wished to produce that approximated well-being.

The coercion bias is crucial here to understand some modern debates over slavery and the American economy. A recurrent claim that has been advanced multiple times is that slavery was a building block of American prosperity (see Magness 2020 for a discussion). In its most recent form, this claim has been advanced by the new historians of capitalism (see Geloso and Glock 2021 for a discussion). They do so by pointing either to the large and rising level of cotton output produced by slaves or to the rates of economic growth in the South as discussed by Fogel and Engerman in their initial work. However, economic historians have widely rejected this view and have argued instead that the United States was impoverished (immediately or/and in the long-run) by slavery (Olmstead and Rhode 2018; Wright 2022).[6] The coercion bias englobes *all* of the rebuttals to the new historians of capitalism and their intellectual predecessors. Indeed, they were fooled by the bias and confused a commanded and coerced output with actual well-being.

ECONOMIC FREEDOM, GROWTH, AND THE COERCION BIAS

The slavery debates are a historical illustration of the coercion bias. A more modern illustration is the set of debates over the importance of economic freedom to economic growth (see De Haan and Sturm 2000; Doucouliagos 2005; Hall and Lawson 2014; Grier and Grier 2021).

Indexes of economic freedom have been widely used for some time now. They use international datasets of institutional indicators about multiple features of government involvement in the economy to measure the level of freedom that individual actors have to make investments and consumption decisions. The main index, that of the Fraser Institute, has five dimensions: the security of property rights, the level of business regulations, the openness to international trade, the soundness of monetary policy, and the size of the government relative to the economy. The vast majority of results available find that economic freedom as a whole is positively associated with higher incomes. The results are stronger for some subcomponents, such as property rights and the level of business regulations.

There are, however, some debates and doubts that persist. These can be divided into two categories. The first is debates regarding the size of the effect of economic freedom, where it is argued that the effect is not as strong as believed (Doucouliagos and Ulubasoglu 2006; Altman 2008). Others point to some components not being relevant to economic growth. Most notable is the finding regarding the size of government that is argued to be less relevant to economic growth (see, e.g., Ott 2018; Bergh 2020; Murphy 2022).[7] The second is the debate regarding whether levels of economic freedom affect *levels* of income but not *changes* in income. Only changes in economic freedom affect economic growth, it is argued by some.

Both categories of arguments are affected by the coercion bias, which forces any empirical test to understate the importance of economic freedom. Exceptionally coercive governments that marshal large quantities of resources to wage war or to preserve the regimes will tend to increase *measured* output in the same way that Higgs discussed for the myth of wartime prosperity during

World War II. However, these goods do not increase well-being. Quite the opposite! This means that countries with high levels of coercion will have a higher ratio of measured GDP to well-being. If coercion is correlated with low values on the index of economic freedom, then statistical tests of the relation between the latter and income levels or economic growth will be biased as well. The effect of economic freedom will be *understated*. As such, we should understand that the lowest values found of the effect of economic freedom are *necessarily* lower-bound estimates.

The same logic applies to the second category. If coercion was used to force people to work more, a change in economic freedom resulting from ending coerced production may lead to a fall in measured output. In such a case, the rate of economic growth may in fact fall, causing us to misinterpret the gain in well-being. Returning to the slavery example is useful here. Indeed, Hummel pointed out that freed slaves worked considerably fewer hours (and much less intensely per hour worked) after emancipation. This caused incomes in the South to fall. If emancipation is—rightfully—understood to be the equivalent of a change in economic freedom that increased well-being, using the change in southern incomes would lead us to the wrong conclusion: that economic freedom slowed down economic growth.

A recent illustration of the importance of the coercion bias has been provided by Luis Martinez (2022). Martinez made a very simple point: dictators can lie about GDP numbers (directly or indirectly).[8] However, satellite imagery allows scholars to estimate the level of nighttime light, which is a strong correlate of economic activity. The satellite imagery cannot lie. Ergo, Martinez posited that free countries would show that actual GDP numbers would generally line up with estimates based on predictions generated from data regarding light intensity at nighttime. His results confirmed that impression. However, when looking at partly free or unfree countries, he found large gaps between the actual GDP and the predicted values. Overall, the gaps he found halved the rate of economic growth in unfree countries, suggesting that improvements in well-being were far smaller than commonly appreciated.

From this he concluded that the gap was the magnitude of the lies made by dictators. I would tend to say that he overstates the lies because the gaps include the coercion bias and the reporting bias that Martinez focuses on. Take the example of China in Martinez's work. Over the 2002–21 period, the official GDP numbers for China reported growth of nearly 400 percent. The numbers based on nighttime light data suggest that that it was less than 200 percent. In many regions of China, there are forced labor camps where prisoners are producing outputs under threat of physical harm (Bown 2021; Caskey and

Murtazashvili 2022; Callais, Caskey, and Peng 2022). This means that there is *some* coercion bias in the gaps that Martinez found. And China is not the only example, as forced labor is a global phenomenon (International Labour Organization 2021).[9]

As such, some of the gaps found by Martinez speak to the coercion bias. Martinez's near-zero difference between predicted values from nighttime light data and actual GDP in free countries can be interpreted as the ratio of 1 in figure 4.3. The gap that increases with the level of coercion (as Martinez moved from free to partly free to unfree) suggests that the greater the coercion, the greater the loss of synonymity between GDP and well-being. Even if only 10 percent of the differences Martinez found speaks to coercion bias, the relationship between economic growth and economic freedom would be massively affected by the coercion bias.[10]

CONCLUSION

This chapter argues for the existence of a coercion bias that foils the reliability of economic measurement for unfree societies. Inspired by the work of Robert Higgs regarding World War II, I argued that this bias is not a trivial one. It is large and economically significant. It affects debates of a historical nature that go to the heart of how prosperous societies came to be. It also affects debates on the importance of economic freedom to economic growth and development.

Few economists—with some exceptions including Robert Higgs—appreciate the importance of this bias. Fewer economists have attempted to assess its empirical importance. Now that I am aware of the existence of the bias, I view this as probably one of the greatest failures of economists since the professionalization of the trade. Empirical efforts should be dedicated to measure its importance and relevance to modern and historical conversations.

NOTES

1. Higgs used GNP rather than GDP data.

2. I omit consideration of whether these frequently used textbook examples really fit the bill of what is a public good. I have elsewhere disputed these examples. For the sake of this chapter's contribution, I will avoid this discussion and refer readers to Candela and Geloso (2018, 2019a, 2019b, 2020) and Callais and Geloso (2022). Essentially, I am assuming that "standard scenario" is the optimally sized state (whatever that is).

3. In his later revisitations of the topic (in *Without Consent or Contracts* and *Slavery Debates*), Fogel toned down this point but did not drop it.

4. In a similar vein, see Bateman, Foust, and Weiss (1975), Vedder and Gallaway (1980), Niemi (1989), Bateman and Weiss (2002), and Atack and Bateman (2008).

5. And this overstates the value because they would have probably preferred $30 to $60 in monetary payment rather than the same value in-kind.

6. In fact, it is worth pointing out that Fogel and Engerman themselves did not credit the faster rates of growth in the South as signs that slavery made the country richer. They do recognize that there was overproduction of cotton in many places, as Hummel points out (see, e.g., 2012, 188).

7. It is worth pointing out that this finding could simply be due to the way the indexes are constructed. The index takes the difference between a country's government size and the minimum size of all countries observed and divides that by the difference between the maximum and minimum sizes found. This is a linear index where smaller governments mean higher scores. However, if the effect of the size of government on economic growth is nonlinear, this is a misspecification (see Scully 1989, 2014; Di Matteo and Summerfield 2020).

8. The indirect route would be taken if dictators set targets of economic growth to be reached under threat of penalty. In such cases, bureaucrats acting as agents of the dictators are incentivized to lie, which props up the numbers. In this case, the fudging is indirect. Berdine, Geloso, and Powell (2018) provide a well-documented process of indirectly making up numbers in the case of Cuba and its infant mortality rate.

9. For example, many countries have a large coerced labor force in their fishing fleets, which increases output from that sector (McDonald et al. 2021).

10. Obviously, the coercion bias and reporting bias combined mean that estimates of this relationship are downwardly biased by a large proportion.

REFERENCES

Altman, Morris. 2008. "How Much Economic Freedom Is Necessary for Economic Growth? Theory and Evidence." *Economics Bulletin* 15 (2): 1–20.

Atack, Jeremy, and Fred Bateman. 2008. "Profitability, Firm Size, and Business Organization in Nineteenth-Century US Manufacturing." In *Quantitative Economic History: The Good of Counting*, edited by Joshua L. Rosenbloom, 72–95. Abingdon, UK: Routledge.

Barzel, Yoram. 1977. "An Economic Analysis of Slavery." *Journal of Law and Economics* 20 (1): 87–110.

Bateman, Fred, James Foust, and Thomas Weiss. 1975. "Profitability in Southern Manufacturing: Estimates for 1860." *Explorations in Economic History* 12 (3): 211–31.

Bateman, Fred, and Thomas Weiss. 2002. *A Deplorable Scarcity: The Failure of Industrialization in the Slave Economy*. Chapel Hill: University of North Carolina Press.

Berdine, Gilbert, Vincent Geloso, and Benjamin Powell. 2018. "Cuban Infant Mortality and Longevity: Health Care or Repression?" *Health Policy and Planning* 33 (6): 755–57.

Bergh, Andreas. 2020. "Hayekian Welfare States: Explaining the Coexistence of Economic Freedom and Big Government." *Journal of Institutional Economics* 16 (1): 1–12.

Bown, Chad P. 2021. "The US–China Trade War and Phase One Agreement." *Journal of Policy Modeling* 43 (4): 805–43.

Callais, Justin T., Gregory W. Caskey, and Linan Peng. 2022. "Repression and International Trade: An Analysis of Chinese Trade Volumes with Islamic Countries." SSRN 4261062.

Callais, Justin T., and Vincent Geloso. 2022. "The Political Economy of Lighthouses in Antebellum America." Working Paper, George Mason University.

Candela, Rosolino A., and Vincent Geloso. 2018. "The Lightship in Economics." *Public Choice* 176 (3): 479–506.

———. 2019a. "Why Consider the Lighthouse a Public Good?" *International Review of Law and Economics* 60 (C): 105852.

———. 2019b. "Coase and Transaction Costs Reconsidered: The Case of the English Lighthouse System." *European Journal of Law and Economics* 48 (3): 331–49.

———. 2020. "The Lighthouse Debate and the Dynamics of Interventionism." *Review of Austrian Economics* 33 (3): 289–314.

Caskey, Gregory W., and Ilia Murtazashvili. 2022. "The Predatory State and Coercive Assimilation: The Case of the Uyghurs in Xinjiang." *Public Choice* 191 (1): 217–35.

Cohn, Raymond L. 1981. "Antebellum Regional Incomes: Another Look." *Explorations in Economic History* 18 (4): 330–46.

De Haan, Jakob, and Jan-Egbert Sturm. 2000. "On the Relationship between Economic Freedom and Economic Growth." *European Journal of Political Economy* 16 (2): 215–41.

Di Matteo, Livio, and Fraser Summerfield. 2020. "The Shifting Scully Curve: International Evidence from 1871 to 2016." *Applied Economics* 52 (39): 4263–83.

Doucouliagos, Chris. 2005. "Publication Bias in the Economic Freedom and Economic Growth Literature." *Journal of Economic Surveys* 19 (3): 367–87.

Doucouliagos, Chris, and Mehmet A. Ulubasoglu. 2006. "Economic Freedom and Economic Growth: Does Specification Make a Difference?" *European Journal of Political Economy* 22 (1): 60–81.

Eggertsson, Gauti B., and Paul Krugman. 2012. "Debt, Deleveraging, and the Liquidity Trap: A Fisher-Minsky-Koo Approach." *Quarterly Journal of Economics* 127 (3): 1469–513.

Fenoaltea, Stefano. 1984. "Slavery and Supervision in Comparative Perspective: A Model." *Journal of Economic History* 44 (3): 635–68.

Fogel, Robert William, and Stanley L. Engerman. 1974. *Time on the Cross: The Economics of American Negro Slavery*. New York: W. W. Norton.

Geloso, Vincent, and Judge Glock. 2021. "The New History of Capitalism and the Methodologies of Economic History." *Essays in Economic and Business History* 39: 206–21.

Geloso, Vincent, and Casey Pender. 2022. "The Myth of Wartime Prosperity: Canadian Evidence." Working Paper, George Mason University.

Grier, Kevin B., and Robin M. Grier. 2021. "The Washington Consensus Works: Causal Effects of Reform, 1970–2015." *Journal of Comparative Economics* 49 (1): 59–72.

Gunderson, Gerald. 1973. "Southern Ante-Bellum Income Reconsidered." *Explorations in Economic History* 10 (2): 151–76.

Hall, Joshua C., and Robert A. Lawson. 2014. "Economic Freedom of the World: An Accounting of the Literature." *Contemporary Economic Policy* 32 (1): 1–19.

Higgs, Robert. 1971. *The Transformation of the American Economy, 1865–1914: An Essay in Interpretation*. New York: John Wiley and Sons.

———. 1977. *Competition and Coercion: Blacks in the American Economy 1865–1914*. Cambridge: Cambridge University Press.

———. 1992. "Wartime Prosperity? A Reassessment of the US Economy in the 1940s." *Journal of Economic History* 52 (1): 41–60.

———. 1999. "From Central Planning to the Market: The American Transition, 1945–1947." *Journal of Economic History* 59 (3): 600–623.

———. 2004. "Wartime Socialization of Investment: A Reassessment of US Capital Formation in the 1940s." *Journal of Economic History* 64 (2): 500–520.

———. 2006. *Depression, War, and Cold War: Studies in Political Economy*. New York: Oxford University Press.

Hummel, Jeffrey Rogers. 2012. *Deadweight Loss and the American Civil War: The Political Economy of Slavery, Secession, and Emancipation.* SSRN 2155362.

International Labour Organization. 2021. *Statistics on Forced Labour, Modern Slavery and Human Trafficking.* Geneva: United Nations.

Lindert, Peter H., and Jeffrey G. Williamson. 2016. *Unequal Gains: American Growth and Inequality since 1700.* Princeton, NJ: Princeton University Press.

Magness, Phillip W. 2020. *The 1619 Project: A Critique.* Great Barrington, MA: American Institute for Economic Research.

Martinez, Luis R. 2022. "How Much Should We Trust the Dictator's GDP Growth Estimates?" *Journal of Political Economy* 130 (10): 2731–69.

McDonald, Gavin G., Christopher Costello, Jennifer Bone, Reniel B. Cabral, Valerie Farabee, Timothy Hochberg, David Kroodsma, Tracey Mangin, Kyle C. Meng, and Oliver Zahn. 2021. "Satellites Can Reveal Global Extent of Forced Labor in the World's Fishing Fleet." *Proceedings of the National Academy of Sciences* 118 (3): e2016238117.

Murphy, Ryan H. 2022. "Freedom Stands: A Rejoinder to Ott." *Econ Journal Watch* 19 (2): 242–46.

Niemi, Albert W. Jr. 1989. "Industrial Profits and Market Forces: The Antebellum South." *Social Science History* 13 (1): 89–106.

Olmstead, Alan L., and Paul W. Rhode. 2018. "Cotton, Slavery, and the New History of Capitalism." *Explorations in Economic History* 67: 1–17.

Ott, Jan. 2018. "Measuring Economic Freedom: Better without Size of Government." *Social Indicators Research* 135 (2): 479–98.

Ransom, Roger L., and Richard Sutch. 2001. *One Kind of Freedom: The Economic Consequences of Emancipation.* Cambridge: Cambridge University Press.

Rauchway, Eric. 2015. *The Money Makers: How Roosevelt and Keynes Ended the Depression, Defeated Fascism, and Secured a Prosperous Peace.* New York: Basic Books.

Scully, Gerald W. 1989. "The Size of the State, Economic Growth and the Efficient Utilization of National Resources." *Public Choice* 63 (2): 149–64.

———. 2014. *Constitutional Environments and Economic Growth.* Princeton, NJ: Princeton University Press.

Vedder, Richard K. 1975. "The Slave Exploitation (Expropriation) Rate." *Explorations in Economic History* 12 (4): 453–57.

Vedder, Richard K., and Lowell E. Gallaway. 1980. "The Profitability of Antebellum Manufacturing: Some New Estimates." *Business History Review* 54 (1): 92–103.

Vernon, J. R. 1994. "World War II Fiscal Policies and the End of the Great Depression." *Journal of Economic History* 54 (4): 850–68.

Wright, Gavin. 2006. *Slavery and American Economic Development.* Baton Rouge: Louisiana State University Press.

———. 2022. "Slavery and the Rise of the Nineteenth-Century American Economy." *Journal of Economic Perspectives* 36 (2): 123–48.

Chapter 5

Regime Uncertainty and Market Uncertainty

Donald J. Boudreaux

W hat put the "Great" in the Great Depression? As with so much about that economic calamity of nearly a century ago, explanations abound. These explanations come from all across the ideological and methodological spectra. The plausibility that you attach to any of these explanations depends on your location on these spectra. I do not differ from you.

As skeptical of government intervention as I am awed by the creative powers of free markets—in each case immensely—I've always been unpersuaded by Keynesian explanations of both the Great Depression's birth and its regrettably long life. As an explanation for the Depression's start, I find some merit in the Austrian theory of the trade cycle (Garrison 2007). Also carrying some explanatory oomph is the complementary explanation supplied by Milton Friedman's and Anna Schwartz's account of the "Great Contraction"—which is the Fed permitting the money supply to decline by 30 percent from 1929 through 1933 (Friedman and Schwartz 1963, 229–419). But in my view neither the Austrians nor Friedman and Schwartz—and certainly none of the countless flavors of Keynesians—adequately explain the Great Depression's length.

To my mind, the first (and, so far, only) plausible explanation of the Great Depression's length didn't come along until 60 years after the fact. That explanation is supplied by Robert Higgs's concept of regime uncertainty, which Higgs defines as "the likelihood that investors' private property rights in their capital and the income it yields will be attenuated by further government action" (Higgs 2006, 9).

As is true of so many pioneering ideas, regime uncertainty, once stated, seems obvious—perhaps *too* obvious to serve as an explanation for such a momentous economic event. Just as, for example, Ronald Coase's (1960) identification of the bilateral (or multilateral) nature of all externalities is "obvious"

For helpful comments, criticisms, and suggestions on an earlier draft I thank Pete Boettke, Veronique de Rugy, Rosolino Candela, Chris Coyne, and Dwight Lee. This chapter's many remaining flaws, alas, are my fault exclusively.

once explained—yet went wholly ignored before Coase offered this explanation—so too with regime uncertainty. But of course the power of any idea is ultimately measured by its ability to give us a sense that that idea improves our understanding of reality. It's a feature and not a bug of such an idea that is so straightforward as to be "obvious" once elucidated.

My purpose here is not to offer a detailed account of Higgs's explanation of how regime uncertainty extended what would likely otherwise have been a much shorter economic downturn into the Great Depression. It is, instead, to compare regime uncertainty to another source of uncertainty—that I will call simply "market uncertainty"—and to ask if there is something unique about regime uncertainty at stifling commercial exchange and the division of labor. Nevertheless, the best way to convey the meaning and power of regime uncertainty is to summarize Higgs's use of it to explain the Great Depression's long duration.

REGIME UNCERTAINTY

Regardless of the precise cause (or causes) of the sudden downturn in economic activity starting in 1930, there is no good reason to believe that this downturn was destined to last for more than a decade and a half.[1] An economic downturn of similar magnitude occurred in 1920 yet is today all but forgotten, as that earlier recession was quickly reversed and followed by the booming 1920s.[2] Something *following* the downturn of 1930 is likely to have differed significantly, perhaps even categorically, from what followed the downturn of 1920. It's that "something" that put the "Great" in the Great Depression.

And that something, according to Higgs, is the much-increased uncertainty that business owners and investors experienced as a result of the unprecedented (in America) government interventions of Franklin Roosevelt's New Deal—especially that period of the New Deal that stretched from 1935 through 1940. This uncertainty was over the degree to which owners of industrial and commercial private properties would retain control of the use of those properties and to enjoy the fruits of deploying those properties profitably. Using survey data, bond yields, and stock-price movements, Higgs demonstrates convincingly that starting in 1935 and extending to 1940, investors were unusually frightened of the economic future. This fear of the future prompted investors to clasp shut their wallets and purses until FDR was dead and New Deal experimentation was largely a thing of the past. In Higgs's words (2006, 5),

The insufficiency of private investment from 1935 through 1940 reflected a pervasive uncertainty among investors about the security of their property rights in their capital and its prospective returns. This uncertainty arose, especially, though not exclusively, from the character of the actions of the federal government and the nature of the Roosevelt administration during the so-called Second New Deal, from 1935 to 1940.

Higgs's account rings true. The higher is investors' perceived risk of committing capital to projects, the less willing are investors to so commit their capital. And because in the 1930s US government economic policy was unprecedentedly interventionist—and interventionist especially in ways that threatened the ability of capital owners to retain control of their properties and of these properties' returns—it's no surprise that too little investment occurred during the 1930s to substantially reduce unemployment and, more generally, to revive the economy. Investors' enthusiasm to be in the capitalist game can only have been furthered dampened by the fact that the general intellectual climate of the era was very favorable to socialism.[3] Actual policy and the intellectual trend both pointed in the direction of increasingly tight and detailed government control over the means of production.

But a skeptic might ask if using regime uncertainty to explain the Great Depression's long duration proves too much. Investors surely do respond negatively to uncertainty regarding the prospects of their investments. But what does it matter that the uncertainty in 1930s America came from fear of excessive government involvement? Might not private investment be no less discouraged by *market* uncertainty?

In short, if what investors care about is the expected returns on their investments, p•R—where p is the probability of actually reaping a return of R—they shouldn't care about what particular events cause p to rise or fall. P might indeed, as Higgs documents, be reduced by government intervention of the sort that was all the rage in the late 1930s, but it might be reduced also by innumerable *economic* occurrences such as increasingly rapid technological innovation that renders investments in specific forms of capital goods obsolete. A 25 percent chance of an investment losing 40 percent of its value next year to government intervention is no more feared by investors than is a 25 percent chance of an investment losing 40 percent of its value next year to an unanticipated technological innovation. At least at first glance, it appears as if the latter prospect should stymie investment spending no less (or no more) than does the former prospect.

Does regime uncertainty threaten economic investment, dynamism, and growth in a way that market uncertainty does not? If so, what is this unique feature of regime uncertainty?

SOURCES OF UNCERTAINTY: THE CHICAGO VIEW

From the perspective of one influential branch of mainstream neoclassical economics—call it the right branch—regime uncertainty does indeed differ categorically from market uncertainty. This "right" branch of mainstream economics is that which is fed by research from economists associated chiefly with, or influenced heavily by, economists at the University of Chicago. According to these economists, the economic efficiency of private markets is remarkably complete, persistent, and robust in the face of all obstacles *except* government interventions. In practice, therefore, investment can be stymied only by regime uncertainty and not by market uncertainty. The reason is that in the "right" branch of mainstream economics, economic agents' ignorance of the future course of markets is confined to Knightian risk. Any genuine economic uncertainty that might infuse markets is assumed away.

This odd assumption is used because mainstream economists are committed to identifying and describing conditions of equilibrium, and the recognition of true uncertainty thwarts this commitment. Suppose that a model's economic agents on Monday cannot know some significant fact that will arise on Tuesday. These agents, thus, are simply unable on Monday to allocate resources in ways that ensure that the resource-allocation decisions that they make on Monday will be revealed to be optimal on Tuesday. This conclusion holds even if the decisions made by the agents on Monday would prove to be unambiguously optimal were the world to *end* on Monday—that is, to end before any new significant facts arise.

A commitment to equilibrium theorizing about markets therefore requires that economists assume away any genuine creativity and change, for the details of creativity and change cannot, by their nature, be predicted even probabilistically. The final result is that nothing truly unknowable, or even unknown, can be admitted into the minds of agents in equilibrium models. And so, it follows, economists committed to equilibrium theorizing can never admit into their models any real change—anything really *new*.

The offspring of such theorizing are remarkably well-behaved. With the future of markets being predictable, if only probabilistically, investment plans are threatened by no true uncertainties or genuine surprises that might arise as a result of the operation of markets. Only exogenous interference with markets, such as the interference that comes from government, can cause people's experience, knowledge, and expectations on Tuesday truly to differ from what people knew and expected on Monday. And come Wednesday, what people know and expect will again be the same as what they knew on Tuesday and on Monday.

And come Thursday. . . . On it goes interminably. As summarized by James Buchanan and Viktor Vanberg, "The equilibrium concept is associated with a world view that treats the future as implied in the present" ([1991] 2001, 293).

Higgs's theory of regime uncertainty seems tailor-made for an audience of market-oriented, equilibrium-obsessed economists in the Chicago mold. The ability of agents in such a modeled free market to anticipate the future, and of the market itself to capitalize agents' rational expectations accurately into the prices of assets today, protects the market from genuine problems. Whatever occurs will be optimal, even if not recognized as such by reporters, pundits, and politicians. This near-omniscience of each of the model's agents also protects him or her from suffering plans being disrupted by unpleasant surprises. Only forces from outside of the market—most notably, government interventions—can be sources of genuine surprise and, hence, of stifling uncertainty. If this uncertainty is sufficiently intense, investors will retreat. The resulting decline in investment will cause economic stagnation. For evidence, see the American economy of the 1930s.

SOURCES OF UNCERTAINTY: THE AUSTRIAN VIEW

A superficial evaluation of Higgs's theory of regime uncertainty might suggest that the story ends here, and satisfyingly so for free-market proponents. Markets left to their own devices do not generate market-destroying—or even market-distorting—uncertainties. And therefore if we encounter in the real world a degree of uncertainty that prevents markets' smooth and successful operation, that uncertainty must be the product either of actual government intervention or of well-grounded fears of such intervention. Without question, the uncertainty that Higgs carefully identified as prolonging the Great Depression is uncertainty caused by investment-stifling government intervention into markets, and intensified by fears that such interventions would continue indefinitely.

But let's dig more deeply. Austrian economists, along with fellow-traveling subjectivists such as James Buchanan and Robert Higgs himself, have long insisted that mainstream equilibrium analyses of markets—including analyses offered by Chicago-oriented scholars—have serious flaws. While appreciating the genuine contributions made by Chicago economists to our understanding of markets, Austrians and allied scholars specifically reject what my old teacher Leland Yeager often referred to derisively as "equilibrium-always thinking."[4] In the Austrian view, markets themselves are *not* so hyperefficient as to be always in equilibrium. At each moment, some resources are misallocated—meaning, some resources are currently being used in ways that yield benefits that fall short of the costs of these uses. Some goods and services for which consumers would be willing to pay prices that fully cover the costs of supplying these goods and services are not supplied. Most significantly, the future features not merely Knightian risks but also genuine uncertainty—and, hence, genuine change.[5]

While some Austrians, such as Ludwig Lachmann, believe that this uncertainty is more pervasive and insurmountable—more "radical"—than do other Austrians, such as Israel Kirzner, one of the marks of all Austrian economic analysis is a recognition of the fact that economic actors, at least in modern market economies, operate not only in a larger world but also in *markets*, in which genuine uncertainty is inescapable. Furthermore, the operation even of the most ideally capitalist free market not only is affected by genuine uncertainty, but also the operation of capitalist markets itself is a *source* of genuine uncertainty.

Consider, for example, James Buchanan's and Viktor Vanberg's discussion in their 1991 paper "The Market as a Creative Process" (2001). Inspired by Lachmann, G. L. S. Shackle, and Jack Wiseman, Buchanan and Vanberg insist that "in human social affairs the future is undetermined but 'created' in the process of choice" (295). And choice itself—to be genuine—is itself a creative act. Favorably quoting Shackle, they write:

> Shackle suggests that every person choosing among different courses of action can be seen "to be making history, on however small a scale, in some sense other than mere passive obedience to the play of all-pervasive causes." Every choice can be seen as the beginning of a sequel that "will partly be the work of many people's choices-to-come whose character . . . the chooser of present action cannot know." (295–96).

Later, Buchanan and Vanberg, quoting Wiseman, describe our world as one "in which creative human choice is a constant source of an 'unknowable future'" (296).

Among the central purposes of this Buchanan and Vanberg paper is to demonstrate that even the Austrian economist Israel Kirzner's recognition of genuine economic uncertainty inadequately captures just how pervasive and significant uncertainty is in real-world market economies. Therefore, in Buchanan's and Vanberg's telling, a major defect mars Kirzner's well-known theory of entrepreneurship as alertness to previously unnoticed profit opportunities.

> Entrepreneurial activity, in particular, is not to be modelled as discovery of that which is "out there." Such activity, by contrast, *creates* a reality that will be different subsequent to differing choices. Hence, the reality of the future must be shaped by choices yet to be made, and this reality has no

existence independent of these choices. With regard to a "yet to be created" reality, it is surely confusing to consider its emergence in terms of
the discovery of "overlooked opportunities." (303)

Entrepreneurs don't merely discover *existing* opportunities to reallocate
resources profitably. Entrepreneurs *create* a future that would not exist were
they to act differently. And in a market economy this creation—this true and
truly unpredictable change—is both incessant as well as the source of vastly
greater value creation than are improvements in the allocation of resources
that better satisfy existing or predictable consumer demands. It's not for nothing that the economic historian Deirdre McCloskey wants to give capitalism
a new name: "innovism."[6]

This Austrian recognition of the inescapability of economic uncertainty,
therefore, perhaps reveals a source of investment-stymying uncertainty that
is rooted not in government interference into markets but in markets themselves. Because every one of the countless genuine choices that each of us—and
especially entrepreneurs—makes daily helps to *create* a future that would not
otherwise materialize and that is inherently unpredictable, surely there exists
at least the possibility that modern capitalism (or "innovism") generates such
a degree of uncertainty in the market that investors become too wary to invest
funds in sufficient amounts to keep the economy buoyant.

Note the irony of this Austrian recognition. Among all schools of economic thought, none is more known—and accurately so—for its defense of
free, open, entrepreneurial markets than is the Austrian school. Mainstream
economists—mainly here those whose work feeds the "left" branch of the
mainstream—offer a long list of private actions that, these economists believe,
can and sometimes do keep private investment at inadequate levels. The most
famous entry on this list is savings. Keynesians are convinced that private individuals and households routinely save too much, thus pushing aggregate demand
down to levels too low to support full employment. The only feasible remedy,
say Keynesians, is a government-engineered increase in aggregate demand
(typically achieved by increased deficit spending by the government). Another
entry on this list is so-called predatory pricing. In this case consumers are
lured to purchase products from producers deviously charging artificially low
prices. These producers aim to monopolize their markets by bankrupting their
rivals and then using the threat of further predatory price cuts to scare away
investors who might be tempted to enter the market once the predator, finally
rid of its original rivals, starts charging monopolistically high prices.

I believe that I can safely say that Bob Higgs joins me in rejecting these and other accounts from the mainstream's "left" branch of how purely private actions within markets might stymie private entrepreneurs and investment.[7] But what about private investment being stymied by entrepreneurial creativity itself—by activity that appears front and center, and with praise, in accounts by Austrian economists of the operation of market processes? Might this market uncertainty produce the same devastating consequences as does regime uncertainty?

MARKET UNCERTAINTY DIFFERS CATEGORICALLY FROM REGIME UNCERTAINTY

Authors writing papers in which genuine uncertainty plays a prominent role should be leery of making firm predictions. Yet looking back at history, and looking forward through the lens of sound economic theory, justifies the confident conclusion that market uncertainty, while real and perhaps even "radical," is highly unlikely to generate stagnation of investment and, hence, highly unlikely to generate economic stagnation of the sort generated by regime uncertainty.

The history is clear. When markets were freed of chains laid on by the state, by tradition, by superstition, or by simple antagonism to commerce, innovation flourished and was able to find sufficient funds to back it. When, in Deirdre McCloskey's (2016) telling, bourgeois pursuits for the first time in history, in the 17th and 18th centuries, became dignified, entrepreneurs sprang into action, each "having a go" at experimenting with new products and new methods of production, distribution, and financing, all in pursuit of honest profit. ("Honest" because buyers, except in relatively rare instances, were neither coerced nor tricked into buying what entrepreneurs were selling. And suppliers—including workers—were gotten by producers offering them better deals and not by enslavement.)[8]

That the economic change that began just over two centuries ago was at a pace unprecedented in any prior age is indisputable. This change has continued ever since, pausing only occasionally (most infamously, and for the longest duration, in the 1930s—and for reasons explained by Bob Higgs). If the uncertainty generated by entrepreneurship, innovation, and creative destruction were *self-destructive*, these productive economic forces would almost certainly have extinguished themselves by now. Yet here we are, nearly a quarter of the way through the 21st century, and entrepreneurial innovations continue to pour forth.

Why? As noted above, from the perspective of the entrepreneur and investor, uncertainty is uncertainty, and lost wealth is lost wealth. Why does market uncertainty not spook investors in the same way as does regime uncertainty?

Part of the answer, I believe, is that market uncertainty might well spook *some* investors in the same way as does regime uncertainty. Yet if it doesn't spook them all—that is, if even only a small handful of investors are sufficiently confident that consumers will enthuse over that entrepreneur's new better mousetrap—the entrepreneur gets his funding and (sorry, mice!) humanity gets a better mousetrap.[9]

Is market uncertainty more likely than regime uncertainty to leave at least some investors sufficiently unfazed that funding will continue to flow to entrepreneurs and businesses who put it to productive, pro-growth uses? I believe so.

Market uncertainty is uncertainty about how private economic actors—consumers, business executives, entrepreneurs, and investors—will spend their own money (or money voluntarily entrusted to them). In contrast, regime uncertainty is uncertainty either about how government officials will spend *other* people's money, or about how government officials will obstruct *other* people from spending their own money. The relevance of this distinction is found in the fact that the range of actions that a person will plausibly take is significantly narrowed by tightly tying that person's material well-being to the actions that he or she decides to take. These actions thus become more predictable than they would absent such a tie. To use an extreme example, I might get great satisfaction by publicly proclaiming a belief that magic crystals will outperform modern medicine at curing people of injuries and diseases. But if my child is seriously injured in an automobile accident, I'm likely to bring my child to a hospital rather than to a new-age healer. And you, as an outside observer familiar with human nature, will predict this outcome with no low level of confidence.

Being human themselves, as well as being participants in the market, investors can with some confidence distinguish opportunities that have plausible prospects of being successful (the parent's use of modern medicine in the earlier example) from prospects that are implausible (the parent's use of magic healing crystals). Choosing only among plausible investment opportunities, investors thereby reduce their exposure to market uncertainty. The five-to-ten-year future created by genuine consumer and entrepreneurial choice, while open, is not wholly unpredictable. Or, at least, the experience of the past couple of centuries in capitalist economies seems to reveal that this future is not so unpredictable as to scare away enough investors to stymie economic growth.

Much more difficult is the attempt to predict the actions of people whose personal, material self-interests are not (or are not very much) affected by the decisions they make. Modern government officials do not, in practice, put their own personal material welfare at risk when making decisions that affect millions of strangers. And so government officials sincerely committed to an ideological agenda hostile to market institutions and activities can pursue that agenda largely on other people's dimes. And if the climate of public opinion also features growing hostility toward commerce and creative destruction, even the constraints posed by the need for reelection—constraints that are never fully reliable even under the best circumstances (Simmons 2011)—become a positive inducement to destructive assaults on private property and market activities. The range of government interventions that might undermine the security of property and contract rights is thus very wide, bounded not by the relatively tight constraints imposed by private interests but, instead, only by the imaginations of ideologically motivated officials and voters.

Not only is the *range* of potential government interventions that threaten the value of private investments wider than is the range of private market activities that threaten the value of particular investments, but the *duration* of destructive government interventions is likely longer (Kirzner 1978). No one likes to encounter evidence that he or she made a mistake. But recognition of mistakes is sure to be faster among market participants than among government officials. The reason, of course, is that the more quickly market participants recognize their errors, the more of their own money they save. The entrepreneur who was confident that consumers would have a high demand for his anchovy-flavored breakfast cereal will be embarrassed to learn of his error, but even more eager to correct that error in order to keep personal losses to a minimum.

In stark contrast to private market actors, government officials are not only less likely to recognize their errors quickly but also, even when such recognition begins to dawn on them, less likely to act as quickly as possible to correct these errors. After all, continuing with erroneous policies generally costs the government office holders responsible for those policies personally very little. But also at work here is an even more perverse incentive: government officials—again, spending only other people's money—often have incentives to double-down on their errors.

Government officials, especially elected ones, obtain and maintain their positions not by actually outperforming rivals at doing whatever tasks they propose to do for citizens. Instead, they secure their positions chiefly by convincing enough voters to put confidence in their—these politicians'—*promises* to fruitfully rearrange reality, often in novel ways. Because the performance of elected officials can almost never be tested "head-to-head" against the contemporaneous performance of rival officials pursuing different policies, the wisdom of putting such confidence in politicians is uncannily difficult to assess (Higgs 2018). No one can ever be sure just how incumbent officials performed. With different policies in place, seemingly good outcomes might have been even better, and seemingly bad outcomes might have been even worse. Further, politicians' promises typically include pledges to stand coura- geously against evil forces working to thwart the fulfillment of their promises. Successful politicians very often win office by convincingly boasting both of their splendid motives and of their rare abilities to achieve what almost no one else can—all without reliable empirical tests of these politicians' claims.

Convinced of their favored government officials' singularly impressive motives and abilities, voters—in the many instances when their preferred politicians' schemes don't work as promised—are open to excuses for why these officials' interventions haven't yet delivered the promised goods. And obviously these officials are strongly motivated to offer such excuses. Rare to the point of nearly nonexistent is the politician who says within a year or two of experiencing disappointing performance of his or her signature policies, "Oops, sorry. That showcase policy that I promised would work is in fact fail- ing spectacularly. I was wrong. Let's change course dramatically." Instead, the typical politician, if he or she doesn't actually spin negative news into positive news, blames the observed poor performance on forces beyond his or her con- trol. This politician promises that with more time and redoubled effort (and, of course, also with more taxpayer money), the results originally promised will indeed materialize.[10]

For politicians to admit failure as quickly as failure is admitted by private market actors is for politicians to expose themselves as ordinary human beings and, thus, people quite different from the secular saviors who were portrayed on the campaign trail and who the voters thought they elected to office. Able for a time—hopefully, at least to the next election—to paper over with other people's money the ill consequences of misguided polices, too many politicians have incentives to persist with bad policies or even to pursue these policies more intensely. When such policies threaten the security of property and contract rights—as in practice many do—investors rationally predict that these destruc- tive policies will be kept in place indefinitely and perhaps even expanded.

The above two considerations—of uncertainty's range and duration— combine to form what is a crucial difference separating market uncertainty from regime uncertainty. Compared to market uncertainty, the fear unleashed by regime uncertainty "closes off" many more investment opportunities across both economic space and time.

Absent regime uncertainty, the investor scared off by competitive market forces from sinking money into, say, a new online retailing venture remains open to sinking money into one or more other opportunities that are believed to be less prone to be undone too quickly by rivalrous market activity. But when government is hostile to investment generally (as it is when regime uncertainty reigns), large swathes of private investment opportunities are discouraged simultaneously, and this discouragement is likely to last a long time. This discouragement, in other words, is not merely of investors rationally worrying that some particular opportunities are today too prone to competitive dissipation, but that nearly *all* opportunities—investment *generally*—are for an extended period too unlikely to pay off.

THE CANCER OF PROTECTING MARKET *VALUES*

Another way—a way perhaps more fundamental—in which regime uncertainty differs categorically from market uncertainty is that interventions of the sort that commonly unleash regime uncertainty often create *de facto* property rights in market values. Depending on the extent of the creation of such "rights" and the determination with which these "rights" are protected, the results range anywhere from economic slowdown to economic calamity.

An essential feature of a successful market economy is that the law protects individuals' properties only against theft and *physical* destruction and obstruction. Not protected are the market *valuations* of individuals' properties. Free to physically use one's person and property in whatever ways one chooses, as long as such use doesn't infringe the same rights of others to use their persons and properties, entrepreneurs pursue profits by physically rearranging resources in ways that give the resulting rearrangements the highest possible market values (as determined by the voluntary expenditures of buyers). Market valuations thus are always changing in uncertain ways, but individuals remain reasonably *certain* that they'll retain unobstructed physical control over whatever goods and assets they own. Consumers who are unhappy with rising prices of particular goods or services are free to increase their savings or to switch their expenditures to other goods and services. Investors who are disappointed with the returns on their assets are free to redeploy those assets in ways that hopefully will yield higher returns.

Precisely *because* the market is and will forever be "imperfect," profit opportunities always exist. Investors who are disappointed with the returns on current uses of their assets can be certain (note the irony) that there exist alternative, more profitable uses of those assets, although of course—because of market uncertainty—these investors cannot know beforehand which *particular* alternative uses will work and which will fail. Free and eager to physically redeploy assets from less profitable uses to what are hoped will be more profitable uses, entrepreneurs and investors ensure that economic activity remains buoyant.

As a matter of logic, one cannot rule out the possibility that the difficulty of correctly identifying or creating particular profitable uses for assets in our uncertain world will discourage such a large number of investors from staying in the capitalist "game" that the economy falls into a recession. But as a practical and historical matter, the desire for profit evidently combines with the certainty that profit opportunities abound in market economies to keep enough investors active.

This conclusion leaves government intervention as the only plausible obstruction of this ongoing redeployment of assets in search of higher profits. This threat is real. It arises most obviously, and in a way that inflicts maximum harm most quickly, when government threatens to seize ownership of assets employed in profitable industries. Assets' economic profitability then becomes, for their owners, a liability. Better to keep assets liquid, in the form of money or precious metals, rather than invested in the likes of factories, machines, R&D, and worker training.

Yet less heavy-handed intervention similarly, if less obviously and more gradually, depresses investment activity. Insofar as government commits itself to protecting the prevailing market values of some particular assets (including labor), it of course discourages those assets from being redeployed from their current uses to different, more efficient uses. Some investors who would otherwise be interested in putting money into a better-mousetrap factory lose their interest because of the resulting higher cost of acquiring the labor and other inputs necessary to operate that factory profitably. Economic growth is thereby slowed.

But the economy-depressing consequences of such intervention don't end there. First, as Hayek warned, when protection of their assets' market values is granted to members of group *A*, government creates a precedent and thus subjects itself to pressure to extend such protection to members of groups *B* and *C*. The greater the number of asset owners and workers whose market values are protected by government from falling, the greater is the pressure to further extend such protection. The inevitable result is economic sclerosis.

Second, even if government's protection of market values remains confined to assets owned by only one or a few groups, government must over time restrict more and more the general public's—including investors'—freedom to determine the physical uses of their properties. Government's commitment to protect the value of, say, existing steel mills might begin with only tariffs on imported steel. But the resulting higher price of steel increases the likelihood of entrepreneurs developing new substitutes for steel.[11] If government is determined to stick to its commitment to prevent the values of steel-producing assets from falling, it then must prevent new substitutes from competing against steel. Whether using assets to produce steel substitutes is directly prohibited or "only" discouraged by punitive taxation, government's determination to prevent the values of steel-producing assets from falling shrinks the range of potentially profitable investment opportunities.[12] A shrinkage of investment naturally follows.

CONCLUSION

Both regime uncertainty and market uncertainty threaten the market values of existing investments. Both sources of uncertainty thus discourage some investments. But there the similarity ends. The uncertainty generated by government intervention regarding the prospects of private investment differs categorically from the uncertainty generated by market processes. Most notably, while government intervention unleashes uncertainty that generally reduces the prospects of profitable uses of assets, market uncertainty itself is a *source* of profit opportunities. And while the government interventions that create regime uncertainty also often obstruct the redeployment of assets, no such obstruction attends market uncertainty. It is therefore unsurprising that markets left to their own devices—unlike markets heavily encumbered with government interventions—do not fall into recession or stagnation of the sort that Bob Higgs so persuasively identified as resulting from regime uncertainty.

NOTES

1. Noting that (1) wartime full employment was artificially created by conscription (and the fear of being conscripted) as well as by the military's enormous need for weapons and materiel, (2) economic data during World War II are simply incomparable to economic data during peacetime, and (3) Americans' living standards did not appreciably improve during the war, Higgs rejects the commonplace assertion that the Great Depression was ended by World War II. Instead, argues Higgs, the most credible date for the end of the Depression is late 1946. See Higgs (2006, 67–80).

2. See Grant (2014).

3. Here's a telling indication of just how thoroughly socialism infused the intellectual air in the late 1930s and early 1940s. In 1941, F. A. Hayek—then living in England—interpreted an April 1938 message of President Roosevelt to Congress as indicating the Roosevelt administration's intention of "restoring competition" (Hayek [1941] 1997, 219). Hayek contrasted what he believed to be America's happy embrace of a liberal market economy with the mania for socialism that then raged throughout Europe, including in Great Britain. It's true that Europeans during those years were so much more enamored of state direction of the economy than were Americans that, from the perspective of a liberal European such as Hayek, FDR's late New Deal interventions seemed in comparison positively promising. But the reality is that *dirigiste* policies were in the late 1930s at unprecedented levels in the United States and showed no signs of retreating. The fact that the intellectual push for socialism had by then advanced further in western Europe than in America was likely taken by investors to mean only that America would soon follow western Europe further down the *dirigiste* road.

4. This account is mainly from my personal recollection of remarks frequently made by Yeager in two macroeconomic theory courses that he taught as a visiting professor at Auburn University in 1983, in addition to many conversations that I had with him then and for many years afterwards. But see also Yeager (1986).

5. This Austrian rejection of equilibrium-always theorizing—and the school's corresponding recognition of the need to account for genuine uncertainty—is rooted in the origins of the school. As noted by Paul Lewis in an annotated footnote in Hayek (2022, 166), "[Austrian-school founder Carl] Menger particularly placed more emphasis on the causal processes through which prices are changed, and the uncertainty faced by economic actors in the course of that process of disequilibrium adjustment, than did the more equilibrium-oriented [Leon] Walras and [William Stanley] Jevons." Samuel Gregg (2022, 164) puts the matter this way: "Those who build economic models typically don't like loose ends. One way to address this is to ignore them."

6. Armen Alchian approved of the name "capitalism" for the modern market economy. He believed this moniker to be singularly appropriate because of the modern market's facility at capitalizing expected future values into today's asset prices. As Alchian ([1978] 2006, 645) explained, "Under private property rights of people to goods and resources, the anticipated future effects of one's current actions are capitalized *now* in to his wealth and hence his current and future exchange opportunities. Precisely for that reason do I like the name 'capitalism' to denote a private property regime. It suggests the capitalization into present market-values of foreseeable events of current actions, which induces the private property rights owner to be responsive to the foreseeable distant effects and even the unforeseen effects." The importance of such capitalization cannot be overstated. But because the net present values of unpredictable events cannot be capitalized into today's asset prices, today's prices cannot possibly reflect these unpredictable future events. Plans made today in response to today's asset prices will therefore not be fully coordinated with plans made, and actions taken, in the future in response to whatever new events occur. Because a key feature of modern market economies is innovation—and because innovation is inherently creative and, hence, unpredictable—the feature of the modern market that McCloskey believes to be preeminent (innovation) is in tension with the feature of the modern market (capitalization) that Alchian believed justifies the name "capitalism." This difference between two of the most insightful and acclaimed champions of the liberal market order is itself revealing. It reveals the fact that the case for the market order includes—as it has long included—*both* its ability, on one hand, to structure prices that incite individuals to predictably respond to market events as if individuals have far more knowledge than they actually have or could possibly have, and, on the other hand, to incite individuals to innovate—that is, to create with neither any guarantees of success nor even the ability to accurately estimate their chances of success. Alchian was of course aware of the productive role of entrepreneurial creativity. (See, e.g., Alchian and Allen 2018, 275–76.) Yet he apparently believed that the *preeminent* feature of the modern market economy is the "marvel" (Hayek's term [1945]) of its pricing system. McCloskey, although herself skilled as a price theorist (McCloskey 1982) and at using price theory to explain various economic phenomena, is very clear that she believes that the preeminent feature of the modern market economy is innovation, especially of the sort famously celebrated by Joseph Schumpeter (1942) as "creative destruction."

7. My purpose here isn't to review the demerits of Keynesianism, theories of predatory pricing, or any other accounts from the "left" branch of mainstream economics of how private market activity might discourage private investment. For sound assessments of Keynesianism, readers can consult Hayek (1995) and Yeager (1973). Easterbrook (1981) remains the single most devastating exposé of the many weaknesses that infect the theory of predatory pricing.

8. See also McCloskey (2019) and McCloskey and Carden (2020).

9. Julian Simon (1996) argued that nothing is a resource until it is made so by human creativity and effort. At some point, some individual recognized, for example, that petroleum can be refined into a variety of products that are useful to humans. This creative spark turned a substance that was previously of no use to humans—and perhaps even a nuisance—into what we misleadingly call a "natural resource." Integral to Simon's explanation is the diversity, across space and time, of how humans perceive reality's details and how individuals respond to their perceptions. A physical object or a prevailing pattern of economic activity can be perceived for months, years, or even centuries by 100 percent of people as X, but then is perceived tomorrow by one individual as Y—where Y differs in at least one essential way from X. This individual's new perception of that object or pattern as Y is a creative act that, if acted upon, changes both the opportunities open to other individuals and the value of resources.

10. As Michael Munger (2022) puts it, "We vote for, and reward, charlatans who pretend to know the answers, and zealots who actually *believe* their own superficial galimatias. Ultimately, it's a collective action problem: it would be better for *society* if our leaders were humble and honest about how little they actually know. But it's better for the *candidates for leadership* if they pretend to be committed to a whole dog's breakfast of truths that just ain't so."

11. See Simon (1996, 12).

12. On the logic of interventionism, see Ikeda (1996).

REFERENCES

Alchian, Armen A. (1978) 2006. "Private Rights to Property: The Basis of Corporate Governance and Human Rights." In *The Collected Works of Armen A. Alchian: Property Rights and Economic Behavior*, vol. 2, edited by Daniel K. Benjamin, 636–49. Indianapolis: Liberty Fund.

Alchian, Armen A., and William R. Allen. 2018. *Universal Economics*. Edited by Jerry L. Jordan. Indianapolis. Liberty Fund.

Buchanan, James M., and Viktor J. Vanberg. (1991) 2001. "The Market as a Creative Process." In *The Collected Works of James M. Buchanan: Federalism, Liberty, and the Law* 18, 289–310. Indianapolis: Liberty Fund.

Coase, Ronald H. 1960. "The Problem of Social Cost." *Journal of Law and Economics* 3: 1–44.

Easterbrook, Frank H. 1981. "Predatory Strategies and Counterstrategies." *University of Chicago Law Review* 48: 263–337.

Friedman, Milton, and Anna Jacobson Schwartz. 1963. *A Monetary History of the United States, 1867–1960*. Princeton, NJ: Princeton University Press.

Garrison, Roger W. 2007. *Time and Money: The Macroeconomics of Capital Structure*. Oxfordshire, UK: Routledge.

Grant, James. 2014. *The Forgotten Depression*. New York: Simon and Schuster.

Gregg, Samuel. 2022. *The Next American Economy: Nation, State, and Markets in an Uncertain World*. New York: Encounter Books.

Hayek, F. A. (1941) 1997. "Planning, Science, and Freedom." In *Socialism and War*, edited by Bruce Caldwell, 213–20. Chicago: University of Chicago Press.

———. 1945. "The Use of Knowledge in Society." *American Economic Review* 35 (4): 519–30.

———. 1995. *Contra Keynes and Cambridge*. Edited by Bruce Caldwell. Chicago: University of Chicago Press.

———. 2022. *Essays on Liberalism and the Economy*. Edited by Paul Lewis. Chicago: University of Chicago Press.

Higgs, Robert. 2006. *Depression, War, and Cold War*. New York: Oxford University Press.

———. 2018. "Principle-Agent Theory and Representative Government." *Independent Review* 22: 479–80.

Ikeda, Sanford. 1996. *Dynamics of the Mixed Economy: Toward a Theory of Interventionism*. Oxfordshire, UK: Routledge.

Kirzner, Israel M. 1978. *The Perils of Regulation: A Market-Process Approach*. Miami: Law and Economics Center.

McCloskey, Deirdre N. 1982. *The Applied Theory of Price*. New York: Macmillan.

———. 2016. *Bourgeois Equality*. Chicago: University of Chicago Press.

———. 2019. *Why Liberalism Works: How True Liberal Values Produce a Freer, More Equal, Prosperous World for All*. New Haven, CT: Yale University Press.

McCloskey, Deirdre N., and Art Carden. 2020. *Leave Me Alone and I'll Make You Rich: How the Bourgeois Deal Enriched the World*. Chicago: University of Chicago Press.

Munger, Michael. 2022. "What Ain't So Can Hurt You." *AIER*, November 3. https://www.aier.org/article/what-aint-so-can-hurt-you/.

Schumpeter, Joseph A. 1942. *Capitalism, Socialism, and Democracy*. New York: Harper and Bros.

Simmons, Randy T. 2011. *Beyond Politics: The Roots of Government Failure*. Oakland, CA: Independent Institute.

Simon, Julian L. 1996. *The Ultimate Resource 2*. Princeton, NJ: Princeton University Press.

Yeager, Leland B. 1973. "The Keynesian Diversion." *Western Economic Journal* 11: 150–63.

———. 1986. "The Significance of Monetary Disequilibrium." *Cato Journal* 6 (2): 369–99.

Chapter 6
Ideology, Crisis, and the Ratchet Effect
Retrospect and Prospects
Abigail R. Hall

I n 1940, the executive branch of the US government employed just under 700,000 people. By 1950, just a decade later, that number had doubled in size to 1.4 million. By 2010, the executive branch employed more than 2.1 million people, excluding the US Postal Service (United States Office of Personnel Management n.d.). In 1929, just under 3 percent of the United States' gross domestic product was federal spending. By 1960, government spending accounted for just under 17 percent of GDP. In 2020, federal government spending as a percentage of GDP had risen to over 31 percent (Federal Reserve Bank of St. Louis n.d.) In 1936, the Federal Register—the official source containing government agency rules, proposed rules, notices, and so on—contained 2,620 pages. By 1950, the number of pages had expanded to over 9,500. In 2018, the Federal Register contained more than 64,500 pages (United States Federal Register 2019).

But it is not only the United States observing this marked expansion in government growth. In the United Kingdom, for example, government spending as a percentage of GDP ballooned from about 32 percent in the early 1960s to over 45 percent in 2011 (International Monetary Fund 2021). Government spending as a percent of GDP in Sweden rose from under 20 percent in the 1950s to nearly 50 percent in 2011 (International Monetary Fund 2021). Indeed, "government expenditure has accounted for a rising proportion of national income in the twentieth century. This result appears to apply to most countries regardless of their level of economic development" (Lindauer and Velenchik 1992).

What has caused this government growth? How do we explain the near universal expansion in governments post–World War II? Many scholars in economics, political science, and elsewhere have attempted to answer this question. In his 1987 book, *Crisis and Leviathan: Critical Episodes in the Growth of American Government*, Robert Higgs offers a profound and insightful look into the growth of the state. Undoubtedly one of his most well-known works, the framework Higgs builds is novel and thought-provoking. It is simple in some ways, yet profoundly complex in others. This chapter aims to discuss the core contribution of Higgs's *Crisis and Leviathan* and the model of the "ratchet effect" developed therein. I discuss the book and model's initial reception and argue that some of Higgs's most important insights as it pertains to government growth have been either neglected or misunderstood. I highlight the extensions of the work in contemporary discourse and offer avenues for further applications of the model and other research.

The rest of the chapter proceeds as follows: In the next section I offer background on the various theories of the growth of government, situating the contribution of Higgs's work and providing the broader context in which his argument is made. The subsequent section provides a detailed overview of the "ratchet effect," its origins, and components. I then turn my discussion to the model's reception, criticisms of the model, and what is commonly missed by those reading or critiquing Higgs's work in this area. I follow with a discussion of applications of the model and its extensions before concluding.

THEORIES OF GOVERNMENT GROWTH

Although it is generally accepted that the size of government has grown significantly in the time since World War II, this does nothing to explain *why* government has grown or precisely *when* government has grown. These questions regarding government growth are not straightforward, and the academic literature is far from a general consensus. In a survey on the literature, Lybeck (1988) identifies *12* different theories of government growth. These 12 theories, however, can be more generally characterized into two broader categories of government growth—"citizen over state" theories and "state over citizen" theories.[1] These categories, and the theories within them, are worth exploring in more detail and are necessary for understanding Higgs's contribution.

Citizen over State Theories

In economic parlance, "citizen over state" theories can be described as "demand-side" explanations for the growth of government. Put simply, consumers or demanders of government services (for reasons discussed below) demand more services for government. This demand ultimately increases the size of government.

There are various hypotheses as to why individual voters would demand more government activity. Meltzer and Richard (1978, 1981, 1983) argue that a key driver behind increased government growth is the ability of voters to use government as a means of income redistribution. Voters can benefit if others with higher incomes are taxed such that those revenues are redirected toward themselves. "With near universal suffrage," they write, "the median voter has less income than the average earner. The voter with an income below the median can gain if incomes above the average are taxed, and the benefits are distributed to himself and others. Large government thus results from the difference between distribution of votes and distribution of income" (Meltzer and Richard 1978, 116).

Government may also have grown in response to the existence and expansion of externalities and the need for public goods. In standard economic theory, both these instances represent instances of "market failure," whereby the market outcome deviates from the efficient outcome. In the case of an externality, actors partaking in a transaction fail to internalize the full cost or benefit of their actions, meaning that a third party, not directly involved in the transaction, incurs a cost (in the event of a negative externality) or acquires a benefit (in the event of a positive externality). As a result, markets will tend to underproduce goods with an associated positive externality and overproduce those goods with an associated negative externality. In theory, these failures leave room for government to step in to correct the externality (via taxation or subsidies). In a similar way, pure public goods are also potentially underprovided by the market. Possessing both the qualities of nonrivalry, whereby consumption of the good by one party does not prevent use by another party, and nonexcludability, whereby users cannot be excluded from use of a good, standard theory suggest that markets will fail to provide or will underprovide the good or service in question. This again leads to potential room for government action.

It could be that consumer (voter) preferences over time have changed such that they prefer more government involvement in cases of market failure. The greater desire on the part of voters for larger expenditures on externality correction and public good provision pushed government expansion. But this is not the only explanation. Baumol (1967), for example, suggests that the relative price of "public goods" has been increasing over time relative to the cost of private-sector goods. Even though productivity gains in the public sector have been slow, wages have nevertheless increased in these sectors in order to remain competitive with more productive sectors. This "cost disease" is particularly likely to impact services provided by government such as government education, law enforcement, and so on (see Baumol 1993, 2012).

Still another account of government growth in the "citizen over state" explanations comes from Olson (1965, 1982) and pertains to special-interest groups. Special interests, or groups of individuals who come together for a common purpose, can exert influence over political actors to enact policies that provide direct, concentrated benefits to group members, but spreads the cost of such policies over the larger population. Olson (1982, 65) argues that interest groups can ultimately retard economic growth as they "slow down a society's capacity to adopt new technologies and reallocate resources in response to changing conditions" as they work to continuously allocate resources toward themselves at the expense of others. Other discussions related to pressure groups are explored by Stigler (1975), Posner (1974), and Becker (1983, 1985).

State over Citizen Theories

Whereas citizen over state theories of government growth emphasize the "demand" factors facilitating government growth, state over citizen theories stress the importance of supply-side influences and how those within government can push for its continued expansion. Many of these explanations place critical importance on the structure of government.

Within this vein, Buchanan (1967) proposes that government officials can mislead voters as to the true size of government. Assuming that voters "measure" the size of government based on their tax burden, he argues that certain forms of taxation are more obvious to voters than others. Elected officials, according to Buchanan, can use these less obvious forms of taxation to allow for effective expansion of government without alerting voters to the increase in size. By engaging in debt financing, whereby the burden of government spending is shifted to a future period, or the printing press, whereby inflation may not be immediately traceable to the preceding government spending, government is able to expand despite what may be preferred by voters.

Niskanen (1971, 2001) highlights how the bureaucratic structure of governments creates incentives that will tend toward continued government expansion. Within the context of markets, producers of goods and services compete for customers. Prices, profit, and loss signals direct resources to their highest valued use, provide incentives to cost save, and so on. Outside of the market context, however, there is no analogous mechanism to the price system. Instead of competing for customers and profit, bureaus are competing with other bureaus for greater portions of their sponsor's (e.g., Congress) budget. Instead of facing an incentive to reduce costs, bureaus have an incentive to exhaust their budgets with the goal of expanding. Alternatively, bureaus may elect to build "slack" into their budgets—maximize the difference between their revenues and their production costs (see Wyckoff 1990). As a result of their organizational structure and the larger institutions in which they operate, government bureaus also have an incentive to engage in "mission creep," whereby the bureau deviates from its initial goals and objectives, allowing again for the agency to seek a larger budget. All these factors increase the size of government.

Tullock (1959, 574–75) discusses how voting systems—namely, majority voting and the bundling of multiple issues—may effectively increase the size of government. By voting on multiple proposals at once and logrolling (vote trading), Tullock shows how bills are more likely to be passed than if each item is voted on individually and votes are not traded. While the system of bundling and logrolling allows for some efficiency gains, these come at a price. Absent constraints to prevent such behavior (e.g., requiring supermajorities), utility-maximizing logrollers are likely to overspend (with regard to median voter preferences) as the result of simple majority rule.

Arguing for the importance of constitutional constraints, Brennan and Buchanan (1977, 1980) develop a "neo-Hobbesian" model of government growth based on the assumption that government is a revenue-maximizing monopolist. This goal of maximizing revenue, combined with other core insights from public choice economics (e.g., rational ignorance of voters, fiscal illusion, etc.), means that government will continuously expand unless appropriately constrained.

Other Theories

Other analyses do not fit cleanly into either of these categories. Lott and Kenney (1999, 1163), for example, posit that women's suffrage expanded the size of government in the United States, noting immediate increases in government expenditures and "more liberal voting patterns" once women were granted access to the polls. Abrams and Settle (1999) found similar results in analyzing women's suffrage in Switzerland. They found that extending voting rights to women increased the overall size of the Swiss government and welfare spending a full 28 percent. Most recently, Cowen (2021) argues that technological innovation provides at least a partial explanation of the growth of government. He contends that the numerous technological changes between 1880 and 1940 (e.g., telephones, radio, etc.), among other things, made it easier for government to collect taxes, thus making it easier for governments to grow. Analyzing the role of technology and state capacity in Ghana, Dzansi et al. (2022) found that new revenue collection technology was able to deliver 27 percent more bills and collect 103 percent more tax revenues than their peers who were not offered the new technology.

The theory of government growth developed and explored by Higgs in *Crisis and Leviathan* does not fit cleanly into either of the two broader categories outlined in the earlier section. Others have referred to Higgs's explanation as a "*Zeitgeist* explanation" of government growth, owing to the importance of ideology in his framework (see Kirchner 2011, 15).

THE RATCHET EFFECT

The ratchet effect Higgs develops was first explored by British economists Alan T. Peacock and Jack Wiseman in their 1961 book *The Growth of Public Expenditure in the United Kingdom*. After exploring many of the aforementioned theories of government growth (what he categories as the "Modernization," "Welfare State," and "Public Goods" Hypotheses), Higgs offers an alternative explanation for government growth, what he terms the "Crisis Hypothesis." The logic of the hypothesis is as follows. Under certain emergency conditions government is able to expand. This expansion, engendered by some critical event, is grown and sustained through many of the elements discussed in citizen-over-state and state-over-citizen theories of government growth (see Higgs 1987, 17–18). It is within this context he introduces the ratchet effect.

The ratchet effect is described as a five-stage process (Higgs 1987, 60). The stages are illustrated in figure 6.1.

Stage I, or "Pre-Crisis Normality," represents government growth in the absence of crisis. The line segment AB reflects an arbitrary growth rate and provides a useful counterfactual that can be used to compare government

Figure 6.1. The ratchet effect

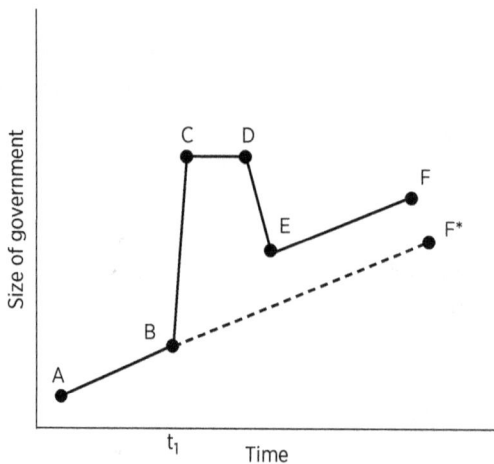

Source: Created by the author based on Higgs (1987, 60).

growth with and without crisis. It is important to note that this pre-crisis period does *not* assume a government growth level of zero. This is to reflect that government growth is not monocausal and may grow as a result of one or more of the factors discussed above (Higgs 1987, 61).

The second state of the model, "Expansion," shows the introduction of a crisis at time t_1 and the subsequent expansion in growth (segment BC). Whether real or perceived, it is at this point where government increases in size (both scale and scope) in response to the emergency. "Modern democratic governments expand . . . during crisis," Higgs writes, "because citizens insist they 'do something'" (1987, 67). These expansions are not costless, however. He continues, "The alternative means of implementing the chosen policies, which is full reliance on pecuniary fiscal and market mechanisms, would reveal the costs of the government's policies so clearly as to threaten the viability of both the policies and the ruling" (1987, 67). Given this, Higgs argues, it is necessary for governments to engage in cost concealment. He suggests several avenues through which this concealment might occur, including moving activities from the market to a command economy, hiding nonpecuniary costs, and increasing indirect forms of taxation (1987, 65–67).

Stage III (segment CD) of the model, "Maturation," depicts the slowing (or complete ceasing) of government growth engendered by the crisis introduced in stage II. It is at this point where growth has reached its peak. In figure 6.1, this stage shows a growth rate of zero, but this is not a necessary assumption and was done for simplicity. Higgs notes elsewhere (2017, 22) that "calling this phase maturity does not imply, however, that government's actions have settled into a fixed pattern or mode of operation." He continues, "In this phase, the opportunists who have succeeded in gaining implementation of their favoured plans and programmes occupy themselves in defending their schemes against critics . . . consolidating their newly gained powers, enlarging their budgets and generally striving to entrench their operations within the government and the overall society" (2017, 23).

The next stage of the model, stage IV (segment DE), is "Retrenchment." At some point after the crisis, the urgency to "do something" abates. Some government policies are reversed, revised, or otherwise eliminated. As a result, the growth rate of government declines.

This leads to the last stage, stage V, or "Post-Crisis Normality." This stage, shown by segment EF, illustrates the government growth path following the crisis. Critically, this path lies above the counterfactual growth path where no crisis occurred, indicated by segment BF*. In figure 6.1, these two lines are shown as parallel, but this not necessary.

But why is the retrenchment in stage IV incomplete? Higgs (1987, 67–72) offers a partial explanation drawing largely from public choice insights. "Many scholars," he writes, "view the incompleteness of the postcrisis retrenchment as a product of the politics of governmental bureaucracies, their private clients, and connected politicians" (1987, 67). But this is not the only reason for this incomplete retrenchment, and Higgs argues that "[this public choice justification] cannot account fully for the incompleteness of the postcrisis retrenchment" (1987, 68). So, what explanation does Higgs offer? He suggests that ideology plays a critical role. It is to ideology that we now turn our focus, as Higgs's discussion of ideology was, and continues to be, one of the most neglected and misunderstood components of his framework.

CRITICAL MISUNDERSTANDINGS

On Ideology

When introduced in 1987, Higgs's conceptualization of episodic government growth via crisis was not universally well received or accepted. One review in the *Cato Journal*, for instance, criticized Higgs for "arbitrarily" restricting his data to 1900 onward. The same review contends that Higgs's framework does not explain the lack of similar expansion prior to this period, nor the "steady shrinkage in the relative size of the federal government [that] appears to have been the pattern for around 40 years prior to the Civil War" (Anderson 1988, 556).

What this reviewer and others have generally failed to understand is that Higgs *does* effectively address this seemingly odd trend in the data. It is not as though crisis did not exist prior to 1900. Why is it only at the beginning of the twentieth century that we see this marked expansion in government? The answer is a critical ideological shift on the part of American (and other Western) societies. In discussing the reception to *Crisis and Leviathan*, Higgs states that few people accepted or truly understood the role of ideology in his framework.[2] Indeed, a major clue to the importance of ideology for Higgs can be found in the name of the chapter in which the ratchet effect is first introduced. The primary title of the chapter is "Crisis, Bigger Government, and *Ideological Change*" (Higgs 1987, 57, emphasis added). But Higgs's treatment of ideology, and the role it plays in government growth, is much more expansive, careful, and critical to the framework than many realize. In the third chapter of *Crisis and Leviathan*, the one immediately preceding the introduction of the framework, Higgs lays out, over the course of more than 20 pages, his conceptualization of ideology and the role it plays in the ratchet effect model.

While most scholars in social sciences would roundly agree that people's beliefs matter (some would even say they are *fundamental*) in understanding human behavior, matters of ideology are often completely ignored. This is likely due to several factors, the first being a lack of a consistent definition of the term. "Settling on a definition of ideology is no mean task," write Hinich and Munger (1994, 9). "Dozens of different definitions exist, each with some claim to primacy" (1994, 9). Higgs defines ideology as "a somewhat coherent, rather comprehensive belief system about social relations" (Higgs 1987, 37). The "somewhat comprehensive" may give us pause, as this phrasing presents as rather nebulous. But Higgs provides further clarification.

> To say that it is somewhat coherent implies that its components hang together, though not necessarily in a way that would satisfy a logician. To say that it is rather comprehensive implies that it subsumes a wide variety of social categories and their interrelations. Not-withstanding its extensive scope it tends to revolve about only a few central values—for instance, individual freedom, social equality, or national glory. (1987, 37)

In the literature on ideology, scholars tend to emphasize a few aspects. Higgs identifies four important ideological features—cognitive, affective, programmatic, and solidary. Ideology, for Higgs, structures a person's belief system. "It [ideology] structures a person's perceptions and predetermines his understanding of the social world" (Higgs 1987, 37). Ideology performs multiple important functions. A person's ideology will "tell" them whether something is "good," "bad," or amoral. "Ideologies perform an important psychological service," he writes, "because without them people cannot know, assess, and respond to much of the vast world of social relations. Ideology simplifies a reality too huge and complicated to be comprehended, evaluated, and dealt with in any purely factual, scientific, or other disinterested way" (Higgs 1987, 37–38).

Elsewhere, Higgs (2008) offers additional exposition on ideological formation and widespread ideological change. The literature on ideological commitments typically falls into one of two categories: (1) interest theories, and (2) strain theories. Interest theories posit that individuals desire personal wealth and power. Various ideologies, according to these theories, allow individuals to legitimize their pursuits of these goals. Strain theories, meanwhile, suggest that ideology provides a mechanism to connect individuals facing economic or other challenges with similar individuals, thus bringing people together (see Higgs 2008, 549–50).

Higgs discusses two broad categories pertaining to ideological change—
(1) the pace of change, and (2) the cause of change. "My causal categories pertain
to the way in which an ideological change spreads from its original source to
penetrate the mass public or a substantial segment of it" (Higgs 2008, 551–52).
The pace category is straightforward. The pace of ideological change may be
temporally *steady* or *irregular*. Put simply, ideological change could hypotheti-
cally occur at some (often assumed incredibly slow) steady pace over time or
irregularly, abruptly, and without consistency.

The causal categorization of ideological change is more complex and worthy of further discussion. In discussing the theories of ideological change,
Higgs considers that change may be theory driven or event driven. Theory
driven conceptualizations of ideological change, Higgs notes, can be seen in
the works of unlikely bedfellows—F. A. Hayek (1949) and John Maynard Keynes
(1936). The idea is straightforward. A relatively small number of "great thinkers"
theorize some new idea or set of ideas. These are then passed to another group,
the individuals Hayek (1949, 372) called "secondhand dealers in ideas." These
"secondhand dealers" then further disperse the original ideas to the broader
population, where they are accepted, or at the very least encountered. In this
way, ideological change comes from the top down, from profound thinkers to
the general public. Alternatively, ideological change may instead result from
the circumstances of time and place. Social structures, proponents argue,
are paramount in shaping people's ideas and beliefs (see Marx [1859] 1979).
Ideology is contingent (or largely depends on) the given social structure and
an individual's position within it.

Higgs rejects the idea that either of these categories alone can explain ideological change. Both great thinkers and social structures influence ideology. But
there is another critical component that shapes and changes ideology—events.
Events, particularly crises, provide the opportunity for ideological shifts to
occur. His argument is worth quoting at length.

> To appreciate how events come into play, we need to recognize that in
> any modern society . . . more than one ideology exists, and hence *ideologi-
> cal competition* occurs all the time. Proponents of rival ideologies take
> various actions to express their beliefs . . . often in the hope of winning
> converts or, at a minimum, raising doubts among opponents and the
> undecided. . . . In this quest, ideologues may labor diligently for years,
> hoping to win converts little by little or to prepare them—to "soften them
> up," as it were—in anticipation of opportunities to bring them over that
> may emerge in a future crisis. . . . Thus, the "softening up" aspect of
> ideological endeavor may have great importance, even though it seems

completely futile during the "normal" stretches of social life, when social, economic, political, and ideological relations change slowly, because when crisis does arrive, its advent creates extraordinary potential for ideological shakeup. . . . [Crises] create new fears, and all tend to discredit established beliefs and to open new possibilities for the successful propagation of novel understandings, evaluations, and political programs. (Higgs 2008, 557–58, emphasis in original)

It is at this juncture we understand how, according to Higgs, we see episodic growth of government. Critically, we understand *why* it is that we fail to see similar growth prior to the early 20th century. Higgs points to a mass shift in ideology during this period that, when coupled with crises like the Great Depression and the World Wars, effectively allowed for government expansion. Higgs (1987, 104) writes that in the 1890s (years that fall squarely outside the period he analyzes) the dominant ideology "held that less government is better than more" and "in the late nineteenth century most activities . . . were considered 'not the proper business of government.'" Ideological conditions in the following decades, he contends, had diverged. "In another crisis, they [progressives] would vanquish the surviving proponents of the classical liberal ideology" (1987, 105). Absent the widespread adoption of progressivism, we fail to observe the same widespread growth of government. Put differently, "correct" ideological preconditions are a *necessary condition* of the ratchet effect model. Other mechanisms of ideological change—social structures and thought leaders—play a critical part in these changes, but it is crisis that lets the horse out of the barn.

When nothing extraordinary seems to be happening in politics, many individuals and groups are working hard to lay the groundwork for future gains, appreciating that ultimate success is unlikely except in a crisis, when a general weakening of offsetting political blockages will occur as the quickening current of "do something" sentiment alters the calculations of the president, the bureaucrats, the legislators and even the judges. (Higgs 2017, 20)

The interactions between these arenas are important for understanding Higgs's ratchet effect and conceptualization of government growth. Figure 6.2 illustrates this dynamic.

Beginning in the upper-left box, "Social Structure" represents those ideas put forward by Marx. The social, ethnic, and other institutions in which an individual finds himself influences his ideology. Moving to the upper-right box, "Ideology,"

Figure 6.2. Ideological relationships between social structures, events, and thought leaders

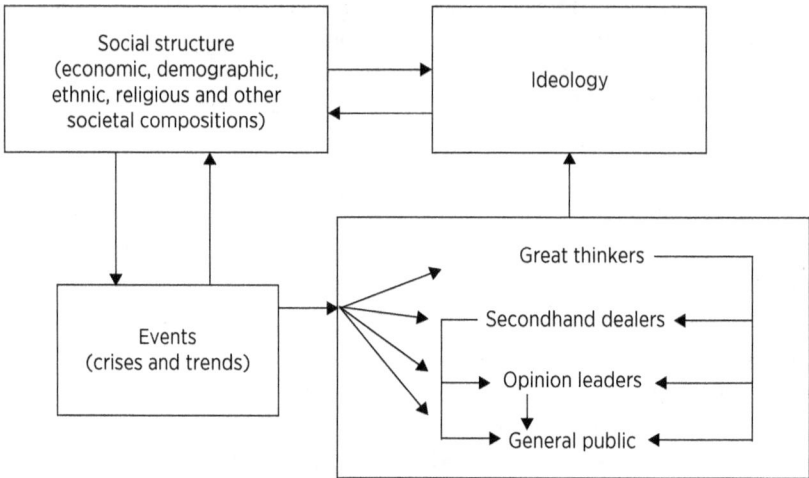

Source: Created by the author based on Higgs (2008, 561).

we see that, according to Higgs, these structures indeed influence ideology. Importantly, however, this arrow runs in both directions. Just as social structures influence ideology, so too does ideology influence social structures. The "Events" box, representing both trends as well as crises, similarly influences social structures. These events and trends likewise inform and influence Hayek's "great thinkers," who with their "secondhand dealers" also exert influence on ideology.

Though the interactions of all these boxes are particularly important, the "Events" box should be taken as critical. Higgs likens the adoption of new policies and government expansion to a logging company sending cut timber (possible policies) down a river. During normal, non-crisis times, political competition often results in a sort of logjam, whereby those who would push for their policies to be enacted must contend with stiff competition from others. This fierce competition limits their success. The "logs" or policies they'd like to see enacted (moved downriver) are caught in the quagmire of political competition with every other actor seeking to push forward their preferred policies. Crisis, however, effectively raises the water level. Once unpopular or unfathomable ideas, perhaps presented for years by "great thinkers" and "secondhand dealers," become possible and popular—or at least tolerable. The river floods its banks, allowing for the forward movement of a whole host of new policies.

The relationship between these components and the critical importance of ideology are one commonly misunderstood part of Higgs's work and model. The framework does *not* offer a singular, monocausal explanation for the growth of government in the earlier 20th century and beyond, but provides a framework for understanding how these components work together. Moreover, Higgs's argument does not suggest that the aforementioned theories of government growth (e.g., citizen-over-state and state-over-citizen theories) are invalid, but rather that they are insufficient individually.

On Scale and Scope

The ideological context of the ratchet effect is one item critics of Higgs's ratchet effect model fail to fully appreciate, but it is not the only one. Some readers of Higgs's work interpret his model too narrowly, interpreting the ratchet effect as working solely on a fiscal level.[3]

But Higgs is careful to point out that his model does not exclusively apply to the *scale* or fiscal dimension of the state, but also to the *scope* of government, or the types of activities undertaken by government. Higgs (1987, 27–33) and Coyne and Hall (2018a, 11–17) highlight how economists often neglect issues of scope. Scale and scope are frequently assumed to be correlated, whereby an increase in scale would imply an increase in scope. Scope is also difficult, perhaps impossible, to measure, while scale is much more conducive to quantitative analysis (e.g., government spending as a percentage of GDP, number of federal workers, etc.). Moreover, in many models of the state, government is assumed to be engaged in activities that benefit the "public interest." Eschewing their own private interests, officials are assumed to be engaged in actions that maximize some knowable, stable social welfare function. In such a model, discussions regarding scope (and scale, for that matter) are irrelevant, as government growth on any dimension is, *by assumption*, fulfilling some notion of the public good.

But neglecting scope fails to appreciate critical dimensions in which government can grow. Changes along these dimensions may, in the long run, be more important than changes in scale. Higgs's careful attention to and focus on changes in scope as a critical piece of his model is unique, particularly for an economist. Higgs's emphasis on changes in scope has been carried forward by some of those drawing upon his work.

INFLUENCE AND EXTENSIONS

Higgs's ratchet effect model has been discussed by *many* contemporary researchers since its inception. He's been cited in studies of fiscal sociology (see Campbell 1993), the collapse of the Soviet Union and Afghanistan (see

Reuveny and Prakash 1999), and studies related to universal healthcare coverage (see McKee et al. 2013). Higgs's ratchet effect has been cited most frequently and applied most clearly, however, to issues related to defense and national security and broader discussions of interventionism (see Desch 2008, Ikeda 1996, Kaempfer and Lowenberg 1999, Krebs 2015, and Rasler and Thompson 1989 for examples).

Coyne and Hall make extensive use of Higgs's original framework and look to extend it. Throughout their work, they draw on Higgs's framework and work to discuss the role of crisis in the growth of government. Like Higgs, they are particularly interested in not only changes in scale, but also changes in scope. Discussing the "crisis" of the war on drugs, for instance, Coyne and Hall (2013) examine how constraints on government agencies relaxed and allowed for the progressive militarization of US domestic police. In later work (2014, 2018a) they develop the "boomerang effect" of foreign intervention. Less constrained than they would be within their own borders, countries engaged in foreign intervention are able to use these foreign conflicts as a testing ground to develop new methods of social control and hone existing methods. Through various channels, these innovations are brought back to the intervening country. Examining the overarching "crisis" of terrorism following the attacks on the World Trade Center and Pentagon in September 2001, they illustrate a variety of ways (surveillance, policing, torture, etc.) in which constraints on government have been largely eroded. Their work looks to directly engage and extend Higgs's discussions on how crises influence critical changes in the *scope* of government and the short- and long-run implications of those changes.

In addition to Higgs's influence on Coyne and Hall, his influence in discussions of war and national defense appear elsewhere. Beetsma, Cukierman, and Giuliodori (2016) examine the effect of wars on the growth of government. Analyzing data on income transfer and taxes following World War II, they find evidence for the ratchet effect, stating, "The evolution of redistribution in the United States would have been substantially slower and possibly permanently lower if WWII had not occurred" (2016, 38). Their findings point to the importance of examining the implications of the ratchet effect from a long-term perspective and that, while events are critical in explaining government growth, the ratchet effect is multifaceted. "The full impact of new programs and the expansion of existing programs materializes only in the longer run, because the eligible groups expand and precedent is taken for further expansions" (2016, 2).

Acknowledging the difficulty in measuring changes in scope, O'Reilly and Powell (2015) attempt to quantify changes in the scope of government during crisis. Drawing directly on Higgs's ratchet effect model, they analyze how wars affect the scale and scope of government, using regulation as a means of measuring scope. They find that, in examining 124 countries over a period of 45 years, "wars permanently expand the scope of government" (2015, 31). Interestingly, they find that wars increase the scale of government only in "highly autocratic regimes."

Most recently, Goodman, Coyne, and Devereaux (2021) apply Higgs's arguments related to crises to the area of public health. Highlighting the critical role of ideology and ideological shifts, they discuss not only the immediate changes to the scale and scope of government activities (e.g., direct government transfers, surveillance for contact tracing purposes, etc.) but also possible long-term effects of the COVID-19 crisis. Taking examples from history, they note how policies implemented in Cape Town, South Africa, during an outbreak of plague laid the groundwork for modern zoning and the myriad of issues that accompany it. They likewise highlight how with compulsory vaccination in the midst of a smallpox outbreak, officials encroached on the rights of individuals in the name of crisis. This extension and application of the framework is a clear illustration of its contemporary relevance and provides an example of one possible avenue for continued research.

CONCLUSION

Though *Crisis and Leviathan* was published over 35 years ago, the ratchet effect Higgs introduces in the book remains relevant. Those analyses that have been completed could be expanded in several ways, and many applications have yet to be explored. I offer seven suggestions for expansion and further research.

The first avenue for future work is relatively straightforward. The scholars who have engaged Higgs's ratchet effect have focused almost exclusively on the United States. This need not remain the case, however. The framework is broadly applicable to other contexts. Analyses and applications of the ratchet effect to other countries in varying time periods would help to show its relevance and explanatory power, and may help to answer critical questions about the size of the ratchet and subsequent retrenchment.

Second, those interested in expanding this area of research may consider applications of the ratchet effect to crises outside of war and economic downturns. Though the framework was never limited, the majority of the applications fall within that category. The aforementioned paper by Goodman, Coyne, and Devereaux (2021) is a relevant example of applying the ratchet effect framework to other crises. In addition to further explorations of the

COVID-19 pandemic and other public health emergencies, other disasters could be fertile ground for exploration. Horwitz (2009), for example, references Higgs, the ratchet effect, and government growth within the context of Hurricane Katrina in 2005, but that is not his primary focus. Understanding the ratchet effect as it pertains to natural disasters like hurricanes, tsunamis, pandemics, and so on would all be relevant applications. In addition to natural disasters, manmade disasters could also be of interest. How might we apply the ratchet effect to disasters linked to human behavior? Does the ratchet effect work similarly or dissimilarly within the context of a nuclear disaster, like that which occurred at Three Mile Island in 1979? Or in Fukushima, Japan, in 2011?

Third, and building from this point, it remains to be seen whether or not particular types of crises engender a greater "ratchet" than others. Are there meaningful differences between disaster "types," and, if so, how could we conceptualize and understand these differences? In their work, Coyne and Hall (2018a) discuss the long and variable changes that may result from crises and the ensuing preparations for and engagement in intervention, but they do not offer an explanation as to why certain changes occur and others do not, or an explanation of the relative speed of the changes that do take place. Further, all their examples relate to the war on terror. In other work, the same authors explore the Cold War crisis and some of its domestic effects, but are far from exhaustive (Coyne and Hall 2022, 2018b). Understanding different types of crises may prove illuminating. Do wars and foreign conflict provide opportunity for the greatest expansions of government (assuming the necessary ideological conditions), or do other crises manifest larger expansions? Are some types of crises more likely to provoke an expansion in government, ignoring the relative size of that expansion? These questions have yet to be explored.

The fourth avenue for future exploration relates to the level at which the ratchet effect is analyzed. In Higgs's original conceptualization, and in the analyses that have followed, emphasis has been exclusively on analysis of the growth of *national* government. The framework, however, is a general one and need not be constrained to the level of the nation-state. How could the ratchet effect be applied to lower levels of government? Though state and local governments would face some alternative constraints relative to their federal counterparts, the logic of the ratchet effect still applies. How does the ratchet manifest at these lower levels of government? Empirically, is retrenchment in these lower levels similar to those at the federal level when experiencing a common crisis? Are there meaningful differences or other relevant constraints necessary to understand at these varying levels? Are particularly changes in scale or scope manifestly different?

Fifth, more work could be done on the duration and timing of the various stages of the ratchet effect. What, for instance, pushes us from "expansion" to "maturation" and "maturation" to "retrenchment? Are there particular circumstances that lead to larger expansions, for example? What dictates the length and duration of the "maturation" phase? What, if anything, is there to say about the relative size of retrenchment? Questions of magnitude are important. Higgs is careful to point out that his effect applies to issues of both scale *and* scope, but scale is by far the more difficult dimension to research. O'Reilly and Powell (2015) and Coyne and Hall (2018a) attempt in different ways to discuss changes in scope, but other tactics could also be employed. Knowing the differences in expansion of scale versus scope could be important in discussing the potency of the ratchet effect.

My sixth suggestion relates to the idea of multiple, or what could be called "compounded" crises. Higgs and those who have expanded upon his framework highlight how interventions and government expansions undertaken following a crisis often lead to additional crises. These additional crises prompt additional responses. Consider, for example, the war on terror paving the way for conditions that led to the rise of the Islamic State in Iraq and Syria (ISIS). How do we account for this within the analysis? How many crises could be considered "exogenous" versus how many crises can be traced to government responses to prior crises?

Seventh, and finally, there is a desperate need for more research on the economics of ideology. Of the questions just mentioned, questions related to ideology are likely the most difficult. Writing on Higgs and other ideological discussions surrounding government growth, economist Stephen Kirchner (2011, 15) notes how discussions of ideology may add to the challenge of discussing government growth.

> Ideas and ideology may be important in driving long-run growth in the size of government. . . . However, this only pushes the question one step back: what drives these changes in opinion and ideas? There is an obvious endogeneity problem. . . . Do ideas drive growth in big government or do collectivist ideas emerge as a rationalisation of growth in the state? Bilateral causality is also possible. . . . Ideology is an important factor in Higgs's crisis-driven model of government growth, but he is compelled to treat ideology as exogenously determined.

These questions are important. It may be that, while economists have been the group to analyze the ratchet effect most extensively, most economists may be ill-equipped to answer these questions. The types of discussions regarding causality, endogeneity, and so on regarding ideology may be out of reach to standard statistical modeling. Given that the term itself is not concretely defined, and we cannot answer very basic questions regarding ideological formation or change, we couldn't expect to quantify it, much less employ econometric models. Researchers in this area should and must be open to adopting a methodological pluralism if they hope to tackle these questions.

It is only through a clear understanding of ideology that we can engage in meaningful discussions about how to limit the ratchet effect, prevent it, or perhaps even reverse it. Discussing government growth and the military, Friedberg (1992) asks why the United States did not become a garrison state after World War II. This is an interesting question and a puzzle for those who utilize and study the ratchet effect to think about. Coyne and Hall (2018a) have discussed how the "crises" of drugs and terrorism in the United States are perpetual. Unlike the World Wars, Vietnam, or other traditional conflicts, there is no clear end point to these crises. They argue that this, in part, helps to explain the militarization of police during these periods but not before. But this discussion of perpetual crises leads us to further questions. At what point does the crisis abate? At what point does the initial fervor that engendered the governmental expansion fade away? What if it never does? Does the original model simply continue perpetually in the "expansion" phase?

Possible solutions to curtail the ratchet effect would be of particular interest. Here scholars in constitutional political economy (CPE) could possibly have much to offer. Are there particular constraints that could be put in place to limit expansions of government in times of crisis? If so, what are those constraints, and how could they be implemented given that policymakers would be clearly disinclined to "tie their own hands"?

Although Higgs has given vast attention to the importance of ideology, and although ideological receptivity is a necessary condition of the ratchet effect, our understanding of ideological development and change remains lacking. Though there is literature on economics *and* ideology or economics *as* an ideology (see Backhouse 2008, Matthews and Mathews 1985, and Söderbaum 2008 for examples), there remains to be seen an economic theory *of* ideology. How can the tools of economics be used to explain ideology and ideological change? As Higgs (2008) notes, scholars from Keynes to Hayek, to Marx to Friedman, have discussed ideology as critical. But Higgs's conceptualization of ideological change, examining the interplay between social structures, events, and great thinkers, has not been given its due. Given the critical importance that ideology plays generally, and in the context of the ratchet effect specifically, could a new or revised theory of ideology help us to understand the ratchet effect? If ideology is critical for episodic growth, then perhaps it is ideology that is the key to its undoing.

NOTES

1. For a more comprehensive overview of these categories, see Garrett and Rhine (2006).
2. Discussed in written correspondence with the author.
3. Discussed in written correspondence with the author.

REFERENCES

Abrams, Burton A., and Russell F. Settle. 1999. "Women's Suffrage and the Growth of the Welfare State." *Public Choice* 100: 289–300.

Anderson, Gary M. 1988. "Review of *Crisis and Leviathan: Critical Episodes in the Growth of American Government*, by Robert Higgs." *Cato Journal* 8 (2): 555–57.

Backhouse, Roger E. 2008. *The Puzzle of Modern Economics: Science or Ideology?* Cambridge: Cambridge University Press.

Baumol, William J. 1967. "Macroeconomics of Unbalanced Growth: The Anatomy of Urban Crisis." *American Economic Review* 57 (3): 415–26.

———. 1993. "Health Care, Education and the Cost Disease: A Looming Crisis for Public Choice." *Public Choice* 77 (1): 17–28.

———. 2012. *The Cost Disease: Why Computers Get Cheaper and Healthcare Doesn't.* New Haven, CT: Yale University Press.

Becker, Gary S. 1983. "A Theory of Competition among Pressure Groups for Political Influence." *Quarterly Journal of Economics* 98 (3): 371–400.

———. 1985. "Public Policies, Pressure Groups, and Dead Weight Loss." *Journal of Public Economics* 28 (3): 329–47.

Beetsma, Roel, Alex Cukierman, and Massimo Giuliodori. 2016. "Political Economy of Redistribution in the United States in the Aftermath of World War II—Evidence and Theory." *American Economic Journal: Economic Policy* 8 (4): 1–40.

Brennan, Geoffrey, and James M. Buchanan. 1977. "Towards a Tax Constitution for Leviathan." *Journal of Public Economics* 8 (3): 255–73.

———. 1980. *The Power to Tax: Analytical Foundations of a Fiscal Constitution.* Cambridge: Cambridge University Press.

Buchanan, James M. 1967. *Public Finance in Democratic Processes.* Chapel Hill: University of North Carolina Press.

Campbell, John L. 1993. "The State and Fiscal Sociology." *Annual Review of Sociology* 19: 163–85.

Cowen, Tyler. 2021. "Does Technology Drive the Growth of Government?" In *Essays on Government Growth: Political Institutions, Evolving Markets, and Technology.* Edited by Joshua Hall and Bryan Khoo. Cham, Switzerland: Springer.

Coyne, Christopher J., and Abigail R. Hall. 2013. "The Militarization of U.S. Domestic Policing." *Independent Review* 17 (4): 485–504.

———. 2014. "Perfecting Tyranny: Foreign Intervention as Experimentation in State Control." *Independent Review* 19 (2): 165–89.

———. 2018a. *Tyranny Comes Home: The Domestic Fate of U.S. Militarism*. Stanford, CA: Stanford University Press.

———. 2018b. "War and Human Rights Abuses in the United States." *Peace Review: A Journal of Social Justice* 30 (2): 184–91.

———. 2022. "Dr. Mengele, USA Style: Lessons from Human Rights Abuses in Post–World War II America." *Cosmos + Taxis* 10 (11–12): 1–14.

Desch, Michael C. 2008. "America's Liberal Illiberalism: The Ideological Origins of Overreaction in U.S. Foreign Policy 2008." *International Security* 32 (3): 7–43.

Dzansi, James, Anders Jensen, David Lagakos, and Henry Telli. 2022. "Technology and Local State Capacity: Evidence from Ghana." *National Bureau of Economic Research*. Working paper 29923. https://www.nber.org/papers/w29923.

Federal Reserve Bank of St. Louis. n.d. "Federal Net Outlays as Percent of Gross Domestic Product." https://fred.stlouisfed.org/series/FYONGDA188S.

Friedberg, Aaron L. 1992. "Why Didn't the United States Become a Garrison State?" *International Security* 16 (4): 109–42.

Garrett, Thomas A., and Russell M. Rhine. 2006. "On the Size and Growth of Government." *Federal Reserve Bank of St. Louis Review* 88 (1): 13–30.

Goodman, Nathan P., Christopher J. Coyne, and Abigail Devereaux. 2021. "Infectious Diseases and Government Growth." *Independent Review* 25 (4): 1086–653.

Hayek, Fredrich A. 1949. "The Intellectuals and Socialism." *University of Chicago Law Review* 16 (3): 417–33.

Higgs, Robert. 1987. *Crisis and Leviathan: Critical Episodes in the Growth of the American Government*. New York: Oxford University Press.

———. 2008. "The Complex Course of Ideological Change." *American Journal of Economics and Sociology* 67 (4): 547–66.

———. 2017. "Crisis without Leviathan?" In *Economic and Political Change after Crisis*. Edited by Stephen H. Balch and Benjamin Powell. New York: Routledge.

Hinich, Melvin J., and Michael C. Munger. 1994. *Ideology and the Theory of Political Discourse*. Ann Arbor: University of Michigan Press.

Horwitz, Steven. 2009. "Wal-Mart to the Rescue: Private Enterprise's Response to Hurricane Katrina." *Independent Review* 13 (4): 1086–653.

Ikeda, Sanford. 1996. *Dynamics of the Mixed Economy: Toward a Theory of Interventionism*. London: Routledge.

International Monetary Fund. 2021. "Government Expenditure, Percent of GDP." https://www.imf .org/external/datamapper/exp@FPP/GBR?zoom=GBR&highlight=GBR.

Kaempfer, William H., and Anton D. Lowenberg. 1999. "Unilateral versus Multilateral International Sanctions: A Public Choice Perspective." *International Studies Quarterly* 43: 37–58.

Keynes, John Maynard. 1936. *The General Theory of Employment, Interest and Money*. New York: Harcourt, Brace and World.

Kirchner, Stephen. 2011. "Why Does Government Grow?" Center for Independent Studies, mono-graph 117. http://www.institutional-economics.com/images/uploads/pm117_-_Why_Does _Government_Grow.pdf.

Krebs, Ronald R. 2015. *Narrative and the Making of US National Security*. Cambridge: Cambridge University Press.

Lindauer, David L., and Ann D. Velenchik. 1992. "Government Spending in Developing Countries: Trends, Causes, and Consequences." *World Bank Research Observer* 7 (1): 59–78.

Lott, John R., and Lawrence W. Kenney. 1999. "Did Women's Suffrage Change the Size and Scope of Government?" *Journal of Political Economy* 107 (6): 1163–98.

Lybeck, Johan A. 1988. "Comparing Government Growth Rates: The Non-Institutional vs. the Institutional Approach." In *Explaining the Growth of Government*. Edited by Johan A. Lybeck and M. Henrekson. New York: Elsevier.

Marx, Karl. (1859) 1979. *Contribution to the Critique of Political Economy*. New York: International Publishers.

Matthews, Alan, and Alan Mathews. 1985. "Economics and Ideology." *The Crane Bag* 9 (2): 52–59.

McKee, Martin, Dina Balabanova, Sanjay Basu, Walter Ricciardi, and David Stuckler. 2013. "Universal Health Coverage: A Quest for All Countries but Under Threat in Some." *Value in Health* 16: 539–45.

Meltzer, Allan H., and Scott F. Richard. 1978. "Why Government Grows (and Grows) in a Democracy." *Public Interest* 52: 111–18.

———. 1981. "A Rational Theory of the Size of Government." *Journal of Political Economy* 89 (5): 914–27.

———. 1983. "Tests of a Rational Theory of the Size of Government." *Public Choice* 41 (3): 403–18.

Niskanen, William A. 1971. *Bureaucracy and Representative Government*. Chicago: Aldine-Atherton.

———. 2001. "Bureaucracy." In *The Elgar Companion to Public Choice*. Edited by William F. Shugart and Laura Razzolini. Northampton, UK: Edward Elgar.

Olson, Mancur. 1965. *The Logic of Collective Action: Public Goods and the Theory of Groups*. Cambridge, MA: Harvard University Press.

———. 1982. *The Rise and Decline of Nations: Economic Growth, Stagflation, and Social Rigidities*. New Haven, CT: Yale University Press.

O'Reilly, Colin O., and Benjamin Powell. 2015. "War and the Growth of Government." *European Journal of Political Economy* 40: 31–41.

Peacock, Alan T., and Jack Wiseman. 1961. *The Growth and Public Expenditure in the United Kingdom*. Princeton, NJ: Princeton University Press.

Posner, Richard A. 1974. "Theories of Economic Regulation." *Bell Journal of Economics and Management Science* 5: 335–58.

Rasler, Karen A., and William R. Thompson. 1989. *War and State Making: The Shaping of the Global Powers*. London: Routledge.

Reuveny, Rafael, and Aseem Prakash. 1999. "The Afghanistan War and the Breakdown of the Soviet Union." *Review of International Studies* 25: 693–708.

Söderbaum, Peter. 2008. "Economics as Ideology." In *Pluralist Economics*. Edited by Edward Fullbrook. New York: Zed Books.

Stigler, George J. 1975. *The Citizen and the State*. Chicago: University of Chicago Press.

Tullock, Gordon. 1959. "Problems of Majority Voting." *Journal of Political Economy* 67 (6): 571–79. Northampton, UK: Edward Elgar.

United States Federal Register. 2019. "Federal Register Pages Published: 1936–2018." https://www.federalregister.gov/uploads/2019/04/stats2018Fedreg.pdf.

United States Office of Personnel Management. n.d. "Historical Federal Workforce Tables." https://www.opm.gov/policy-data-oversight/data-analysis-documentation/federal-employment-reports/historical-tables/executive-branch-civilian-employment-since-1940/.

Wyckoff, Paul Gary. 1990. "The Simple Analytics of Slack-Maximizing Bureaucracy." *Public Choice* 67: 35–47.

Chapter 7

The History, Ideology, and Shape of Leviathan

Researching the American State's Ratchet Effect, Growth, and Transformation

Anthony Gregory

I n delivering both narrative and analysis, few critics of American Big Government have the scholarly stature of Robert Higgs. Some of his best work, most famously *Crisis and Leviathan: Critical Episodes in the Growth of American Government* (Higgs 1987), has performed at the heavy intersection of history and theory, neither of which can replace the other (Mises 1957). Among those of similar political outlook, Higgs stands out for his fluency across fields and his research ambitions, a rare writer capably juggling three or more sets of intellectual commitments with both expertise and humility. Higgs's research summons scholars of all persuasions to bring interdisciplinary rigor to the history of the state. Indeed, its importance is sometimes obscured by temptations to employ his most renowned contribution toward reaffirming clean narratives of liberty and government.

As an empiricist and theoretician Higgs has indeed equipped fellow travelers, whom we might call either libertarians or radical liberals, with scholarly reinforcement for their ideological priors.[1] An alluring caricature repeats itself in popular discourse: Higgs's *Crisis and Leviathan* demonstrates that government expands during crises and afterwards retreats only partway. This "ratchet effect" has become a cautionary parable with dour implications: partisans of freedom must mobilize against state expansion, and yet it will likely prove futile as some liberty lost will never return. This normatively inflected pessimism accommodates a common libertarian folk myth: Americans were once much freer, but then the exogenous central state arose to rob their ancient liberties. This would be a fatalistic takeaway indeed, as every crisis leads asymptotically toward total subjugation. Thankfully Higgs's actual insights are more interesting and less depressing. In fact, they point to research questions that might divide committed ideologues. The main thesis of *Crisis* is not that the ratchet effect is a fixture of social nature but rather that something accounts for the US government's ratcheting growth in some times and not others, and the main factor is ideology. In pursuing its relationship to state power, Higgs theorizes ideology and identifies it as a historical actor, and these are the intellectual projects that make *Crisis* worth reading and rereading.

Complicating matters, as its subtitle expressly cautions, *Crisis* is an episodic treatment not a comprehensive one. As both a theoretical and historical treatment it cannot, in under 400 pages, do justice to his larger body of work in both domains. *Crisis* does not attempt an exhaustive master narrative of power and liberty, even within the topics it treats with some care, and yet the danger exists of reading it that way. Consulting *Crisis* alongside his other theoretical elaborations on ideology, as well as some of his focused economic history, reveals Higgs's research as compelling far beyond its force as political ammunition.

Here is a good place to disclose that Bob is dear to me as a friend and mentor, whose passionate opposition to state violence has inspired me for two decades. For years I was his junior colleague at the Independent Institute, during which his work helped motivate me to return to academia. In preparing this chapter I realized more than ever how profoundly indebted I am to him for his intellectual and scholarly influence in addition to his personal and philosophical inspiration. I am no economic historian, much less an economist, but as a political and legal historian I have embraced his venture of integrating ideological and institutional history to advance our understanding of the American state. Despite his training in economics, Bob has often stressed legal and social history, political agency, and the interplay between societal conditions and ideology, factors that highlight the value of qualitative historical study. I have moreover inherited his affinity for the puzzles presented by the decades between the late-19th and mid-20th centuries—namely the transitions from the Gilded Age to the Progressive Era and from the New Deal to the Cold War.

In critically drawing from Higgs's masterpiece and other works I aim to show how pondering the qualitative dimensions of state power, ideology, and theory of history might inform historians seeking to build richer, more sophisticated narratives of the growth and transformation of American government. While humanists and historians could always use more modesty toward the lessons of quantitative social science, we must not surrender our responsibility to interpret the contours of state power. What the state has done, how it has transformed, and the contingent and particular ways institutions and ideas shape each other are at bottom historical questions. The answer to these questions is complicated. A long-term pessimism entices with its simple declension tale of a central state mechanically swelling through the epicycles of real and manufactured emergencies. But Higgs's insights about history, ideology, and government's ratcheting growth should not merely reaffirm libertarian folk wisdom. They might instead reinforce a long-term and less despondent outlook, though not always a philosophically convenient one, and fuel new research into the histories of law, federalism, and the modern contingency of ideology itself.

A THEORY OF GOVERNMENT AND IDEOLOGY

Among its major contributions, *Crisis* offers a nuanced and often overlooked theorization of government expansiveness. A crude quantification of government growth would be apparent in a few pages of line graphs with the wars and recessions marked on the x axes. Assessing the size or very fact of "Big Government" must transcend quantitative measures and consider qualitative factors through such sources as "laws, regulatory directives, executive orders, court decisions, and similar documents" (Higgs 1987, x). Economic output alone might make for a vivid elevator pitch, but Higgs's account conjures something more cultural—the *ways* that government and people interact. What we might call the *shape* of state power, its contours and texture, cannot be found in GDP alone. Not even its "Bigness" can be. Higgs distinguishes capitalized "Big Government" from mere "big government," where the former broadens its scope beyond the quantitatively visible. Big Government arises through undertaking "new functions, activities, and programs" (Higgs 1987, x). Even if crises mechanically ratcheted up government spending, as Higgs explains elsewhere, such an automatic effect would be "bigger government but not Bigger Government" (Higgs 1985, 7).

Higgs nevertheless understands Big Government as a matter of economics broadly construed: Big Government achieves "wide scope of effective authority over economic decision-making" (Higgs 1987, 32). What qualifies as authority over the economic? *Crisis* and Higgs's other work suggest that the power to compel or prohibit activity in nearly any domain could count. And when it most matters, the personal is political, the political economic, by the government's own reckoning. Higgs describes the judiciary's acquiescence to military conscription as a "keystone" to leviathan (Higgs 1997). As the Supreme Court reasoned during World War II, if the state could legitimately force its subjects to fight and die, its lesser economic interventions would seemingly be legitimate (Higgs 1987, 222–25). Higgs might question the premise that conscription is defensible, but he appears sympathetic to the logic that most wartime economic interventions were no less so. Perhaps conscription counts as narrowly economic given its impact on labor markets, yet at least one of the period's great legal minds also defended censorship on this basis.[2]

Defined qualitatively, we might ask what brings about Big Government. Higgs defies simplistic and monocausal explanations. Assumptions that the modern state emerged due to societal modernization and complexity do not satisfy Higgs. Complexity might justify state power in some minds, but cannot alone explain it (Higgs 1987, 7). Turning to crises, which others have understood as spawning government growth, Higgs affirms that crises punctuate the "critical episodes" in which government grew (Higgs 1987, 61). But crisis alone does not create Big Government (Higgs 1987, 78). Each crisis, moreover, unfolds in the historical context of past crises. In government growth, timing matters (Higgs 1987, 57). Institutions change in capital-intensive ways, teaching future generations the supposed benefits of governmental mobilization (Higgs 1987, 71). While stressing historical conditions, Higgs does observe something akin to an axiom in the way crisis affects people: "Crisis, by its very nature, creates heightened insecurities" and even "widespread bewilderment" (Higgs 1987, 16–17). But this focuses on the attitudes people have, and thus on the factor that truly drives *Crisis*.

For Higgs, the most salient variable is ideology. Drawing on Clifford Geertz, Higgs finds that ideology "seeks to motivate action" and that those driving government expansion were historically constrained by beliefs (Higgs 1987, 56, 58). Part I of *Crisis* explores ideology before part II offers a narrative test of the ratchet effect across different ideological conditions. In the 1890s depression, he argues, classical liberal ideology accommodated no significant government growth and thus no ratchet effect. From the Progressive Era through World War II, in contrast, ideology had changed to welcome federal expansion with each crisis. Yet unlike those seeing crisis and government as a force of nature, Higgs, writing at the end of the Cold War, muses with scholarly humility that the long-term impacts of Vietnam and the Great Society are yet to be seen (Higgs 1987, 261).[3] We will return to *Crisis*'s historical account, but first we will more deeply consider ideology. Along with drawing attention to the qualitative character of Big Government, Higgs's insights about ideology reveal ways that the state cannot fully be grasped through formulaic assumptions of theory or economic science.

To track ideology's transformative role Higgs endeavors to define it: ideology is a "somewhat coherent, rather comprehensive belief system about social relations" that has cognitive, affective, programmatic, and solidaric elements (Higgs 1987, 37). An ideology has to "hang together," with its internal tensions plausibly managed, and it must address a wide array of social questions (Higgs

2008, 548). It must appeal to human logic as well as emotion, and inform its adherents what to do and not to do on its behalf. Ideology is partly visceral, and it gives one a sense of good and evil (Higgs 1987, 44).[4]

Perhaps most important, ideology entails solidarity. This concept of solidarity is central to understanding Higgs's approach to the interaction between the subjective and objective conditions surrounding government power. It is through solidarity that ideology overcomes the limitations of Mancur Olson's "logic of collective action." Public choice, taken too uncritically, cannot reconcile the reality of social behavior in clear contradiction to narrow self-interest. (Higgs 1987, 38–40). Solidarity implies a sense of community, and true believers afford palpable affinity to others in their ideological camp and will sacrifice for it (Higgs 1987, 42–43).

The aspect of ideology perhaps most conducive to qualitative analysis, and most elusive to reductive social science theory, is solidarity. This consequential and yet unquantifiable factor in the history of government means that the relationship between crisis and ideology cannot be mechanical. The way people interpret crises matters, and those crises can stir solidaric passions and disrupt the explanatory power of economic axioms. A major war and the art that depicts it can together alter society far beyond any theory's predictions.

In order to test ideology as a factor of government growth, and not as a dependent variable, requires careful qualitative examination. We must understand the ideas of historical actors (Higgs 1987, 35). At the same time, to recognize that ideology is not a purely independent variable—that the reduction of institutional conditions down to changing ideologies is no more viable than the reduction in reverse—is where things get tricky. And here we get to Higgs's contributions to the theory of history.

HISTORICIZING IDEOLOGY

Higgs's concern for ideology does not itself differentiate him from other luminaries of his discipline or philosophical tradition. Rather, it is Higgs's understanding of how ideology and materialist factors interact that drives his nuanced, and more historicist, approach to state building. While *Crisis* does not focus much on theory of history, Higgs elsewhere gives more sustained attention to historicizing ideology. In a 2008 article, "The Complex Course of Ideological Change," Higgs considers "theory-driven" and "event-driven" explanations of ideological change (Higgs 2008, 551). Among those stressing theory are economists John Maynard Keynes and F. A. Hayek, as well as Ludwig von Mises. Meanwhile, the materialist focus, beyond Karl Marx, has had its own adherents at least since the interwar popularity of sociologies of knowledge. Pushing against Marx's materialism, Mises, as Higgs words it, "expressed his disagreement in the form of an adamant denial that social structure affects ideology at all." In his postwar treatise *Human Action*, Mises argued that "society and any concrete order of social affairs are an outcome of ideologies; ideologies are not, as Marxism asserts, a product of a certain state of social affairs." Caught between Marx and Mises, Higgs could not "accept" Mises's "claim" as written, "except in the trivial sense that for any individual act, an idea of possibility and an idea of purpose must always precede a specific deliberate action" (Higgs 2008, 555). Instead, Higgs believes that "the relationship between 'ideas' and their sustaining social processes is always a dialectical one" (Higgs 2008, 556). Higgs thus urges a careful examination of both materialist and ideological trajectories in their complex and changing relationship to one another—which, I might add, would create a lot of work for historians.

Unapologetic dialectic thinking distinguishes Higgs from other radical liberal thinkers and has at least a surface resonance with the theories of history arising from the continental philosophical tradition. But unlike dialecticians who distill all historical forces into spirit or ideas (like Hegel) or power differentials parasitic on economic power (like Marx), Higgs practices a dialectic sensibility toward the very interplay between ideas and structures. Higgs favorably quotes at length Berger and Luckmann's 1966 book *The Social Construction of Reality: A Treatise in the Sociology of Knowledge*, which is worth partially reproducing:

> Definitions of reality have self-fulfilling potency. Theories can be realized in history, even theories that were highly abstruse when they were first conceived by their inventors. . . . Consequently, social change must always be understood as standing in a dialectical relationship to the "history of ideas." Both "idealistic" and "materialistic" understandings of the relationship overlook this dialectic, and thus distort history. (Berger and Luckmann 1966, 128)

While he rejects Marx's reductive materialism, Higgs also rejects Mises's reductive idealism. Regarding Higgs's dialectic approach, the most consonant libertarian intellectual might be philosopher Christopher Matthew Sciabarra, whose works on libertarianism and theory of history are worth consulting in conversation with Higgs's institutional histories (Sciabarra 2000).

Higgs stands athwart the ahistorical theorists and dissents, and prioritizes the intellectual task of understanding how "ideology and society are linked"

(Higgs 1987, 53). The relationship is indeterminate—it depends on the society, its ideas, and historical setting. There are some axioms about ideology Higgs admits to assuming, and he would be unlikely to reject compelling evidence of counterexamples to these general tendencies he takes up as working assumptions. We will return to some of these later. For now, let us note that Higgs begins fundamentally with the fact of history's importance: ideological change is a "truly historical process," one that is path dependent and "motivated and constrained" by its historical conditions (Higgs 1985, 2–4). Since the dialectic between ideas and conditions is so vital, history as both a qualitative and empirical discipline is indispensable. Neither theoretically weighty social science nor a priori reasoning can predict how materialist and ideological changes affect each other.

But Higgs's insights about ideology pose a problem for historians. One might even conclude that Higgs's thoughts on ideology and history set up an ideal that historians cannot fully achieve. In its most idyllic form, Higgs differentiates social science from ideology: "Social science," writes Higgs, is "diagnostic and critical; ideology is justificatory and apologetic" (Higgs 1987, 56). Whether we categorize history as a social science or one of the softer humanities, its reliance on both empiricism and interpretive liberties helps explain why it is described both ways. Straddling the divide between disciplines, it is "diagnostic and critical" but at least a little "justificatory and apologetic." Most theorists of history admit that ideology inflects historical writing. Even without reducing the field down to mere literary genre, we detect ideology in history's narrative form. Higgs notes that ideological language employs rhetoric, "metaphor, analogy, irony, sarcasm, satire, hyperbole, and overdrawn antithesis" as "common devices." Political campaign propaganda, Higgs remarks, does not typically promise "a Slightly Improved Society" (Higgs 1987, 48–49). But even the blandest historical storytelling generally relies on literary devices (White 1990). At a minimum it entails periodization, and even the decision of when to begin and end a story is laden with judgment calls about what is most important.

When it comes to historicizing ideology itself, how do historians, themselves ideological, avoid producing propaganda? Historians, unavoidably shaped by their own ideology, should resist the allure of seeking answers or framing questions in ways that privilege ideological comfort over historical understanding. Those motivated by libertarianism (or anything else) might pursue valuable and neglected questions, but must take extra care in their answers. Historical work arises from its own dialectic between research and exposition—asking questions, finding answers, reframing questions to make sense of the answers that are found. Ideally, historians should not shy away when their research moves in directions dissonant with their priors. Each of Higgs's four elements of ideology could obviously bias historical exposition. Moral judgment might cast history as an oversimplified struggle between good and evil. Affection competes with honest analysis. Programmatic commitments are especially perilous, discouraging honest insights in tension with convenient advocacy.

For historians, perhaps ideology's most fraught dimension is solidarity. Solidarity not only tilts narratives in favor of some actors and movements over others. Even when an ideologically driven historian concedes that pure heroes and villains did not characterize the past, each narrative risks becoming a teleology where ideological contradictions—as understood from the vantage of the historian's supposed ideological coherence—become clarified toward a struggle between genuine right and wrong. Solidarity can moreover cause scholars to overvalue the research produced by fellow travelers and discount the work by adversaries. This danger, I submit, is plainly in evidence all around. Libertarian scholars, socialist scholars, and conservative scholars tend to favor work within their own camp—even when particular interpretations contradict one another as much as they clash with specific interpretations from outside their camp. In emphasizing this, I recognize I am fighting several uphill battles and must confront a glaring irony in my own intellectual development: while ideological solidarity first inspired me to read Higgs, it is now methodological solidarity that inspires me to plead libertarians and radical liberals to take his insights beyond their politics, and to plead scholars of different politics to value his methodology.

In considering the danger of intellectual solidarity to honest scholarship, we can distinguish between two distinct meanings of solidarity, one of which might help counteract the other. Here I invoke another thinker, Richard Rorty, rarely seen in conversation with Higgs. I hope if this pairing is not persuasive of my point it can still be discursively generative.[5] As Higgs formulates solidarity, it is a sectarian affinity to those of like mind and shared social goals. Rorty, in comparison, stresses solidarity for humanity itself (Rorty 1989, 189). Rorty relies on this universal solidarity to reinforce his own politics, a Rawlesian liberalism, but I would argue that Rortian solidarity can be orthogonal to what sort of liberalism one finds best: those who believe their politics best serve humankind both as societies and individuals can ground their value system in solidarity.[6]

In another related area, Higgs and Rorty might fruitfully if counterintuitively be discussed together. Higgs concedes a subjectivity and uncertainty haunting all ideologies (presumably including his): "all ideologies contain unverified elements, some of which, including their fundamental commitments to certain values, are unverifiable. In relation to those elements, which are neither true nor false, the allegation of distortion has little or no meaning" (Higgs 2008, 549). It is a major admission that everyone's ideology relies on beliefs that are at bottom unprovable. Higgs's insight resonates with Rorty's discussion of how each worldview has its own distinctive and irreducible "final vocabulary" (Rorty 1989, 73). Rorty holds that in the end different ideologies can be comparably and impressively sophisticated and comprehensive, and because none is provable, only a universal solidarity spares the liberal from the temptations of relativism slipping into nihilism. Rorty's solidaric empathy thus accommodates an intellectual humility toward rival beliefs and the contingency on which his own beliefs depend. For both Rorty and Higgs, solidarity, in their different meanings, overcomes narrow and reductive findings that clinical social science and reason alone produce. For Higgs, economic reasoning alone cannot overcome the collective action problem; for Rorty, moral reasoning alone cannot overcome the contingency and irony that render all ideologies unprovable.

While Rorty and Higgs see solidarity as vital to ideology, for better or worse, the question is how to compensate for it in historical writing. For starters, the inescapability of unprovable ideology ought to bring humility, but surely not the mirage of objectivity, to historical writing. More pointedly, Rortian solidarity relies on a willingness to consume literature and art from people of different walks of life to appreciate their shared humanity. This sort of task complements the sort of analytical empathy that helps historical writing avoid the worst of ideological bias. Attempting to understand historical actors on their own terms goes a long way.

For even the most honest ideologues writing history, the most inescapable blind spot will be the propensity toward narratives of ideology and institutions that reinforce comforting explanatory lines. Higgs seeks to avoid this trap, but *Crisis* nevertheless highlights the sorts of questions that fellow travelers like to ask about government power. It is ideological solidarity, not methodological affinities, that explain Higgs's prominence in libertarian folk wisdom. By leveraging universal solidarity against the distorting temptations of sectarian solidarity, we can direct Higgs's research methods toward a richer understanding of the shape of American state power and avoid pessimistic and unnuanced declension narratives.

ON THE TEMPTATION OF A DECLENSION NARRATIVE

If the libertarian movement's intellectuals and its masses agree on anything, they generally see the rising modern state and individual liberty as at odds. *Crisis* understandably has a resonance as a fable for the masses—it gives credulity to popular anxiety about the ever-encroaching national government and the shrinking domain of the sovereign individual. A superficial reading of *Crisis*, uninformed by Higgs's other work, could forgivably reinforce such a simple declension narrative. A surface reading also gives comfort to oversimplified understandings of ideological battle lines. To be sure, *Crisis* eschews one-dimensional models of left against right or libertarianism against statism. Higgs instead outlines the main American ideologies as populist, conservative, liberal, and libertarian (Higgs 1987, 46). But the narrative judgment calls necessary to chronicle the "widely noticed change in prevailing ideology" appropriately bring focus to national state power (Higgs 1985, 2). Higgs does not, moreover, seek to explain the "twists and turns of ideology among opinion leaders," which he considers a "separate question." While he maintains that legislatures are hardly pristine reflections of public opinion (Higgs 1987, 16), it is easy to overlook these nuances. *Crisis* does not have time to show how sharply different nonlibertarian groups understand their own historical roles. The interest that drives the theoretical and narrative core of the book is thus largely comforting to modern libertarian sensibilities.

If a superficial reading divines an intractable declension narrative driven by social-scientific law, Higgs's work elsewhere undermines such complacency. On the one hand, yes, Higgs concedes that a "broad perspective" of both "technological and ideological changes," coupled with historical grasp of "belief and practice" and social structures, tends to give "collectivism an edge over the free market" (Higgs 1985, 16). On the other hand, despite "a presumption in the theory sketched above that the 'progressive' movements of ideology will outweigh such reactionary ones, . . . we need not attempt to settle where the balance lies a priori" (Higgs 1985, 18). As important, I would add, what is "progressive" and what is "reactionary" does not actually exist along one dimension, especially with the US government, whose leaders have historically pitched their projects in the name of freedom. A dialectical approach paints a complex picture, where individual liberty has expanded in some areas even as the government has as well. Higgs's historicizing of structures and ideals invites not only nuanced understanding of the ratchet effect but also hard questions about where the quantitative and qualitative contours of state power give different impressions about the Bigness of Government.

Indeed, Higgs's explanation of government winning the people over implicates a great paradox of modern liberal states. In respect to novel interventions, "like all forms of knowledge, technology and ideology must be learned" (Higgs 1985, 16). And so, for example, after World War I's regulations on gold, Americans more readily tolerated the "monetary departures of 1933–1934" (Higgs 1985, 22). But the American state's path-dependent trajectory also suggests a nonbinary reality of state oppression. The modern liberal state's "bureaucrats and other rulers will improve their devices for making the command economy work better; new information systems, allocation rules, procedures for resolving inter-bureau disputes, and reconciling inconsistencies in the overall plan." And such "improvements," I would stress, "help to render the controls less obnoxious to aggrieved parties" (Higgs 1985, 17). If state innovations recognize the alienating danger of state power, uncomfortable questions follow: What truly is liberal about the modern liberal state? How do the state's emancipatory promises serve Big Government while observing some individual liberties better than in the past?

If we concede that government can advance liberal ends, whatever the contradictions, the quirks of American political history become a lot more coherent, even as the history undercuts libertarian folk wisdom. Historians, whatever their ideologies, must resist simple meta-narratives of Big Government inexorably invading individual liberty if they are to understand the complexities and shape of Big Government as well as its complicated relationship to ideology.

READING HIGGS BEYOND THE DECLENSION NARRATIVE

Despite its nuances, the arc of *Crisis and Leviathan* shares a cursory similarity with the popular libertarian declension narrative. We might consider a key periodization where *Crisis* seemingly jibes with the folk wisdom. For both ideology and institutions, Higgs finds a central pivot between Reconstruction and the New Deal. This period features both the control case and the operational break in *Crisis*. In the early 1890s, classical liberalism restrained government expansion, most unlike the case in most 20th-century federal expansions. In choosing Grover Cleveland for president in 1892, Americans "elected an ideal leader" given their own classical liberalism. This ideological atmosphere constrained federal and state government responses to the 1890s depression. "Most people resisted radical pleas for Bigger Government," writes Higgs in his strongest claim about the period's public temper, "because they believed that such a government would be not only counterproductive but immoral" (Higgs 1987, 83). In response to real threats of impoverishment, monetary instability, and labor unrest, Cleveland championed classical liberalism: he promoted confidence in gold through closed-door dealings with the Morgan financial empire, imposed law and order in response to the Pullman strike, and avoided major deviations from the minimal constitutional state. The judicial resistance to a new income tax typified the era's liberalism (although Cleveland's ambivalence about the tax might complicate his personification of the age's spirit) (Higgs 1987, 89, 91–92).

One limitation in this formulation is the use of the national government to stand for public ideology. In linking ideology to institutions, we might pause on the question of constitutional federalism. Some historical work has highlighted the states' welfare and regulatory capacity, which, while limited, tell an inconsistent story about a general public moral objection to government aid (Novak 1996). Higgs nevertheless persuasively shows that the 1890s crisis did not cause state governments to expand much either, and he has addressed criticism that he did not focus on federalism (Higgs 1992). But more attention to federalism reminds us of the peculiar path-dependent relationship between national power and liberal ideology.

It is at least arguable that America's classical liberal spirit peaked only after, and partly because of, the massive and sometimes constitutionally suspect national mobilization in support of Civil War, Lincolnian free-soil political economy, slavery abolition, Reconstruction, and westward conquest. The Yankee Leviathan helped chaperone general incorporation, the proliferation of free wage labor, and the triumph of contractual individual liberty over patronage and republican civic duty (Bensel 1990; Stanley 1998). The aspirations of the conquering political elite really mattered, and Higgs has recognized how even disagreements among the Reconstructionist Republicans could translate into serious distinctions in political economy for the Black labor force (Higgs 1977, 37–43). After Reconstruction, the weak national state, even under Cleveland, only tenuously represented public ideology, at least defined as a comprehensive, coherent system with cognitive, affective, programmatic, and solidaric elements.

How classical liberal was the American public really? To some degree the liberal state, especially at the federal level, was contingent on the public *lacking* coherent public ideology. The Republican Party was divided among conflicting liberal commitments—contractual liberties and civil rights at the expense of subsidiarity; limited federal power; law and order in the frontier west. Rural populists, northern working-class radicals, and rank-and-file Democrats were not genuinely classically liberal, nor were most southern elites emboldened by the redemption of white supremacist social control. Resistance to national mobilization arose from very different, even contradictory, motivations. What is more, the Gilded Age's political atmosphere was also an aberration. Neither political party dominated convincingly, which political scientists argue reinforces polarization that can limit state activity (Lamis et al. 1990). Populists decried political machine corruption but criticized modern capitalism; anti-Black racism and northern fatigue blunted civil rights enforcement; Indian wars served as a rationale and release valve for federal power, as well as a warning about the limits of mobilization (Higgs 1987, 81). While the Civil War and Reconstruction empowered liberalism in some ways, the collapse of federal power in wars of attrition empowered it in other, paradoxical ways.

The late 19th century was perhaps above all a vexing period—a confounding interregnum between cleaner chapters of national history organized around activist presidential administrations and positive statist agendas. Historians struggle to structure a master narrative around Victorian America's ideological temper. Deceptively, the national state's selective federalism meant that ideology perhaps did less work than in the next century. Where federal and local power were robust, as well as where rights protection was less vigorous, marginalized Americans most suffered. Higgs conscientiously notes the era's greatest shortcomings, the oppression of Black Americans and Native Americans (Higgs 1987, 3). If *Crisis*'s self-consciously "episodic" chronicle cannot capture all this, its theoretical apparatus urges such qualitative consideration. Higgs's other work demonstrates such careful consideration of both ideological and materialist factors in this revolutionary era of industrialization, urbanization, and demographic and social change. He has studied the economic conditions for African Americans after emancipation and Reconstruction (Higgs 1982). While Higgs has done more than his share, much more can be said. The challenges remain in understanding the shape of the Gilded Age state.

Other paradoxes arise in what we might call the Big Government aspects of small government. Higgs summarizes 1890s ideology as a belief in less government except "where extraordinary action is required to maintain law and order, including the monetary order of the economy" (Higgs 1987, 104). When writing *Crisis* Higgs believed, "We need government," and might since becoming an anarchist less charitably narrate Cleveland's efforts against domestic disorder (Higgs 1987, 3). Of course, an anarchist's normative radicalization does not preclude recognition of classical liberal constraints on power. Yet a characteristic insight among anarchists is the difficulty in restricting government to "minarchist" confines. Anarchist scholars stress the coerciveness of the state's "limited" nightwatchman powers. This insight reinforces the understanding of war as "the health of the state," as Randolph Bourne put it in

1918 (Bourne 1998). Nothing illustrates the paradox of limited government like "national defense." Every government gives promises of security, and yet through security the state most reliably aspires toward total power. The horrors of totalitarianism—its detentions, its interrogations, its show trials, executions, and murderous territorial conquests—ironically turn on the first powers states use to lay claim to territory, impose law and order, and satisfy Weberian definitions of a state in the first place.

Returning to *Crisis*, its narration into the 1900s seemingly gives further comfort to libertarian folk wisdom. Classical liberal America stood firm under Cleveland, but some agitators, namely the populists, challenged the limited-government status quo and rallied behind William Jennings Bryan's condemnation of the gold standard in 1896. Higgs describes William McKinley's 1896 defeat of Bryan as evidence that "the challengers' time had not yet come" (Higgs 1987, 105). As *Crisis* moves into the 20th century, the key ingredients for the declension narrative appear. Higgs's 1890s control case ends as Americans abandon their classical liberalism and the modern ratchet increasingly defines the long arc of crisis and mobilization.

But *Crisis*'s episodic treatment cannot give full consideration to ideological continuity and rupture and their complex overlay with institutional changes. Such consideration appears in Higgs's other work—for example, he has taken some populist economic grievances seriously (Higgs 1970, 291), but selective readers would not know that. And while McKinley's 1896 victory is described as a break against populist-friendly collectivism, McKinley's presidency also inaugurated presidential progressivism: it catapulted Teddy Roosevelt up the executive branch, and McKinley himself waged the Spanish-American War, which Higgs has elsewhere faulted as the birth of modern American empire[7]— the chief propellant of 20th-century state power. What is more, Teddy Roosevelt, as Higgs relays, cast off Cleveland's ambivalence and backed an income tax in 1908 (Higgs 1987, 112).

The temptation to read *Crisis* as straight declension narrative becomes stronger with the late Progressive Era, although as in other areas Higgs's economic history work gives the period textured consideration.[8] As *Crisis* tells it, in the early 20th century ideology had matured to "such conditions" to allow Big Government (Higgs 1987, 107). By the 1910s, progressive consensus over "economic decision-making" was in place (Higgs 1987, 113). Higgs compellingly describes the Adamson Act as a Progressive Era high point, a dress rehearsal for war powers (Higgs 1987, 116). By this time, the old populists "must have taken much pressure in the momentous shift" in favor of central economic policy (Higgs 1987, 121).

Yet the populists and progressives were, by their own lights, very different groups with divergent priorities. The relationship between war and state accentuates the distinctions. If the 1896 election had been a referendum where Bryan, representing the potent challenge to classical liberalism, lost to McKinley, the ultimate irony becomes clear with foreign policy. From McKinley through Woodrow Wilson the United States embarked on a series of imperial adventures throughout the hemisphere and Pacific, culminating in US involvement in World War I, in pacifist protest against which Secretary of State Bryan resigned.

A related tension arises in the discussion *Crisis* offers on 1890s law and order and Progressive Era repression of labor and war dissidents. The historiography, dominated by scholars with solidarity for organized labor, typically stresses continuity from Gilded Age suppression of disruptive strikes to the repression under Progressive politicians who generally represented the middle-class sensibility they inherited from the liberals. This invites a painful question for libertarians: whether it was the populists who were the true progenitors of the progressives, or whether it was the classical liberals. An inconvenient explanation stresses the continuity between classical liberals and progressive liberals, both representing a similar socioeconomic slice of the professional and journalistic middle class with outsize political influence. Their frustrations in representing this population help explain the transformation of liberalism.[9] A tale of classical liberalism developing into progressivism, circumventing the confounding story of the populists, is possible (Cohen 2002). Whereas in the Gilded Age, opposing factions within liberalism had competing demands for government power and for freedom, perhaps their 20th-century reshuffling proved more compatible to federal expansion. They had different policy reasons and tactics for seeking to preserve social order, but a narrative of continuity helps explain the maintenance of labor repression from the 1870s through Wilson's war. Wilson favored organized labor more than previous administrations, as Higgs reminds us (Higgs 1987, 143). But from much of organized labor's point of view, Wilsonian repression before and after World War I was a climax of Gilded Age class warfare.

After World War I came the New Deal and World War II, occasioning the most significant crises and ratchets. Higgs's work on these episodes, in *Crisis* and elsewhere, is for good reason among his most well-known. *Crisis* has more space for nuance in explaining the 1930s and 1940s than the hinge between the 1890s and 1900s. Higgs distinguishes between the early and late New Deal, while still seeing continuity as important to his ideological story (Higgs 1987, 167–72). Higgs adeptly handles the curious overlap between New Deal activism and the peak of federal judicial scrutiny of progressive legislation (Higgs 1987, 183). Elsewhere he has shown that not only ideology but anxieties about the climate of ideological and institutional uncertainty hampered 1930s capital investment. Volatility in governing policy provoked "fear that the market economy might not survive in anything like its traditional form and that even more drastic developments, perhaps even some kind of collectivist dictatorship," might follow (Higgs 2006, 12). Economics helps illuminate how this might have worsened the Great Depression, but the feedback loop between that anxiety and the politics surrounding more New Deal policies is another question for the historians.

However strained the relationship beforehand, World War II was the consummation of America's marriage to Big Government, which has never since been annulled (Higgs 1987, 198). From the war's ashes arose a seemingly durable system that Higgs calls "participatory fascism" (Higgs 1987, 258). And yet, returning to the shortcomings of the declension narrative, World War II brought qualitatively different state building from past crises. World War I spawned less restrained and therefore less sustainable experimentations with state power—unbridled repression, government-vigilante relations, nativism, and alcohol prohibition. World War II led to a more polite and sustained state expansion, finally creating the modern state as we know it. Yet it did so with more liberal branding—both rhetorically devoted to universal human rights and yet more cautious in its promises about the state's socially transformative capacity (Brinkley 1998). Perhaps disillusioned by the progressives' utopian promises, culminating in alcohol prohibition, and with the foils of fascism and communism abroad, their unapologetic sympathizers discredited at home, midcentury leaders paradoxically had confronted unprecedented global and domestic challenges and yet brought a newfound appreciation of *certain* limits to power and hostility toward *certain* outdated forms of illiberalism.

As Higgs has noted, policymakers learn from mistakes and excesses as they refine the technology and ideology of state building—and in some uncomfortable ways the modern state and modern American liberalism became both more statist and individualist after World War II, just as they had after the Civil War. The postwar state better respected civil rights, racial equality, and even civil liberties like free speech and aspects of bodily autonomy. Of course, after World War II, modern libertarian ideology finally took root in institutions and flourished. One way to reconcile this to declension narratives is to disregard modern social liberties or take their advancement for granted. Or we might question the whole one-dimensional declension narrative and try to better understand the ideological contours and qualitative shape of Big Government.

TOWARD MULTIPLE RESEARCH AGENDAS

Higgs's work leaves us with insights and tensions that invite multiple research questions, the pursuit of which could complicate the libertarian declension narrative. One big task is to apprehend the differences between qualitatively potent Big Government and quantitatively measurable big government. It is very possible for a leaner state, imposing a relatively small tax burden, to operate quite coercively in everything it does, while a redistributive state has larger budgets but commits less violence and aggression overall. A second big task is to better track the indeterminate relationship between ideology and institutions. A diversity of approaches could fruitfully serve both tasks. In particular I would urge further historical inquiry into constitutional federalism, the substance of the law, and the historical contingency of 20th-century liberal ideologies on the conditions of modernity.

Contests over the distribution of power, particularly across jurisdictions, drive much of US history. This seems clearest from the Revolution through Reconstruction, and from the New Deal onward, but in the period between, where Higgs locates a consequential ideological shift, the story of federalism is harder to narrate. Responding to historian Ballard Campbell's review of *Crisis*, which criticized Higgs for overemphasizing federal power, Higgs replied: "This is not the whole story . . . but it is a very important part of the story . . . that had never been carefully and fully developed before. It is plenty for one book." Higgs concurred "entirely with Campbell that future research on the growth of government might fruitfully be focused on federalism" (Higgs 1987, 1992). What would such research, informed by Higgs, look like?

In linking institutions to ideology, federalism is essential, particularly in light of the paradoxes surrounding liberalism after Reconstruction. The challenge arises even at the level of theory. According to Higgs, government is not itself a "coherent institution" (Higgs 1987, 6). American government especially consists of horizontally and vertically separated and overlapping authorities. Its lack of "coherence" must sit alongside Higgs's definition of ideology as itself mostly "coherent." Can an ideology coherently appreciate federalism? Given ideology's structural propensity toward coherence, how does it make sense of an incoherent institution?

My own research suggests that major transformations of American government tend to entail a dialectic transformation of liberalism, broadly defined, and federalism. These shifts are rarely more or less libertarian in a straightforward way, but rather amount to rearrangements of competing liberal values. The Lincolnian state birthed the classical liberal era and yet it was the 20th century social state that more fully pursued the nightwatchman aspirations of "law and order" (Gregory 2024). Out of World War II and the Cold War came a new liberalism more attentive to equal rights and even free speech.[10] Over the ages, the centralizing state has often accompanied individualism, even as intermediary centers of power have been swept away or incorporated into the modernizing regime. Historians and other scholars have considered such paradoxes. Brian Balogh has considered how the national government nurtured and benefited from the strengthening of civic associations (Balogh 2015). Social scientists like Theda Skocpol (Skocpol 1995) and historians like Gary Gerstle (Gerstle 2015) have grappled with the development of American state power through the limiting contexts of federalism. But the relationship between federalism and liberalism remains a great problem of American political history, deserving more theorization and archival attention.

Gerstle's apt description of the United States as a "liberal state" (Gerstle 2015) poses challenges to how libertarian folk wisdom understands US history. Much of the liberalism of this "liberal state" appears in limitations on federal power. The most pronounced paradoxes have concerned slavery and civil rights. The national government's rise imposed basic liberal standards. Was the American political project more or less liberal before or after the Civil War? Classical liberalism, rooted in free labor, seemingly became more salient afterward. The possibility that federal power could be more genotypically liberal before the Civil War but more phenotypically liberal afterward highlights the core tension in the history of liberalism and federalism. It also challenges nightwatchman libertarianism, since the federal government's rights-defending functions turned on a permissive reading of constitutional authority. The federal government's original "limited functions," moreover, were not particularly liberal. As a general matter, the few powers exercised by a "limited" government are among the most patently coercive and hierarchical. The antebellum national security state's involvement in ethnic cleansing and slavery enforcement are not exceptions proving any rule, but serve to refute any immaculate conception of American power. Over time, the most constitutionally legitimate wars were among the most important in expanding the welfare state.

The twists of constitutional federalism more generally implicate questions of law. Law serves to mediate ideology, and institutions must meet in formation of political authority. In *Crisis* Higgs identifies the content of judicial decisions as a key dimension of "Big Government" (Higgs 1987, 68). While courts have legible quantitative costs regardless of their rulings, how they rule actually determines the relationship between government and the individual

(Higgs 1987, 29). American law, along with its politics, reconciles the ideals of freedom with the realities of state violence. These mechanisms serve in civilizing, moderating, and liberalizing state domination. But law, like politics, is not a clean reflection of public ideology, nor of private interests, nor of the state itself. Nor is it a purely autonomous force. As critical legal historians have persuasively argued, society and law, both written and unwritten, have an indeterminate relationship (Gordon 1984). Historical examination thus can shed light that jurisprudential philosophies or public choice theory cannot uncover.

Libertarian and radical liberal scholars, confronted with histories of legal construction, are tempted to write vindicatory or condemnatory genealogies hoping that one particular school of legal interpretation will most reliably accommodate individual liberty. But even federal jurisprudence undermines any reductive master narrative. Legal history from the 1890s through the 1940s especially defies analysis. The federal judiciary was discernibly classical liberal on the freedom of contract, as enforced through a federal usurpation of state powers. The states were meanwhile the main laboratories for progressive regulation until the New Deal. This dynamic somewhat reversed in the middle of the century with the Warren Court, yet judicial activism spelled a continuity of nationalizing substantive due process from *Lochner v. New York* in 1905 to *Roe v. Wade* in 1973. Did the Court's ideology become more or less libertarian over time? On the issue of privacy, an individualist conception that went beyond physical boundaries became possible with judicial activism in *Katz v. New York* in 1967 (Gregory 2016). Whether conservative-leaning libertarians admire or renounce this construction of privacy rights has been breathtakingly conditional—whether the question before them was Barack Obama's NSA wiretapping or abortion or same-sex marriage decisions.

This speaks to the historically contingent construction of ideas and ideology themselves. On such questions, Higgs's dialectic between ideas and material conditions could not be more relevant. Consistent with libertarian declension narratives is the assumption that urban modernization tends to promote left-progressive politics overall hostile to so-called traditional liberties. If this were consistently true, there would be little long-term hope for liberty. In popular conservative and right-libertarian discourse these anxieties have metastasized into fears of contemporary corporate culture—finally resolving the paradoxical simultaneous admiration of industrial capitalism and disdain for urban modernity in favor of a coherent pessimism about the future altogether. But Higgs's own granular studies undercut many of the assumed premises at play. First, industrialization and urbanization are not exactly the same process (Higgs 1969). Second, if ideas and material conditions have a consequential dialectical relationship in any area, it is in technological advancement. Higgs has taken up the question of inventiveness, a palpable but nebulous concept, finding it better served by the density and market activity of urban centers. Higgs has further suggested that the South's traditionally strident social hierarchies impeded inventiveness, even putting aside rural versus urban differences (Higgs 1971, 662–64).

More generally, we must wonder how much of our own ideas, and our own political contests, only make sense in light of our modern historical setting. We can raise two inconvenient questions—one about the general definability of ideology as a static analytical category, and the second about the dialectic between anti-state ideology and modern state power. In order to have at least one target that remains constant enough to track over time, Higgs persuasively formulates a definition of ideology, working through the abstract lens of a social scientist to build a theory with broad applicability. Higgs discloses numerous assumptions. One is that ideology both limits and propels political action (Higgs 1987, 48). This cannot be disputed without rejecting the very core of Higgs's dialectical thinking. Another assumption is vital to his story if not his framework: because of their comprehensiveness and coherence, only a few ideologies will likely have "much importance in a given time and place" (Higgs 1987, 45).[11]

Yet, elsewhere Higgs stresses that "more than one ideology exists, and hence *ideological competition* occurs all the time" (Higgs 2008, 557). There is no contradiction here, but it suggests a narrow range for the number of true ideologies—more than one, but not too many. Another assumption is that ideology becomes more pronounced during social crisis (Higgs 1987, 47). This seems to me dependent on the prevalence of ideologies when the crisis began. A possible proviso might hold that when several well-articulated and comprehensive ideologies occupy discursive space, a crisis that defies their confident expectations could produce a scramble of ideology in favor of more pragmatic seat-of-the-pants politics. And even if such pragmatic politics can still be understood as ideological, are some political ideologies more coherent and comprehensive and thus more platonically ideological than others?

Such considerations lead one to wonder whether Higgs's formulation relies somewhat on the conditions surrounding modern political, economic, and historical discourse—whether by "modern" we mean post-Enlightenment, post–World War II, or something in between. Higgs remarks that "notwithstanding its extensive scope"—its solidaric, moral, programmatic, affective elements, its comprehensiveness and coherence—ideology "tends to revolve about only a few central values, such as individual freedom, social equality, national glory, or social security" (Higgs 2008, 548). Higgs's description of these pillars of ideology might not so easily describe what most people believed before the Reformation or Enlightenment. Before Westphalian national consciousness, did "national glory" enter into many ideologies? Was "individual freedom" a common social worldview before the 18th or even 19th century? Were "social equality" or "social security" recognizable fixtures in political thought before the 19th or even 20th? If the DNA of most visible ideologies comprise these four "central values" as their nucleotides, one wonders how primordial this life of ideology is. Is ideology itself a late-modern phenomenon? If so, are the dominant strains of aspirational collectivism and radical individualism truly progeny of the same historical moments? This would make some sense of how libertarian individualism came to truly flourish after the horrors of World War II, fascism, and communism—especially in America, where the national ethos at once defined and collectively mobilized itself in opposition to totalitarianism. Nothing better lined up with that ethos, in both patriotic harmony and radical subversion, than modern libertarianism.

Perhaps ideology itself, even in its solidaric power, is the product of an individualist era. The suggestion seems too clever by half. Yet in discussing his key concept of solidarity, Higgs emphasizes something rather self-oriented. In considering such economics-oriented "interest theories" of self-serving legitimation and "strain theories," Higgs sees solidarity as largely having an "important connection with the maintenance of personal identity" (Higgs 2008, 549–50). The groups, including ideological groups, one "chooses" to inhabit "is closely connected with the kind of person he or she takes himself or herself to be" (Higgs 2008, 550). The way people have valued personal identity has itself shifted across time and place.[12] This appeal to individual identity to bolster solidarity resonates in profoundly ironic ways with historians who have explained Rawlesian liberalism as a product of late postwar individualist retreat from the planning state (Rodgers 2011)—and it also jibes with Rorty's understanding of solidarity as something obtained through individual pursuit of the arts. The personal is political, indeed.

CONCLUSION

I may have taken this chapter into somewhat unconventional places. Among the many scholars Higgs has deeply influenced, I am discernibly on the historicist periphery, bordering on a relativism some might find unforgiveable. I indeed have some anxiety that Bob himself will find objectionable the directions I take my research. With great scholars we might associate both a blessing and a curse: as one of them, Higgs has inspired others who will for generations take his ideas into areas none of us can predict or necessarily endorse.

Fundamentally, my primary aim as a historian of the American state is to better understand how ideas, beliefs, passions, and culture have interacted with institutions, structures, and material conditions in the construction of both power and freedom. This topic's importance as well as my emphasis on qualitative analysis came into sharp focus for me when I first read *Crisis and Leviathan* in 2002, uncertain about my own future as well as the nation's as we all bore witness to the cascading momentum for waging the Iraq war. In the past 20 years Higgs's admonitions have resonated, even among ideologues. But that must not distract us from his deeper intellectual contributions to theorizing and historicizing the relationship of ideology to government power. Higgs's work demands that we take seriously the study of history itself, even as we question our own ideological assumptions, emerging as they do from the historical moment we inhabit. Bob has touched so many lives and minds, and his students will stubbornly take his ideas in strange directions while his brilliant work continues to be caricatured to serve the folk wisdom. This is the curse he will have to abide. But the blessing is all ours.

NOTES

1. I reserve "classical liberalism" for those of a bygone age; I refer to those inspired by its traditions, operating in modern context, as radical liberals.

2. Drawing on Ronald Schaffer (Schaffer 1991), Higgs cites John Henry Wigmore and Louis Brandeis (Higgs 1997).

3. In a striking example of the time *Crisis* was written, Higgs notes that "Contagious diseases . . . historically . . . caused tremendous harm; and government's public health regulations were generally framed and enforced to bring about a more efficient condition" (Higgs 1987, 9). This passage raised few eyebrows in the late 1980s but today libertarians would likely read it differently.

4. I have in casual conversation shared Higgs's definition of ideology with scholars occupying a wide range of belief, and they have found the definition resonant.

5. An exception is James Livingston's critical review of *Crisis and Leviathan*, although his discussion of Rorty in a footnote is tangential to questions of solidarity (Livingston 1988, 313n2).

6. I admit that the methodological implications might not appeal to historians working outside of the larger liberal tradition. I should give more thought to whether my attempts to protect historical rigor from ideological distortion betray a privileging of liberal ideologies, broadly construed.

7. "Strange to say it," wrote Higgs in the beginning of his foreword to a 2003 collection, but "the U.S. 'war on terrorism' has its roots in events that took place in 1898" (Higgs 2003).

8. Higgs discusses how "many persons of minority and ethnic status perceived that business enterprise offered an important opportunity for joining the mainstream of American economy life" and generally had the best "chance in the city" (Higgs 1976, 153–54). Higgs elsewhere discusses the complex challenges for Japanese immigrants as they adjusted to increasingly onerous state policies as well as local discrimination (Higgs 1978, 215).

9. Another confounding factor in the ideological relationship between anti-government liberalism and the rising progressive state is the importance of anarchist activism. See Willrich 2023.

10. On the interwar construction of free speech principles around a new consensus, both more liberal and consistently anti-state, see Weinrib 2016.

11. One way to reconcile this assumption with my own skepticism about the supposedly classical liberal 1890s is to stipulate that classical liberalism was one of the few true ideologies of prominence, and won the day by default due to the conditions of post–Reconstruction governance.

12. See a somewhat related discussion in Henrich 2020.

REFERENCES

Balogh, Brian. 2015. *The Associational State: American Governance in the Twentieth Century.* Philadelphia, PA: University of Pennsylvania Press.

Bensel, Richard Franklin. 1990. *Yankee Leviathan: The Origins of Central State Authority in America, 1859–1877.* New York: Cambridge University Press.

Berger, Peter L., and Thomas Luckmann. 1966. *The Social Construction of Reality: A Treatise in the Sociology of Knowledge.* Garden City, NJ: Doubleday.

Bourne, Randolph. 1998. *The State.* Tuscon, AZ: See Sharp Press.

Brinkley, Alan. 1998. "The Two World Wars and American Liberalism." In Alan Brinkley, *Liberalism and Its Discontents,* 79–94. Cambridge, MA: Harvard University Press.

Cohen, Nancy. 2002. *The Reconstruction of American Liberalism, 1865–1914.* Chapel Hill: University of North Carolina Press.

Gerstle, Gary. 2015. *Liberty and Coercion: The Paradox of American Government, from the Founding to the Present.* Princeton, NJ: Princeton University Press.

Gordon, Robert W. 1984. "Critical Legal Histories." *Stanford Law Review* 36: 57–125.

Gregory, Anthony. 2016. *American Surveillance: Intelligence, Privacy, and the Fourth Amendment.* Madison, WI: University of Wisconsin Press.

———. 2024. *New Deal Law and Order: How the War on Crime Built the Modern Liberal State.* Cambridge, MA: Harvard University Press.

Henrich, Joseph. 2020. *The WEIRDest People in the World: How the West Became Psychologically Peculiar and Particularly Prosperous.* London: Penguin.

Higgs, Robert. 1969. "The Growth of Cities in a Midwestern Region, 1870–1900." *Journal of Regional Science* 9 (3): 579–82.

———. 1970. "Railroad Rates and the Populist Uprising." *Agricultural History* 44 (3): 291–98.

———. 1971. "American Inventiveness, 1870–1920." *Journal of Political Economy* 79 (3): 661–67.

———. 1976. "Participation of Blacks and Immigrants in the American Merchant Class, 1890–1910: Some Demographic Relations." *Explorations in Economic History* 13: 153–64.

———. 1977. *Competition and Coercion: Blacks in the American Economy, 1865–1914.* Cambridge: Cambridge University Press.

———. 1978. "Landless by Law: Japanese Immigrants in California Agriculture to 1941." *Journal of Economic History* 38 (1): 205–25.

———. 1982. "Accumulation of Property by Southern Blacks before World War I." *American Economic Review* 72 (4): 725–37.

———. 1985. "Crisis, Bigger Government, and Ideological Change: Two Hypothesis on the Ratchet Phenomenon." *Explorations in Economic History* 22: 1–28.

———. 1987. *Crisis and Leviathan: Critical Episodes in the Growth of American Government.* Oxford: Oxford University Press.

———. 1992. "Federalism, State Action, and 'Critical Episodes' in the Growth of American Government: Reply to Ballard Campbell." *Social Science History* 16 (4): 579–82.

———. 1997. "War and Leviathan in Twentieth-Century America: Conscription as the Keystone." In *The Costs of War: America's Pyrrhic Victories,* edited by John V. Denson, 375–88. Piscataway, NJ: Transaction Publishers.

———. 2003. Foreword to *Liberty, Security, and the War on Terrorism.* Edited by Richard M. Ebeling and Jacob G. Hornberger. Fairfax, VA: Future of Freedom Foundation.

———. 2006. *Depression, War, and Cold War: Studies in Political Economy.* Oxford: Oxford University Press.

———. 2008. "The Complex Course of Ideological Change." *American Journal of Economics and Sociology* 67 (4): 547–65.

Lamis, Alexander P., Everett C. Ladd, William Schneider, Philip Meyer, and John K. White. 1990. "Symposium on the Work of Samuel Lubell." *PS: Political Science and Politics* 23 (2): 184–91.

Livingston, James. 1988. "Review: Radicals All." *Reviews in American History* 16 (2): 307–13.

Mises, Ludwig von. 1957. *Theory and History: An Interpretation of Social and Economic Evolution.* New Haven, CT: Yale University Press.

Novak, William J. 1996. *The People's Welfare: Law and Regulation in Nineteenth-Century America.* Chapel Hill: University of North Carolina Press.

Rodgers, Daniel T. 2011. *Age of Fracture.* Cambridge, MA: Harvard University Press.

Rorty, Richard. 1989. *Contingency, Irony, and Solidarity.* Cambridge: Cambridge University Press.

Schaffer, Ronald. 1991. *America in the Great War: The Rise of the War Welfare State.* New York: Oxford University Press.

Sciabarra, Chris Matthew. 2000. *Total Freedom: Toward a Dialectical Libertarianism.* University Park, PA: Penn State University Press.

Skocpol, Theda. 1995. *Protecting Soldiers and Mothers: The Political Origins of Social Policy in the United States.* Cambridge, MA: Harvard University Press.

Stanley, Amy Dru. 1998. *From Bondage to Contract: Wage Labor, Marriage, and the Market in the Age of Slave Emancipation.* Cambridge, UK: Cambridge University Press.

Weinrib, Laura. 2016. *The Taming of Free Speech: America's Civil Liberties Compromise.* Cambridge, MA: Harvard University Press.

White, Hayden. 1990. *The Content of the Form: Narrative Discourse and Historical Representation.* Baltimore: Johns Hopkins University Press.

Willrich, Michael. 2023. *American Anarchy: The Epic Struggle between Immigrant Radicals and the US Government at the Dawn of the Twentieth Century.* New York: Basic Books.

Chapter 8

The Ratchet Effect

War Powers and Presidential Unilateralism

Sarah Burns

From the beginning of the republic, Americans have always had a paradoxical self-perception. The great experiment was, at once, "an empire in many respects the most interesting in the world," as well as a peaceful republic that saw itself as morally superior to European empires. These two contrasting polarities would push and pull the United States for over 100 years as leaders struggled to decide which one to value, and which one was morally or strategically beneficial.

Those who adhered to the constraining ideology claimed the United States had to stay small to stay free. Over time and over many battles, these voices became increasingly marginalized as the expansionist ideology became attractive to a larger portion of the population. The more expansionists won, the more we see the balance of power between Congress and the country's executive shift. As the United States expanded west, east, and south, the powers that had once been co-equal rapidly became unequal. The biggest watershed moment occurred during and after the Spanish-American War in 1898. In previous eras, during a war, the powers of the president would expand, and military spending would increase. After the war, the power and military spending would contract to their pre-war levels. The events of the late 19th century, however, changed this dynamic.

This was the beginning of what Robert Higgs describes as the "ratchet effect." As he notes in his seminal work, *Crisis and Leviathan*, there was a strong "link between crisis and changes in the prevailing ideology posture" (Higgs 2013, 69). This period was a perfect storm of depressions and other economic pressures. When America entered the Spanish-American War, it solidified the establishment of the ratchet effect to set the United States on a path of growing state power (Higgs 2013).

Starting with William McKinley, presidents began taking it upon themselves to increase their powers at the expense of Congress's co-equal status. For decades, Congress fought back. This changed with the attack on Pearl

Harbor. While presidents had always tried to usurp congressional power, after World War II, Congress let them. Members of the US government collectively decided their constitutional system had to change.

As Higgs notes, "Whereas World War I was followed by relative international calm for the United States, the Big One merged almost immediately into the Cold One—not to speak of Korea, Vietnam, and assorted smaller military adventures around the world during the four decades after 1945" (Higgs 2013, 198). At this point, the ratchet effect increased dramatically. In particular, the unilateral powers of the president grew, too, especially in the realm of war as Congress after Congress authorized the expansion of a large peacetime military deployed all over the world.

The creation of such was problematic for a healthy balance of power that restrained military adventurism. Now, presidents could simply ignore congressional objections, removing any deliberation about the nature of the operation, how it should be conducted, or if it was worth conducting at all. Despite continued failures and evidence of this systemic fault, presidents often continue to make the very same mistakes in military operations again and again, regardless of their size or objective.

In this chapter, I will use Higgs's notion of the ratchet effect to show how the growth of government threatens liberty not only at home, but also abroad. In particular, we see that the ideological shift that occurred in the late 19th century combined with the Spanish-American War to change the size of the government and coincidentally sparked a steady increase in spending on the military. As time went on and the United States entered two world wars followed by the Cold War, presidents collected more and more power in their hands, and Congress allowed them to do so in two critical ways. First, they allowed presidents a lot more unilateral control over foreign policy decision-making. Second, they sanctioned the creation and maintenance of a large peacetime military. The following will offer an explanation of how that shift occurred. I will begin with a discussion of the ideological foundation of the American state. There was an ideological battle involving those like the Antifederalists, who saw America as morally superior to European states because it was a small peaceful republic that respected the right to self-rule. Others sought to expand the power of the American military, the size of the state, and its influence internationally. When combined with the racial and religious hierarchy that coexisted within American liberalism, we see an explanation for why the United States expanded into certain territories and not others. In the following sections, I discuss the sea change that occurred during the period around the Spanish-American War, the World Wars, the Cold War, and finally, the war on terror.

EARLY AMERICA

Just a few decades after securing its freedom, the United States bought a huge swath of land from France. While some feared what this expansion would do to freedom, others clamored for even more territory. Eventually termed Manifest Destiny, through aggression and through purchases the United States ultimately spanned the entire continent. Even in the 19th century, when some claim the United States was isolationist, it was clear that the imperial expansionist tendency had already started winning out over those who saw the perils to liberty, especially given the calls to expand slavery further west.

Fortunately, during this period there was still a healthy debate among the political branches. The president would dutifully come to Congress and ask for permission to purchase new territory or start a war.[1] Congress, in turn, would engage in a meaningful debate about the merits of the action, and make a decision. Subsequently, if the war effort proved questionable or problematic, Congress would again debate the prosecution of the war and hold the executive accountable. Finally, money and power would flow to the executive branch *during* an operation; at the end of the operation, spending would drop to pre-war levels, and the power balance between the political branches would be restored.

Over the course of the second half of the 18th century and most of the 19th century, there were many who tried to keep the United States small, pacific, and morally superior to the corrupt European empires with their large standing militaries maintained for the very purpose of suppressing rebellions at home and in their colonies. Men like the Antifederalist Brutus warned that a republic cannot survive over a large territory (Storing and Dry 1985, 113). Some even objected to the new powers of the federal government in the Constitution. Patrick Henry noted, "The American spirit, assisted by the ropes and chains of consolidation, is about to convert this country to a powerful and mighty empire. . . . Such a Government is incompatible with the genius of republicanism" (from Patrick Henry's June 5, 1788, speech before the Virginia Ratifying Convention, quoted in Storing and Dry 1985, 305).

After the Constitution was ratified, these voices continued to hold sway, especially during the debates over greater territorial expansion. At first, leaders like Alexander Hamilton and John Adams were against territorial expansion, advocating instead for "conventional state capacity in order to sustain the new nation's authority over a vast and vulnerable hinterland" (Adams 1821). Conversely, Thomas Jefferson and the Democratic-Republicans claimed they should decentralize power and aggressively expand the size of the United States.

The Jeffersonians were the predominant winners of this debate while the Hamiltonians and Antifederalists struggled against the growing power of western states and the sustained power of the southern slave states. Despite the Jeffersonian narrative about an agrarian republic filled with peace-loving yeoman farmers, starting with the Seminole Wars in 1818 it was clear that a sufficient number of elites were comfortable using illiberal tools like military power to assert their dominance and steal the land of others.

In the name of acquiring territory, the US government forcibly pushed the Seminoles out of their own lands and punished those who helped them attempt to defend it. In particular, Andrew Jackson aggressively expanded the displacement of Native peoples during his presidency, to provide their land to white settlers (Meacham 2009).

Anti-expansionists may have had a kind of ally in the Hamiltonians, who wanted to build the nation-state and expand *trade* rather than expand territory, but they could stop neither the expansion of the United States nor the clamor for that expansion coming from both citizens and some elites. Furthermore, Hamilton may have favored trade over expansion, but he also favored expanding the power of the US military, especially the US Navy, to protect that trade (Burns 2019, 88–95). Ideologically, those who shared Hamilton's views about trade and the military would join forces with those who wanted the United States to become an empire. In the 19th century, however, there was an added and perhaps unexpected impediment to the most ambitious expansionists. The racial and religious hierarchy that existed awkwardly alongside American liberalism stopped the United States from acquiring heavily populated areas on the continent.

THE PICKY EAGLE

Despite the consensus among many in power, the United States did not ever achieve its greatest territorial ambitions: the annexation of Canada, Mexico, and parts of the Caribbean. It expanded massively through war and aggression during the 19th century, a time when there was a consensus among imperial powers that ruling over others was justified through the prism of a racial hierarchy that placed those of European descent at the apex of civilization. What explains the rather unusual expansion pattern of the United States?

Unlike their European counterparts, Americans did not have formidable neighbors or political competitors capable of restraining them (Maass 2020, 13). Even the Europeans, who uniformly disliked US expansion, did not mount any considerable effort to impede their movement across the continent. Some historians have looked at regional clashes, especially between slave and free states, as a constraint on more aggressive expansion. In some ways, this did restrict leaders, especially those who sought to develop a large enough military to achieve such goals. In the 19th century, there was enough of a consensus that a republic cannot rule *over* a large population from a different background. This consensus would give way by the end of the 19th century.

Another restraint prior to the Civil War was nullification, especially among the slave states. Many governors claimed the power to refuse to enforce federal law, and there was little the federal government could do to stop their actions short of using the military to enforce federal laws, which threatened clashes with state militias. Along with nullification, according to Scott Silverstone, prior to the Civil War the complicated separation of powers system and varied regional interests kept the federal government from having the power to develop a large military and an ambitious foreign policy (Silverstone 2004, 59–62). This did not change dramatically right after the Civil War due to the continued divisions within the federal government, the battles among regional interests in the legislative branch, and the relative weakness of the executive branch, especially in contrast to the power asserted by the legislative branch (Hendrickson 2009, 242–85).

Despite these impediments, there were many voices in Congress calling for certain kinds of annexation, and few voices able to constrain. When looking at the congressional record, however, we don't see uniform support for all annexations. Instead, in the antebellum republic, we see enthusiastic support for annexation of areas that were sparsely populated and more reticence regarding populated areas (Maass 2020, 13–14). As Richard Maass notes, Americans may have expanded, but they were "picky eaters."

Problematically, the ideology behind the objections cannot be traced back to the principle of self-rule. What often restrained the ambition of those who sought to expand were racial and religious prejudices against populations that were not white Anglo-Saxon Protestants. American leaders in both the executive and legislative branches eschewed places like Canada due to its large French and Catholic population and the more populated parts of Mexico for similar reasons. This is why American expansion both did and did not overcome the peaceful Enlightenment principles that should have informed its policies; in practice, they only did so selectively.

Adding to these restraints was the nature of American economic growth. The diffuse nature of economic development around the country prevented Congress from solidifying control over the growing economic power of the United States and asserting a more expansionist foreign policy (Zakaria 1999,

11–12). Observing this dysfunctional state of affairs, Woodrow Wilson wrote *Congressional Government* in 1885, claiming that Congress is both too powerful compared to the executive and too disorganized to assert itself effectively (Wilson 2005).

This restraint suited the American people. As Higgs notes, if the nation is dedicated to limited government, it needs a leader with a similar inclination. In 1892, Americans elected Grover Cleveland, who demonstrated a strong adherence to this principle. He wanted to avoid having the "government . . . support the people" through welfare programs (Higgs 2013, 84). The desires of the people, however, and the state of the economy together started to change during this era. Unemployment in 1893–98 was estimated to be around 20 percent of the labor force. These unemployed men would march to Washington demanding relief, and there was an increasing push for it among politicians (Higgs 2013, 84–85).

Meanwhile, the economically powerful moved from the agricultural sectors to industry. The Gilded Age represented an unprecedented concentration of wealth in the hands of a few, fueling their capacity to influence the government to serve their industrial interests. They were not uniformly protectionist or laissez-faire. They would demand tariffs or expanded free trade (or both) depending on what suited their self-interest (Campbell 1976). The political branches underwent a sea change, as well. Power transferred from the legislative branch to the executive. The war with Spain became a flashpoint in 1898. As Woodrow Wilson notes in the forward to his 15th edition of *Congressional Government*, this war "greatly increased power" and created what he deemed an "opportunity for constructive statesmanship." As a consequence, "the new leadership of the Executive . . . will have very far-reaching effect upon our whole method of governing" (Wilson 1900). As will be discussed below, what Wilson labeled "constructive statesmanship" would receive a different title during the tenure of Lyndon Johnson and Richard Nixon. At this point it received the name it deserves: the imperial presidency (Schlesinger [1973] 2004). Whereas presidents like McKinley only reluctantly adopted the broad executive powers thrust upon him, his successor, Theodore Roosevelt, would greedily absorb as much power as possible.

THE ROOSEVELT COROLLARY

As the United States claimed to take its place among the great nations of the world, there was no president better poised to take full advantage of the newly aggrandized military and the further concentration of power in the hands of the executive. Unfortunately for Theodore Roosevelt and fortunately for the separation of powers, he did not have a major military crisis during his presidency to ratchet up executive power further. He had to content himself with more symbolic demonstrations of the changing political order.

Roosevelt sent the Great White Fleet on a global tour. There were a few objectives involved: increase the visibility of America's military power, improve relations with friendly governments, and deter Japan from threatening war (Love 2017). Beyond projecting power, he also developed the stewardship theory of the presidency and created the Roosevelt Corollary to supplement the Monroe Doctrine.

The stewardship theory states, alarmingly, that presidents can do whatever the Constitution and laws do not strictly prohibit. The expansion of presidential power to interpret laws, treaties, and the ambiguities associated with their constitutional powers would change the way presidents interpreted the Constitution moving forward (Tulis 1988). Similarly, the Roosevelt Corollary attempted to alter the meaning of the Monroe Doctrine. Where it originally claimed that European powers should respect the sovereignty of newly formed democracies in the Western Hemisphere, Roosevelt demonstrated a change in the ideology. Respect for self-determination was replaced with a justification for meddling in the internal affairs of any country. It was, allegedly, in the name of the "peace of justice," and he rationalized this change in policy by claiming there is "yet no judicial way of enforcing a right in international law." The United States would intervene if a nation "wrongs another." He tried to align it with liberal principles by claiming the United States would not do this out of "land hunger," but rather for the "welfare of all in the Western Hemisphere" (Roosevelt 1904).

It was clear that Roosevelt was asserting the power to make and apply the rules. In doing so, he was rejecting the notion that you cannot rule over others and remain free as most of the founders had thought. More disturbingly, the United States would enforce its self-interest—which it also claimed to be in the interests of all—through its own growing military power. This would get worse during the World Wars.

WOODROW WILSON AND WORLD WAR I

By the time Wilson became president, he had a well-established reputation as someone who did not adhere to the founding ideology and actively sought to place the presidency at the center of decision-making. He thought executives better represented the people and could act in their interests more effectively than the messy actions of the legislature. At the same time, there were still enough people who saw Congress as co-equal, and they struggled against his attempts at an ideological shift. The constitutional system had not yet become fully warped, so Congress still had the power to constrain presidential action. Furthermore, there was not a large standing military, so Wilson had to go to Congress to justify entering the war and receive the necessary authorization and funding.

Germany forced Wilson's hand after the sinking of the British-owned but American-occupied passenger ship *Lusitania*. He called a joint session of Congress to explain that Germany failed to respect American neutrality. He was careful, however, to maintain the American rhetoric that the nation itself was "but one of the champions of the rights of mankind." It does not seek any "conquest" or "dominion"; it does not seek "material compensation for the sacrifice [it] shall freely make"; it is merely attempting to make the world "safe for democracy" (Wilson 1917). Congress authorized the war by claiming there was a "state of war" between "the Imperial German Government and the Government and people of the United States." As a consequence, the United States declared war. Congress gave the president authority to conduct the war using the following language:

> That the president be, and he is hereby, authorized and directed to take immediate steps (not only) to put the country in a thorough state of defense, and also to exert all of its power and employ all of its resources to carry on war against the Imperial German Government and to bring the conflict to a successful termination. (US Congress 1917)

In this case, Congress gave the president permission, and precise direction. They told him what he was commanded to do, what resources he had at his disposal, who he was authorized to fight (the government, not the people of Germany, or the country Germany), and what would conclude this authorization (the end state of peace).

Nothing illustrates the expansion stage of the ratchet more clearly than the Wilson administration's conscription program and other government programs during the war. Even before the United States entered the war, Congress passed the Lever Act, which allowed the government to control the creation and distribution of food and fuel. Wilson could require anyone importing or exporting any vital products to procure a license, and he could control when they could distribute goods. The crisis of the war had convinced Congress to give the president unprecedented control over private industry out of fear that

Americans might be drawn into the war without access to the needed materials. Perhaps more significantly, the people didn't object to showing a shift from the more laissez-faire model of the late 19th century to a more socialized system of government. Similarly, the Army Appropriations Act of 1916 proved to be sufficient authorization to nationalize the railroads held by private owners once the United States entered the war (Higgs 2013, 129).

As Higgs's theory demonstrates, Wilson could go even further to shift the ideology once the United States entered the war. Existential threats to the nation facilitate these opportunistic shifts. As Higgs notes, "Wilson proposed to rearrange and strengthen some existing agencies and to fortify the reorganized bodies with an explicit statutory mandate." He asked Congress to give him this "authority . . . without the case-by-case approval of Congress," and Congress granted it (Higgs 2013, 139).

The most shocking expansion was Wilson's conscription program. Rather than calling it conscription, he claimed, "It is in no sense a conscription of the unwilling: it is, rather, selection from a nation which has volunteered in mass" (Higgs 2013, 132). Showing the depth of the ideological shift, even the more market-oriented Democrats like Secretary of the Navy Josephus Daniels claimed these expanded government controls were beneficial. He said, "We will not be afraid in peace to do revolutionary things that help mankind, seeing we have become accustomed to doing them in war" (as quoted in Higgs 2013, 156).

While we do see a ratchet effect in terms of military spending at the conclusion of World War I, fortunately, at this point, we also see that there is still a healthy balance of power between the president and Congress in the realm of war powers. At the conclusion of the war, Wilson spearheaded the movement to create the League of Nations in the hope that an international body would prevent future world wars. Without discussing the merits of that international body, when looking at how the president presented the treaty to the Senate and how it reacted, we see members of Congress attempting to maintain their position as a co-equal branch in the realm of war.

Wilson presented the 14 Points to the Senate as a *fait accompli*, instructing senators to sign the document into law without any changes. Senators pushed back because they feared that the super-sovereign body would have the power to decide when the United States used military force. They claimed the Constitution gave Congress the exclusive right to declare war in Article I, Section 8. They wanted to change the document to reflect that fact. Wilson refused, and the treaty did not pass. We see here the restraining impact of Congress maintaining its co-equal status. Presidents will always push farther and attempt to follow the logic of executive power. Like all individuals with governmental energy, they want to increase their own power. Like many leaders, they want to expand the power of their state. Congress has the power to hold the nation's leader accountable. If they guard their own power, they have to force presidents to justify their desired outcomes by requiring legislative permission for any actions that require the blood or treasure of the American people. This is exactly what the Senate did at this moment.

Rather than accept their decision, however, Wilson used the newly expanded rhetorical powers of the presidency to do a tour of the United States to rally the people to his cause. He was successful with the people, the majority of whom supported the measure. The Senate, however, stood firm. It would not give up its war powers (Burns 2019, 137–39). This would change when Franklin Roosevelt faced off against Congress during World War II.

FRANKLIN ROOSEVELT AND WORLD WAR II

At its beginning, Americans viewed World War II through a similar lens as World War I: someone else's fight. The problems seemed far away from the "fortress" of American-led North America in the eyes of the public, and Congress reflected this view. This did not hold back Franklin Roosevelt, who saw the battle with Germany and Japan as a competition between authoritarianism and liberty. For that reason, he was willing to work around the constraints placed on him by neutrality acts and other constitutional limitations. Roosevelt thought it was his duty to help the Allies in any way he could.

In some ways, Congress attempted to restrain him. It passed several neutrality acts to keep the United States out of the fight, and its stance did not falter much as Germany and Japan enjoyed remarkable success on the battlefield. Roosevelt became frustrated and started to engage in reckless and unconstitutional actions. He signed an executive order extending the American security zone further into the Atlantic. Above all, he had the intention of helping the British and daring the Germans to attack American vessels despite the Neutrality Acts explicitly stating he could not do such (Beschloss 2018, 379).

In other ways, the other branches of government behaved in the same way they did during World War I due to the compelling draw of the expansionary stage of the ratchet effect. They created the first war powers act in 1941. As Higgs notes, it gave Roosevelt the power "to redistribute functions, duties, powers, and personnel among existing executive agencies as he saw fit" (Higgs 2013, 205). By 1942, once the United States was in the war, they delegated the power to distribute "material or facilities in such manner, upon such conditions and to such extent as he shall deem necessary or appropriate in the public interest and to promote the national defense." No other Congress has ever delegated such immense economic power to a president (Higgs 2013, 206).

These, evidently, were not enough for Roosevelt. He displayed a flagrant disregard for the limitations Congress had put on his war effort. One of the most dramatic examples occurred in September 1940 when he signed the executive agreement with England to trade American destroyers for strategically important bases throughout the British empire. The decision to act unilaterally would become the first moment in US history when the president blatantly circumvented congressional war powers, in this case involving treaties. On a plain reading of the constitutional text, the Senate has to "advise and consent" on treaties. In this instance, rather than go to the Senate, Roosevelt turned to his attorney general, Robert Jackson.

Starting a long tradition of warping Article II that would eventually be dubbed the imperial presidency, Jackson claimed the deal didn't violate the Constitution (even though it circumvents the Senate's power to advise and consent). He said the president has the power as commander in chief, and this power is "not defined or limited" (Jackson 1940). He then cited the Supreme Court decision in *Curtiss-Wright* where it says the president is the "sole organ of the nation in its external relations" (299 US 304 [1936]). He said the president didn't need new legislation to sign this agreement because he was not violating existing neutrality laws. He did not have the authority to *sell* ships, but he was merely trading them (Jackson 1940). As I have noted elsewhere, "It is shocking to see how far FDR and his lawyers pushed the concept of executive power in what should have been a balanced system, with the political branches working in tandem" (Burns 2019, 147). We see in this action, and in congressional inaction, the effect of changing ideology. Whereas the Senate had stopped Wilson from becoming a member of the League of Nations, in this case the Senate did not stop Roosevelt, nor did it create legislation to restrain his unilateralism. The shift in ideology was nearly complete.

On December 7, 1941, the Japanese drew the United States into World War II. This was the proverbial breaking point for Congress. A joint session of Congress quickly passed what would be the last American declaration of war. It looked much like the WWI declaration. In it, Congress provided authorization to the president and commanded him to act. He was told what resources he had at his disposal, who he was fighting (the governments of the Axis powers), and what would end the war (see US Congress Senate Joint Resolution 1941).[2]

This is the last period wherein we see any real effort from Congress to stand up to the president and defend its co-equal status in the realm of war. Interestingly, at the end of the war when the Senate was negotiating the creation of the United Nations and the North Atlantic Treaty Organization (NATO), it did not take the same stance as the Senate had with Wilson.

As an example, Senator Warren Austin noted that if he and other senators were to sign this document, "We recognize that a breach of the peace anywhere on earth which threatens the security and peace of the world is an attack upon us." Showing a completely different perspective on the constitutional powers of the president than previous senators, he said that "the President is the officer under the Constitution in whom there is exclusively vested the responsibility for maintenance of peace" (as quoted in Burns 2019, 160, 161). Congress consented to the creation of the UN and soon after also consented to the creation of NATO.

According to American elites, the UN Security Council was a few years later thwarting American interests due in meaningful part to the Russian veto on the Security Council. To demonstrate how ambiguous the nature of the power at the UN was, however, and the power it had to declare war, it is noteworthy to look at how the international community initiated the Korean War. President Harry Truman didn't go to Congress to get a declaration of war: he would never have received one. Instead, he used the Security Council to pass a resolution authorizing the action. This should not have happened, however. The Russians opposed the war. It *could* happen because the Americans, French, and British refused to seat the new Communist representative from China on the council. They still recognized the exiled Taiwanese government as the official Chinese government. In reaction, the Russian representative, Jacob Malik, refused to attend meetings of the Security Council. He presumed the council could not conduct business without him. Instead, the four remaining members passed resolutions, which Truman used to claim he had authorization to launch the Korean War (Burns 2019, 171).

When the Russian representative was on the council, however, the UN proved to be a body incapable of many actions desired by Western allies. As a consequence, Americans and European allies wanted a defensive pact that would "keep the Russians out, the Americans in, and the Germans down," to quote Lord Ismay, the first secretary general of NATO (Hurowitz 2018). Like the League of Nations, these international bodies would usurp congressional wars—and did so very soon after their creation, in 1950 when Truman started a war in Korea without congressional permission. Unlike the League of Nations, however, members of Congress accepted this usurpation in the late 1940s.

Self-consciously and with the same power-hungry rhetoric used previously by European and Asian empires, Americans shed the restraining ideology of the Antifederalists that restrained the worst elements of the imperial impulses. The country embraced its role as an international police force, and Congress made its two most consequential moves. First, it stopped forcing presidents to seek its permission to initiate any military operation, large or small; instead, Congress provided broad grants of power. It rarely, if ever, used its power to force presidents to stop and consider the merits of their intended military operation, nor did Congress force presidents to consider whether the military was the right tool to address the problem. Second, it funded a large peacetime military that the president could send all over the world to engage in military operations at his whim. Even though the Cold War era provided a litany of poorly developed and poorly executed military actions all over the world, Congress remained passive.

While there were still members of Congress that asserted their legislative powers, it was clear that after World War II, due to a variety of circumstances, there was a consensus about a shift in the balance of power between Congress and the president. It was not presidents grasping for power. It was Congress willingly giving up its powers to the president, reducing the intended functioning of the separation of powers. The Madisonian system requires "Ambition . . . to counteract ambition" (Hamilton, Madison, and Jay 2003). If Congress shirks its responsibility, it is in the hands of the president to decide when and where he will use the military; and this is exactly what was delivered.

THE COLD WAR AND THE GULF OF TONKIN RESOLUTION

Besides Congress shirking its responsibilities starting with the Spanish-American War, we see American military spending start to ratchet up. In the decade following that war, military spending rose to $50/per capita from $2/per capita in 2020-equivalent dollars. In the 1910s, it rose to $60/per capita. It spiked in World War I but only returned to $73/per capita in the 1920s. In the following decade it increased to $153/per capita and spiked again during World War II. We do not see the same drawdown in presidential power, nor do we see a reduction of the military to pre-war standards. As Higgs notes, the Supreme Court had "acquiesced in an exercise of presidential war power that would seem to have infinite and explosive possibilities" (Higgs 2013, 224). We also don't see a serious reduction in the size of the US military. Truman asked for and Congress granted him the Selective Service Act in 1948, which continued conscription. He would use these forces two years later with the start of the Korean War (a war that was never authorized by Congress and was deemed a "police action" by the United Nations).

This occurred because the Cold War appeared to many in and out of government to be one of the worst crises the United States had ever faced. More problematically for the ratchet effect, it was a *sustained* crisis. During the Cold War, military spending exploded into thousands per capita, waffling between $2,000/per capita to $3,000/per capita. It fell briefly below $2,000/per capita during the 1990s, only to return to Cold War spending levels during the war on terror (See appendix 8.1 and figure 8.1). As Higgs explains:

> Virtually everyone who considered the matter, from influential economists, bureaucrats, and congressmen right up to Supreme Court justices and the President himself, used and accepted the validity of the moral argument: if A is all right, then X is certainly all right; where A was military conscription and X was any governmental suppression of individual rights whatsoever, especially any denial of private property rights. (Higgs 2013, 235)

It was a consequence of this newly expanded presidency that we see what would have been obvious to any member of the founding generation: if you place so much power into one set of hands, that person will be unable to avoid abusing his power. It took the failures of the Vietnam War for those in and out of government to see that providing presidents with this amount of power

Figure 8.1. Military expenditure from the Civil War to 2010

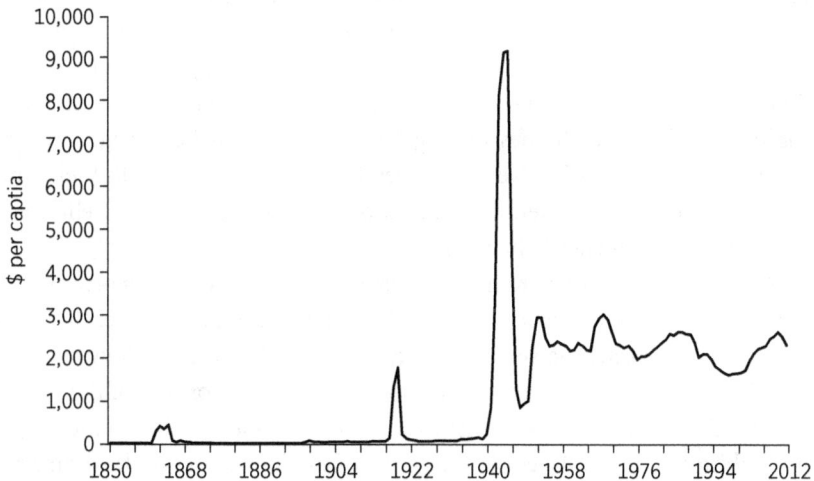

Note: The figure provides military expenditures per capita, adjusted for inflation, in 2020 dollars.

Source: See appendix 8.1.

would cause them to act in an imperial fashion and start or perpetuate wars of ambition.

For a long period after World War II, many thought of Americans as a liberator. As the narrative goes, America entered the World Wars and emerged from the second war as the only liberal democracy capable of defending that form of government (Ikenberry 2011; Herring 2011; Lundestad 1986). It *had* to create a large military to compete against the forces of communism threatening to oppress people around the world (Kennan 1946). This narrative fails to address the dramatic change to the ideology that was caused by the ratchet effect. Furthermore, this is only a portion of the story and one that many people, both domestically and internationally, see as far too generous. While many in Central and South America have long viewed American meddling for what it is, there are few nations that have suffered from America's foolish and misguided military policy more than Vietnam.

In the Americanization of the Vietnam War in 1965, we see how it is that an oversized executive with a huge standing military can create and execute extremely damaging policy. In a classic example of path dependency, President Johnson inherited the Vietnam War from the actions of his three immediate predecessors.

Despite the call for self-determination and the elimination of imperialism, Harry Truman allowed the French to keep Vietnam after World War II in order to solidify their support for NATO.[3] When the French started losing what was then Indochina, Dwight Eisenhower saw the need to support an ally (France) and maintain a partner in Asia (then Indochina) (Eisenhower 1954). John Kennedy shifted the direction somewhat, implementing a development program while still also providing some military assistance to the South Vietnamese government. The Kennedy program would end up displacing villagers from their homes, forcing them into newly created villages. When combined with the ineffective and oppressive government in South Vietnam, there was growing sentiment for unification with the North and the elimination of foreign influence (Chamberlin 2018, 185–98).

After the tragic death of Kennedy, President Johnson saw an opportunity to pass the ambitious domestic legislation Kennedy had hoped to usher through Congress. As a former powerful legislative leader, Johnson knew how to work members of Congress to craft bills associated with the concept of the Great Society. Besides the warped constitutional system and the shifted ideology, his ambition to pass this legislation is one of the root causes of the dramatic increase in the US military presence in Vietnam.

In Johnson's opinion, the reason Truman couldn't pass more legislation is because he "lost" China in 1949 when it became Communist. Johnson believed that Truman had lost his political capital. If he "lost"' South Vietnam, it would have the same impact. Adding fuel to this fire were the large US standing military, the growing military-industrial complex, the strong desire to avoid a direct fight with the Soviets, and an unswerving adherence to domino theory. Policy leaders during the Cold War staunchly believed that if one country fell to communism, the countries around it would fall as well.

When the North Vietnamese fired on the USS *Maddox* in 1965, there were few who took the time to determine whether the North Vietnamese had truly fired on the US ship twice—which they hadn't. Members of the American government claimed this second and mythologized confrontation was an unprovoked attack. This was the spark that caused Johnson to bring the Gulf of Tonkin Resolution to Congress. He wanted the political cover of receiving congressional authorization.

While there is and should be plenty of blame heaped on Johnson's shoulders for the policy he created without enough deliberation and that he implemented even more poorly, it is important to remember that Congress did not fulfill its constitutional responsibilities. Unlike the Declarations of War created in previous eras, Congress chose to create an ambiguous Authorization for the Use of Military Force (AUMF) whereby Congress claimed the president could "take all necessary measures to repel any armed attack against the forces of the United States and to prevent further aggression." More ambiguous still, "The United States regards as vital to its national interest and to world peace the maintenance of international peace and security in Southeast Asia." To keep the peace in Southeast Asia, the president could "take all necessary steps, including the use of armed force, to assist any member or protocol state of the Southeast Asia Collective Defense Treaty requesting assistance in defense of its freedom" (US Congress 1964).

We see here that Congress was not holding the president accountable, let alone telling him who to fight, what resources he had to fight them, and what a conclusion to the conflict would look like. Johnson had a free hand to make all of these decisions without significant congressional oversight. As I have noted elsewhere, "By housing so much power in the executive branch, we have come to rely heavily on the character of the president rather than relying on the moderating force of the constitutional order which maintains checks and balances" (Burns 2019, 1–2). When men lack the character to lead well, elites and citizens alike start to see the extreme consequences associated with the shifts created by the ratchet effect. We see in the Gulf of Tonkin Resolution (US Congress 1964) that it may actually be worse when Congress *does* authorize military actions because it legitimizes overly broad discretionary power by the executive. This has been made even more clear by the war on terror AUMFs.

THE 2001 AND 2002 AUMFS

Americans were well aware of radical Islamic terrorism in the 1990s. There had been a few attacks, but, generally, they were all concentrated abroad. It may even appear that the United States had yet to really shed the image of a continental fortress that had blinded it to the 1941 attack by Japan in Hawaii. Enjoying a period of peace and prosperity that did not show any signs of ending, the nation and the world were ill prepared for an event as monumental as 9/11.

The international reaction to the terrorist attacks of September 11, 2001, was overwhelmingly sympathetic to the Americans. Vladimir Putin was the first to call George W. Bush and offer his condolences. For the first time in its history, NATO triggered Article V and vowed to stand by the United States in the fight against terrorism. Congress stood behind the president, providing him with a broad grant of power to engage in this fight. He was

> authorized to use all necessary and appropriate force against those nations, organizations, or persons he determines planned, authorized, committed, or aided the terrorist attacks that occurred on September 11, 2001, or harbored such organizations or persons, in order to prevent any future acts of international terrorism against the United States by such nations, organizations or persons. (US Congress 2001)

This broad granting of power arguably shows support for a president in the middle of the worst attack on the United States since World War II. While this is a legitimate sentiment, it demonstrates how much the ideology had shifted, allowing a warping of the separation of powers system. Presidents could now exploit such crises to imbue an executive with far too much unilateral power. Congress was complicit. This legislation claims that the president has complete control over how and when to use the military force to carry out an ambiguous mission without a date of conclusion.

What does it mean to say someone "aided the terrorist attacks"? How broadly does that reach? What can a president do to prevent "future acts of international terrorism"? Congress does not answer these questions. This is the new dynamic between the branches: Congress provides endless funding for whatever presidents want without holding them accountable for military adventurism. This authorization and the subsequent one provided George W. Bush and his successors with immense power. These authorizations further demonstrate that when Congress fails to engage in its constitutional duty and instead grants the president control over decision-making, it provides political cover for poorly developed and poorly executed policy.

By the summer of 2002, the Bush administration started beating the drum for war in Iraq, claiming that Iraq had weapons of mass destruction (WMD). Due to the monumental failure of the intelligence community, the press, and the administration, there was growing support for the war (Pew Research Center 2008). Bush asked Congress for a war authorization. Many in both houses thought such an authorization would be used to perform gunboat diplomacy, likely threatening a military operation to bring Saddam Hussein to heel (Clinton 2014). Once again, we see that members of Congress failed to per-form their constitutional duties. After listing the problems caused by Hussein and the attempts by the UN Security Council to stop him, Congress authorized the president to

> Use the Armed Forces of the United States as he determines to be neces-sary and appropriate in order to 1) defend the national security of the United States against the continuing threat posed by Iraq; and 2) enforce all relevant United Nations Security Council resolutions regarding Iraq. (US Congress 2002)

The ambiguity and enormity of this grant of power are breathtaking. This is the logic of the ratchet effect. In this unprecedented move, Congress allowed the president to decide what was necessary and appropriate when it came to the use of force. The president was defending "national security." What isn't within the scope of national security? It is an umbrella term that covers a multitude of possible forms of security and ways to address them with little to constrain presidential action. It allows presidents more political cover when they want to engage in a military operation and a variety of other things (Burns 2021). The military-industrial process had already started kicking in and was developing a path to war. By March 2003, Bush had launched a military operation in Iraq.

The rest of the decade would see a civil war in Iraq followed by a surge authorized by a Democratic Congress that had taken over in the House vow-ing to drawdown the war in Iraq. We see in this authorization that members of Congress suffered from fallacious sunk-cost thinking. For them, the past costs of the Iraq war, which they could not recuperate, were a justification for incurring additional costs. The US military could not fail, even in a war of choice. Thanks to the ideological change that had been solidified during the Cold War, even the opposition will continue to fund foolish and poorly executed military operations rather than holding executives accountable for their failures.

When Barack Obama assumed office, some thought it would usher in the promised hope and change as well as the promised drawdown of the war in Iraq. Instead, we saw division and intransigence. Even more disappointing was his use of war powers. Obama claimed the war in Afghanistan was the "good war" while the war in Iraq was the "dumb war." As a consequence, he decided to create a surge in Afghanistan. Congress gave him the extra funding, once again, failing to review the plan or assess whether the extra 30,000 troops would produce the desired result. There was little scrutiny and even less evidence of what Obama hoped to achieve besides avoiding ending the war failure.

The added 30,000 troops brought the total US presence to 90,000 starting in 2012. Obama claimed the plan was to impede the growing power of the Taliban and improve the capacity of the government. There was not, however, any sign of success, so the drawdown occurred in 2014. The administration continued to justify a few thousand troops to continue fighting the determined insurgency. The war in Afghanistan would continue until 2021, without achieving any of the multiplicity of its goals. The Taliban regained power and continued its relationship with Al-Qaeda. We know the latter fact due to a US drone strike against the leader of Al-Qaeda in the summer of 2022. He was staying with Gulbuddin Hekmatyar, the Foreign Minister of Afghanistan.

Besides his actions in Afghanistan, we see a continuation of presidential unilateralism throughout Obama's presidency for smaller operations and the continued impact of the ratchet effect as power over the military concentrates further in the executive's hands while Congress shirks its responsibility. The first clear instance was the regime change in Libya. Without asking Congress and without much clarity in the mission, in March 2011 Obama casually announced that NATO allies were going to create a no-fly zone in Libya for the sake of "national security" and "regional stability" (as quoted in Burns 2017). While claiming this publicly, the administration prepared for regime change (Burns 2019). Libya remains unstable to this day.

Simultaneously, the Syrian leader, Bashar al Assad, continues to crack down on his people; but unlike Muamar Qaddafi, he has close allies in Iran and Russia. As a consequence, NATO has decided not to act, allowing a civil war to draw out for years. This instability has a variety of consequences, from the refugee crisis to the growing influence of Iran in the region. By far the most consequential result for international security, however, has been the rise of the Islamic State. Starting in 2013, this group split from Al-Qaeda and became a more violent force. The world was stunned when the Islamic State took the dam at Mosul in the summer of 2014 and started to claim that it is a sovereign state (Gerges 2017). Obama immediately deployed a US military force in Iraq to address the very real threat. The American-trained and -equipped Iraqi military had run away from the fight.

Once again, we saw Congress shirking its responsibility and the president acting unilaterally to address an issue. Jack Goldsmith notes an interesting decision in the administration. Each time the United States deployed the air force in the summer of 2014, Obama submitted a new letter to Congress. Goldsmith postulated that Obama was trying to reset the War Powers Resolution clock each time. By that fall, however, he changed tactics (Goldsmith 2014). Here we see the lasting impact of Congress providing a broad and ambiguous grant of power. Obama used the 2001 and 2002 AUMFs to claim he had congressional authority to combat ISIS (Burns 2019). True to its warped position within the constitutional system, Congress did not push back against this claim. Presidents Trump and Biden have used the AUMFs to carry out a variety of operations. Congress has made limited and entirely unsuccessful attempts at creating a new law that would restrict presidential unilateralism or restrain their military actions.

CONCLUSION

There were arguably six important moments in which we see the United States commit questionable actions to increase the size or power of the state, and these began to warp the separation of powers to place more power in the hands of the executive. The first three are found in the 19th century. These are the Mexican-American War, the Civil War, and the Spanish-American War. The most consequential of these was the Spanish-American War. As Higgs notes, "The underlying behavioral structure," in this case the comparative restraint on US imperial actions, "could not revert to its prior condition" (Higgs 2013, 59). As time progressed, these problems compounded as the ratchet effect continued to facilitate a shift in ideology among those who exercised political power.

The United States' military spending changed as if a release valve had opened, and those with imperial ambitions dominated policy while those who wanted to maintain a small pacific republic were pushed to the side. Military spending did not return to pre-war levels. It stayed higher and then ballooned during the Cold War and remained at that level to the present day, only to take a brief dip in the 1990s.

The Spanish-American War changed how the United States perceived itself in the world and how it acted in foreign affairs. Following this shift, the United States defeated a European empire, annexed Hawaii and Puerto Rico, forced Cuba to accept humiliating terms that favored Americans, and started a lengthy war of oppression against Filipinos trying to rid their state of foreign influence.

While it did not possess the number of territories of the French or English empires, Americans were, in no uncertain terms, an imperial power ruling over foreign people without their consent and against their will. This war set the United States on a fundamentally different path and initiated the ratchet effect in the expansion of government power, most perniciously in the executive and the military. The culmination of the ambitions of those who wished to see a more powerful state with an enormous military would take another 45 years, however, as the anti-imperialist sentiments in and out of government kept the size and scope of American government somewhat contained. There would be another ratchet effect after World War I, followed by an enormous one after World War II. At this point, the ideology within government and the nation had shifted. Presidents collected more power in their hands, and Congress no longer resisted presidents acting as the dominant power. This compounded the power executives already enjoyed in foreign affairs, and military affairs in particular. Congress continued to authorize a large and growing standing peacetime military.

After this point, the Cold War represents the opposite of what John Lewis Gaddis called the Long Peace. The stalemate between the United States and the Soviet Union took the fighting into other parts of the world in order to ensure there was not a direct war between the two powers. Finally, the war on terror marks the end of what may have been an opportunity for Congress to reassert itself and the possibility that the United States would draw down its international military presence. Arguably more problematic than the Cold War, the war on terror demonstrates an explosion of executive unilateralism and congressional acquiesce alongside a dramatic expansion of failed or less than effective military activities around the world.

There have been a few attempts to reverse or at least slow down this ideological shift. Early in the 20th century, commercial leaders such as Andrew Carnegie created the Anti-Imperialist League, but they had limited success. As time went on, many of these voices became fringe elements of the political class. But there were some efforts to address the growing militarism. Eisenhower warned of the military-industrial complex. Jimmy Carter tried to reduce the US military presence abroad. Walter Mondale tried to continue Carter's focus on diplomacy and force reduction, only to see the American people soundly reject that message in the 1984 election. They preferred Ronald Reagan's continued promise of "peace through strength." Since that time, Republicans and Democrats alike echo Reagan's message. The number of vested interests pushing for the United States to maintain a large and well-equipped military stationed all over the world far outweighs those calling for its reduction.

What, if anything, can be done about presidential unilateralism and overspending on the military? There was some hope in the Trump era that Congress would reassert itself more aggressively. There were a few instances where it did, as with the passage of sanctions against Russian actors who meddled in the 2016 election. Congress did not, however, use the opportunity to reevaluate its decision to remain a secondary player in the realm of war.

It is possible, however, that the current chaos is due to the end of a political era. As Stephen Skowronek noted, presidents exist within what he calls "political time." Leaders like Abraham Lincoln and Franklin Roosevelt fundamentally reshaped the politics around them and created a new ideological moment that lasted for decades (Skowronek 1997). According to Jack Balkin, we are at the end of the Reagan era. He notes that at the end of an era, the ideologically dominant power can no longer use the political branches to effectively govern, so it turns to the courts. We saw the Republican Party doing this aggressively throughout Donald Trump's time in office at every level of the federal system (Levinson and Balkin 2019).

It is possible that if we are at the end of an era, there could be a leader or group of leaders actually dedicated to the concept of limited government. Like Grover Cleveland or Jimmy Carter, the desire to restrain the government and keep it more restrained still exists among the American people and among some political elites. However, just how to elevate these individuals and what it would take for them to succeed is an important question. At present, it appears increasingly unclear who would act in this way and how might the body politic elevate them.

APPENDIX 8.1

References for Data on US Wars

- **Correlates of War Project** was the primary source of data on US national level production and consumption.

- **Inflation** was calculated using average yearly values since 1913, using the US government Bureau of Labor Statistics (BLS) Consumer Price Index (CPI) obtained from the Official Data Foundation, https://www .officialdata.org/current-inflation-rate. Inflation data from 1634 to 1912 is sourced from a historical study conducted by political science professor Robert Sahr at Oregon State University and from the American Antiquarian Society, http://oregonstate.edu/cla/polisci/sahr /sahr [no longer available].

- Historical data used to create the timeline and make determinations needed to categorize and analyze US military actions was derived from the sources in the reference list.

NOTES

1. Thomas Jefferson purchased Louisiana prior to asking permission, but he assumed if Congress did not see the value of the purchase, it could impeach him or at least refuse to pay for it. John Tyler may have asked Congress to annex Texas, but it was done under dubious circumstances and Congress reluctantly agreed. Finally, as will be discussed below, James Polk lied to Congress by saying the Mexicans had killed Americans on American soil when in fact he had ordered them into disputed territory with the intention of agitating the Mexican soldiers.

2. Some are puzzled by the fact that the United States has five declared wars and yet there are 11 declarations of war. Congress passes an individual declaration against each belligerent *government* to clarify that the United States is at war with each government rather than allow more ambiguity. This practice fell by the wayside with the Authorizations for the Use of Force starting with the Gulf of Tonkin Resolution and the subsequent authorizations against Iraq in 1991 and 2002, and against those individuals associated with the attack on 9/11 in 2001.

3. The French were equivocating on the decision to join NATO. Truman knew he needed their support to make NATO viable (Chamberlin 2018). He traded the goal of self-determination and an end to imperialism for a large military alliance with Western European countries that saw the permanent deployment of over 3 million troops in various countries. West Germany alone saw the deployment of over 2 million members of the military through all of the Cold War, only to see the number halved in the 1990s and continue to reduce from there, but never falling below several hundred deployed at a time (Kane 2006).

REFERENCES

Adams, John Quincy. 1821. "Address on U.S. Foreign Policy." Presidential Rhetoric. http://www .presidentialrhetoric.com/historicspeeches/adams_jq/foreignpolicy.html.

American Antiquarian Society. 2007. *Robert Sahr, Inflation Study 1634–2000.* http://oregonstate .edu/cla/polisei/sahr/sahr [no longer available].

Beschloss, Michael. 2018. *Presidents of War.* New York: Crown.

Burns, Sarah. 2017. "Debating War Powers: Battles in the Clinton and Obama Administrations." *Political Science Quarterly* 132 (2): 203–23.

———. 2019. *The Politics of War Powers: The Theory and History of Presidential Unilateralism.* Lawrence: University Press of Kansas.

———. 2021. "Legalizing a Political Fight: Congressional Abdication of War Powers in the Bush and Obama Administrations." *Presidential Studies Quarterly* 51 (3): 462–91. https://doi.org /10.1111/psq.12729.

Campbell, Charles S. 1976. *Transformation of American Foreign Relations, 1865–1900.* New York: Harper Collins.

Chamberlin, Paul Thomas. 2018. *The Cold War's Killing Fields: Rethinking the Long Peace.* New York: Harper.

Clinton, Hillary Rodham. 2014. *Hard Choices: A Memoir.* New York: Simon and Schuster.

Conference of Army Historians. 2008. *The U.S. Army and Irregular Warfare 1775–2007, Selected Papers from the 2007 Conference of Army Historians.* Edited by Richard G. Davis. Washington, DC: US Army Center of Military History.

Congressional Research Service. 2002. *CRS-RL30172, Instances of Use of United States Armed Forces Abroad, 1798–2001.* Washington, DC: Congressional Printing Office.

———. 2010. *CRS-RL32170, Instances of Use of United States Armed Forces Abroad, 1798–2009.* Washington, DC: Congressional Printing Office.

Correlates of War Project. (1963) 2021. *Data Sets.* https://correlatesofwar.org/.

Department of Defense. 2021. *DOD Global War on Terrorism Service (GWOT-S) Medal—Approved Operations.* Washington, DC: Office of the Under Secretary of Defense for Personnel and Readiness.

Eisenhower, Dwight. 1954. "The President's News Conference (March 10)." American Presidency Project. http://www.presidency.ucsb.edu/ws/index.php?pid=10177.

Gerges, Fawaz. 2017. *ISIS: A History,* rev. ed. Princeton, NJ: Princeton University Press.

Goldsmith, Jack. 2014. "A New Tactic to Avoid War Powers Resolution Time Limits?" Lawfare. September 2. https://www.lawfareblog.com/new-tactic-avoid-war-powers-resolution-time-limits.

Hamilton, Alexander, James Madison, and John Jay. 2003. *The Federalist Papers.* Edited by Clinton Rossiter and Charles R. Kesler. New York: Signet Classics.

Hendrickson, David C. 2009. *Union, Nation, or Empire: The American Debate over International Relations, 1789–1941.* Lawrence: University Press of Kansas.

Herring, George C. 2011. *From Colony to Superpower: U.S. Foreign Relations since 1776.* New York: Oxford University Press.

Higgs, Robert. 2013. *Crisis and Leviathan: Critical Episodes in the Growth of American Government,* 25th anniversary ed. Oakland, CA: Independent Institute.

Hurowitz, Richard. 2018. "What Is NATO For?" *Washington Examiner* (blog). July 25. https://www .washingtonexaminer.com/weekly-standard/what-is-the-purpose-of-nato-keep-the-russians -out-the-americans-in-and-the-germans-down.

Ikenberry, G. John. 2011. *Liberal Leviathan: The Origins, Crisis, and Transformation of the American World Order.* Princeton, NJ: Princeton University Press.

Jackson, Robert H. 1940. "Opinion on Exchange of Over-Age Destroyers for Naval and Air Bases." *American Journal of International Law* 34 (August): 728.

Kane, Tim. 2006. "Global U.S. Troop Deployment, 1950-2005" (May 24). Available at SSRN: https://ssrn.com/abstract=1146649 or http://dx.doi.org/10.2139/ssrn.1146649.

Kennan, George. 1946. "The Long Telegram." National Security Archives. https://nsarchive2.gwu .edu/coldwar/documents/episode-1/kennan.htm.

Legends of America. 2021. *Indian Wars List and Timeline.* https://www.legendsofamerica.com/na -indianwartimeline/.

Levinson, Sanford, and Jack M. Balkin. 2019. *Democracy and Dysfunction.* Chicago: University of Chicago Press.

Love, Robert W. 2017. *History of the U.S. Navy: 1775–1941*. Reprint. Mechanicsburg, PA: Stackpole Books.

Lundestad, Geir. 1986. "Empire by Invitation? The United States and Western Europe, 1945–1952." *Journal of Peace Research* 23 (3): 263–77.

Maass, Richard W. 2020. *The Picky Eagle: How Democracy and Xenophobia Limited U.S. Territorial Expansion*. Ithaca, NY: Cornell University Press.

Meacham, Jon. 2009. *American Lion: Andrew Jackson in the White House*. New York: Random House.

Peters, V. B. 1979. *The Florida Wars*. Hamden, CT: Archon Books.

Pew Research Center. 2008. "Public Attitudes toward the War in Iraq: 2003–2008." *Pew Research Center* (blog), March 19. http://www.pewresearch.org/2008/03/19/public-attitudes-toward -the-war-in-iraq-20032008/.

Phillips, C., and A. Axelrod. 2005. *Encyclopedia of Wars*. 3 vols. New York: Facts On File.

Ramsey, R. D. 2006. *OP19 Advice for Advisors: Suggestions and Observations from Lawrence to the Present*. Fort Leavenworth, KS: Combat Studies Institute Press.

Roosevelt, Theodore. 1904. "3rd Annual Message to Congress." National Archives and Records. https://www.archives.gov/milestone-documents/roosevelt-corollary.

Schlesinger, Arthur M. (1973) 2004. *The Imperial Presidency*. Reprint. Boston: Mariner Books.

Silverstone, Scott A. 2004. *Divided Union: The Politics of War in the Early American Republic*. Ithaca, NY: Cornell University Press.

Skowronek, Stephen. 1997. *The Politics Presidents Make: Leadership from John Adams to Bill Clinton*, rev. ed. Cambridge. MA: Belknap Press.

Storing, Herbert J., and Murray Dry. 1985. *The Complete Anti-Federalist*. Chicago: University of Chicago Press.

Tulis, Jeffrey K. 1988. *The Rhetorical Presidency*. Princeton, NJ: Princeton University Press.

US Army Center of Military History. 2021. *The Campaigns of the U.S. Army*. https://history.army .mil/html/topics/campaigns/index.html.

US Congress. 1917. "Declaration of War against Germany, S.J. Res 1." https://www.senate.gov /about/resources/pdf/sjres1-wwi-germany.pdf.

———. 1964. "Tonkin Gulf Resolution (H.J. Res 1145)." National Archives and Records. https:// www.archives.gov/milestone-documents/tonkin-gulf-resolution#:~:text=It%20stated%20 that%20%22Congress%20approves,President%20Nixon%2C%20relied%20on%20the.

———. 2001. "Authorization for the Use of Military Force, Public Law 107–40." Washington, DC: US Government Printing Office.

———. 2002. "Authorization for the Use of Military Force, Public Law 107–243."

US Congress Senate Joint Resolution. 1941. "Declaration of War against Japan, S.J. Res. 116." https://www.senate.gov/artandhistory/history/common/image/SJRes116_WWII_Japan.htm.

War-Memorial.net. 2021. *Wars since 1900*. http://war-memorial.net/wars_all.asp?q=3.

Wilson, Woodrow. 1900. *Congressional Government*, 15th ed. New York: Houghton Mifflin. https:// www.gutenberg.org/files/35861/35861-h/35861-h.htm.

———. 1917. "Transcript of Joint Address to Congress Leading to a Declaration of War against Germany." Our Documents. https://www.ourdocuments.gov/doc.php?flash=true&doc =61&page=transcript.

———. 2005. *Woodrow Wilson: The Essential Political Writings*. Edited by Ronald Pestritto. Lanham, MD: Lexington Books.

Zakaria, Fareed. 1999. *From Wealth to Power: The Unusual Origins of America's World Role*. Princeton, NJ: Princeton University Press.

Chapter 9
Crisis and Hydra
The Ratchet Effect and Government Control over Money and Banking

Jonathan Newman

I n *Crisis and Leviathan*, Robert Higgs (1987) shows that government expands nonlinearly. Higgs analyzes the timing of new US government programs, laws, executive orders, budgets, court decisions, regulations, public sector employment, and taxation throughout the 20th century, and finds that crisis episodes bring about "Bigger Government." While there is certainly some underlying secular institutional creep as politicians and bureaucrats behave predictably according to their incentives, the size and scope of government spike during times of crisis, well above the trend. As the crisis period subsides, the government never returns to the status quo, not only compared to the pre-crisis levels, but also compared to the pre-crisis growth trend. According to Higgs, an important reason for this "partial retrenchment" is the post-crisis ideological change toward more tolerance of expanded government. In *Crisis and Leviathan*, Higgs discusses the topics of inflation and monetary policy, like the advent of the purely fiat US dollar and the creation of the Federal Reserve, but they are in the background of the broader analysis. This chapter brings these issues to the forefront by applying Higgs's analytical framework to the topic of money and banking.

Higgs's analysis of government growth employs three main ideas: the Crisis Hypothesis, the ratchet effect, and the Cost-Concealment Hypothesis. The Crisis Hypothesis "maintains that under certain conditions national emergencies call forth extensions of government control over or outright replacement of the market economy" (Higgs 1987, 19). Wars and economic crises are common culprits. Indeed, Higgs's work is centered around three major episodes: World War I, the Great Depression, and World War II. The Crisis Hypothesis hinges on acute changes in public opinion at the onset of a crisis. When survival is at stake—whether the survival of the nation at war or the financial survival of individual households during the bust phase of a business cycle—

public opinion changes dramatically in a way that favors or at least tolerates government intervention.

Higgs points to thought leaders that corral and reflect public opinion: "Ideologies reveal themselves most clearly in the crisis-time pronouncements of opinion leaders" (1987, 55); the speeches and texts of these opinion leaders comprise an important part of Higgs's data. In each episode, Higgs shows how the effect of the changes in public opinion during a crisis is that long-standing constitutional limitations are discarded (1987, 17–18), many times with the expectation that the intervention will only be temporary. This contributes to a "ratchet effect," such that the size and scope of government does not return to the pre-crisis trend.

In introducing the concept of the ratchet effect, Higgs quoted William Graham Sumner: "It is not possible to experiment with a society and just drop the experiment whenever we choose. The experiment enters into the life of the society and never can be got out again" (Sumner, quoted in Higgs 1987, 58). While a popular explanation for the permanence of government growth points to "entrenched bureaucrats, their clients, and connected politicians" (Higgs 1987, 73), Higgs notes that a complete explanation of the ratchet effect must include the acquiescence of the public with the crisis in hindsight. Thus, ideological changes explain both the expansion of government in the crisis and the impossibility of a symmetric contraction after the crisis. The government's actions during a crisis set both legal and attitudinal precedents. According to Higgs, "The underlying behavioral structure could not revert to its prior condition because the events of the crisis created new understandings of and new attitudes toward governmental action; that is, each crisis altered the ideological climate" (1987, 59).

Even though the public demands government growth during times of crisis, this is not enough to account for the enormous expansion of government that occurs. Everything comes at a cost, especially when the public wants the government to "'do something,' and to do it immediately" (Higgs 1987, 64). Government officials understand that while the public demands new government interventions in a crisis, they are not willing to pay the tax bill. If the costs of the new government interventions are directly and transparently imposed on the citizenry via taxation, this would temper their intense demands. Thus, Higgs offers a Cost-Concealment Hypothesis as a factor contributing to the dramatic expansion of government during a crisis.

> Inability to levy taxes and then purchase on the open market everything it wishes to use in carrying out its policy shows that the government values the activity more than the citizens, that it takes from them coercively

more than they are willing to supply voluntarily at a free-market price. The government might get away with such takings because . . . the costs are concealed so that politically influential citizens fail to appreciate the magnitude of the burden even though they bear much of it. (1987, 67)

In what follows, I apply these three concepts (the Crisis Hypothesis, ratchet effect, and Cost-Concealment Hypothesis) to government control over money and banking. I consider four applications: (1) government control over money and banking is by itself an example of expanded government scope, since both money and banking could be (and have been) provided in private markets; (2) inflation and debt monetization allow the government to conceal, delay, and distribute the costs of government actions during a crisis; (3) the government's use of inflation to conceal costs in one crisis leads to another crisis, as explained by Austrian business cycle theory; (4) finally, inflation leads to psychological and cultural changes that further encourage the public's acceptance of government intervention, exacerbating the ratchet effect.

While Higgs treated crises as exogenous, I offer an endogenous view of crises, and therefore a dynamic, self-feeding ratchet effect. Austrian business cycle theory presents one mechanism by which one crisis results in another crisis. Austrian business cycle theory explains that artificial credit expansion creates an unsustainable boom that ends in a bust, and that if the government responds to the economic crisis with more intervention, as Higgs's overwhelmingly validated hypothesis predicts, then the cycle begins again.

Another mechanism by which the ratchet effect is self-feeding works through the psychological and cultural consequences of inflation. As Hülsmann (2008) and Salerno (2013) explain, inflation has far-reaching implications, beyond the economic consequences on prices, economic calculation, and the business cycle. The deterioration of human personality and social institutions creates a dependent and vulnerable population that is more tolerant of government expansion in crises. Thus, government control of money and banking is more than just an example of the ratchet effect—it institutionalizes and intensifies the ratchet effect through both economic and ideological means.[1]

In the conclusion, we will consider the bank war between Andrew Jackson and the Bank of the United States as a possible exception to the ratchet effect rule. Political cartoonists at the time depicted the central bank as a many-headed Hydra monster, which betrays a view of central banking (and, more broadly, government control over money and banking) as an indomitable foe. Nevertheless, Jackson was victorious, which offers a glimmer of hope for proponents of limited government and a free society.

GOVERNMENT CONTROL OVER MONEY AND BANKING

There is a wide literature on the theory and history of money and banking that confirms that both money and banking are market institutions that have been appropriated by governments for their own purposes (Menger 1892; Mises [1953] 2009; Salerno 2010; Selgin 1988; Rothbard 2002; Rothbard 2008; White 1999). Menger showed that money originates from market participants overcoming the double coincidence of wants problem of barter by discerning that some goods (eventually one good) have superior "saleableness." Market participants begin using the especially saleable good as a medium of exchange to have greater success in obtaining the goods they desire (Menger 1892). Banking services also originate on the market as individuals demand secure storage and management of their money (like gold) or other banking services, such as a convenient way to "undertake large or distant exchanges" (Selgin 1988, 19).

Despite the fact that money and banking originated in the market economy, governments have commandeered these institutions to serve their own interests. Let us consider a few historical examples of expanded government control of money and banking in crisis episodes. Higgs (1987) notes that the crises that trigger the ratchet are usually wars or financial crises, so we will consider both.

Wars

Murray Rothbard (2002) outlined the US colonies' experiments with paper fiat money from the late 17th to the early 18th century. The typical historical experience flows this way:

1. A government incurs huge debts by waging war.

2. The war does not yield the anticipated spoils that could have been used to repay the debts.

3. The government tries to convince soldiers and other debt holders to accept paper with the promise of future redemption.

4. Redemption is postponed and ultimately defaulted upon, while the government continues the cycle with additional wars and paper inflation.

5. The decrease in demand for paper money causes the government to enact legal tender laws and other controls with strict enforcement to keep the paper money in use.

Rothbard summarizes, "Dramatic inflation, shortage of specie, massive depreciation despite compulsory par laws—ensued in each colony" (2002, 53–54). Of course, large debts were incurred during other pre-20th-century wars involving the United States, with similar results. For example, both the War of 1812 and the War Between the States brought about pivotal precedents in the form of outlawing state banknotes, unbacked currencies, and inflation (Rothbard 2002, 122–23). Wars in the 20th century were not exceptions to this rule, either, as Higgs shows in *Crisis and Leviathan*. For example, Higgs outlines the provisions of the Second War Powers Act, enacted in 1942.

> Title IV of the act liberalized the authority of the Federal Reserve System to purchase government securities "without regard to maturities either in the open market or directly from" the Treasury. This allowed the Treasury to use the Fed as a de facto printing press, which it did on an enormous scale to help finance the government's gargantuan deficits. (1987, 206)

He notes that the lack of ordinary tax revenue required that the government impose "the hidden tax of inflation" and that rising prices gave Roosevelt the political leeway to impose price controls (1987, 207). Intervention begets intervention.[2]

The ratchet effect is on full display in these examples. The government goes to war, and the size and scope of government expand in the form of debt, spending, and the powers associated with delaying and defaulting on debt. A chain of interventions, including legal tender laws, follows in the aftermath of the crisis of war, leaving a lasting impact on the laws and attitudes of the populace. Importantly, these examples also show that government control over money and banking expands even if the precipitating crisis is not primarily economic or financial in nature.

Economic Crises

Governments also exert control over money and banking institutions during economic crises. The Federal Reserve's response to the financial crisis of 2008 included unprecedented actions in both size and scope. The Federal Reserve's balance sheet quintupled in size from 2008 to 2014, along with a flurry of new "policy tools" that were announced and implemented, representing a momentous shift from the status quo. As Murphy (2010) notes, the Federal Reserve's actions during the 2008 crisis align precisely with Higgs's *Crisis and Leviathan* thesis.

> We see Higgs's thesis of the ratchet effect on brilliant display with the Federal Reserve in the wake of the financial crisis of 2008. . . . It's difficult to imagine it now, but just three years ago it would have been inconceivable that the Fed would quickly double the monetary base, or would start buying nongovernment assets in an attempt to rescue specific markets. Most homeowners wouldn't have expected that Fed chairman Bernanke would be buying their mortgages, either.
>
> Yet all of this came to pass, largely spurred by the worldwide financial panic of September 2008. Since then, the Fed has started a wide range of new programs, and it has been busy creating and testing its arsenal of "unconventional policy measures," or what are simply called the Fed's "tools." (Murphy 2010)

Indeed, the Federal Reserve acquired a range of new "policy tools" in the 2008 financial crisis and subsequent recession. These include paying interest on reserve balances, new facilities like the Overnight Reverse Repurchase Agreement Facility and the Term Deposit Facility, buying and selling assets other than Treasury securities (like mortgage-backed securities), and purchasing assets in unprecedentedly large quantities (called "Quantitative Easing").[3] While some of these tools were allowed to expire, many remain in effect today.

Moreover, the Federal Reserve's overall scope and posture toward the economy has widened and come to the forefront of financial news media. The Fed is no longer in the background—investors, borrowers, lenders, and many consumers wait with bated breath for the Federal Open Market Committee's press releases, which announce new targets for the Federal Funds Rate and new rounds of open market purchases in the order of billions of dollars. Consider this example of boilerplate daily reporting on the stock market: "Stock market today: Wall Street swings to mixed close as Fed hints of rate hikes to come" (Kageyama 2023). This heightened interest in the Fed's announcements is also evidenced by Google Trends data; figure 9.1 shows that the search term "FOMC meeting" spiked during times of economic uncertainty, including 2007–08 and 2022–23, but the search interest in the latter period is much higher than it was before (Google Trends 2022).

The Federal Reserve has grown into a position of great influence over financial markets. Instead of evaluating firms' profitability, investors look to the Fed as a "Big Player" with an outsized influence on the market. Koppl (2002) documents the way the Fed attained this position in a stepwise fashion (much like a ratchet) via successive "regime shifts" punctuated by crises.

Figure 9.1. Google Trends search interest for "FOMC Meeting"

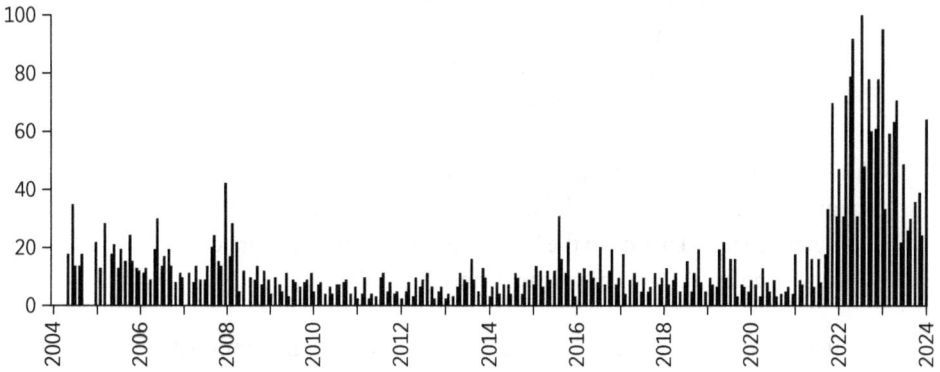

Source: Created by author.

Following each shift to a new regime, there was a significant period of experimentation and modification on the part of the Federal Reserve policymakers as they sought the best way to implement their new objectives. During these periods, the market was characterized by greater uncertainty, as small players could not clearly distinguish signals reflecting discretionary interventions from those reflecting shifts in underlying economic fundamentals. Furthermore, following a shift, the market would reward entrepreneurs who could correctly anticipate the actions of the Big Player, resulting in a reallocation of resources toward "Fed watching." ... Likewise, private actors' market expectations would now have to be based not only on their theories of what the market would do in the absence of intervention, but also on their theories of what the Fed would do. (Koppl 2002, 188)

Executive Orders during Crises

Both FDR and Richard Nixon exploited crises and conjured scapegoats in their own incursions against sound money. FDR invoked a "national emergency" of gold hoarding in his executive order to confiscate private citizens' gold.

By virtue of the authority vested in me by Section 5 (b) of the Act of October 6, 1917, as amended by Section 2 of the Act of March 9, 1933, entitled "An Act to provide relief in the existing national emergency in banking, and for other purposes," in which amendatory Act Congress declared that a serious emergency exists, I, Franklin D. Roosevelt,

President of the United States of America, do declare that said national emergency still continues to exist and pursuant to said section do hereby prohibit the hoarding of gold coin, gold bullion, and gold certificates within the continental United States by individuals, partnerships, associations and corporations. (Roosevelt 1933)

And Nixon closed the Bretton Woods system, reneging on the US government's promise to redeem dollars for gold for foreign governments. In so doing, he assigned blame to the "international money speculators" who "have been waging an all-out war on the American dollar."

In the past 7 years, there has been an average of one international monetary crisis every year. Now who gains from these crises? Not the workingman; not the investor; not the real producers of wealth. The gainers are the international money speculators. Because they thrive on crises, they help to create them.

In recent weeks, the speculators have been waging an all-out war on the American dollar. The strength of a nation's currency is based on the strength of that nation's economy—and the American economy is by far the strongest in the world. Accordingly, I have directed the Secretary of the Treasury to take the action necessary to defend the dollar against the speculators.

I have directed Secretary Connally to suspend temporarily the convertibility of the dollar into gold or other reserve assets, except in amounts and conditions determined to be in the interest of monetary stability and in the best interests of the United States. (Nixon 1971)

These executive orders demonstrate more than the mere encroachment of government into money and banking matters. They also serve as the texts of opinion leaders, providing a view of the ideological grounds for the government's expansion. Higgs (1987) relies on such texts to highlight the changes in public opinion that drive the ratchet effect.

Opinion leaders are the producers and distributors of (a limited number of) ideologies; the masses are mainly consumers. This fact—if indeed the assumption is valid—creates an opportunity to view ideologies. Although one cannot hope to penetrate the minds of the millions, certainly not in much detail, one can ascertain with some reliability the publicly expressed beliefs of the important elite disseminators of ideological messages. (45)

Both executive orders characterize the scapegoated groups as profiteering and self-serving: "gold hoarders" and "international money speculators." The executive orders malign these groups and imply that they are exacerbating and exploiting the crisis to enrich themselves at the expense of their neighbors. Of course, in both instances, neither group was the root cause of the crisis in which they were involved, and their actions (holding and withdrawing their own gold or trading currencies) were not only within their rights but were reasonable responses to the incentives they faced. Nevertheless, providing such scapegoats allowed FDR and Nixon to corral public opinion, making use of both "grand classes" of economic debates identified by Higgs: one over the "character of the economic order" (e.g., "capitalism versus socialism") and the other over distributional conflicts (often posed in terms of "the rich versus the poor") (Higgs 1987, 43–44).

INFLATION AND COST-CONCEALMENT

While government officials may find that public opinion demands quick action by the government, even bypassing constitutional processes that would slow such action, it is "something else to carry out the plan when it requires widespread compliance or sacrifice" (Higgs 1987, 64). Higgs notes that "it behooves a government wishing to sustain a policy that entails suddenly heightened costs to find ways of substituting nonpecuniary for pecuniary costs. The substitution may blunt the citizens' realization of how great their sacrifices really are and hence diminish their protests and resistance" (65). In a crisis, the public demands immediate government action, and government officials are happy to oblige, but the tax bill for such action would shock even the most fervent supporters. Thus, Higgs explains that government officials must (1) impose costs by force, (2) distribute costs to the politically weak, or (3) conceal costs (1987, 67). Higgs considers the last option the most likely, though all three can be seen in the major US crisis episodes he dissects, and all three are accomplished by monetary inflation.

Monetary Inflation as Government Force

Inflation (properly defined) always originates outside the market. As Hansen and Newman conclude, "Inflation is always and everywhere an interventionist phenomenon," and this is in accordance with the older meaning of the term (2023, 167). The original definition of *inflation* made a distinction between the supply of money and the stock of specie backing it up. Inflation was an "undue expansion or increase of the currency of a country, esp. by the issuing of paper money not redeemable in specie" (Hazlitt 1960, cited in Hansen and Newman 2023). This implies that an increase in the stock of gold in a gold standard does not constitute inflation, even if it does represent an increase in the supply of money. Only an increase in fiat paper or fiduciary media represents an inflation with the corresponding distortive Cantillon effects[4] and initiation of the boom-bust cycle. Even if one does not accept this older definition of inflation, governments cannot create gold ex nihilo, which means that the only way the government can surreptitiously impose the immense costs of its actions in a crisis via monetary expansion is by issuing paper money in excess of the stock of gold.

This process is necessarily forceful, as it relies on the government's monopoly of note issue (which is virtually costless, and therefore not restrained by the law of costs), legal tender laws, and other coercive restraints on what would occur in an unhampered market (Hansen and Newman 2023, 158–59). No matter the legality of inflation, the government is, from the economic point of view, in the same position as an ordinary counterfeiter who may command additional goods and services on the market. In this way, the government may acquire vast resources for its crisis response without increasing tax revenues. The only constraint is the voting public's tolerance of the lagged, indirect, and complex effects of the inflation, including higher prices and financial crises. And even this constraint is tenuous, as it depends on the public's knowledge of the causal connection between monetary expansion and the effects of inflation.

Hülsmann (2008) suggests that inflation is what enabled the political centralization during the 17th and 18th centuries and eventually the creation of the powerful modern nation-states of the 19th and 20th centuries. The wealth acquired via debasement and coin-clipping by the governments of antiquity enabled political centralization, but centralization also occurred due to the temptation of the scale of inflation that could be achieved by a centralized nation-state with paper money. Hülsmann claims that this prospect of the ability to forcefully acquire resources via inflation on a massive scale "made the nation state irresistible" (2008, 176). Hülsmann, like Higgs, also comments on the way inflation allows governments to wage war to a greater extent than the population will tolerate.

> The more protracted and destructive a war becomes, therefore, the less is the population inclined to support it financially through taxes and the purchase of public bonds. Fiat inflation allows the government to ignore

the fiscal resistance of its citizens and to maintain the war effort on its present level, or even to increase that level. (2008, 177)

This observation was succinctly expressed by Ron Paul: "It is no coincidence that the century of total war coincided with the century of central banking" (2009, 63).

Monetary Inflation Distributes Costs to the Politically Weak

Higgs also suggests that government officials who want to avoid the unpopularity of increasing taxes could resort to methods of imposing costs on the politically weak (1987, 67). Monetary inflation accomplishes this via Cantillon effects, that is, the way inflation distorts relative prices, the allocation of resources within the economy, the flow of incomes, and the value of assets. In short, increases in the money supply are non-neutral—new money enters the economy at a particular point, in the form of income to the first recipients. These first recipients, typically banks, large financial institutions, and the contractors who sell goods and services to the government, benefit from higher incomes before prices increase generally.[5] As a result, these beneficiaries can acquire resources and invest at the expense of those whose nominal incomes rise later or never.

Thus, the "losers" of the Cantillon effects of fiat inflation are those with lower or fixed incomes, few assets, and less access to credit, that is, the politically weak. Their real incomes decrease as prices rise, inhibiting their ability to acquire the resources that could give them more political power, as is wielded by the leaders of large firms with substantial lobbying efforts. This dynamic exacerbates existing wealth disparities, as those who hold assets that appreciate with inflation (e.g., real estate, stocks) further consolidate their wealth, while those with limited assets struggle to keep pace with rising prices.

Monetary Inflation as Cost-Concealment

Of course, costs can be concealed only, and not diminished or eliminated. Through inflationary finance, governments can acquire vast resources without facing the political consequences that might accompany substantial increases in tax revenues. Governments use monetary inflation as a method of cost concealment to fund war efforts or other large-scale projects while minimizing the political backlash that would arise from heavy taxes or borrowing. Thus, the full costs of the government's actions are concealed—citizens pay for it via higher prices instead of seeing the costs directly in their tax bill. Higgs points out that this enables governments to implement potentially unpopular policies and projects, or to participate in wars to a greater extent than the public would otherwise tolerate.

> Inability to levy taxes and then purchase on the open market everything it wishes to use in carrying out its policy shows that the government values the activity more than the citizens, that it takes from them coercively more than they are willing to supply voluntarily at a free-market price. (1987, 67)

This cost concealment pervades the economy beyond the government's initial purchases of goods with monetized debt. Inflation distorts prices, which serve as essential guides for entrepreneurs in allocating resources and making investment decisions. Mises emphasizes the way monetary inflation distorts the process of economic calculation.

> In accordance with the rise or fall in purchasing power there emerge between items reflecting earlier prices and those reflecting later prices specific differences; the calculus shows profits or losses which are merely produced by cash-induced changes effected in the purchasing power of money. If we compare such profits or losses with the result of a calculation accomplished on the basis of a kind of money whose purchasing power had been subject to less vehement changes, we can call them imaginary or apparent only. ([1949] 1998, 421)

Thus, inflation finance burdens the economy in many ways. First, the Cantillon effect "losers" face higher prices before their incomes increase. Second, the production of the goods and services demanded by the government are favored at the expense of the production of goods and services that consumers demand.[6] Finally, the distortion of economic calculation causes the entire structure of production to go into disarray.

CRISIS BEGETS CRISES: AUSTRIAN BUSINESS CYCLE THEORY

The precipitating cause of the upswing in the ratchet is always a crisis. We have seen that the widespread panic and uncertainty during economic crises provides fertile ground for government expansion. Austrian business cycle theory (ABCT) provides an explanation for the source of economic crises: artificial credit expansion. Moreover, ABCT explains how one crisis leads to another, owing to the central bank's reaction to recessions with further credit expansion. Thus, ABCT implies a continuing cycle of ratchets of government growth and control over money and banking.

Rothbard made a distinction between "ordinary business fluctuations" and business cycles (2000, 4). A dynamic economy will have unending changes in specific industries and markets, but these do not constitute a business cycle. Business cycles refer to the economy-wide booms and busts that feature "a general cluster of business errors" (8). This observation leads us to consider a cause of the business cycle that would have economy-wide consequences for how entrepreneurs select which lines of production to pursue. Rothbard narrows it down to intervention within the realm of money and credit (10). Only artificial credit expansion and the consequently reduced interest rates can explain why entrepreneurs would pursue new longer lines of production at the same time consumption spending increases. The artificial credit generates an unsustainable boom as employment, spending, and firm values are boosted (Rothbard 2000).

The new projects that are started cannot be completed, however, because the real savings that are needed to sustain them do not exist. On the contrary, real savings diminish as inflation encourages overconsumption (Mises [1949] 1998, 428–29). The increased scarcity of capital is usually realized by entrepreneurs when the artificial credit is cut off, causing them to reevaluate their ambitious projects and ultimately liquidate them. The bust, then, features dramatic increases in unemployment and uncertainty. Salerno (2012) adds that entrepreneurs become especially reluctant to start new projects, even if they appear profitable, due to the recent memory of being fooled by apparent profitability in the artificial boom. When exacerbated by government interventions like additional credit expansion, this can turn what would have been a quick and easy correction into a long and painful depression (Salerno 2012).

When the Federal Reserve expands credit, it increases the supply of reserves in the banking system, which results in a lower Federal Funds Rate. A long-term view of this rate, as shown in figure 9.2, shows that in recessions, the Fed responds by attempting to "stimulate the economy" with new credit and lower interest rates (Board of Governors of the Federal Reserve System n.d.).

According to ABCT, however, this only sets the stage for another unsustainable boom to occur. Thus, an economic crisis caused by government intervention creates another economic crisis, giving the government and the central bank opportunity to expand even further.

This cycle is notably evident in the connected economic crises in 2001 and 2008. The Federal Reserve responded to the early 2000s recession

Figure 9.2. Federal funds effective rate, 1960–2023

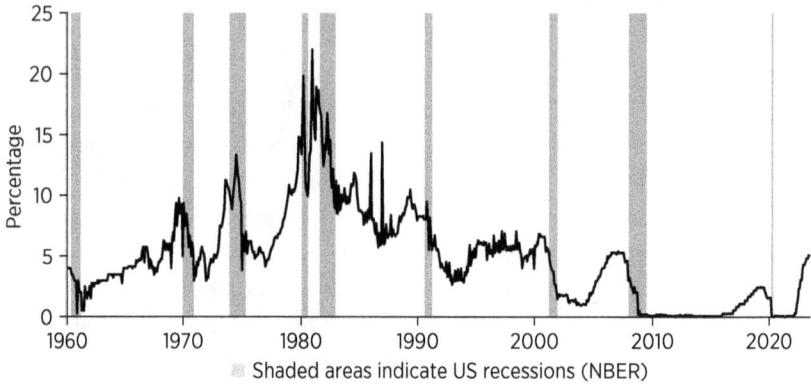

Shaded areas indicate US recessions (NBER)

Source: Created by author with data from Federal Reserve Economic Data (FRED), Federal Reserve Bank of St. Louis.

with expansionary monetary policy, driving the Federal Funds Rate from over 6.5 percent in 2000 to below 1 percent by 2003 (Board of Governors). Thornton (2009) documents economists' views on the potential development of a housing bubble after the bursting of the "dot-com bubble" in 2000–01, including that of Fed chair Alan Greenspan in 2002.

> The ongoing strength in the housing market has raised concerns about the possible emergence of a bubble in home prices. However, the analogy often made to the building and bursting of a stock price bubble is imperfect. . . . Even if a bubble were to develop in a local market, it would not necessarily have implications for the nation as a whole. (Greenspan 2002, quoted in Thornton 2009)

This shows that the Fed chair was not concerned about the potential long-term effects of expansionary policy in response to the early 2000s crisis. Meanwhile, 30-year fixed rate mortgages dropped from 8.24 percent in May 2000 to 5.21 percent by 2003 (Freddie Mac n.d.), and adjustable-rate mortgages as a share of all mortgages exploded from below 10 percent in 2001 to 35 percent in 2004 (Mortgage Bankers Association n.d.). The Case-Shiller home price index shows an 85 percent increase in home prices from 2000 to 2006 (S&P Dow Jones Indices LLC n.d.). Over the same time period, there was a 22.8 percent surge in residential building construction employment (US Bureau of Labor Statistics n.d.).

Of course, this infamous housing bubble and general economic boom did not last. The 2007–08 crisis and ensuing recession was a painful correction of the malinvestment and overconsumption of the earlier part of the decade. True to Higgs's *Crisis and Leviathan* thesis, the severity of the economic crisis led to a host of new banking regulations, fiscal stimulus packages, and Federal Reserve policy tools. This self-perpetuating cycle illustrates how the government's own interventions in the realm of money and banking led to a crisis that resulted in an even broader scope of government control over these institutions.

THE PSYCHOLOGICAL AND CULTURAL CONSEQUENCES OF INFLATION

The psychological and cultural consequences of inflation also drive a self-perpetuating cycle of ratcheting government growth. Since Higgs's thesis in *Crisis and Leviathan* depends on ideological change, it makes sense to consider the personal and social effects of inflation. Higgs defines ideology as "a somewhat coherent, rather comprehensive belief system about social relations" (1987, 37). He continues,

> [Ideology] structures a person's perceptions and predetermines his understandings of the social world, expressing these cognitions in characteristic symbols; it tells him whether what he "sees" is good or bad or morally neutral; and it propels him to act in accordance with his cognitions and evaluations as a committed member of a political group in pursuit of definite social objectives. Ideologies perform an important psychological service because without them people cannot know, assess, and respond to much of the vast world of social relations. (37)

This is closely related to the human personality concept as employed by Salerno (2013). Salerno does not consider personality as "a cluster of psychological attributes and qualities; rather it is a mode of being and becoming based on economic calculation and the ownership of property" (18). Social action and participation in the social division of labor are indispensable for the goal-oriented person, according to Salerno (18).

This conception of personality allows Salerno to explore how inflation hampers people's ability to plan for the future (2013, 19). Inflation makes planning difficult due to the added uncertainty regarding the value of money in the future. Saving and production are discarded for the sake of immediate gratification and consumption. Once respectful lifestyles involving "productive work, thrift and sober investment" are exchanged for scams and gambling

(Salerno 2013, 19). Salerno remarks that a hyperinflation "brings about a social revolution" in this way, as social and economic classes that were rewarded for their productivity and future-mindedness are replaced by those who thrive in economic chaos ("gamblers, con artists and swindlers") (2013, 19).

To illustrate his thesis, Salerno (2013) gathers commentary from German citizens who lived through the great hyperinflation episode of the early 1920s. Their stories validate, in a terrifying way, Salerno's hypotheses about the connection between money and property and human personality. Consider the testimony of Erna von Pustau:

> Referring to a popular song of the day, Pustau quoted the following line: "We are drinking up our grandma's little hut and the first and second mortgage, too." She then remarked, "Saving is the very source of wealth and health of a sound nation. But, we have no longer a sound nation. We are on our way to become a crazy, a neurotic, a mad nation." Pustau also lamented the spiritual trauma inflicted by the sudden collapse of the social structure: "It was a sad world, a world in which none was better than the other and all was a matter of chance and degree. A sad world, and a sad conception for a girl who still remembered the good old times of Grandmother! Our times made us cynical." (Buck [1947] 1969, cited in Salerno 2013, 20)

Pustau alludes to the fact that money savings protect individuals from calamity, which is why the destruction of the value of savings via hyperinflation made the citizenry vulnerable and desperate for help from any source. Normally, social institutions like the family, churches, and charitable organizations could fill this need for an individual or household, but hyperinflation destroys everybody's savings and way of life. Thus,

> Social and economic institutions long taken for granted disintegrated and disappeared, and the social structure itself began to dissolve causing human existence to become atomized and aimless. Thought, language, values, culture—all were deformed, as the interior life of the individual was inexorably drained of meaning and purpose and, in large measure, extinguished. (Salerno 2013, 22)

Salerno (2013) concludes that the psychological and cultural consequences of inflation lead to expanded roles for the state in the lives of its citizens. In the case of the German hyperinflation, "The State was the conqueror and successor of money. And thus the State was everything" (Heiden

[1944] 1969, cited in Salerno 2013, 22). Like FDR, Adolf Hitler was able to exploit public dissatisfaction with inflation for the sake of consolidating political power.

> There was nothing definite left but the State to fill the economic and spiritual void created by the German hyperinflation. Now, a shrewd and cunning German politician, Adolf Hitler, understood the nature of inflation as a gigantic material and spiritual swindle and recognized the deforming of German souls and personalities and the corresponding disintegration of German society. Hitler both taunted the German people for acquiescing in the swindle and at the same time promised them material relief and spiritual regeneration in the State, the successor of money. (Salerno 2013, 22)

Hülsmann (2008) takes a broader view but reaches the same conclusion: fiat inflation brings about a more powerful and centralized state. Governments can extract more wealth from their citizens than they would with just taxation, and these enriched central governments expand at the expense of local governments and civil institutions. As the government expands in scope, providing ever more services for its citizens, it crowds out families and other institutions that formerly provided them (Hülsmann 2008, 176).[7]

Thus, the ratchet of government growth is intensified by inflation, through its lasting psychological, social/cultural, and ideological effects. Both the initial crisis expansion and the incompleteness of the post-crisis retrenchment are exacerbated by these "soft" or indirect effects of inflation. Higgs (1987) remarks that the initial expansion of government is partially explained by citizens' inclination to respond to a crisis by calling on the government to "do something" without regard to the due process and checks and balances that are followed in normal times. This knee-jerk response may be encouraged by the psychological and cultural effects of inflation. And Higgs's explanation of the incompleteness of the retrenchment points to the more permanent ideological and attitudinal shifts. Fiat inflation exacerbates both stages of the ratchet in two ways. First, by hampering citizens' ability to plan and save, the population becomes more vulnerable to crises, such that when crises come, prior convictions about the proper role of government are put aside for the sake of survival. Second, both Salerno (2013) and Hülsmann (2008) point out that inflation brings about a revolution in the social nexus as trustworthy people, organizations, and institutions are replaced by political power. Inflation is a kingmaker; but instead of installing a wise and benevolent monarch, it imposes permanently Bigger Government.

CONCLUSION: JACKSON VS. THE MANY HEADED MONSTER

In 1836, political cartoonist Henry Robinson lampooned Andrew Jackson's campaign against the Bank of the United States. Jackson famously eliminated the bank by vetoing its recharter bill and transferring US Treasury deposits to several state banks (Rothbard 2002, 93). Robinson, who was anti-Jackson, intended to make fun of him by giving him a cane as a weapon as he fights alongside his bumbling allies. Interestingly, Robinson chose to depict Jackson's enemy, the Bank of the United States, as a many-headed monster, known as a "Hydra" in Greek mythology. The monster's heads represented the state banks' support of the central bank. Robinson intended to show the central bank through Jackson's eyes, making him out to be a quixotic hero who thinks he is battling a terrible monster, when in reality he is tilting at windmills (Robinson 1836). Another way to interpret the artist's depiction of this scene, in a way the artist probably did not intend, is that it highlights how difficult it is to oppose powerful institutions. The cartoon depicts an old man fighting a fierce many-headed Hydra with nothing but a cane. The cartoon's dialogue also contributes to this view. Major Downing, who represents the common man, exclaims, "Now, now, you nasty varmint, be you imperishable?" The artist probably intended this line to reflect the public's increasing fatigue of Jackson's bank war, but it also betrays a view of the permanence of government control over money and banking. Even though the Bank of the United States was eventually dissolved, central banking returned to the United States with the Federal Reserve Act less than a century later. This raises the question: Is the expanding reach of government into money and banking perishable?

Regarding the question of inevitability, Higgs concludes *Crisis and Leviathan* with a glimmer of hope. If ideological change is not predetermined and can be swayed "through rational consideration in the light of historical evidence and moral persuasion, then there remains a hope, however slight, that the American people may rediscover the worth of individual rights, limited government, and a free society under a true rule of law" (1987, 262). Unfortunately, the endogenous view of self-perpetuating cycles of crises and ideological change presented in this chapter casts a shadow on this glimmer of hope.

And yet, Jackson's victory is an exception to the ratchet effect rule. He annihilated the central bank that was instituted in the aftermath of a crisis: the War of 1812 and the ensuing economic mess. This complete retrenchment deserves a close look as a case study or model for how the ratchet of government growth and government control over money and banking may be unwound.[8] Does it require an exceptional, anti–central bank leader and popu-list rhetoric? How can such a leader buck entrenched interests? To what extent can a political leader redirect the tides of ideological change? Was it inevitable for a central bank to reappear 75 years later? Does the state ever overplay its own hand, igniting a countermovement? In answering these questions, we may find a way to turn the ideological gears in the other direction, away from Big Government, central banking, and fiat money, and toward liberty.

NOTES

1. Higgs hoped for "a general theory of ideological change expressed at an empirically useful level of generality" (1987, 54). This chapter seeks to make additional steps toward this goal. However, Higgs did propose some explanations for ideological change based on learning, government propaganda, and individuals' self-justification of new benefits: "Occupants of privileged positions naturally develop more than an appreciation of the personal advantages; they tend to view the whole apparatus of governmental control as essentially benign" (Higgs 1987, 72).

2. See Mises ([1950] 2018), *Middle of the Road Policy Leads to Socialism*, and Ikeda (2004), "The Dynamics of Interventionism."

3. Ramin Toloui (2020) explained the policy tools in a Stanford Institute for Economic Policy Research brief, "How Do the Federal Reserve's New Tools Really Work?"

4. Of course, increases in the amount of gold in a gold standard have non-neutral effects, but these changes would be in accordance with the preferences of market participants, and so would not be "distortive." For example, an unhampered market economy would have a certain level of income and wealth inequality, but these would be exacerbated by fiat inflation.

5. See Rothbard (1984), *Wall Street, Banks, and American Foreign Policy* and, for a few good examples of favored contractors, Higgs (1989), "Beware the Pork-Hawk: In Pursuit of Reelection, Congress Sells Out the Nation's Defense."

6. For more on the problems with this kind of "non-comprehensive planning," see Coyne and Goodman (2020), "Economic Pathologies of the State."

7. Relevant to Higgs's thesis, Hülsmann also claims that inflation "contributed, indirectly at least, to the popularity of nationalistic ideologies, which in the twentieth century ushered in a fre-netic worshipping of the nation-state" (2008, 176).

8. See also Rothbard (1974), "Economic Determinism, Ideology, and the American Revolution." Here, Rothbard convincingly shows that truly libertarian revolutions, like the American Revolution, have as a prerequisite the writing and speaking of opposition intellectuals who can distill and distribute anti-state ideology to the masses. The ideological groundwork must be laid before a critical mass of the population are sufficiently passionate to set aside their economic interests and "lead them out of their morass of daily habit into an uncommon and militant activity in opposition to the State" (5).

REFERENCES

Board of Governors of the Federal Reserve System. n.d. Federal Funds Effective Rate [FEDFUNDS]. Retrieved from FRED, Federal Reserve Bank of St. Louis. https://fred.stlouisfed.org/series /FEDFUNDS.

Buck, P. S. (1947) 1969. "How It Happens: Talk about the German People, 1914–1933, with Erna von Pustau." In *The German Inflation of 1923*, edited by Fritz Ringer, 120–46. New York: Oxford University Press.

Coyne, C., and N. P. Goodman. 2020. "Economic Pathologies of the State." In *The Routledge Handbook of Anarchy and Anarchist Thought*, edited by Gary Chartier and Chad Van Schoelandt, 247–61. New York: Routledge.

Freddie Mac. n.d. 30-Year Fixed Rate Mortgage Average in the United States [MORTGAGE30US]. Retrieved from FRED, Federal Reserve Bank of St. Louis. https://fred.stlouisfed.org/series /MORTGAGE30US.

Google Trends. 2022. "FOMC Meeting." June 15, 2022. https://trends.google.com/trends/explore ?date=all&q=fomc%20meeting&hl=en-US.

Greenspan, Alan. 2002. "Monetary Policy and the Economic Outlook." Testimony before the Joint Economic Committee of the US Congress, April 17, 2002. http://www.federalreserve.gov/board docs/testimony/2002/20020417/default.htm.

Hansen, Kristoffer J. Mousten, and Jonathan R. Newman. 2023. "What Is Inflation? Clarifying and Justifying Rothbard's Definition." *Quarterly Journal of Austrian Economics* 25 (4): 147–70.

Hazlitt, Henry. 1960. *What You Should Know about Inflation.* New York: D. Van Nostrand.

Heiden, K. (1944) 1969. *Der Fuehrer: Hitler's Rise to Power.* Translated by Ralph Mannheim. In *The German Inflation of 1923*, edited by Fritz Ringer, 164–218. New York: Oxford University Press.

Higgs, Robert. 1987. *Crisis and Leviathan.* New York: Oxford University Press.

———. 1989. "Beware the Pork-Hawk: In Pursuit of Reelection, Congress Sells Out the Nation's Defense." *Independent Institute*, June 1, 1989. https://www.independent.org/publications /article.asp?id=98.

Hülsmann, Jörg Guido. 2008. *Ethics of Money Production.* Auburn, AL: Ludwig von Mises Institute.

Ikeda, Sanford. 2004. "The Dynamics of Interventionism." In *The Dynamics of Intervention: Regulation and Redistribution in the Mixed Economy*, edited by P. Kurrild-Klitgaard, 21–57. Leeds, UK: Emerald.

Kageyama, Yuri. 2023. "Stock Market Today: Wall Street Swings to Mixed Close as Fed Hints of Rate Hikes to Come." *AP News*, June 14, 2023.

Koppl, Roger. 2002. *Big Players and the Economic Theory of Expectations.* London: Palgrave Macmillan.

Menger, Carl. 1892. "On the origin of money." *Economic Journal* 2 (6): 239–55.

Mises, Ludwig von. (1949) 1998. *Human Action.* Auburn, AL: Ludwig von Mises Institute.

———. (1950) 2018. *Middle of the Road Policy Leads to Socialism.* Auburn, AL: Ludwig von Mises Institute.

———. (1953) 2009. *The Theory of Money and Credit.* Auburn, AL: Ludwig von Mises Institute.

Mortgage Bankers Association. n.d. "Weekly Applications Survey." https://www.mba.org/news-and -research/research-and-economics/single-family-research/weekly-applications-survey.

Murphy, Robert P. 2010. "The Fed and the Ratchet Effect." *Mises Wire*, September 6, 2010. https:// mises.org/library/fed-and-ratchet-effect.

Nixon, Richard. 1971. "Address to the Nation Outlining a New Economic Policy: The Challenge of Peace." American Presidency Project. https://www.presidency.ucsb.edu/documents/address -the-nation-outlining-new-economic-policy-the-challenge-peace.

Paul, Ron. 2009. *End the Fed.* New York: Grand Central.

Robinson, Henry R. 1836. *General Jackson Slaying the Many Headed Monster.* Pennsylvania, 1836. Printed and published by H. R. Robinson. Photograph. https://www.loc.gov/item/2008661279/.

Roosevelt, Franklin D. 1933. "Executive Order 6514 of December 19, 1933." American Presidency Project. https://www.presidency.ucsb.edu/documents/executive-order-6514.

Rothbard, Murray N. 1974. "Economic Determinism, Ideology, and the American Revolution." *Libertarian Forum* 6 (11): 4–5.

———. 1984. *Wall Street, Banks, and American Foreign Policy*. Auburn, AL: Ludwig von Mises Institute.

———. 2000. *America's Great Depression*. Auburn, AL: Ludwig von Mises Institute.

———. 2002. *A History of Money and Banking in the United States: The Colonial Era to World War II*. Auburn, AL: Ludwig von Mises Institute.

———. 2008. *The Mystery of Banking*. Auburn, AL: Ludwig von Mises Institute.

S&P Dow Jones Indices LLC. S&P/Case-Shiller U.S. National Home Price Index [CSUSHPINSA]. Retrieved from FRED, Federal Reserve Bank of St. Louis. https://fred.stlouisfed.org/series/CSUSHPINSA.

Salerno, Joseph T. 2010. "Gold Standards: True and False." In Joseph T. Salerno, *Money, Sound and Unsound*, 355–73. Auburn, AL: Ludwig von Mises Institute.

———. 2012. "A Reformulation of Austrian Business Cycle in Light of the Financial Crisis." *Quarterly Journal of Austrian Economics* 15 (1): 3–44.

———. 2013. "Hyperinflation and the Destruction of Human Personality." *Studia Humana* 2 (1): 15–27.

Selgin, George A. 1988. *The Theory of Free Banking: Money Supply under Competitive Note Issue*. Washington, DC: Cato Institute.

Thornton, Mark. 2009. "The Economics of Housing Bubbles." In *Housing America: Building Out of a Crisis*, edited by Randall Holcombe and Benjamin Powell, 237–62. New Brunswick, NJ: Transaction.

Toloui, Ramin. 2020. "How Do the Federal Reserve's New Tools Really Work?" Policy Research Brief. Stanford Institute for Economic Policy.

US Bureau of Labor Statistics. n.d. All Employees, Residential Building Construction [CES2023610001]. Retrieved from FRED, Federal Reserve Bank of St. Louis. https://fred.stlouisfed.org/series/CES2023610001.

White, Lawrence. 1999. *The Theory of Monetary Institutions*. Oxford: Wiley-Blackwell.

Chapter 10

COVID and Leviathan

Laurie Calhoun

T
he years 2020–23 were marked by an unprecedented disruption to
the lives of free people. Yes, there was a novel coronavirus circulating,
and it did kill many people. But what was truly unprecedented about
this disruption, in particular, was the nearly uniform and universal political
reaction to it.

Humanity had certainly seen its share of virus-induced baleful diseases and
swift-acting plagues throughout history, but only in 2020, with the announce-
ment of the onset of a *global pandemic*, did the governments of the world take
action in concert against this nonhuman killer. All societies were affected by
the sweeping measures imposed on the populace by elected officials and their
appointees, from border closures and business lockdowns to the "emergency"
wealth transfer of untold sums to the pharmaceutical and biotech—among
other—industries (including the military, which was enlisted in various ways),
to the imposition of a moratorium on mortgage foreclosures, along with rent
and loan freezes. In terms of sheer magnitude of coordinated policy-induced
disruption, nothing like this had been seen before in human history. In World
War II, a number of governments did of course mobilize massively, and disrupted the lives and activities of citizens in countless ways, but in that case,
there were two sides: the allies and their enemies. In this case, the governments
of the world formed a united front in what was claimed to be a war on a nonhuman enemy: the COVID-19 virus.

In some countries, direct cash payments were made to select sectors of
the populace by the government in order to help them to weather the pandemic storm, but many other persons were left to their own devices, as leaders implemented policies making it illegal for them to work or to welcome
customers to their businesses. Notably, lawmakers themselves remained
well-salaried as they drafted legislation that prevented others from seeking or
retaining gainful employment. As a result of the new restrictions, thousands
upon thousands of small businesses were permanently shuttered, having been
rendered unnecessary by the companies christened "essential" by the govern-

ment, including Amazon, Walmart, and other big box stores, all of which flourished as salaried people stuck at home ordered everything they needed to be delivered to their door.

Billions of masks were worn and discarded in cities all over the world, and children were forced to attend classes online and prevented from socializing in public. Curfews were enacted, and people were forbidden from congregating even in their places of worship. An array of "vaccines" were developed by companies funded by governments, and citizens were vigorously encouraged, if not threatened, through widespread propaganda campaigns (paid for by the citizens themselves), to undergo experimental medical treatments. Those who dissented were punished and censored. Doctors and scientists critical of the government's narratives were discredited and deplatformed. Many persons lost their means of gainful employment for daring to decline to participate in the largest experimental trial of a novel medical device (the mRNA shots) in history. Businesses were shut down for refusing to shut down.

In the end, the effects of all these massive interventions by governments into the lives of citizens, carried out under the pretext of public health, were mixed. Despite being denounced by the most draconian advocates of emergency measures for its less restrictive approach to the virus, Sweden did relatively well (Statista 2019). Among all Western nations, the United States had the worst outcome, in terms of virus and excess nonvirus deaths, despite having doled out more money as a percentage of GDP than any other government on the planet, save Singapore (Our World in Data 2023).

Is there any way to understand what we just witnessed, including the creeping expansion of state power since March 2020? There is, and it was presciently outlined in great detail by Robert Higgs in his *chef-d'œuvre*, *Crisis and Leviathan* (1987), more than three decades before the SARS-CoV-2 (COVID-19) virus appeared on the scene. In his study of major disruptions of human societies, Higgs elucidates key concepts to explain the residual and seemingly permanent expansion of government, what becomes a "ratchet effect" subsequent to periods of war and economic depression: the fallacy of *post hoc ergo propter hoc*, the role of *ideology*, and the perception of *emergency* as necessitating government intervention. The multifaceted apparatus presented in *Crisis and Leviathan* explains, too, what we witnessed throughout the COVID-19 upheaval as veritable armies of petty despots emerged at the local, state, and federal levels to issue arbitrary dictates, and impose onerous penalties on those who dared to defy the new laws.

"EMERGENCY!"

On September 18, 2022, President Joe Biden told a CBS News reporter: "The pandemic is over" (Biden 2022). This did not, however, prevent him from extending the declared state of emergency yet again. Two months later, on December 15, 2022, the president announced that, effective immediately, every US household would once again be able to order four cost-free, at-home COVID-19 tests (Kimball 2022), as he had announced about a year earlier (White House 2022b). Each winter, flu season arrives on the scene, with frail, elderly persons apt to succumb as the elements become more difficult to bear. The current COVID-19 tests identify all sorts of things, up to and including run-of-the-mill coronaviruses, better known as "colds" (Surkova, Nikolayevskyy, and Drobniewski 2020).

Where there is no testing, no cases are detected, so the most obvious and predictable effect of millions of people suddenly testing themselves "free" at home for infection by a virus that had morphed to a number of weaker variants than the original, more lethal, strain, was a rekindling of the fear and hysteria that drove COVID-19 policy from 2020 to 2022, thereby shaping the perceived need to keep the declared "state of emergency" in place. Indeed, the government's "state of emergency" (FEMA 2020) was scheduled to expire in early January 2023, but on December 30, 2022, the Transportation Security Administration (TSA) effectively extended the term by issuing a prolongation of its vaccine requirement on visitors through April 2023 (Boyd 2023).

By late 2022, the United States had become one of the few countries still requiring vaccination for any noncitizen attempting to visit. While some exceptions were granted, including to those individuals attempting to immigrate to the United States, the vaccination requirement for noncitizens wishing merely to do a bit of tourism or visit relatives not seen for years was not changed. This inconvenient, restrictive, and illogical policy remained in place despite the fact that well-known examples abound of persons fully vaccinated who nonetheless contracted COVID-19 postvaccination. Among them is the president himself, Joe Biden, who has tested positive for the virus on multiple occasions, despite being "fully vaccinated" and "up-to-date" on his booster shots (Liptak and Judd 2022).

Obviously, if vaccinated persons can contract and spread COVID-19, then the requirement of vaccination on anyone is utterly arbitrary, serving no public health pretext whatsoever, and yet vaccination status continued to be used as a means of dividing people into distinct social classes and restricting the rights of those who chose not to comply. Given that the TSA requirement allowed infected persons into the country, whether because they sought immigrant status or because they had been vaccinated, but did not permit the entry of uninfected persons who are unvaccinated, this emergency law served a primarily punitive purpose: to restrict the liberty of those who refused to buy into the hype over this new medical product, which does not act in the manner of any of the time-tested vaccines to stop the spread of a pathogen.

In the 2023 National Defense Authorization Act (NDAA), the US Congress included a provision lifting the vaccine mandate on persons serving in the military, a policy imposed by the Pentagon on its employees shortly after the experimental shots became available. Lawsuits challenging this mandate had been struck down, so a number of science-savvy congresspersons (including, notably, Representative Thomas Massie) mobilized to render the requirement illegal. Interestingly enough, the rationale offered in the written text promoting the new legislation was not based on any compelling belief in bodily autonomy or the right of a human being not to be experimented on against his will. Instead, the argument was made that the mandate was harming battlefield readiness. During a time of dwindling enlistment and missed recruitment quotas, more than 8,000 persons were relieved without pay by the Pentagon for refusing to accept the injections—again, despite the fact that they prevent neither transmission of nor infection by the virus, and mitigate illness severity only in cases where a person is in fact vulnerable to severe illness or death through infection by COVID-19.

Despite the ever-augmenting mountain of data demonstrating that the shots serve primarily to make a bout of the virus less deadly and reduce the need for hospitalization, many Americans appear to continue to believe on some level that "The vaccinated must be protected from the unvaccinated!" as a surprising number of ardent promoters of the shots chirped throughout what is aptly termed the "Coronapocalypse." As though "The Science" came to a screeching halt in March 2020, President Biden, ignoring all that we learned in the intervening years, agreed at the G20 meeting in Bali on November 15–16, 2022, that the United States would support a "Global Health Passport" system to regulate the movement of persons based on their vaccination status (White House 2022a).

Throughout this extraordinary period of history, as restrictions became more arbitrary and abrupt, it became difficult to stifle the suspicion that the more intransigent the authority, the less actual understanding of science the person possessed. Thus the most vehement figures in the United States, including Governor Whitmer of Michigan, Governor Newsom of California, and Governor Cuomo of New York, those who imposed the most illogical, stringent, and arbitrary restrictions of all, appeared to base all of their "governance" on the ever-oscillating pronouncements of the Centers for Disease Control (CDC) and the deliverances of the newfound health messiah, Dr. Anthony Fauci.[1] One of the most disastrous examples of counterproductive measures was Governor Cuomo's decision to send infected elderly persons to nursing homes to convalesce (Lahut 2020), thereby spreading the virus rapidly through clusters of persons in the most vulnerable cohort, resulting in many preventable deaths (Condon, Sedensky, and Hoyer 2020). Other dubious, and arguably deadly, policies included the neglect of mildly infected persons until they were ill enough to require hospitalization, the use of the toxic treatment Remdesivir (Gérard et al. 2021), and the concerted refusal to consider the use of any alleged remedy, including hydroxychloroquine (Erb 2021) and ivermectin (Kory et al. 2021), which might diminish the sales of the newly patented vaccines.

New Zealand prime minister Jacinda Ardern and Canadian prime minister Justin Trudeau demonstrated extraordinary zeal in attempting to force their compatriots to undergo inoculation for a disease to which many of them were not vulnerable and which some had already survived.[2] Trudeau went so far as to block access to the bank accounts of those who supported the protesters in the truck convoy in January 2022, thus effectively outlawing dissent and inflicting punishments from on high upon "the criminals" with no due process whatsoever (Fung 2022).

In their militant fervor to save their compatriots from the virus, it seems unlikely that such leaders had any idea that key terms in the central health authority's narrative had been entirely *redefined* so that the words no longer meant what they used to mean, once upon a time. Nor did they seem to have any understanding of how vaccines are supposed to work. But so long as their constituents also remain ignorant in these regards, they will never challenge the laws imposed upon them by the central government authority.

Post Hoc Ergo Propter Hoc and Ideology

As is the case with major government interventions more generally, during this inordinately disruptive period of history, many persons have fallen prey to the seductive line that "I did not die because the government kept me alive," a version of the *post hoc ergo propter hoc* fallacy diagnosed by Higgs in cases of world wars and economic depressions. The fallacy has proven to be even more rhetorically effective in the case of the COVID-19 crisis because the medical profession has always benefited from patients' inclination to believe that they are alive only because of their doctors. (No matter that approximately 250,000 persons suffer iatrogenic death each year, making it the third leading killer.[3]) But with the government now forming an impenetrable alliance with powerful forces in the medical and pharmaceutical industries, political leaders, too, capitalize on the illusion that anyone who survived COVID-19 did so because of the government, even though, in truth, the US outcomes were the worst among all industrialized nations.

In *Crisis and Leviathan*, Higgs explains how, in part because of the ease with which people succumb to the *post hoc ergo propter hoc* fallacy, the incessant growth of government is brought about through a ratcheting effect, whereby some of the implemented measures remain in place in the aftermath of a major crisis. The cases examined in scrupulous detail by Higgs are war and economic depression, both of which give rise to vast expansions of government power under the guise of protecting the people in the face of an emergency. The operative term is *emergency*, which invariably sets the stage for widespread popular support of even very restrictive policies and indeed the usurpation of private wealth and property, up to and including, in the case of war, the lives of persons conscripted to fight, kill, and die for the "greater good" of the group.

When citizens have been told by their government that the situation has reached the dire state of *emergency*, then not only elected and appointed officials themselves but the populace more generally tend to support the expansion of power and the shrinking of individual liberties under the circumstances, which are claimed and believed by many to be temporary. Both war and economic depression are cases where the populace is not merely unhappy not to be flourishing but in apparent danger of losing their very lives. So fearful have they become that they may (illogically enough) agree to sacrifice their own lives or, in the case of involuntary conscription, those of their compatriots, in order to save the greater group.

One sort of emergency is of course the public health emergency of a *pandemic*, and the pronouncement of that word by officials in 2020 struck fear into the hearts of billions of persons the world over. What most of them did not know, however, was that, as though in preparation for the political cataclysm to come, the definition of *pandemic* had been weakened by the World Health Organization (WHO) so as to omit the former requirement of causing death to large numbers of people over a broad geographic area.

In earlier times, before the H1N1 swine flu appeared in 2009, the term *pandemic* was reserved for simultaneous outbreaks worldwide involving much higher than usual death rates. Removing the requirement of severity from the definition allowed the use of the term *pandemic* nonetheless to trigger WHO measures to promote swift vaccine development and distribution. Similarly, in

2020, the new definition was instrumental in causing the lockstep lockdowns by governments all over the world (Day 2020). Historically, *pandemic* was reserved for cases where a disease would likely cause the death of significant portions of the population—such as the Black Plague, which killed millions of people swiftly and indiscriminately, across all age and health cohorts, rather than specifically posing a danger to the elderly and the already infirm.

Likewise, the term *vaccine* was defined by the CDC in 2018 as

> *a product that **stimulates a person's immune system to produce immunity to a specific disease**, protecting the person from that disease. Vaccines are usually administered through needle injections, but can also be administered by mouth or sprayed into the nose.*[4] [my emphasis]

But in 2021, the CDC redefined *vaccine* as

> *a preparation that is **used to stimulate the body's immune response against diseases**. Vaccines are usually administered through needle injections, but some can be administered by mouth or sprayed into the nose.* (CDC 2021b) [my emphasis]

Under the new definition, anything that "stimulates" the immune system would qualify as a vaccine, including, notably, the mRNA shots. By the same definition, however, many items not promoted by Fauci and Co. would also count as vaccines. Using zinc and vitamin C and D supplements, eating leafy green vegetables, and getting exercise all meet the weak requirement stipulated in the new definition of *vaccine*.

To say that these slick neologistic tricks (or rebranding) were somehow deployed by officials in the public health establishment is not to take sides on the conspiracy theory according to which the development and release of the novel coronavirus—likely a product of gain-of-function research (Husseini 2020)—was an intentional plot devised to set the stage for a one-world government as envisioned by the World Economic Forum (WEF) (Schwab and Malleret 2020; Schwab 2016). For it suffices to explain these developments that one recognize that *any* measure that is likely to increase the consumption of pharmaceutical products (any of them, not just the COVID-19 vaccines) will be promoted by industry-coopted persons in the various government regulatory agencies, just as occurred in the preamble to the opioid addiction crisis.

There can be little doubt, with the benefit of hindsight, that hundreds of thousands of narcotic deaths in the United States in recent years were caused—

whether directly or indirectly—by the Food and Drug Administration (FDA) decision to permit product companies such as Purdue Pharma to claim that their products were nonaddictive and could be prescribed with virtually no limits in addressing what was blitz-marketed at the time as a "pain epidemic."[5] But, as in the case of COVID-19, in order to explain the opioid crisis, there is no need to adduce any hypothesis grander than the "conspiracy theory" according to which companies in the for-profit pharmaceutical industry were trying to sell as many of their wares as possible. The effects of this debacle have been all too real, but the ascription of a conscious intention to kill what became the victims of opioid overprescription is implausible and explanatorily superfluous.

The entanglement of private industry and government invariably leads to conflicts of interest, which incline lawmakers to enact legislation favored by those who stand to profit from the arrangements, as Higgs has highlighted especially in the case of the crony capitalist military-industrial complex (Higgs 1987, 212–16). In the case of Big Pharma, which deploys more lobbyists in Washington, DC, than there are congresspersons, we should expect the same (Facher 2020). And, indeed, as though the opioid overdose crisis were nonexistent, the pharmaceutical industry managed, with the help of the government's massive propaganda campaign launched in the name of public health, to burnish its image and augment its power significantly in 2020.

With the arrival of COVID-19, companies such as Pfizer, which had paid the largest fine for healthcare fraud in history (US Department of Justice 2009), successfully portrayed themselves, again, with the aid of government agencies, as the saviors of humanity. The usual cast of opportunists crawled out of the woodwork to profit from the situation, with massive government allocations of funds to everything under the sun said to be necessary in order to combat the virus run amok. Public health consultancy, signs and stickers, masks and tests, industry-sponsored "news" programs and advertisements—all of these were a part of the massive propaganda campaign to induce citizens to roll up their sleeves through a combination of bribery and shaming, rationalized by politicians and pundits alike as a part of the government-led initiative to stop the virus, ostensibly to save people's lives.

Having survived two years of what was politically stoked trauma and strife, many citizens during this period appear to have come to believe that it is now the government's role to decide for them which medical treatments they should undergo. In 2021, the state of Massachusetts mandated flu shots for all attendees of schools, from elementary through graduate students (Commonwealth of Massachusetts 2020). Such a policy might seem reasonable enough to someone with no awareness that the efficacy of the flu shots in recent years has ranged only from 19 percent to 48 percent, which implies that, even in the best-case scenario, fully half of those injected are not helped by the treatment at all (CDC 2022). Because any and every new chemical ingested by human beings will have adverse effects, up to and including death, on a small portion of the population, a risk-benefit analysis must be made by individuals themselves in deciding whether to undergo such treatments. The new mandatory flu shot policy of the state of Massachusetts, a radical encroachment on the liberty of formerly free students, was made possible by the aggressively promoted idea that vaccines and shots are always and everywhere good, and anyone who disagrees with that claim is some sort of enemy of science—having been incessantly and effectively portrayed and denounced by the mainstream media (on behalf of the government and pharma) as "antivaxxers."

In reality, many of those who demurred from the COVID-19 shots were acting perfectly rationally, given the experimental nature of the treatment, and given that their own prospects for survival of the virus were already quite good, according to all available statistical data. Understandably enough, among those who declined the treatment were people who had already contracted and recovered from the illness. The preposterousness of the idea that individuals who already survived a bout of the virus should submit to treatment *ex post facto* is manifest to anyone who understands how vaccines actually work. And yet, somehow millions of people were propagandized into denying the reality of natural immunity, and insisting on the government-imposed vaccination of everyone everywhere, despite the fact that the efficacy of any vaccine is predicated on the soundness of the body's own immune system. If natural immunity were insufficient to combat COVID-19, then no vaccine whose mechanism involves precisely the commandeering of the body's own immune system preemptively could possibly work.

THE ROLE OF IDEOLOGY AND SELF-IMAGE IN SCAFFOLDING POLICY

What we have witnessed since 2020 is a radical change in the thinking of people themselves, many of whom now appear sincerely to believe that the fact that the government has ordered them to take a shot is the necessary and sufficient condition for their doing so. When President Biden solemnly admonished unvaccinated Americans in September 2021 that "our patience is wearing thin," not only were many people not troubled by his implied threat, but they came to support even more adamantly the mandated vaccination of unwilling persons (Rogers and Stolberg 2021).

Higgs carefully explains how ideology plays a decisive role in the expansion of government power, as persons become invested in the narratives which they support, and this gets tied in with their very self-image. In the case of war, those who oppose state policies of mass homicide as a foreign policy "tool" are denounced as cowards, if not traitors. In the case of the COVID-19 public health emergency, the notion that those who agreed with the government were pro-science and that those who did not were not only ignorant but also self-ish became a powerful inducement to compliance, particularly on the part of educated persons with no formal science background.

For fear, not of losing their lives, but because they want to be good and right, many citizens will retain their commitment to "the official story," even as the emergency conditions serving as the pretext for draconian measures are alle-viated and the perceived danger of their own death subsides. Throughout the initial period of the crisis, what is made to seem the need for the government's fear-fueled emergency interventions transforms citizens' beliefs, particularly when the crisis drags on for years. By the time the danger has passed, much of the populace remains favorably disposed to keeping the new policies in place, even though they were introduced as temporary, emergency measures.

War and economic depression have both been clear cases, Higgs demon-strates, where the beliefs among the citizenry about the appropriate role of government have altered permanently as a result of policies implemented in their name and allegedly on their behalf under the pretext of an emergency. The Coronapocalypse has presented a third such case, where the people have, once again, largely deferred to the government—out of both habit and fear—in the hopes that their leaders will keep them safe and figure out a way to bring the nation back to its pre-crisis state. What remains post-crisis was accurately labeled by promoters of the government's COVID-19 narrative as "The New Normal."

No matter how temporary the emergency may be claimed to be, full rever-sion never really happens. In other words, every major crisis results in a "New Normal." This is partly because each time the government usurps more of the rights of the citizenry, the less likely it becomes that the direct executors of the liberty-restricting policies will want to relinquish their newfound power. But, again, it is not only a matter of the new czars wanting to maintain control of this or that aspect of society once left to private persons to sort out. Nor is it merely a case of politicians hedging their bets, as we witnessed throughout the "war on terror" waged in response to the crimes of September 11, 2001.

Many of the emergency policies implemented in the early part of the 21st century remain in place still today, even after revelations of the strict illegality of measures such as the mass surveillance of citizens' digital data (Satter 2020). Lawmakers play an important role in the retention of policies crafted in emergency situations because they wish not to be blamed if anything negative should happen subsequent to the lifting of restrictions. But, as Higgs persuasively argues, the most important factor of all is that, as the populace lives through a declared emergency, they become progressively more accustomed to signing off to the government, just as they have always done during wartime, allowing elected and appointed officials to control more and more aspects of their lives, under the assumption that leaders actually know what they are doing.

This is despite the fact that we know that government officials often have no idea what they are doing. (The "war on terror" is a case in point, given the outcome in Afghanistan [Horton 2017].) Yet the overwhelming fear inculcated in the populace works wonders to persuade them to decline to question even dubious policies, such as were imposed throughout the Coronapocalypse. Among the most glaring of those policies were surely the extreme lockdowns of the societies of nearly all countries on the planet beginning in the spring of 2020, supposedly for the benefit of everyone, even though the virus itself was not considered especially dangerous to nonelderly persons in otherwise good health (not suffering from comorbidities, and also not obese).

From the outset, the CDC, the WHO, and their affiliated health professionals had access to data from China and Italy, and they initially issued pronouncements (which were later suppressed) according to which most people would suffer "mild symptoms," and only the very old and the already ill were especially vulnerable to the novel coronavirus. And yet, as the crisis unfurled and emergency laws proliferated, the establishment conducted itself as though we were in the midst of the Black Plague, with the 99.5 percent chance of survival apparently assumed by many to be their chance of death.

When President Donald Trump announced that he would be closing US borders in March 2020, thousands of Americans located abroad descended upon the major airports attempting to get home before the deadline. Because these persons were coming in some cases from places with much higher incidences of COVID-19, it seems likely that their congregation for hours on end in congested airport settings, as the government processed the sudden influx of arrivals, may have facilitated the spread of the virus throughout what was at that time the largely uninfected US populace.

Similarly, when universities sent all of their students home, they in all likelihood spread the virus to the farthest corners of the country.[6] At that time, there was so little understanding of what was going on that nearly everyone complied with whatever they were told by persons in positions of authority. The leaders, also no doubt personally fearful of the ominously announced *global pandemic*, operated under the perceived need to "do something, do anything!"

It is plausible that the reason for the overwhelming willingness of the populace all over the world to comply with the dictates of their overlords was the natural inference on the part of individuals themselves that the virus must be incredibly dangerous and deadly for the government to adopt such extreme and unprecedented measures as to close off the borders. The abrupt shutdown of businesses and the policies preventing citizens from leaving their homes, except in cases where they performed duties deemed "necessary" to the basic functioning of society, seemed to many to imply that the world was being crippled by the virus, not the lockdowns themselves.

The whole slippery slope began, as usual, with modest claims: "Two weeks to stop the spread!" This seemed like the sort of sacrifice to which any reasonable person would be willing to acquiesce. Surely a small price to pay to keep everyone's grandparents safe! But when the virus did not stop spreading after two weeks of lockdowns, government officials and many citizens alike inferred that what were needed were even more restrictive policies. The conclusion drawn by some of the officials who crafted the initial emergency orders was not that they had been wrong and their measures nugatory (given the nature of the virus), but that portions of the citizenry were to blame for having defied the new laws intended to keep everyone safe.

In this way, and quite ironically, as a result of their sheer inefficacy, the lockdowns were not curtailed but extended after two weeks. In some countries, they continued on for months and months, making it impossible for the inhabitants of those lands to make plans spanning anything more significant than the next day or so, about mundane and trivial matters such as what they would next eat and which movie to add to their viewing queue. Grocery store managers did their part to ensure that contact between fellow human beings be minimized by pasting arrow and circular stickers all over the floors to indicate where patrons were permitted to walk or to stand. All "nonessential" stores were shuttered and, in some supermarkets, entire aisles were closed off on the grounds that the items in them were "nonessential," and no one should be mulling around in public without a pressing quest to purchase something needed for basic survival.

Many restaurants, cafes, and bars went out of business, although some enterprising owners innovated to stay solvent by transforming their offerings into take-out fare, which people were permitted to purchase at the counter but then had to consume in their homes. City managers as well got onboard with the "humanitarian" mission to stop the virus, by closing parks and beaches, and in some awe-inspiring displays of enthusiasm, even filling skate parks with sand so that they could not be used. People caught walking alone on public trails were issued warnings and told to go home, as it had suddenly become illegal in some places even to be outside.

The lockdowns were disastrous, and not only for the social life and education of people. Indeed, they had the opposite of their intended effect, resulting in excess nonvirus deaths the world over (Dowd 2022). Precisely because of restrictive measures put in place by administrators in health facilities, millions of people, including grandparents, who likely would not have succumbed to COVID-19 (for they were not especially vulnerable to the virus) ended up dying for various other reasons, including the refusal of hospitals to treat persons not suffering from COVID-19. Once the vaccines were readily available, persons who opted not to roll up their sleeves were denied even acute care by facilities, on the grounds that they were not doing their part and thus posed a threat to other patients and the staff. The postponement of cancer treatments and surgeries, and the failure rapidly to respond to minor strokes and heart conditions, proved to be devastating in some cases.

Many persons in the gig economy were financially ruined by the lockdowns, having no access to the generous government funds doled out to salaried persons. The travel industry was essentially shut down for more than a year (although major airlines received generous aid packages from governments), and many of those formerly employed in temporary contract arrangements were reduced to penury. Depression and anxiety soared, and some people succumbed to excessive drug or alcohol use, having lost not only their jobs but also their homes. Overdose deaths in the United States exceeded 100,000 for the first time in 2021 (CDC 2021a), and it is plausible that the epidemic created by the gross overprescription of opioids conjoined with the flooding of fentanyl and its derivatives into street-market supplies was made measurably worse by the fact that idle persons began to self-medicate as a means of coping with the pandemic restrictions.

IS EVERYTHING PERMITTED?

In addition to showing how ideology and perceived emergency incline toward the expansion of government through the retention of supposedly temporary laws, Higgs analyzes how emergency legislation and executive orders upheld in the courts subsequent to crises can be understood as the result of a mode of reasoning on the part of judges schematized thus: "If A is all right, then X is certainly all right" (Higgs 1987, 235). The example considered by Higgs is that of military conscription, but the same schema applies in the case of government-mandated medical treatments and imposed penalties for failure to comply.

In September 2021, President Biden announced a broad mandate, to be administered by the Occupational Safety and Health Administration (OSHA), which would require companies with 100 employees or more to make vaccination and/or frequent testing for COVID-19 a condition of employment (Wiseman 2021). The arbitrariness of such a mandate, which was eventually struck down by the Supreme Court (Patterson, Belknap, Webb, and Tyler LLP 2022), was troubling enough on its own, given that a company with 99 employees is only slightly less likely to spread germs from workers to the greater community than is one with 100 employees. Even worse, the mandate ignored altogether the issue of natural immunity, as though it had and should have no relevance in individuals' decision of whether or not to undergo an experimental treatment.

At the same time, Biden issued a sweeping mandate for healthcare professionals, many of whom had worked through the early months of the pandemic and therefore had already been infected by and recovered from the virus. The Pentagon had already, on its own, required vaccination of all military personnel—again, with no provision for exception based on previous infection. To claim that such mandates were based on "The Science" is only to betray one's basic ignorance of how vaccines protect people, when in fact they do.

Ludicrously, the entire pretext behind the universal vaccination scheme, "Listen to the Science!" ignored all the knowledge accumulated about vaccines and immunity up to 2020. It was as though public health officials had all somehow forgotten that the way in which vaccines work is by spurring the body's immune system to produce antibodies and T-cells in advance of one's encounter with a wild virus. In the case of every person previously exposed, this had already happened. To claim that natural immunity is insufficient to fend off COVID-19 is simultaneously to deny the efficacy of *any* possible vaccine. Ultimately, the OSHA mandate was struck down by the Supreme Court for reasons relating to the stated mission of OSHA. But enough of the justices had been taken in by the massive pro-vaccine marketing campaign that they left the healthcare worker mandate in place. Those judges clearly labored under the ideology and self-image effect described by Higgs, assuming sincerely (but erroneously) that patients needed to be protected from people who had already recovered from the virus.

The failings of the government witnessed throughout this period, which resulted in the financial ruin of many citizens and the preventable deaths of persons not even vulnerable to the virus itself, were not merely of an intellectual or logical sort, committed by officials seemingly discombobulated by the manifest fear induced by ticker-tape displays of death tolls on every major television network for months on end. Even more egregious than the lockdowns, the government's attempt to force citizens to introduce experimental elixirs into their arms effectively rejected the finding of the Nuremberg Court, which concluded in 1947 that it is immoral, illegal, and fully unacceptable to experiment on human beings (as was done during Nazi Germany) against their will and without their free and fully informed consent (United States Holocaust Memorial Museum 2023).

Despite the fanfare with which the vaccines were bestowed upon the world by pharmaceutical companies, with optimistic claims of 95 percent efficacy, in reality, the experimental shots were effective at preventing neither transmission nor infection (Olliaro, Torreele, and Vaillant 2021). More people died after the massive vaccination campaigns than before, which makes sense when one considers the mechanism of the novel mRNA technology being used (Tebor and Bacon 2021). Rather than introduce traces of the viral offender (whether live or dead) into the human body, what these new shots did was to introduce foreign mRNA coding for a small part of the virus, the spike protein, which would galvanize the body to produce it. In the second stage of this *in vitro* experiment, the body would then produce antibodies and T-cells to combat the presence of the pseudo-foreign protein.

The use of mRNA for medical purposes had long seemed promising to innovators in biotechnology, and the hope in this case was that when a person later encountered a virus using the spike protein to gain access to the body's cells, the antibodies and T-cells would already exist in the person's system, with the result that the infection would be much less severe than it would otherwise have been. This procedure was not new, but every previously attempted mRNA shot had failed to make it to the stage of human testing (Edwards 2020). Only with the Emergency Use Authorization (EUA) by the FDA, made possible by the declared global pandemic, were companies permitted to experiment on the entire species with the mRNA technology. As a result of the highly visible sticks and carrots of governments, billions of shots were ultimately injected into the arms of human beings.

Completely ignored by the optimists was the role that virus mutation would play in rendering in short order the original vaccines entirely nugatory against rapidly multiplying variants. Viruses mutate in order to be able to continue to propagate themselves. Since the only things keeping the original strain of COVID-19 out of the cells of vaccinated persons were the spike protein antibodies, mutant strains needed only to evolve other strategies for cell entry to be able to propagate themselves. Accordingly, when vaccinated persons began becoming infected *en masse*, this demonstrated that the virus had already mutated to create new pathways to cell entry, which would not be obstructed by the spike protein antibodies.

If there was a conspiracy in this case, it was surely a conspiracy on the part of marketers who capitalized on the scientific illiteracy of much of the populace. We witnessed over the past two years countless dutifully vaccinated celebrities and politicians confidently pronouncing that, despite the fact that they had tested positive for COVID-19, they were grateful for the vaccine, since as a result they did not die and needed no hospitalization. This is perhaps one of the most glaring cases of the *post hoc ergo propter hoc* fallacy in history. Crediting the vaccine with saving the life of a healthy young person such as former press secretary Jen Psaki is nothing short of sophistry. According to all available statistical data, Psaki and those of her and many other age and health cohorts were never at any significant risk of dying from COVID-19.

Yet the fallacious reasoning continued on, propagating itself like a virus, not only because marketers were keen to sell the vaccines, but also because government officials had vested interests in keeping the narrative alive. The last thing government bureaucrats ever want is for their general incompetence to be exposed. Thus we saw officials pushing worthless "booster shots" (indistinguishable from the original formula) on the populace long before any new versions of the vaccine were developed, and despite the fact that infection among vaccinated persons had already demonstrated that the virus had mutated so as to be able to evade the spike protein antibodies.

Perhaps there would seem to be no cause for complaint in any of this (beyond the tax dollars dumped down the drain) to those who survived, provided only that the shots were truly innocuous. But the Vaccine Adverse Events Reporting System (VAERS) database catalogues thousands of deaths, some among previously healthy young persons, including professional athletes, who dropped dead of heart attacks or suffered debilitating cardiac myocarditis injury or strokes subsequent to vaccination. Yet the allegation or even suggestion that these "sudden deaths after a short illness" may have been caused by the vaccines has been systematically suppressed by those under sway of the importance of universal vaccination. Time will tell how all of this will be sorted out in the future by scientists whose reputations are not at stake and will therefore be able competently to investigate whether the biological activity of the spike protein itself, which even the current slate of public health officials has acknowledged can lead to blood clotting and artery clogging, in fact caused the deaths of persons coerced to undergo vaccination.

What is indisputable is that what we have witnessed since 2020 has involved a qualitative change in the government's general tendency to expand its power, as is clear upon considering the implications of mandated medical treatments. Higgs observes that, during wartime, once conscription has been imposed on men, effectively coercing them to fight, kill, and possibly die in defending the nation, then the natural inference on the part of judges assessing the legality of further provisions effectively becomes: *If conscription (and therefore the sacrifice of one's own life) is permitted, then everything is permitted.*

In the United States, military conscription, when imposed, at least up to now, has involved only half of the population (the males). With the dawning of the Drone Age, this is likely to change, given that physical strength is no longer required of government killers, who can dispatch by remote control anyone who has been labeled "the enemy" (Calhoun 2015). Once the Selective Service Registration requirement is expanded to include persons of all genders, then the draft, when called, will require every military-age citizen to kill on behalf of the government, though they may or may not risk death, given the development of remote-control technology (Calhoun 2022).

Strikingly, the newly asserted authority of governments (contested in some but not all countries to date) to force *all* of their citizens to undergo experimental treatments, which have as possible side effects severe injury and even death, implies that the government to which such powers are granted is tantamount to a tyranny, no matter what it may call itself. For if the government can force citizens to undergo experimental treatments against their will (and in the United States, thanks to the Public Readiness and Emergency Preparedness [PREP] Act[7] [US Department of Health and Human Services 2021], this is with no possibility of restitution in the case of injury or death), then the government effectively owns its citizens, who are no longer free persons but the subjects of a tyrannical regime.

This is why the push among leaders such as President Biden, Prime Minister Trudeau, Prime Minister Hipkins, European Commission president Ursula von der Leyen, and others for a global health passport preventing citizens from exercising their rights without first having complied with public health measures handed down by a single, unelected government authority is incredibly dangerous, ushering in, as it would, a new centralized system akin to that of the Soviet Union, where dissent is sharply curtailed and free thinkers are criminalized.

CONCLUSION

As we have seen, a global one-world oligarchic conspiracy is unnecessary to explain what happened from 2020 to 2023. History certainly suggests that government bureaucrats do not generally possess the level of competence, knowledge, and intelligence found in the sort of evil genius who might be capable of devising such a scheme. That said, looking back over all that has transpired, it may nonetheless be difficult to suppress the suspicion that we were all laboring under a carefully orchestrated psyop designed to weaken our natural resistance, not to a virus, but to government intervention in our lives.

The contradictions and omissions in the coverage of the pandemic were so flagrant as to cause one to wonder whether people may have lost all capacity for critical thought during this period, so cowered and confused were they by the government and the media's overbearing carping and incessant insinuations that everyone was in mortal danger from the virus. From 2020 through 2022, the role of government-produced and -propagated propaganda was undeniable, with President Biden himself issuing ominous proclamations in attempting to mandate injections of experimental pharmaceutical products for citizens in the process of being transformed into subjects. It matters little whether Biden himself had any conscious awareness of what he was doing.

It is entirely possible, for example, that Biden has done no more and no less than loyally to support his generous donors in the pharmaceutical industry (Roche 2020). Yet it is equally plausible that, while waving the "Listen to the Science!" banner, Biden has been laboring in a state of scientific ignorance, along with many in the populace who have helped to push the shots on their family members, friends, and colleagues. Either way, the all-too-familiar "divide and conquer" wartime playbook was undeniably deployed throughout the government's campaign to peddle as many mRNA shots as possible, with the harsh denunciation of anyone who dared to demur and a constant exaggeration of the threat so as to frighten people into compliance. Notably, the White House authoritatively pronounced just before Christmastime 2021 that the unvaccinated could look forward to "a winter of severe illness and death" for refusing to fall in line (Malloy and Velazquez 2021).

However it was that all of the mainstream media and much of social media managed to be captured by government propagandists and their trusty allies in the biomedical industry, the numbers do not lie. Billions of dollars ended up being transferred from citizens to pharmaceutical, biotechnological, and related industries as a result of the COVID-19 pandemic relief bills, in yet another crony capitalist coup (Parlapiano et al. 2022). Even worse, throughout the COVID-19 crisis, an astonishing number of citizens were prepared to support the government in its efforts to force participation in an experimental trial for a medical treatment of which many persons had no need, given the statistical likelihood of their survival, which had already been definitively demonstrated in many cases through previous infection.

Initially, citizens were told that "vaccination" would prevent them from killing other people, but even after it emerged that the shots prevented neither infection nor transmission, the push to mandate inoculation forged ahead, bolstered by pharmaceutical industry forces entirely analogous to those operating in the for-profit military industry and demonstrating yet again that crony capitalism is, above all, a social program of specifically corporate welfare, with government-allied companies prioritized above the lives of the human beings for which the government presumably exists.[8]

People are by now quite accustomed to answer, "How high?" whenever government authorities tell them to jump, and this was never more evident than in the three exceedingly strange years of history spanning the COVID-19 crisis. If the government can legally force you to undergo an experimental medical treatment with injury and even death as possible side effects, then the government can kill you. This implies that the powers of the government are limitless. Citizens whose bodies are owned by their government to do with as it pleases are in fact slaves. Robert Higgs expressed hope that he was wrong to be pessimistic at the end of *Crisis and Leviathan*. Alas, he was right.

NOTES

1. Robert F. Kennedy Jr. (2021) has produced a scathing and compelling critique of the administrative role that Anthony Fauci has played for decades in the medical and pharmaceutical industries, and also academic medicine: *The Real Anthony Fauci: Bill Gates, Big Pharma and the Global War on Democracy and Public Health*.

2. On January 19, 2023, Jacinda Ardern resigned from her position as New Zealand prime minister. Initially this may have seemed to be a tacit acknowledgment of the failure of her "Covid Zero" policy. The new prime minister, Chris Hipkins, however, was in fact the person in charge of New Zealand's COVID-19 response. He ominously indicated in July 2021 that the government would be "chasing down" citizens who refused to "come forward" for their vaccines voluntarily (Hipkins 2021).

3. This number has increased significantly in recent years because of the widespread polypharmaceutical approach to illness now favored by doctors as a result of their industry-influenced professional training. The more medications patients take, the more likely it becomes that there will be a dangerous or even deadly interactive effect (Holistic Sanctuary n.d.).

4. The definition of *vaccine* from 2018 is found in the earlier document, "Immunization: The Basics," which has been archived (Web Archive 2018).

5. Many insightful books are now available about the opioid crisis (e.g., Macy 2018; McGreal 2018; Quinones 2015; Westhoff 2019). In addition, Alex Gibney (2021) has produced a com-

pelling two-part documentary film miniseries covering many of the key factors in producing what became an overdose epidemic: *The Crime of the Century*.

6. Curiously, Harvard University acted in this regard even before the government announced the border closures (Isselbacher and Su 2020).

7. The Public Readiness and Emergency Preparedness (PREP) Act provides liability immunity to certain individuals and entities [companies] as specified by the Secretary of the Department of Health and Human Services, "against any claim of loss caused by, arising out of, relating to, or resulting from the manufacture, distribution, administration, or use of medical countermeasures." The Act does not protect from "willful misconduct," so lawsuits on that basis would be permitted. Manufacturers and distributors of COVID-19 vaccines were included under this protection from liability claims in a series of amendments issued throughout and after the pandemic.

8. In *Questioning the COVID Company Line: Critical Thinking in Hysterical Times* (Calhoun 2023), a volume of essays composed throughout the Coronapocalypse, I chronologically chart the many stages of this latest crony capitalist fiasco.

REFERENCES

Biden, Joe. 2022. "President Joe Biden: The 2022 Sixty Minutes, Interview." *CBS News*, September 18. https://www.cbsnews.com/news/president-joe-biden-60-minutes-interview-transcript-2022 -09-18/.

Boyd, Connor. 2023. "America Quietly Extends Covid Vaccination Entry Requirement for Travels until APRIL—Making US an International Outlier." *The Daily Mail*, January 4. https://www .dailymail.co.uk/health/article-11600173/US-extends-Covid-vaccination-entry-requirement -travelers-APRIL.html.

Calhoun, Laurie. 2015. *We Kill Because We Can: From Soldiering to Assassination in the Drone Age*. New York/London: Bloomsbury/Zed.

———. 2022. "The Pentagon Is neither Woke nor Based." *Libertarian Institute*. November 1. https:// libertarianinstitute.org/articles/the-pentagon-is-neither-woke-nor-based/.

———. 2023. *Questioning the COVID Company Line: Critical Thinking in Hysterical Times*. Austin, TX: Libertarian Institute.

Centers for Disease Control and Prevention (CDC). 2021a. "Drug Overdose Deaths in the U.S. Top 100,000 Annually." Last modified November 17, 2021. https://www.cdc.gov/nchs/pressroom /nchs_press_releases/2021/20211117.htm.

———. 2021b. "Immunization: The Basics." September 1. https://www.cdc.gov/vaccines/vac-gen /imz-basics.htm.

———. 2022. "CDC Seasonal Flu Effectiveness Studies." December 22. https://www.cdc.gov/flu /vaccines-work/effectiveness-studies.htm.

Commonwealth of Massachusetts. 2020. "Flu Vaccine Now Required for all Massachusetts School Students Enrolled in Child Care Pre-School, K-12 and Post-Secondary Institutions." August 19. https://www.mass.gov/news/flu-vaccine-now-required-for-all-massachusetts -school-students-enrolled-in-child-care-pre-school-k-12-and-post-secondary-institutions.

Condon, Bernard, Matt Sedensky, and Megan Hoyer. 2020. "New York's True Nursing Home Death Toll Cloaked in Secrecy." *AP News*, August 10. https://apnews.com/article/virus-outbreak -ap-top-news-understanding-the-outbreak-new-york-andrew-cuomo-212ccd87924b69060 53703a00514647f.

Day, Joel. 2020. "WHO Exposed: How Health Body Changed Pandemic Criteria to Push Agenda." *Express*, May 12. https://www.express.co.uk/news/world/1281081/who-world-health -organisation-coronavirus-latest-swine-flu-covid-19-europe-politics-spt.

Dowd, Edward. 2022. *"Cause Unknown": The Epidemic of Sudden Deaths in 2021 and 2022*. New York: Skyhorse Publishing.

Edwards, Erika. 2020. "Pfizer Vaccine Relies on New Technology Never before Used in Mass Human Vaccination." *NBC News*, November 10. https://news.yahoo.com/doctors-excited -cautious-pfizers-covid-202616468.html?guccounter=1.

Erb, Robin. 2021. "Henry Ford Study on Hydroxychloroquine for COVID Quietly Shut Down." *Bridge Michigan*, January 11. https://www.bridgemi.com/michigan-health-watch/henry-ford -study-hydroxychloroquine-covid-quietly-shut-down.

Facher, Lev. 2020. "Prescription Politics: Pharma Is Showering Congress with Cash, Even as Drug Makers Race to Fight the Coronavirus." *STAT*, August 10. https://www.statnews.com/feature /prescription-politics/prescription-politics/.

Federal Emergency Management Agency (FEMA). 2020. "COVID-19 Emergency Declaration." Updated March 18, 2021. https://www.fema.gov/press-release/20210318/covid-19 -emergency-declaration.

Fung, Katherine. 2022. "Banks Have Begun Freezing Accounts Linked to Trucker Protest." *Newsweek*, February 18. https://www.newsweek.com/banks-have-begun-freezing-accounts -linked-trucker-protest-1680649.

Gérard, Alexandre O., Audrey Laurain, Audrey Fresse, Nadège Parassol, Marine Muzzone, Fanny Rocher, Vincent L. M. Esnault, and Milou-Daniel Drici. 2021. "Remdesivir and Acute Renal Failure: A Potential Safety Signal from Disproportionality Analysis of the WHO Safety Database." *National Library of Medicine*, January 16. https://pubmed.ncbi.nlm.nih.gov /33340409/.

Gibney, Alex, dir. 2021. *The Crime of the Century*. HBO. https://www.hbo.com/the-crime-of-the -century.

Higgs, Robert. 1987. *Crisis and Leviathan: Critical Episodes in the Growth of American Government*. New York: Oxford University Press.

Hipkins, Christopher. 2021. "New Zealand COVID Minister to Chase Down the Unvaccinated." YouTube. https://youtu.be/htxuJD2zQiI.

Holistic Sanctuary. N.d. "Iatrogenic Disease: Treatment for Iatrogenic." https://www.theholistic sanctuary.com/holistic/iatrogenic-disease-silent-killer/.

Horton, Scott. 2017. *Fool's Errand: Time to End the War in Afghanistan*. Austin, TX: Libertarian Institute.

Husseini, Sam. 2020. "Peter Daszak's EcoHealth Alliance Has Hidden Almost $40 Million in Pentagon Funding and Militarized Pandemic Science." *Independent Science News*, December 16. https://www.independentsciencenews.org/news/peter-daszaks-ecohealth -alliance-has-hidden-almost-40-million-in-pentagon-funding/.

Isselbacher, Juliet E., and Amanda Y. Su. 2020. "Inside Harvard College's Decision to Send Students Home during the Coronavirus Pandemic." *Harvard Crimson*, April 1. https://www .thecrimson.com/article/2020/4/1/harvard-coronavirus-khurana-decision/#_blank.

Kennedy, Robert F., Jr. 2021. *The Real Anthony Fauci: Bill Gates, Big Pharma and the Global War on Democracy and Public Health*. New York: Skyhorse Publishing.

Kory, Pierre, Gianfranco Umberto Meduri, Joseph Varon, Jose Iglesias, and Paul Marik. 2021. "Review of the Emerging Evidence Demonstrating the Efficacy of Ivermectin in the Prophylaxis and Treatment of Covid-19." *American Journal of Therapeutics* 28 (3).

Kimball, Spencer. 2022. "Biden Administration Makes At-Home Covid Tests Available for Free Again This Winter." *CNBC*, December 15. https://www.cnbc.com/2022/12/15/biden-admin -free-covid-home-tests.html.

Lahut, Jake. 2020. "NY Gov. Cuomo Reportedly Ordered over 4,300 Recovering COVID-19 Patients to Be Sent to Nursing Homes." *Business Insider*, May 22. https://www.businessinsider

.com/cuomo-executive-order-4300-recovering-coronavirus-patients-ny-nursing-homes
-2020-5?r=US&IR=T.

Liptak, Kevin, and Donald Judd. 2022. "President Biden Tests Positive for Covid-19—Again." *CNN*,
July 30. https://www.cnn.com/2022/07/30/politics/joe-biden-covid-19-positive/index.html.

Macy, Beth. 2018. *Dopesick: Dealers, Doctors, and the Drug Company That Addicted America*. New
York: Little, Brown.

Malloy, Alley, and Maegan Velazquez. 2021. "Biden Warns of Winter of 'Severe Illness and Death'
for Unvaccinated Due to Omicron." *CNN*, December 16. https://www.cnn.com/2021/12/16
/politics/joe-biden-warning-winter/index.html.

McGreal, Chris. 2018. *American Overdose: The Opioid Tragedy in Three Acts*. New York: Public
Affairs.

Olliaro, Piero, Els Torreele, and Michel Vaillant. 2021. "COVID-19 Vaccine Efficacy and
Effectiveness—the Elephant (not) in the Room." *The Lancet*, April 20. https://www.thelancet
.com/journals/lanmic/article/PIIS2666-5247(21)00069-0/fulltext.

Our World in Data. 2023. "Coronavirus Country Profiles." February 24. https://ourworldindata.org
/coronavirus#coronavirus-country-profiles.

Parlapiano, Alicia, Deborah B. Solomon, Madeleine Ngo, and Stacy Cowley. 2022. "Where $5
Trillion in Pandemic Stimulus Money Went." *New York Times*, March 11. https://www
.nytimes.com/interactive/2022/03/11/us/how-covid-stimulus-money-was-spent.html.

Patterson, Belknap, Webb, and Tyler LLP. 2022. "Legal News: Supreme Court Rejects OSHA
Mandate." *JDsupra.com*, January 19. https://www.jdsupra.com/legalnews/supreme-court
-rejects-osha-mandate-3515744/.

Quinones, Sam. 2015. *Dreamland: The True Tale of America's Opiate Epidemic*. New York:
Bloomsbury.

Roche, Darragh. 2020. "Big Pharma Backs Joe Biden, but People Don't Think He'll Fix Drug Price."
Newsweek, September 20. https://www.newsweek.com/big-pharma-joe-biden-fix-drug
-pricing-1534809.

Rogers, Katie, and Sheryl Gay Stolberg. 2021. "Biden Mandates Vaccines for Workers, Saying 'Our
Patience Is Wearing Thin." *New York Times*, September 9. https://www.nytimes.com/2021/09
/09/us/politics/biden-mandates-vaccines.html.

Satter, Raphael. 2020. "U.S. Court: Mass Surveillance Program Exposed by Snowden Was Illegal."
Reuters, September 2. https://www.reuters.com/article/idUSKBN25T3CJ/.

Schwab, Klaus. 2016. *The Fourth Industrial Revolution*. Geneva: World Economic Forum.

Schwab, Klaus, and Thierry Malleret. 2020. *COVID-19: The Great Reset*. Geneva: Forum
Publishing.

Statista. 2019. "Number of Novel Coronavirus (COVID-19) Deaths Worldwide, by Country."
February 3, 2023. https://www.statista.com/statistics/1093256/novel-coronavirus-2019ncov
-deaths-worldwide-by-country/

Surkova, Elena, Vladyslav Nikolayevskyy, and Francis Drobniewski. 2020. "False-Positive COVID-
19 Results: Hidden Problems and Costs." *The Lancet* 8 (12).

Tebor, Celina, and John Bacon. 2021. "COVID-19 Deaths in 2021 Have Surpassed Last Year's
Count." *USA Today*, November 22. https://news.yahoo.com/2021-us-covid-death-count
-100257576.html.

United States Holocaust Memorial Museum. 2023. "Nuremberg Code." https://encyclopedia
.ushmm.org/content/en/article/the-nuremberg-code

US Department of Health and Human Services. 2021. "Public Readiness and Emergency Preparedness
(PREP) Act," Administration for Strategic Preparedness and Response website. https://aspr.hhs
.gov/legal/PREPact/Pages/default.aspx.

US Department of Justice. 2009. "Justice Department Announces Largest Healthcare Fraud Settlement in Its History." September 2. https://www.justice.gov/opa/pr/justice-department -announces-largest-health-care-fraud-settlement-its-history.

Web Archive. 2018. "Immunization: The Basics." May 17. http://web.archive.org/web/2021082611 3846/https://www.cdc.gov/vaccines/vac-gen/imz-basics.htm.

Westhoff, Ben. 2019. *Fentanyl, Inc.: How Rogue Chemists Are Creating the Deadliest Wave of the Opioid Epidemic*. New York: Grove Press.

White House. 2022a. "G20 Bali Leaders' Declaration." November 16. https://www.whitehouse.gov /briefing-room/statements-releases/2022/11/16/g20-bali-leaders-declaration/.

———. 2022b. "FACT SHEET: Biden Administration to Begin Distributing At-Home, Rapid COVID-19 Tests to Americans for Free." January 14. https://www.whitehouse.gov/briefing -room/statements-releases/2022/01/14/fact-sheet-the-biden-administration-to-begin -distributing-at-home-rapid-covid-19-tests-to-americans-for-free/.

Wiseman, Paul. 2021. "Biden Tasks OSHA with Vaccine Mandate." *Associated Press*, September 16. https://www.pbs.org/newshour/politics/biden-tasks-osha-with-vaccine-mandate.

Chapter 11
The Military-Industrial Complex and the Militarization of Society

Nathan P. Goodman

In his farewell address, President Dwight Eisenhower warned of the pernicious influence of the "military-industrial complex" (Eisenhower 1961). This referred to emerging relationships between government officials, scientific researchers, and private defense contractors associated with the American state's ongoing militarization and armament. The rise of the military-industrial complex is one particularly pernicious example of the growth of government throughout the 20th and 21st centuries. Economic historian Robert Higgs's groundbreaking research program on the growth of government includes eye-opening works on the origins and development of the military-industrial complex (MIC) (Higgs 2006a, 2012). In addition to analyzing its history, Higgs offers insightful theory and analysis that illuminates the ongoing harms caused by the MIC (Higgs 2007). Moreover, Higgs's core theoretical framework for understanding the growth of government, namely the "ratchet effect" he analyzed in his seminal work *Crisis and Leviathan* (Higgs 1987), provides useful analytical tools for understanding the origins, development, and consequences of the MIC.

The purpose of this chapter is twofold. First, it explains Higgs's distinctive contributions to our understanding of the MIC. Second, it builds on these contributions to explain how the MIC contributes to an ongoing militarization of society. How does Higgs's analysis of the MIC differ from other accounts of the topic?

Higgs's analysis of the MIC addresses many well-known issues with defense contracting, including rent-seeking, the revolving door, and perverse incentives that encourage a vicious cycle of militarization. But he also highlights several aspects that are underappreciated. These aspects can all be interpreted through the lens of Higgs's work on the ratchet effect, which explains why government grows during crises and does not return to its pre-crisis growth path. This theory emphasizes that the growth of government is heavily shaped by ideology, and that expansions in government have persistent post-crisis consequences, partially because of the interest groups they bring together and partially because of the way they alter the ideology and expectations of the citizenry.

This framework helps us understand the origins of the MIC, which Higgs traces to institutional changes made to the defense procurement process during one significant crisis period: World War II. Once the MIC was established, it created a set of interest groups, relationships, and ideological shifts that sustained the post-crisis system of militarized state power. Higgs documented various features of these interest groups, relationships, and ideological shifts. One aspect of this is the crucial role that legislators play in the MIC. Higgs sees their position within the military-industrial complex as so crucial that he follows an earlier draft of Eisenhower's farewell address in calling it the military-industrial-congressional complex (MICC) (Greenwalt 2021).

Higgs's emphasis on how the MICC sustains a broader scope of state power in post-crisis periods also draws his attention to an aspect of the MICC that pure rent-seeking accounts neglect. Higgs recognizes that the MICC corrupts not only government, but also business and society. In addition to rent-seeking by private contractors distorting the priorities of political leaders, defense spending creates incentives for private individuals to support war, militarism, and state power. By increasing incentives for individuals to embrace militarism, the MICC militarizes society. This occurs not just at the level of material incentives, but also at the level of ideology.

These Higgsian insights provide us with a framework for understanding the ongoing consequences and expansion of the MICC. As Higgs recognized in his later work, the post-9/11 expansion of the domestic security state gave rise to a broader phenomenon: the security-industrial-congressional complex (SICC). The SICC creates similar dynamics of cronyism and ideological statism, thereby entrenching the post-9/11 security state. Moreover, it undermines the civil liberties of domestic citizens.

The next section explains Higgs's theory of government growth, which emphasizes how crises create opportunities to expand government. The sections that follow explore how Higgs applied this theory to understand several aspects of the MIC. I begin by exploring the origins of the MIC in a crisis period: World War II. Then I discuss the role of legislators in perpetuating and maintaining the MIC, followed by a section that explores how the MIC militarizes society by coopting private citizens and placing them in entangled relationships with the militarized national security state. I then explain how the MIC has shaped the growing domestic security state, especially the Department of Homeland Security that was formed after the 9/11 attacks. Finally, the chapter concludes with a discussion of avenues for future research.

CRISES, IDEOLOGY, AND THE RATCHET EFFECT

Robert Higgs's seminal contribution to our understanding of the growth of government is *Crisis and Leviathan*, a book that uses both theory and economic history to explain the growth of the US government over time. It's important to be clear about what Higgs means by the growth of government.

Discussions of government growth often focus narrowly on the *scale* of government, which we can define in terms of the quantity of resources the government uses. Along this margin, an increase in military expenditure is an increase in the scale of military activity. By contrast, the *scope* of government refers to the range of activities government carries out. If the national security state acquires new surveillance powers or if the military becomes involved in domestic law enforcement in ways that previously were not permitted, then this is an expansion in the *scope* of government activity. Higgs was interested in the growth of government in both *scale* and *scope* dimensions, which meant that merely looking at growth of government spending as a percentage of GDP was not sufficient to capture the phenomenon he was studying. Instead, both qualitative and quantitative evidence were important for understanding the growth of government over time.

Higgs clearly explained that his theory of government growth was not monocausal. There may therefore be relevant factors outside the scope of his core theory. However, two factors were crucial to his explanation of government growth: (1) crises and (2) ideology. Crises, whether real or perceived, create opportunities to expand the scope of government, as they create a situation where people clamor for something to be done about a pressing problem. Whether these opportunities are taken up varies depending on the prevailing ideology, which refers to a system of broadly accepted beliefs that shape which political activities are seen as legitimate.

Higgs argues that prior to the Progressive Era, the prevailing ideology significantly limited the scope of the federal government's power. As a result, major crises did not always lead to significant expansions in the scale and scope of the federal government. However, Higgs argues that progressive ideology treated action by the national government as a legitimate means of addressing all manner of social ills. As a result, crises that occurred during and after the Progressive Era, such as wars and economic recessions, resulted in significant expansions in the scale and scope of government.

After a crisis concludes, there is often some amount of retrenchment. Not all of the crisis measures remain in place. For instance, many wartime measures are repealed, and military budgets decline after major wars end. However, this retrenchment typically does not return the scale and scope of government to their pre-crisis growth paths. That is, after the crisis the state remains larger than it would have been absent the crisis. Why does the state remain larger in the post-crisis period? There are at least two reasons.

One is that the expansion of government creates concentrated interest groups that benefit from a large state and have incentives to lobby for the continuation of powers and programs established during the crisis. Defense contractors and others involved in the MIC are examples of such interest groups. A second reason that government remains larger after the crisis is that expansions in the size of government impact the prevailing ideology. Government activities that would have seemed strange, dystopian, or otherwise unacceptable prior to the crisis become normalized. Ideology therefore shifts in a manner that expands the scope of permissible state action even after the crisis concludes. The MIC does this in several ways, including by normalizing entanglements between the state and private business, normalizing participation in militarism, and placing individuals in a position where they are part of the national security state. When individuals are part of the national security state, this shapes their ideology in several ways. Many people's careers become part of their identity, so those who identify with the operations of the national security state will become ideologically attached to its legitimacy. Moreover, the friendships and relationships that individuals form with their colleagues will increase their sympathy for others within their industry. If one's industry is part of the national security state, then these sympathies will result in greater ideological support for the national security state's operations.

ORIGINS OF THE MILITARY-INDUSTRIAL COMPLEX

After World War II, the US government "continued to maintain a military establishment that, by historical standards, can only be called immense. Keeping large numbers of men heavily armed with ever more sophisticated weapons has created a tremendous demand for munitions" (Higgs 2006a, 30). These munitions are produced by private contractors, who receive lucrative procurement contracts from the US Department of Defense (DoD). This contracting process leaves substantial room for cronyism and favoritism. Higgs attributes much of this cronyism to institutional features of the procurement process that he traces back to "the rearmament program of 1940–41" (Higgs 2006a, 33).

In the period between World War I and World War II, the United States did not maintain a significant military establishment or arms industry. Public attitudes toward weapons manufacturers were quite negative, and they were widely condemned as "merchants of death" (Engelbrecht and Hanighen 1934). As Higgs explains, "Military suppliers and financiers were subjected to prolonged investigation before the Nye Committee of the Senate during 1934–36, and they were widely blamed for U.S. participation in the Great War. In a public opinion survey in 1936, 82 percent of the respondents agreed that the manufacture and sale of munitions for private profit should be prohibited" (Higgs 2006a, 33). Moreover, 1939 polls found that "business executives opposed war even more than the general public," partially because they feared that a war economy would undermine property rights (Higgs 2006a, 33). In other words, ideology acted as a constraint on this type of entanglement between the state and private industry.

However, as Nazi Germany escalated its aggression throughout Europe, public opinion shifted. A crisis in Europe created demands for rearmament in the United States. Congress responded to the new demand for munitions, and "between June 1940 and December 1941, about $36 billion was made available to the War Department alone—more than the army and navy combined had spent during World War I" (Higgs 2006a, 35). While a large amount of funding was made available, turning this funding into munitions required investing in factories and other capital goods.

Business leaders were hesitant to invest in such projects, as they feared that Franklin Delano Roosevelt's administration would use wartime concerns as a justification to further erode their property rights. The Roosevelt administration alleviated these concerns by establishing "the Advisory Commission to the Council of National Defense (NDAC)" and appointing executives from companies such as General Motors, Sears, and U.S. Steel to key positions (Higgs 2006a, 35). In 1941 Roosevelt established the Office of Production Management (OPM), another federal bureau headed by wealthy businessmen. Despite these concessions to business, many were still reluctant to accept military contracts for three reasons.

First, at this point it was uncertain whether the United States would enter the war. Any capital investments made for war production might become unprofitable after the war. Second, government policies might limit their rates of return during the war, and public officials might use leverage associated with financing war production to control businesses that accepted military contracts. Third, there was no guarantee that war profits could be kept. After World War I, the government had sued firms "for recovery of funds advanced to stimulate investment in war facilities" (Higgs 2006a, 36). Businessmen largely saw defense production as a risky investment. Yet public officials had committed funds to a rearmament program. Direct government production of munitions, much less the underlying materials for weapons production, was not a viable option given the ideological commitments at the time. Persuading private firms to enter the arms industry was therefore vital for the rearmament program.

To convince private firms to participate, policymakers began to alter the contracting process in order to insulate defense contractors from risk. Competitive bidding was largely replaced by negotiated contracts, which created greater leeway for cronyism, favoritism, and higher payments. Under this new system, "only rarely would large defense contractors have to bear the burden of submitting the lowest bid in order to get the business" (Higgs 2006a, 39). Cost-plus-fixed-fee contracts were also introduced, which essentially offered guaranteed profits for defense contractors. Ultimately, the result was a shift "from an 'arm's length' relationship between two more or less equal parties in a business transaction [to] an undefined but intimate relationship" (Smith [1959] 1991, 312). As a result, "deals came to turn not on price, but on technical and scientific capabilities, size, experience, and established reputations as a military supplier—vaguer attributes that are easier to fudge for one's friends" (Higgs 2012, 217–18).

World War II laid the groundwork for the military-industrial complex. As with other instances of the "ratchet effect," this involved a crisis creating opportunities to expand the scale and scope of government, in this case by expanding both the public and private elements of the military sector (Higgs 1987). The profitable cronyism that the new contracting process enabled has persisted ever since. Higgs empirically examined later incarnations of the military-industrial complex and found similar patterns. For example, in a paper with Ruben Trevino, Higgs found that between 1970 and 1989 defense contractors made significantly higher profits than firms from outside the defense industry (Trevino and Higgs 1992). The military-industrial complex had been cemented, creating a contracting system that protected firms from risk and secured supernormal profits for them at taxpayer expense.

THE ROLE OF LEGISLATORS

The phrase "military-industrial complex" draws attention to the relationship between the military and private firms. However, this leaves out some key players. The defense budget, after all, is determined by Congress. Eisenhower emphasized this in an early draft of his speech by referring to the military-industrial complex as the "military-industrial-congressional complex"

(MICC), which is a phrase Higgs also uses throughout his writings as a more accurate description of the arrangement.

Higgs points out that "a single member of Congress can create magnificent gifts for his friends by making 'earmarks,' furtive amendments to an appropriations bill that everyone understands to be nothing but an individual legislator's pound of flesh taken out of the taxpayer's unfortunate corpus" (Higgs 2007, 309). The discretionary power legislators possess creates substantial incentives for defense contractors to expend resources on rent-seeking in order to influence these legislators. "To keep this gravy train on the track, contractors and their trade associations, as well as the armed forces themselves, devote great efforts to increasing the amount of money Congress appropriates for 'defense' and now also for 'homeland security.' Campaign contributions and other favors go predominantly to the incumbent barons—congressional leaders and committee chairmen—and to the military 'hawks' who have never met a defense budget big enough to satisfy them" (Higgs 2007, 309).

Legislators engage in frequent logrolling, which refers to vote trading between legislators, in order for each to secure sufficient support to pass their desired legislation. Consider, for instance, a scenario where one legislator supports a project that employs another's constituents and, in exchange, he receives support for a project that lines the pockets of a contractor that donated to his campaign. These types of exchanges are mutually beneficial for legislators. But they impose significant costs upon taxpayers, not to mention those who may eventually be brutalized by American weapons. Ultimately, however, "their interests do not count: they are not 'players' in this game, but merely victims of its depredations" (Higgs 2007, 309).

In an idealized model of the democratic state, legislators oversee the military on behalf of their constituents. If officials act in a manner that is counter to the law, basic ethics, or the preferences of voters, then in principle legislators can use their oversight powers and their powers of the purse to hold officials accountable. If voters are unsatisfied with how legislators are using their powers, then in principle they can vote these legislators out of office. However, in practice democratic politics is characterized by multiple frictions, principal-agent problems, and information asymmetries that limit the applicability of this idealized form of democratic accountability. In the realm of national security policy, these information asymmetries are particularly intense, as a great deal of relevant information is classified (see Coyne, Goodman, and Hall 2019).

These information asymmetries create significant scope for opportunism. Ordinary voters represent a dispersed group with little incentive to monitor the details of military policy, while defense contractors and other members of the MICC constitute a concentrated interest group with incentives to pay attention to public policies and engage in rent-seeking. Therefore, legislators have strong incentives to appeal to these concentrated interest groups rather than to the general voting public or to more public-spirited concerns. In a similar vein to their oversight powers, Congress is constitutionally vested with the power to declare war, which is intended to limit the discretionary power of the executive in entering the United States into new conflicts. Over the years, however, legislators have become hesitant to check presidential war powers (Burns 2019). Symbiotic relationships between legislators and defense contractors can help explain this troubling trend.

MILITARIZING SOCIETY

Defense contractors engage in rent-seeking, convincing legislators and bureaucrats to reshape defense policy in a manner that benefits narrow private interests, not the purported "public interest" or "national interest." One way to understand the MICC is that it involves private interests capturing and corrupting government. Yet Higgs argues that the MICC also corrupts the private sector, creating incentives for individuals to support state power, militarism, war, and violent conflict. Commerce, civil society, and other spheres of life that might operate in the realm of peaceable voluntary cooperation become militarized. Individuals who might oppose state power instead are paid off and incorporated into an apparatus of coercion.

Higgs suggests that this makes the MICC worse than a situation in which the military apparatus operates entirely through public bureaucracies. If militarism operates entirely through public bureaucracies, then "people are oppressed by being taxed, conscripted, and regimented, but they are not co-opted and corrupted by joining forces with their rapacious rulers; a clear line separates them from the predators on the 'dark side'" (Higgs 2007, 300). By contrast, the MICC coopts many private individuals, places them in close relationships with public figures, and renders them dependent upon military spending.

This has perverse ideological effects, because "by empowering and enriching wealthy, intelligent, and influential members of the public, [the MICC] removes them from the ranks of potential opponents and resisters of the state and thereby helps to perpetuate the state's existence and its intrinsic exploitation of people outside the precinct of the state and its major supporters. Thus, it simultaneously strengthens the state and weakens civil society, even as it creates the illusion of a vibrant private sector patriotically engaged in supplying goods and services to the heroic military establishment" (Higgs 2007, 300). This fuels the militarization of society, shifting the incentives and beliefs of the public.

In some sense, this type of ideological shift was a major goal of the early military-industrial complex. During World War II, the Roosevelt administration gave business leaders significant power in war mobilization and defense contracting, largely to quell businessmen's fears that war would cause regimentation and undermine their property rights. Today the MICC corrupts and coopts a wide range of individuals, not just business leaders but also scientists, engineers, and university administrators. The MICC militarizes society by coopting those who might otherwise embrace peaceful, voluntaristic civil society.

THE RISE OF THE DOMESTIC SECURITY STATE

When we think about the military-industrial complex, we often think about relationships between defense contractors and the Department of Defense. Yet the same dynamics of cronyism, weapons purchasing, logrolling, and militarization also occur in the rising domestic security state, which consists of a variety of federal law enforcement agencies. Since the 9/11 attacks in 2001, the US government has built up a substantial domestic security state centered around the Department of Homeland Security (DHS). The DHS exacerbated the preexisting militarization of domestic law enforcement, which had been occurring at the federal, state, and local levels for decades, largely fueled by the war on drugs (Coyne and Hall 2018). The war on terror was a perceived crisis that created a new impetus to militarize domestic law enforcement and security policy, and it created a centralized federal bureau, the DHS, that had "homeland security" as its primary ideological justification.

Just as the military contracts extensively with private firms, so does the DHS. During the war on terror, the DHS created something comparable to the MICC, namely "a completely new and even more menacing apparatus, which I call the security-industrial-congressional complex (SICC)" (Higgs 2006b). Billions of dollars in federal homeland security contracts create a strong incentive for rent-seeking by private firms (Bennett 2006; Mueller 2009).

The ongoing militarization of border security illustrates how the security-industrial-congressional complex works. Border security has become increasingly militarized since the 1970s, a process that has occurred via the acquisition of military hardware, incorporation of military tactics and training, and collaboration with the military (Coyne and Goodman 2022; Goodman 2024). After the 9/11 attacks, this process accelerated when the Border Patrol became part of DHS. The Immigration and Naturalization Service (INS) was split up into Immigration and Customs Enforcement (ICE) and Customs and Border Protection (CBP), both of which became part of DHS. The Border Patrol is part of the CBP. As such, their power is reinforced using rhetoric about "homeland security," and their budgets are heavily influenced by legislators that sit on the House Homeland Security Committee (Coyne and Goodman 2020a; Miller 2019).

As a result, homeland security contractors, many of which have long been part of the military-industrial complex, expend significant resources to influence the House Homeland Security Committee. "Between 2006 and 2018, Lockheed Martin, General Dynamics, Northrop Grumman, Raytheon, [and] Boeing contributed a total of $6.5 million to members of the committee. In the 115th Congress (2017–2018), Northrop Grumman donated $293,324, General Dynamics $150,000 and Lockheed Martin $224,614" (Miller 2019, 4). These firms receive lucrative contracts to provide weaponry, surveillance equipment, and other services to the Border Patrol.

The House Appropriations Committee also has significant influence over the federal budget, impacting both the homeland security budget and the defense budget. This committee is therefore a crucial decision-making center for both the MICC and the SICC, and its members receive significant campaign contributions from contractors involved in both complexes. As journalist Todd Miller explains:

> Between 2006 and 2018, Lockheed Martin, General Dynamics, Northrop Grumman, Raytheon, Boeing contributed a total of $27.6 million to members of the committee. During the 115th Congress (2017–2018), Northrop Grumman and Lockheed Martin were the top two contributors with $866,194 and $691,401 respectively offered to members of the Appropriations Committee, along with Raytheon, Boeing, Deloitte, and General Dynamics, all making donations of over $500,000. While these were all companies winning military contracts and were also lobbying on military issues, they also received substantial contracts from CBP. (Miller 2019, 3–4)

The SICC and the MICC involve many of the same key players in both the private sector and the legislature. Both rely on the rhetoric and ideology of national security and counterterrorism to secure government largess. Moreover, legislators on key committees have significant discretionary power within both complexes, which creates strong incentives for private contractors to donate to their campaigns, lobby them, and build relationships with them.

Another crucial way that the SICC operates is through trade shows that help cement social ties between contractors and public officials. For instance, at the annual Border Security Expo numerous private contractors advertise their wares to officials at the Border Patrol and other law enforcement agencies. In addition to advertising their products, contractors forge social ties with public officials at coffee breaks, shooting range events, and an annual golf game (Coyne and Goodman 2020a; Miller 2019).

Social ties between individuals in the private and public sectors are further reinforced by the revolving door by which individuals move between these sectors. This revolving door operates at the highest levels of the DHS and CBP, as "between 2003 and 2017, at least four CBP commissioners and three DHS Secretaries went onto homeland security corporations or consulting companies after leaving government" (Miller 2019, 5). From 2006 to July 2019, "177 people have gone through the DHS revolving door and 34 have worked both for the House Homeland Security Committee and for a lobbying firm" (Miller 2019, 5).

This arrangement blurs the line between the public and private sectors. It places various private individuals and firms in close crony relationships with the state and provides them with strong incentives to support militarized border security approaches intended to enforce draconian immigration restrictions. These immigration restrictions drastically restrict the labor market, prohibiting mutually beneficial exchanges between migrants and businesses. Many business leaders would have an incentive to oppose these restrictions, but border security contracts coopt some of these firms, turning them into beneficiaries of immigration enforcement rather than mere victims of it.

In addition to coopting private individuals and turning them into lackeys for the security state, border militarization undermines civil liberties and privacy. These harms begin in border regions, where surveillance, invasive searches, and violence by the Border Patrol are most common. However, the powers and tools granted to the Border Patrol are often shared with other law enforcement agencies and used for purposes with a tenuous relationship to border security and homeland security. For instance, the Border Patrol has lent its unmanned aerial vehicles, or drones, to numerous other law enforcement agencies, thereby expanding domestic surveillance capacities in the interior of the United States (Lynch 2013; Coyne and Goodman 2020a; Goodman 2024).

Border militarization, and the broader SICC, illustrate that the dynamics of the MICC can be turned inward. Legislators, generals, and private contractors make lucrative deals at taxpayer expense in order to prepare for wars abroad. But legislators, bureaucrats, and private contractors also make lucrative deals at taxpayer expense in order to build a homeland security state at home. Both complexes—the MICC and the SICC—undermine civil liberties, militarize society, and divert private parties from civil society toward participation in the violent and militarized operation of state power.

CONCLUSION

Robert Higgs's work provides us with powerful theoretical and empirical insights into the military-industrial-congressional complex. His scholarship sheds light on the MICC's historical origins, the role of crises in its expansion over time, the crucial role that legislators play in its operations, how it shapes ideology and is shaped by ideology, and the way it coopts and militarizes business and civil society. While Higgs has shed significant light on these issues, there are many opportunities for further research on these issues.

One direction for further research involves studying recent developments in the MICC and the SICC. How does the contemporary MICC operate? Does the current approach to the war on terror generate different contracting patterns than earlier periods? How are relationships and projects within the MICC developing as tensions escalate with Russia and China? Do contemporary domestic events and civil unrest influence the lobbying strategies or outputs of homeland security contractors? Where we see firms experienced in the MICC entering the SICC to militarize border security and law enforcement, do any firms start out in the SICC and then enter the MICC? Have the supernormal profits documented by Trevino and Higgs (1992) persisted in the years since? Do similar profit rates prevail in the SICC, or just in the MICC?

Researchers could further investigate Higgs's theories about the ways militarism corrupts business and civil society. Are those involved in defense contracting firms, military-funded research labs, and military-funded university centers individuals who would otherwise work in the public security sector under a different system? Or would they otherwise be working in the private sector and civil society? Causal identification is difficult here, but researchers may devise ways to tease out how many in the MICC and SICC are simply drawn to militarism and security and how many have been coopted by contemporary arrangements.

One especially important question for future research concerns what, if anything, can be done to break the power of the MICC and the SICC. Can these distributional coalitions and crony relationships be disrupted? Can we demilitarize a militarized society and move toward a stable peace? Higgs is pessimistic. To the question "Can anything be done?" he has written, "The short answer is probably not. The MICC is deeply entrenched in the U.S. political economy" (Higgs 2007, 311). Despite its severe costs to the lives, liberties, prosperity, and security of people around the globe, the MICC serves its key stakeholders quite well. They therefore have strong incentives to preserve the current system.

Yet there may still be hope for change. One way forward would involve shifting the prevailing ideology. To Higgs, ideology is crucial, as it sets the parameters of what the public will accept and what political decision makers see as feasible and permissible. To end the MICC and the SICC, the prevailing ideology must shift away from militarism, American hegemony, and the security state. An ideological shift like this would require imagining alternatives to militarized security provision. Conflict and security threats are real problems. Yet militarism and state power are not the only conceivable ways to address them.

People resolve conflicts peaceably in many contexts, and they also provide security through a wide variety of organizational forms at multiple scales. Researching polycentric security, defense, peacebuilding, and conflict resolution can help us imagine feasible alternatives to militarism (Coyne and Goodman 2020b). An ideological shift toward prioritizing such approaches may seem radical. But it is grounded in a practical understanding of the real ways people resolve conflict and resolve context-specific security dilemmas. It may be the only way to end the military-industrial complex and demilitarize society.

REFERENCES

Bennett, James T. 2006. *Homeland Security Scams*. New York: Routledge.

Burns, Sarah. 2019. *The Politics of War Powers: The Theory and History of Presidential Unilateralism*. Lawrence: University Press of Kansas.

Coyne, Christopher J., and Nathan P. Goodman. 2020a. "The Political Economy of the Virtual Wall." *Peace Review* 32 (2): 172–80.

———. 2020b. "Polycentric Defense." *Independent Review* 25 (2): 279–92.

———. 2022. "U.S. Border Militarization and Foreign Policy: A Symbiotic Relationship." *Economics of Peace and Security Journal* 17 (1): 5–16.

Coyne, Christopher J., Nathan P. Goodman, and Abigail R. Hall. 2019. "Sounding the Alarm: The Political Economy of Whistleblowing in the US Security State." *Peace Economics, Peace Science, and Public Policy* 25 (1): 1–11.

Coyne, Christopher J., and Abigail R. Hall. 2018. *Tyranny Comes Home: The Domestic Fate of U.S. Militarism*. Stanford, CA: Stanford University Press.

Eisenhower, Dwight D. 1961. "Farewell Address." Avalon Project. https://avalon.law.yale.edu/20th _century/eisenhower001.asp.

Engelbrecht, H. C., and F. C. Hanighen. 1934. *Merchants of Death: A Study of the International Armament Industry*. New York: Routledge.

Goodman, Nathan. 2024. "Border Militarization and Domestic Institutions." *Constitutional Political Economy*. https://doi.org/10.1007/s10602-024-09440-5.

Greenwalt, Bill. 2021. "Ike Was Wrong: The Military-Industrial Congressional Complex Turns 60." *Breaking Defense.* January 25. https://breakingdefense.com/2021/01/ike-was-wrong-the -military-industrial-congressional-complex-turns-60/.

Higgs, Robert. 1987. *Crisis and Leviathan: Critical Episodes in the Growth of the American Government.* New York: Oxford University Press.

———. 2006a. *Depression, War, and Cold War: Studies in Political Economy.* New York: Oxford University Press.

———. 2006b. "The Security-Industrial Congressional Complex: SICC." The Independent Institute, October 19, 2006. https://www.independent.org/news/article.asp?id=1835.

———. 2007. "Military-Economic Fascism: How Business Corrupts Government and Vice Versa." *Independent Review* 12 (2): 299–316.

———. 2012. *Delusions of Power: New Explorations of State, War, and Economy.* Oakland, CA: Independent Institute.

Lynch, Jennifer. 2013. "Customs & Border Protection Logged Eight-Fold Increase in Drone Surveillance for Other Agencies." Electronic Frontier Foundation. July 3. https://www.eff.org /deeplinks/2013/07/customs-border-protection-significantly-increases-drone-surveillance -other.

Miller, Todd. 2019. *More Than a Wall: Corporate Profiteering and the Militarization of US Borders.* Amsterdam: Transnational Institute. https://www.tni.org/files/publication-downloads/more -than-a-wall-report.pdf.

Mueller, John. 2009. *Overblown: How Politicians and the Terrorism Industry Inflate National Security Threats, and Why We Believe Them.* New York: Free Press.

Smith, R. Elberton. (1959) 1991. *The Army and Economic Mobilization.* Washington, DC: Center for Military History, United States Army.

Trevino, Ruben, and Robert Higgs. 1992. "Profits of U.S. Defense Contractors." *Defence Economics* 3 (3): 211–18.

Chapter 12

The War Industry as Economic Cancer

Christopher J. Coyne and Yuliya Yatsyshina

I n testimony before Congress in 1969, economist Kenneth Boulding argued that "the war industry is a cancer within the body of American society. It has its own mode of growth, it represents a system which is virtually independent and indeed objectively inimical to the welfare of the American people, in spite of the fact that it still visualizes itself as their protector" (quoted in Joint Economic Committee 1969, 140). Boulding's point was that the military system has harmful effects, which metastasize throughout society. Studying these effects has been a central part of Robert Higgs's research program.

Higgs's most well-known work on the topic explores the connection between crisis and the growth of the state through a ratchet effect (Higgs 1987, 2007a). Beyond this, Higgs has made important contributions to our understanding of the relation between war and the economy. One aspect of his scholarship in this area examines the historical war economy, including a reconsideration of the American economy during World War II and the ortho-dox story that the war increased economic growth, reduced unemployment, and increased consumer well-being (Higgs 2006a). Higgs's work on this topic employs the tools of economics to differentiate between increases in output and increases in value-added output in terms of improved human well-being. A second aspect focuses on the contemporary war economy and the interplay between private and public actors in the military system (Higgs 2006a, 2007b). This research explores the direct effects of military activity on economic activ-ity, as well as the broader effects on the economic system itself.

This chapter engages Higgs's work on the political economy of the military system. Whereas Boulding identified the overall harmful effect of the military system on American society, Higgs's scholarship offers insight into the specific mechanisms that contribute to the emergence and spread of the harmful effects of the military system. Understanding the operations and economic effects of the US military system is important given its significant magnitude.

We would like to thank Amy Crockett for useful comments and suggestions on an earlier version.

The US government spends over $1 trillion per year on national-security activities (Smithberger and Hartung 2021). The Department of Defense is among the world's largest employers; in 2015 it was estimated to be the world's largest, employing 3.2 million people (see Taylor 2015). It is estimated that over 200,000 companies provide supplies, parts, and manufacturing to the Department of Defense (US Government Accountability Office 2022, 1). The real estate portfolio of the Department of Defense spans all 50 states, eight US territories, and 45 foreign countries (US Department of Defense 2018, 7). In many cases military establishments become focal points of local economic activity, with entire communities built around their existence and operation. As these statistics indicate, the US military system is entangled with private economic activity. As such, military activity has real economic effects, both in the immediate term and in the long term.

In what follows, we explore the US military system—by which we mean the integrated network of public and private actors involved in the federal government's military activities. Public actors include elected officials and bureaucrats (civilian and military) employed in military-related bureaus. Private actors include private firms and people connected to the military sector.

We proceed as follows: the next section explores the unique nature of the military system so that we may understand its overarching structure and features. After that, we explore the machinery of the military system. We discuss the incentives facing private and public participants and the important role played by the revolving door between the two arenas. We also explore the cancerous economic effects of the military system, and we discuss the immediate and long-term effects of the military system on the broader economic system.

THE NATURE OF THE MILITARY SYSTEM

The US government has a monopoly on defense provision at the national level and is the sole buyer of military supplies not legally obtainable by civilians. Higgs (2006a) pinpoints a notable institutional change that fostered the current state of the US military system. In building military capabilities for World War II, the Roosevelt administration encouraged cooperation between public and private interests by dramatically changing procurement laws from the sealed-bid type to a negotiated form of cost-plus-fixed-fee contracts (Higgs 2006a, 31–33).

This shifted the existing process from open advertising and competitive bidding to contract negotiation with firms. In doing so it elevated the importance of personal connections between members of the military and private sectors. Drawing on the insights of Wilberton Smith, the U.S. Army's historian on economic mobilization during the war, Higgs (2007b, 307) writes about

> the buyer-seller dealings as constituting "an undefined but intimate relationship" and his [Smith's] recognition that "contracts ceased to be completely binding." Thus, the institutional changes made in 1940–41 and the war-time operation of the military-industrial complex in the context of these new rules put permanently in place the essential features of the modern procurement system, which has repeatedly demonstrated its imperviousness to reform for the past sixty years.

This relationship between public and private entities has extended over time due to the buildup and maintenance of the military after the war. "The tight budget constraints of the pre-1940 peacetime periods become vastly looser thereafter as trillions of dollars poured out of the congressional appropriations process during the endless national emergency of the Cold War, and the spigot has remained wide open in its sequel, the so-called war on terror" (Higgs 2007b, 308). During the Cold War, the defense contracting industry was represented by a handful of dominant firms working exclusively for the defense needs established by the government.

The number of defense contractors in all size categories—the "Big Five" corporations and smaller firms—dramatically increased during the past two decades due to the spending associated with the "war on terror." The "Big Five" defense contractors—Lockheed Martin, Raytheon Technologies Corp., General Dynamics, Boeing, and Northrop Grumman—typically receive about a quarter to a third of the annual contract budget allocation. For example, in 2020, these companies received about 35 percent of the defense contracting dollars—$156.4 billion of the $445.5 billion allocated to contracting (Levinson 2021). The amount of defense spending dollars received by medium to small contractors providing a variety of services has also grown over time. "In 2019, the Pentagon spent $370 billion on contracting—more than half the total defense-related discretionary spending, $676 billion, and a whopping 164% higher than its spending on contractors in 2001" (Peltier 2020, 1).

Defense procurement is a complex and multilevel process involving numerous stakeholders including Pentagon officials who initiate the budget process, as well as the congressional subcommittees that review budgets and submit for final approval. Following approvals, the US government purchases defense products directly from private firms. These products range from basic uniforms and vehicles to weapons, planes, drones, and defense systems. The result is that numerous firms are entangled in the broader defense system and are incentivized to participate in the political process to secure government contracts. This process has been plagued by systematic waste, fraud, and corruption throughout time (see Fitzgerald 1972, 1989; Burton 1993; McCartney 2015). Discussing these systematic pathologies, Roland (2021, 128) notes, "Neither structural changes nor cycles of reform, however, could meliorate the chronic flaws in government procurement of goods, services and R&D."

The resulting system is not capitalism or socialism. It is not capitalism, which is defined by private ownership over the means of production and voluntary exchange. A crucial feature of a capitalist system is the absence of a single hierarchy of ends. No person, or group of people, imposes their ends on a market system. Instead, people within the system pursue their own individual ends through exchange and experimentation. Nor is the resulting system socialism, which is defined as national ownership over the means of production. Instead, Higgs (2007b) argues that the system is best characterized as one of "military-economic fascism" or "participatory fascism."

On a fundamental level, "the essence of fascism is nationalistic collectivism, the affirmation that the 'national interest' should take precedence over the rights of individuals" (Higgs 1987, 241). At the same time, private property over the means of production remains. "Fascism recognizes people's desire to possess private property and admires the strength of the profit motive" (Higgs 1987, 241). However, voluntary exchanges are allowed to operate only "insofar as they do not conflict with the national interest as formulated by fascism's political authorities" (Twight 1975, 14). So, while private ownership over the means of production exists in this system, the administrative state dictates and shapes production.

This stands in contrast to a private, competitive market in a capitalist system where private firms produce value-adding goods in response to diverse market demand absent a single hierarchy of ends imposed by political authorities. Instead, the political control over private productive capabilities that defined the military system, coupled with "extensive interchange of positions between ranking civil servants and high corporate executives," sets up a coalition of big business and government (Twight 1975, 22).

The participatory aspect refers to the reality that private people have the perceived ability to actively participate in the process of government (Twight 1975, 21; Higgs 1987, 242–43). For instance, people are able to vote, voice their political opinions publicly, and voice their opinions to their representatives. This gives people the sense that political outcomes are driven by "the people." The reality, however, is that much of the political process is outside of the reach of the ordinary members of society. This is due to the complexity of the political apparatus and the ability of political insiders to use that complexity favorably to pursue their own ends.

Holcombe (2018) offers a detailed analysis of the workings of what he calls "political capitalism," which offers insight into the foundations of the system discussed by Twight and Higgs. He defines the system of political capitalism as follows:

> Political capitalism is an economic and political system in which the economic and political elite cooperate for their mutual benefit. The economic elite influence the government's economic policies to use regulation, government spending, and the design of the tax system to maintain their elite status in the economy. The political elite who implement those policies are then supported by the economic elite, which helps the political elite maintain their status: an exchange relationship that benefits both the political and economic elite. The elite cooperate to use their political and economic power to retain their positions at the top of the political and economic hierarchies. (2018, 1)

In this system, the means of production are privately owned, but political elites have significant influence over how these productive capabilities are used through the regulatory-administrative state. The reason, according to Holcombe, is that there are insiders—the political and economic elite—and outsiders—the general populace—who face different costs of transacting. The insiders are part of a low transaction cost group that allows them to bargain among the elites in pursuit of their ends. The outsiders face high transaction costs as it relates to influencing political outcomes. This allows insiders to concentrate benefits on their members while imposing costs on outsiders who have little recourse given the relatively high transaction costs they face.

This poses a challenge because the stated purpose of the military system is to serve "the people" by protecting their person, property, and the broader institutions of freedom. However, the system operates in a way that creates space for insiders to engage in narrow opportunism that threatens the very things it is designed to protect, hence Kenneth Boulding's concern that the war industry was a cancer on American society. It is important to note that these concerns are not the result of malicious actors, but instead the nature of the system itself. As Holcombe notes, "The problem is not caused so much by specific individuals engaging in some specific misdeeds, but rather is due to the incentive structure within a system of political economy that leads the political elite to cooperate with the economic elite for their mutual benefit" at the expense of the masses they purport to protect (Holcombe 2018, 252).

THE MACHINERY OF THE MILITARY SYSTEM

The US military system is best described as military-economic, or participatory, fascism. But how does this system operate? The following mechanisms offer insight into how the elite use their insider position to entrench and extend their interests.

Private Incentives

Well-established connections are crucial in a system of participatory fascism. "When business profitability depends on connections and cronyism, businesses have to participate in that system to remain profitable. Political capitalism not only gives business interests the incentive to use political connections for private benefits, it makes their profitability dependent on connections" (Holcombe 2018, 41). This is certainly the case in the military system, where many firms are highly dependent on the federal government for revenues. This incentivizes rent-seeking, which refers to the use of resources to secure favorable political privileges.

This rent-seeking can take on a number of forms, including campaign contributions, lobbying efforts through meetings and entertainment, and donations to causes linked to specific political officials. The purpose of these expenditures is to create a quid pro quo expectation. As Higgs notes, "Business interests seek to bend the state's decisions in their favor by corrupting official decision makers with outright and de facto bribes" (2007b, 299). Moreover, "both the givers and the receivers understand these payments in exactly the same way that they understand illegal forms of bribery, even though they never admit this understanding in public" (2007b, 305).

One illustrative example of defense contractor lobbying is Northrup Grumman's efforts to reauthorize the Global Hawk drone program despite its routine cost overruns and subpar performance. When defense officials considered cutting the program from the budget, the producer and defense contractor, Northrup Grumman, engaged in an intense political lobbying campaign that included significant sums to the key House defense panels in the form of campaign contributions to political action committees (PACs) in the 2012 election cycle. "Members of the full House Armed Services Committee received about $584,000, in total, during the 2012 election cycle, 46 percent more than in the 2010 cycle" (Sia and Cohen 2013). Shortly after, the costly and ineffective Global Hawk program was extended. These same political dynamics apply to a myriad of public-private partnerships in the military system from the end of World War II to the present (see Roland 2021).

As another illustration, consider that the US Navy recently announced that it would be retiring eight of its 10 Freedom-class littoral combat ships following numerous breakdowns and engine and transmission dysfunctions (Lipton 2022). In response, the private entities that produce and maintain the ships— Lockheed Martin and Fincantieri Marinette Marine—exerted pressure on key decision makers of Congress to reverse course. Soon thereafter, members of Congress amended the 2023 Pentagon spending authorization to allow for the retirement of only four of the ships.

Even in rare instances where programs are ultimately canceled, lobbying can delay the process for years. Consider, for instance, the case of the Joint Land Attack Cruise Missile Defense Elevated Netted Sensor System (JLENS). The JLENS was a tethered aerial radar system that was intended to surveil for aircraft, cruise missiles, and ground vehicles. The program, which began in the late 1990s and received increased support in the wake of the 9/11 attacks, was a joint venture between Hughes Aircraft and Raytheon. The program ran into significant issues throughout its existence, including software issues, a lack of flexibility in movement and detection of key threats—for example, crude rockets and improved explosive devices—an inability to differentiate between friendly and enemy aircraft, and an inability to operate in bad weather. Efforts to cancel the program in 2010 were met with intense lobbying efforts from Raytheon, which blocked these efforts, keeping the program in operation (Willman 2015). The JLENS program was ultimately canceled in 2017 with more than $2.7 billion spent over the life of the project.

The ability of defense contractors to secure contracts through political relationships insulates them from losing business in the face of repeated wrongdoing. To provide an example, Boeing has repeatedly settled cases brought against it for overcharging the military. In 2011, for instance, it was revealed that the company routinely overcharged the army for helicopter parts (Schwellenbach 2011), and in 2014, the company paid $23 million in fines for labor charges in building aircraft for the Air Force (US Department of Justice 2014). In 2021, after a three-year investigation, the company repaid $10.7 million for double billing the government for taxes paid to foreign governments on Boeing's foreign employees (Capaccio 2021). These types of publicly revealed malfeasance often do not prevent contractors from receiving lucrative deals in the defense budget.

In general, there is a lack of accountability in the military system. Part of this is due to the lack of a clear residual claimant, or owner. The military system represents "the people" and is paid for by "the people." When everyone is responsible, no one is, with the result being weak incentives to check abuses and opportunism. Part of the issue is due to the sheer size of the US military apparatus. The military apparatus is enormous, with dysfunctional accountability rules and systems—as evidenced by the Pentagon's repeated failure of financial audits (Echols 2022). This dysfunction creates an environment ripe for unchecked abuse and waste by private contractors.

Because voters are part of the out group, they have little influence over specifics of outcomes in the military system. Voting is a weak form of feedback due to bundling (voters choose politicians representing a number, or bundle, of complex issues), election timing (elections are held relatively infrequently), the limitations of votes to express the intensity of their preferences (each voter gets one vote, which counts the same as everyone else's vote, meaning there is no way to differentiate between the intensity of each voter's preferences), and the limited impact of each vote (as the number of voters increase, the likelihood of a single vote impacting the outcome falls) (Buchanan 1954).

This incentivizes rational ignorance whereby voters lack the inducement to collect detailed information on the actions of their representatives. Beyond this, the complexity of the military system makes it nearly impossible for even the most interested voters to collect accurate information. Because of its sheer size, the military system is characterized by significant information asymmetries between the elites and the masses (Coyne, Goodman, and Hall 2019; Coyne and Hall 2021).

Another factor limiting the influence of the masses is ideology. As Higgs (1987, 2008) has documented, ideology plays a crucial role in the way citizens perceive their relationship to the state and its activities. Government responses to past crises can reshape citizens' ideology such that the masses become more accepting of expansions in the overall size (scale and scope) of government activities. Further, Higgs (2006b) has emphasized that governments take active steps to cultivate citizens' fear to foster acceptance of expansions in state power. These factors, combined with the incentives inherent in democratic politics, limit the ability of citizen-voters to check the opportunism of the private elite who are able to leverage their relationship with the political elite for their own gain.

As a result, foreign policy outcomes partially reflect the interests of the private elite. As John Kenneth Galbraith (1978, 323) noted, private defense firms shape "the official view of defense requirements and therewith of some part of the foreign policy. These will be a broad reflection of the firm's own goals; it would be eccentric to expect otherwise." These private interests interplay with those of the public elites to shape the activities and policies of the military system.

Public Incentives

Private firms seek to use their connections and resources to secure revenues from political gatekeepers. Rent-seeking is the expenditure of resources to gain political favor. However, political actors are not passive in this process. Because of their decision-making power, these gatekeepers possess a property right over the allocation of defense-related resources. This allows them to extract resources from private parties seeking to secure government transfers (see McChesney 1987, 1997). This rent extraction can be understood as private expenditures to avoid political disfavor by political decision makers possessing the power to determine resource allocations; that is, it is a "pay-to-play" arrangement.

In practice, rent-seeking and rent extraction can be difficult to disentangle, and it is likely that both forces are at work simultaneously. Private actors spend resources to both curry favor and avoid disfavor. Political actors certainly recognize the power they possess, and the potential benefits attached to that power. Consider, for instance, the House Subcommittee on Defense, a permanent subcommittee of the US House Committee on Appropriations, which controls the flow of military-related funding to private firms. Schweizer (2013, 37) notes that the final report of the subcommittee is "the sort of document that can make or break the programs of defense contractors, both large and small." This grants significant discretion to political decision makers sitting on the committee. As one would expect, defense firms invest significant resources building and maintaining relationships with members of this, and other congressional committees (e.g., the House Armed Services Committee), with control over resource allocations (see Giorno 2022; Wooten and Claypool 2022). Among other things, these entanglements between the private and public sectors undermine the supposed oversight function of these committees.

The prevalence of rent-seeking and rent extraction sheds important light on the machinery of the military system. Appreciating these features calls into question the common claim that the military system is pursuing the "national interest" or to provide for the "common defense" of "the people." Decisions and activities are not based on some vague notion of the "national interest" (which does not, and cannot, exist), but instead on political relationships between the public and private elite.

The absence of a grand pursuit of a "national interest" becomes even more evident when one considers the incentives facing elected officials. In principle, representatives would work together for the "common good." In reality, these officials respond to incentives by pursuing the narrow interests of their local constituents even when this deviates from the interests outside of that local constituency.

To illustrate this point, consider the reflections offered by Robert Gates, a former secretary of defense who served under both President George W. Bush and President Barack Obama, regarding his experience with Congress. "I was more or less continuously outraged by the parochial self-interest of all but a very few members of Congress. Any defense facility or contract in their district or state, no matter how superfluous or wasteful, was sacrosanct. I was constantly amazed and infuriated at the hypocrisy of those who most stridently attacked the Defense Department as inefficient and wasteful but fought tooth and nail to prevent any reduction in defense activities in their home state or district" (Gates 2014). People respond to incentives, and in the context of the military system this means that elected officials will compete to secure benefits for themselves and their constituents. The military system is an ideal setting to do this because it allows elected officials to concentrate benefits while dispersing costs on others who foot the bill, all under the name of protecting "the nation."

Private firms recognize the incentives facing private firms and organize their activities accordingly. For instance, consider Lockheed Martin's F-35 Joint Strike Fighter, whose production is spread over 307 congressional districts across 45 states (Cockburn 2019). This has created a dense network of elected officials who have a vested interest in seeing this project continue and expand despite a varieties of failures within the F-35 program.

The final aspect of the public side of the military system is government bureaus. These bureaus are populated by nonelected political actors (bureaucrats). The national security state apparatus is enormous. A study by Priest and Arkin (2011) of the post-9/11 US security state (including private and public actors) found that it is so extensive and hidden that it was impossible to identify its exact magnitude, cost, or the range of actions being undertaken by those populating these positions. As noted previously, the US military bureaucracy is plagued by fraud and waste and is unable to satisfy even the most basic accounting and financial standards. Bureaus face an incentive to expand their discretionary budgets and to spend to demonstrate that they are doing things (Tullock 1965; Niskanen 1971, 1975). And in the absence of a clear residual claimant (owner), there is a weak incentive to exercise prudence with resources.

In principle, Congress serves as a check on the activities of bureaus, and in some instances it does. But there are two factors that weaken the efficacy of this oversight. First, Congress is often reliant on bureaus for the provision of information that is used in oversight (Coyne, Goodman, and Hall 2019). Bureaus, however, can act strategically to control the flow and content of information in a way that benefits them. In one case, for instance, the Pentagon concealed a study that indicated a potential savings of $125 billion from reduced waste out of fear that Congress would use this information to reduce its budget (Whitlock and Woodward 2016).

Second, many members of Congress have a strong incentive to contribute to expansions in the military bureaucracy. "The Armed Services Committee has a tradition of uniting its members on both sides of the aisle, since many have a military background or home-state interests in defense" (Steinhauer 2015). Members of Congress are reliant on bureaus to direct resources to both private firms (which make payments to members of Congress) and to their constituents who vote for them. This creates a strong incentive for members of Congress to be advocates for bureau expansion.

Coyne, Michaluk, and Reese (2016) argue that the perverse incentives that exist in the military system during peacetime significantly intensify during times of war. "Times of war are especially unique because the incentives for unproductive behavior are magnified due to the injection of significant amounts of additional funds with the added pressure to spend quickly in a rapidly changing conflict environment" (2016, 3). This magnifies already dysfunctional oversight and accounting mechanisms, leading to further waste, fraud, and abuse. These dynamics were evident in the US occupations of Afghanistan and Iraq.

In 2011, the Commission on Wartime Contracting in Iraq and Afghanistan released its final report for Iraq and Afghanistan. The report concluded that "between $31 billion and $60 billion of taxpayers' funds have been lost to contract waste and fraud in Iraq and Afghanistan. It is outrageous" (2011, 5). A 2020 report by the Special Inspector General for the Afghanistan Reconstruction (SIGAR) further reviewed $63 billion of the $134 billion that Congress had appropriated to Afghanistan between 2002 and 2019 and found that $19 billion—nearly a third of the total—was lost due to waste and fraud (Special Inspector General for the Afghanistan Reconstruction 2020, 2).

The Revolving Door

The structure of the military system creates opportunities and incentives for elites to transition between key roles in the private and the public sectors. This back-and-forth movement of high-ranking government officials and defense industry executives is known as the "revolving door" (Duncan and Coyne 2015). One effect is to contribute to the private-public entanglements, and resulting cronyism, in the military system.

The Project on Government Oversight (2018) established a database to track senior-level Pentagon officials who leave their government roles to work at corporations serving as defense contractors. In 2019–21, the project identified 170 companies hiring 479 former senior Pentagon officials. In 2021, 36 government officials left the Pentagon to join defense firms (some holding roles in multiple firms), with those firms receiving over $89.3 billion in defense contract obligations (Summers 2022). The revolving door, which is considered legal, is an important element in the military-system machinery. Like oil in a car engine, the revolving door serves as a type of lubricant to reduce frictions, via reduced transaction costs, and facilitate interactions between the public and private elite.

Attempted limitations on revolving-door activity have been ineffective. For example, early in his first term President Obama issued an executive order to bar lobbyists from joining his administration in roles connected to the agencies they lobbied. However, shortly afterward the administration issued a waiver to William Lynn, previously the top lobbyist for Raytheon, the fifth-largest defense contractor, who was able to secure the deputy defense secretary position within the administration (Thompson 2009). A report by the Project of Government Oversight "found federal ethics laws to be a tangled mess and insufficient to prevent conflicts of interest" (2018, 2) associated with revolving-door activity.

More broadly, Higgs (2007b, 311) notes that "decades of studies, investigations, blue-ribbon commission reports, congressional hearings and staff studies, and news media exposés detailing the MICC's [military-industrial-congressional complex] workings from A to Z have scarcely dented it." What appear to be inefficiencies from those outside the military system can actually be seen as efficiencies to the insiders within the system, who face low transaction costs in feathering their own nests at the expense of members of the outside group—that is, taxpayers.

THE CANCEROUS EFFECTS OF THE MILITARY SYSTEM

The machinery of the military system generates a range of deleterious economic effects. Some of these effects are immediate while others are long and variable. These effects are cancerous in that they metastasize beyond the parties directly involved in the military system and affect broader economic activity.

Immediate Effects

There are four immediate effects generated by the military system machinery. The first is a distortion in the allocation of physical resources. The second is the distortion in the allocation of labor. These two categories are distinct but related in their underlying logic. They are distinct in that labor entails human beings with agency to choose and to act entrepreneurially. This is fundamentally different than raw materials. However, the two are related in that the institutional environment influences how physical resources and labor are employed.

In order to operate, the military system requires resources. The government redirects, via its coercive power to tax, resources from the private sector into the public sector. Once in the public coffers, these resources are then directed into the military system. The key issue is the difference in the institutional environments in private markets and in government decision-making.

There are two key features of private markets. The first is that markets are a competitive discovery process (Hayek 1948, 92–106). The knowledge of the best use of scarce resources is not predetermined and given. Instead, it emerges through the process of market competition and cannot exist absent that process. "The market process is one that is generated, at each and every moment, by entrepreneurial decisions. These decisions are not to be understood as merely selecting the highest out of an array of given and ranked alternatives" (Kirzner 2016, 21). How do entrepreneurs navigate this discovery process?

The answer lies in the second feature of markets—the ability of economic decision makers to rely on economic calculation to guide their decisions as they engage in a process of discovery. Economic calculation refers to the ability to gauge the expected value of alternative resource uses. Entrepreneurs are alert to potential profit opportunities. They then gauge the expected value of alternative uses based on market prices and expected profitability. Assuming they pursue the project under consideration, they then "test" their conjecture by carrying out their plan and subjecting it to the profit-and-loss test. This ongoing process of rivalry, discovery, and learning leads to a constant reshuffling of scarce resources.

Political decision makers cannot rely on the market process because government is designed to operate outside of competitive markets. Prices are paid, but those prices are determined through the political process (in the military system this is the procurement process), not the competitive market process. The government is a nonprofit by design, meaning there is no profit-and-loss test to determine whether private consumers value the use of scarce resources. The result is that political decision makers can increase the output of predetermined outputs through top-down planning and administrative dictates, but without the confidence that resources are being channeled (and rechanneled) to their highest-valued uses as judged by the private actors. Higgs (2006a, 68) summarizes the issue as follows:

> Economics is not a science of hammers and nails, or of production or consumption in the raw; it is a science of choice, and therefore of values. Valuation is inherent in all national income accounting. In a command economy, the fundamental accounting difficulty is that the authorities suppress and replace the only genuinely meaningful manifestation of people's valuations, namely, free market prices.

As this indicates, the political process cannot mimic the market process, and this has real effects on economic welfare.

The operation of the military system pulls initial resources from the private sector and then spends those resources to fulfill the plans of political decision makers. This distorts the market allocation of physical resources and labor. Steel employed in the private sector is not the same as steel employed in the political sector because of the differences in the processes guiding the respective decision makers regarding *how* scarce resources are used. The activities of the military system have immediate distortionary effects on the physical resource and labor markets.

The military system redirects scarce physical resources from private use into government use. Because the counterfactual (the private use of these resources absent the government use) never occurs, there is no way to gauge the opportunity cost of the scarce physical resources that is the central economic question. The economic problem, Hayek (1948, 77–78) noted, is "not merely a problem of how to allocate 'given' resources—if 'given' is taken to mean given to a single mind which deliberately solves the problem set by those 'data.'" Instead, it is one of discovery and coordination, or a "problem of the utilization of knowledge which is not given to anyone in its totality" (Hayek 1948, 78).

In diverting labor, government diverts the efforts of laborers (e.g., the effort to produce and manufacture) while also redirecting the entrepreneurial alertness of these people. As Boulding (1981) noted, "The war industry, with its non-market intrusion into the economy, creates instability and sucks the intellectual lifeblood from the civilian sector" (6). Similar to the resource market, the opportunity cost cannot be gauged because that alternative path is never taken. We cannot know what labor would have produced or what value-added profit opportunities those people would have been alert to in the private-market setting.

The third effect is that the military system elevates political competition as a means of allocating resources and labor. Politics is a negative-sum game; for any given period, budgets are fixed, meaning that if one person earns a contract, another person cannot. Private markets are wealth creating, meaning that wealth is not fixed and given but instead is variable; it can expand due to productive entrepreneurship or contract due to unproductive entrepreneurship. The fixed resources available in politics leads to intense competition among potential recipients to secure resources before others can do so. This results in rent-seeking and rent extraction, as discussed earlier, with the aim of winning the political competition. This competition is negative sum because scarce resources are spent to secure a transfer of existing resources, with nothing new being created. This means that the process is inherently wealth destroying rather than wealth creating.

Finally, the fourth effect is fostering waste, fraud, and abuse. "War and preparation for war systematically corrupt both parties in the state-private transactions by which the government obtains the bulk of its military goods and services" (Higgs 2007b, 299). The underlying causes for this corruption were discussed earlier—the lack of a clear residual claimant, convoluted rules, dysfunctional accounting and financial processes, and a lack of effective oversight and punishment. This further contributes to the destruction of wealth in the immediate term by furthering the negative-sum aspect of the military system.

Long and Variable Effects

There are four harmful long-term effects of the activities of the military system. The first is the distortion of the capital structure. "Capital" refers to intermediary goods used to produce final consumer outputs. Capital is heterogeneous, meaning that capital goods are different, and multispecific, meaning that they have multiple, albeit limited, uses. In order to produce consumer goods, heterogeneous and multispecific capital needs to be combined in a specific manner over time. These capital combinations constitute the capital structure, which refers to the overall order of the relationship between different capital goods. In an economy characterized by advanced material production, the capital structure is extremely complex. It is also constantly changing as individual economic decision makers adjust their plans. The market process—the prices, economic calculation, and profit and loss discussed in the prior subsection—guides entrepreneurs in their individual decisions, which together yields the broader capital structure.

By redirecting resources from the private sector to the government sector, the activities of the military system distort the capital structure. This is a broader effect than the immediate reallocation of resources, labor, and entrepreneurship discussed previously. To understand why, consider the concept of derived demand, which holds that capital goods derive their value from their contribution to the final consumer goods. A capital good is not valuable because of its inherent nature, but because it contributes to some final good that consumers value. When government actors intervene in markets as a consumer, it necessarily influences the capital structure. When the government contracts for fighter jets, for instance, it will influence the value of the capital goods that are used in producing the fighter jet. This has ripple effects throughout the capital structure precisely because capital is heterogeneous. There are multiple potential uses, but the government demand pulls the capital goods away from private use into uses that satisfy government planners as consumers. These effects are long, variable, and heterogeneous. As Melman (1974, 288) noted, the "war economy does not have a homogeneous effect across the economy but is differentiated in its effects by industry, region, and occupational class" through time.

The second effect is to undermine the dynamism of markets. In a market economy, the role of government (to the extent it has one) is to enforce the rules of the game. Where government intervenes by offering profit opportunities, it creates the expectation that government is an active consumer making purchases from firms. This results in the cronyism and corporate welfare discussed earlier. Firms receiving government largesse do not need to compete in markets for the business of private consumers. Discussing the current state of the military system, Roland (2021, 196) writes that

> corporate welfare and bailouts also continue. . . . As the number of prime defense contractors shrank and the size of the integrators swelled, more and more became too big to fail. Lockheed and Lockheed Martin have been bailed out several times. Newport News Shipbuilding remains the only contractor for aircraft carriers, immune from both competition and collapse.

This undermines the dynamism of markets because well-connected military firms no longer need to respond to the disciplinary forces of competitive markets in order to earn a profit. It also creates a dependency on corporate welfare, which fosters cronyism and associated nefarious effects.

Melman (1974) noted another harmful effect of the military system on the private economy—inefficiencies in management and operations. As he put it,

> The sustained normal operation of a large cost- and subsidy-maximizing economic system produces a major unintended effect in the transfer of inefficiency into the civilian economy. Insofar as the cost-maximizing style of operation is carried with them by managers, engineers, or workers as they move individually from the military to civilian employment, the civilian economy becomes infected with the standards and practices that these men and women learned in the military sphere. (69)

As this suggests, the military system has a wide effect on the way people understand and perceive business practices. Moreover, it is not just the movement of people between the military and private sectors. The entanglements between the public and private sectors leads to the carryover of these practices—for example, the red tape of government bureaucracy—as a necessity for success in business. This contributes to the transformation of the market economy.

The third effect is the creation of a culture of rent-seeking and corruption. As government becomes normalized as a means of profit, entrepreneurs will intensely compete to secure a slice of the pie. This fosters rent-seeking behavior with the aim of securing, and maintaining, government privilege. In doing so it contributes to a broader "culture of rent seeking" where this type of behavior becomes a widely accepted pathway to becoming a successful entrepreneur (Choi and Storr 2019). Where this type of culture emerges, it further contributes to undermining the dynamism of markets. As Olson (1982, 42) noted when discussing the decline of nations, in diverting resources to secure more income for their members, special-interest groups not only reduce social output directly but also shift the "pattern of incentives in the society . . . in ways that can vastly reduce the level of production." This shift in incentives both contributes to and reinforces a culture of rent-seeking that reduces wealth both in the immediate term and in the long term by contributing to economic decline and stagnation.

Finally, the operation of the military system erodes self-governance, or the ability of people to exercise their individual agency and freedoms without external interference. It does so in two ways. First, the military system is an exercise in noncomprehensive state planning based on top-down dictates administered through the military-administrative state (see Coyne and Hall 2019). As Galbraith (1978, 321) noted, "The Department of Defense supports the most highly developed planning in the planning system." Planning of this magnitude requires extensive interventions into private markets, which reduce the scope of self-governance—people's ability to engage in voluntary social cooperation and to allocate their person and property as they see fit.

Second, the sheer size of the military system makes it impossible for ordinary people to exercise democratic influence or control. The structure of the military system is such that there is a firm dividing wall between insiders and outsiders. To borrow a distinction from Vincent Ostrom (1997, 52–53), the US military system does not govern with the American people, but rather over them through top-down administrative control. It has significant antidemocratic and antiliberal features and tendencies despite its existence being justified on the grounds of protecting liberal values (Coyne 2022). As Higgs (2007b, 309) notes, "Only the taxpayers lose, but their interests do not count: they are not 'players' in this game, but merely victims of its depredations."

CONCLUSION

Robert Higgs's scholarship offers insight into the nature, machinery, and effects of the US military system. His work also offers insight into what is required to change course. "Until the scope of the U.S. government's geopolitical aspirations and hence the scale of its military activities are drastically reduced, not much opportunity will exist for making its system of military-economic fascism less rapacious and corrupt" (Higgs 2007b, 312). It is unlikely that this will occur endogenously, for there is no incentive for the main stakeholders to reduce the scale and scope of the military system; just the opposite. Higgs's (1987, 2008) emphasis on the importance of ideology, in contrast, does offer a pathway to change. Enough citizens have to demand a change in the operations of the military system for change to occur.

This might sound daunting, but there is evidence of the role of "people power" in limiting the activities of the military system. For instance, Wittner (2009) documents the crucial role played by citizen activism in limiting the testing and use of nuclear weapons. This grassroots global movement demonstrates the power of the general populace to constrain the military activities of the state. If anything, this serves as an existence proof—evidence that ordinary people do possess the power to limit the activities of the military system.

We have focused on the harmful economic effects of the military system. It is important to note that this is only one slice of Higgs's research program on the broader pernicious effects of the war-making powers of the state. As he notes, the state's power to engage in national security policymaking is a "master key" because it "opens all doors, including the doors that might otherwise obstruct the government's invasion of our most cherished rights to life, liberty, and property" (Higgs 2015, 276). A key part of Robert Higgs's legacy is his scholarship on these topics that serve as a model for the systematic and careful study of the realities of war-making and its impact on human well-being.

REFERENCES

Boulding, Kenneth. 1981. "Defending Whom from What?" *Technology Review* (July 1981): 6–7.

Buchanan, James M. 1954. "Individual Choice in Voting and the Market." *Journal of Political Economy* 62 (4): 334–43.

Burton, James G. 1993. *The Pentagon Wars: Reformers Challenge the Old Guard.* Annapolis, MD: Naval Institute Press.

Capaccio, Anthony. 2021. "Boeing Pays Pentagon $10.7 Million to Settle Double-Billing Case." *Bloomberg*, April 27. https://www.bloomberg.com/news/articles/2021-04-27/boeing-pays-pentagon-10-7-million-to-settle-double-billing-case?leadSource=uverify%20wall.

Choi, Seung Ginny, and Virgil Henry Storr. 2019. "A Culture of Rent Seeking." *Public Choice* 181 (1/2): 101–26.

Cockburn, Andrew. 2019. "The Military-Industrial Virus" *Harper's Magazine*, June. https://harpers.org/archive/2019/06/the-pentagon-syndrome/.

Commission on Wartime Contracting in Iraq and Afghanistan. 2011. "The Final Report of the Commission on Wartime Contracting in Iraq and Afghanistan." https://www.govinfo.gov/content/pkg/CHRG-112shrg72564/pdf/CHRG-112shrg72564.pdf.

Coyne, Christopher J. 2022. *In Search of Monsters to Destroy: The Folly of American Empire and the Paths to Peace.* Oakland, CA: Independent Institute.

Coyne, Christopher J., Nathan Goodman, and Abigail R. Hall. 2019. "Sounding the Alarm: The Political Economy of Whistleblowing in the US Security State." *Peace Economics, Peace Science, and Public Policy* 25 (1): 1–11.

Coyne, Christopher J., and Abigail R. Hall. 2019. "State-Provided Defense as Non Comprehensive Planning." *Journal of Private Enterprise* 34 (1): 75–85.

———. 2021. *Manufacturing Militarism: U.S. Government Propaganda in the War on Terror.* Stanford, CA: Stanford University Press.

Coyne, Christopher J., Courtney Michaluk, and Rachel Reese. 2016. "Unproductive Entrepreneurship in U.S. Military Contracting." *Journal of Entrepreneurship and Public Policy* 5 (2): 221–39.

Duncan, Thomas K., and Christopher J. Coyne. 2015. "The Revolving Door and the Entrenchment of the Permanent War Economy." *Peace Economics, Peace Science, and Public Policy* 21 (3): 391–413.

Echols, Connor. 2022. "The Pentagon Fails Its Fifth Audit in a Row." *Responsible Statecraft*, November 22. https://responsiblestatecraft.org/2022/11/22/why-cant-the-dod-get-its-financial-house-in-order/.

Fitzgerald, A. Earnest. 1972. *The High Priests of Waste*. New York: W. W. Norton.

———.1989. *The Pentagonists: An Insider's View of Waste, Management, and Fraud in Defense Spending*. New York: Harper and Row.

Galbraith, John Kenneth. 1978. *The New Industrial State*. Boston: Houghton Mifflin.

Gates, Robert. 2014. "The Quiet Fury of Robert Gates." *Wall Street Journal*, January 7. http://www.wsj.com/articles/SB10001424052702304617404579306851526222552.

Giorno, Taylor. 2022. "Defense Sector Donors Contributed $3.4 Million to House Armed Services Committee Members in the 2022 Election Cycle." *Open Secrets*, July 13. https://www.opensecrets.org/news/2022/07/defense-sector-donors-contributed-3-4-million-to-house-armed-services-committee-members-in-the-2022-election-cycle/.

Hayek, F. A. 1948. *Individualism and Economic Order*. Chicago: University of Chicago Press.

Higgs, Robert. 1987. *Crisis and Leviathan: Critical Episodes in the Growth of American Government*. New York: Oxford University Press.

———. 2006a. *Depression, War, and Cold War: Studies in Political Economy*. New York: Oxford University Press.

———. 2006b. "Fear: The Foundation of Every Government's Power." *Independent Review* 10 (3): 447–66.

———. 2007a. *Neither Liberty nor Safety: Fear, Ideology, and the Growth of Government*. Oakland, CA: Independent Institute.

———. 2007b. "Military-Economic Fascism: How Business Corrupts Government, and Vice Versa." *Independent Review* 12 (2): 299–316.

———. 2008. "The Complex Course of Ideological Change." *American Journal of Economics and Sociology* 67 (4): 547–66.

———. 2015. *Taking a Stand: Reflections on Life, Liberty, and the Economy*. Oakland, CA: Independent Institute.

Holcombe, Randall G. 2018. *Political Capitalism: How Economic and Political Power Is Made and Maintained*. New York: Cambridge University Press.

Joint Economic Committee. 1969. "The Military Budget and National Economic Priorities." Hearings Before the Subcommittee on Economy in Government of the Joint Economic Committee Congress of the United States, First Session. Washington, DC: US Government Printing Office.

Kirzner, Israel M. 2016. *Discovery, Capitalism and Distributive Justice*. Edited by Peter J. Boettke and Frederic Sautet. Indianapolis: Liberty Fund.

Levinson, Robert. 2021. "Fiscal 2020 Pentagon Contracting Hits Record $445 Billion." *Bloomberg Government*, January 6. https://about.bgov.com/news/fiscal-2020-pentagon-contracting-hits-record-445-billion/.

Lipton, Eric. 2022. "The Pentagon Saw a Warship Boondoggle. Congress Saw Jobs." *New York Times*, February 4. https://www.nytimes.com/2023/02/04/us/politics/littoral-combat-ships-lobbying.html.

McCartney, James. 2015. *America's War Machine: Vested Interests, Endless Conflicts*. New York: Thomas Dunne.

McChesney, Fred S. 1987. "Rent Extraction and Rent Creation in the Economic Theory of Regulation." *Journal of Legal Studies* 16 (1): 101–18.

———. 1997. *Money for Nothing: Politicians, Rent Extraction, and Political Extortion*. Cambridge, MA: Harvard University Press.

Melman, Seymour. 1974. *The Permanent War Economy: American Capitalism in Decline*. New York: Simon and Schuster.

Niskanen, William A. 1971. *Bureaucracy and Representative Government.* Chicago: Aldine-Atherton.

———. 1975. "Bureaucrats and Politicians." *Journal of Law and Economics* 18 (3): 617–43.

Olson, Mancur. 1982. *The Rise and Decline of Nations: Economic Growth, Stagflation, and Social Rigidities.* New Haven, CT: Yale University Press.

Ostrom, Vincent. 1997. *The Meaning of Democracy and the Vulnerability of Democracies: A Response to Tocqueville's Challenge.* Ann Arbor: University of Michigan Press.

Peltier, Heidi. 2020. "The Growth of the 'Camo Economy' and the Commercialization of the Post 9/11 Wars." Watson Institute International and Public Affairs at Brown University, June 30. https://watson.brown.edu/costsofwar/files/cow/imce/papers/2020/Peltier%202020%20-%20Growth%20of%20Camo%20Economy%20-%20June%2030%202020%20-%20FINAL.pdf.

Priest, Dana, and William M. Arkin. 2011. *Top Secret America: The Rise of the New American Security State.* New York: Little, Brown.

Project on Government Oversight. 2018. "Brass Parachutes: Defense Contractors' Capture of Pentagon Officials through the Revolving Door." November 5. https://s3.amazonaws.com/docs.pogo.org/report/2018/POGO_Brass_Parachutes_DoD_Revolving_Door_Report_2018-11-05.pdf.

Roland, Alex. 2021. *Delta of Power: The Military-Industrial Complex.* Baltimore: Johns Hopkins University Press.

Schweizer, Peter. 2013. *Extortion: How Politicians Extract Your Money, Buy Votes, and Line Their Own Pockets.* New York: Houghton Mifflin Harcourt.

Schwellenbach, Nick. 2011. "Leaked Audit: Boeing Overcharged Army up to 177,000 Percent on Helicopter Spare Parts." *Project on Government Oversight*, June 28. https://www.pogo.org/investigation/2011/06/leaked-audit-boeing-overcharged-army-up-to-177000-percent-on-helicopter-spare-parts.

Sia, Richard, and Alexander Cohen. 2013. "The Drone That Wouldn't Die: How a Defense Contractor Bested the Pentagon." *The Atlantic*, July 16. https://www.theatlantic.com/politics/archive/2013/07/the-drone-that-wouldnt-die-how-a-defense-contractor-bested-the-pentagon/277807/.

Smithberger, Mandy, and William Hartung. 2021. "America's Nearly $1.3 Trillion National Security Budget Isn't Making Us Any Safer." *Responsible Statecraft*, July 2. https://responsiblestatecraft.org/2021/07/02/americas-nearly-1-3-trillion-national-security-budget-isnt-making-us-any-safer/.

Special Inspector General for the Afghanistan Reconstruction. 2020. "Update on the Amount of Waste, Fraud, and Abuse Uncovered through SIGAR's Oversight Work between January 1, 2018 and December 31, 2019." October. https://www.sigar.mil/pdf/special%20projects/SIGAR-21-05-SP.pdf.

Steinhauer, Jennifer. 2015. "With Chairmanship, McCain Seizes Chance to Reshape Pentagon Agenda." *New York Times*, June 8. http://www.nytimes.com/2015/06/09/us/politics/mccain-uses-committee-post-to-press-for-defense-agenda.html?_r=0.

Summers, Ryan. 2022. "The Pentagon's Revolving Door Keeps Spinning: 2021 in Review." *Project on Government Oversight*, January 20. https://www.pogo.org/analysis/2022/01/the-pentagons-revolving-door-keeps-spinning-2021-in-review/.

Taylor, Henry 2015. "Who Is the World's Biggest Employer?" *World Economic Forum*, June 17. https://www.weforum.org/agenda/2015/06/worlds-10-biggest-employers/.

Thompson, Mark. 2009. "Obama's Lobbyist Ban Meets a Loophole: William Lynn." *Time*, January 27. https://content.time.com/time/politics/article/0,8599,1874165,00.html.

Tullock, Gordon. 1965. *The Politics of Bureaucracy.* Washington, DC: Public Affairs Press.

Twight, Charlotte. 1975. *America's Emerging Fascist Economy.* New Rochelle, NY: Arlington House.

US Department of Defense. 2018. "Base Structure Report—Fiscal Year 2018 Baseline: A Summary of the Real Property Inventory Data." https://www.acq.osd.mil/eie/Downloads/BSI/Base%20Structure%20Report%20FY18.pdf.

US Department of Justice. 2014. "Boeing Pays $23 Million to Resolve False Claims Act Allegations." October 10. https://www.justice.gov/opa/pr/boeing-pays-23-million-resolve-false-claims-act-allegations.

US Government Accountability Office. 2022. "U.S. Defense Industrial Base: DOD Should Take Actions to Strengthen Its Risk Mitigation Approach." July. https://www.gao.gov/assets/gao-22-104154.pdf.

Whitlock, Craig, and Bob Woodward. 2016. "Pentagon Buries Evidence of $125 Billion in Bureaucratic Waste." *Washington Post*, December 5. https://www.washingtonpost.com/investigations/pentagon-buries-evidence-of-125-billion-in-bureaucratic-waste/2016/12/05/e0668c76-9af6-11e6-a0ed-ab0774c1eaa5_story.html?utm_term=.22ea909d8c61.

Willman, David. 2015. "How a 2.7 Billion Air-Defense System Became a 'Zombie' Program." *Los Angeles Times*, September 24. https://graphics.latimes.com/missile-defense-jlens/.

Wittner, Lawrence S. 2009. *Confronting the Bomb: A Short History of the World Nuclear Disarmament Movement*. Stanford, CA: Stanford University Press.

Wooten, Savannah, and Rick Claypool. 2022. "Military-Industrial Complex Clinches Nearly 450,000% Return on Investment." *Public Citizen*, July 7. https://www.citizen.org/article/military-industrial-complex-contributions-report/.

Chapter 13
The Continuing Costs of the Permanent War Economy
Thomas K. Duncan

Throughout his career, Robert Higgs has made several significant contributions to the permanent war economy literature. In *Crisis and Leviathan*, Higgs (1987) makes his first and likely primary contribution in the formulation of "crisis theory" and the "ratchet effect" as a cause of government growth. The ratchet effect has a plethora of implications, not the least of which is its use in explaining the growth and entrenchment of the military-industrial complex (Higgs 1985, 1987, 1988a, 2001, 2012a, 2019; Trevino and Higgs 1992). A second, but no less important, contribution is Higgs's rejection of the theory of "war prosperity" and his efforts to calculate the actual costs of military buildups and the permanent war economy (Higgs 1988b, 1992, 1994, 1997, 1999, 2001, 2005, 2006, 2007, 2011).

The "permanent war economy" was first noted in 1944, the year prior to the end of World War II, when Walter Oakes published a very prescient article foretelling the rise of what he termed a permanent war economy in the United States. In this permanent war economy, Oakes (1944, 12) warned, "government's expenditures for war (or "national defense") [would] become a legitimate and significant end-purpose of economic activity." His article suggested a shift was occurring within US culture. Prior to the war, the "legitimate end-purpose of economic activity" was viewed to be the "satisfaction of human wants." However, as the war and its changes on the US economy and institutions continued, the view increasingly became supplanted by the idea that "peacetime expenditures for a war of a sizable nature" were now a legitimate economic activity (1944, 12). In the decades that have followed, Oakes's projection has become reality, and the permanent war economy has become a fixture of American life (Duncan and Coyne 2013a, 2013b, 2015; Hooks 1991).

Oakes was far from the last to analyze the permanent war economy. President Dwight Eisenhower (1961) warns of further shifts in the structure of national defense in his farewell address. Raymond (1964) offers evidence of creeping bureaucratic processes in business from its ties to the military.

Melman (1971, 1985) provides an in-depth analysis of the politics of the permanent war economy. Bacevich (2007, 2010) argues that the United States has not only been in a permanent war economy but has remained in an actual state of permanent war through most of the post–World War II era. Johnson (2008) argues that the permanent war economy will continue to strain U.S. government debt. Duncan and Coyne (2013a, 2013b, 2015) analyze the rise and continuation of permanent war. Each of these authors, and others not listed here, have made important contributions to the permanent war economy literature.

This chapter will illustrate how Higgs's ratchet effect remains relevant as an explanation for the creation and continuation of the permanent war economy. It will also discuss how the continued existence of a large defense sector necessarily affects and reshapes the private economy of the United States (see also Duncan and Coyne 2013b, 2015). The formation of the military-industrial complex (MIC) is an important aspect of these phenomena that must be touched upon in brief. However, as the MIC is a subject of another chapter in this volume (Nathan Goodman's "The Military-Industrial Complex and the Militarization of Society"), the primary focus here will be on ratchets and costs as illustrated through the permanent war economy. As such, this work contributes to the literature on the origins of the permanent war economy (Oakes 1944; Vance 1951a, 1951b, 1951c, 1951d, 1951e, 1951f; Baran and Sweezy 1966; Melman 1971, 1985; Vatter 1985; Woods 2010; Duncan and Coyne 2013a, 2013b, 2015; Coyne and Duncan 2019).

The remainder of the chapter will be organized as follows: the next section will illustrate the existence of the permanent war economy and provide the historical path through which it emerges. This section will also focus on the ratchet effect that coincides with major US involvement in overseas conflicts. After that, the chapter will illustrate the continuing costs associated with the permanent war economy, including the oft-mischaracterization of military spending as a viable option to create prosperity. The final section will offer further avenues of research and a conclusion.

THE SHAPE OF A PERMANENT WAR ECONOMY

Higgs (1987, 2004, 2005, 2006, 2012b) describes how government extends its power through historical crises, particularly wars, increasing in size to deal with each one and never quite giving up as much power as it gained once the crisis passes. This pattern gives rise to what he refers to as the "ratchet effect," with incremental growth in state size and authority over time. As Higgs (1987, 30) defines the ratchet, "after each major crisis, the size of government, though smaller than during the crisis, remained larger than it would have been had the precrisis rate of growth persisted during the interval occupied by the crisis." While raw statistics do not tell the full story, as will be discussed further in this chapter,[1] they can provide a basic illustration of the ratchet effect. Figure 13.1 provides one such illustration in terms of military expenditures following World War II.

The data in figure 13.1 begins in 1948, after the end of World War II. During World War II, federal spending surged. The US government spent over $5 trillion on defense between 1940 and 1945, with defense spending consuming more than 40 percent of GDP in 1943–44.[2] With the end of the war, military spending dropped precipitously. The drop, however, was short lived. As figure 13.1 illustrates, military expenditures began to rise dramatically once again by 1950 with the beginning of the Korean War (1950–53). With the end of active engagement in Korea, military spending saw a decline, though not nearly so far as the 1948 level. With the beginning of heavy US involvement in the Vietnam War, expenditures rose again. Though the Vietnam War itself extended from 1955 and ended in 1975, the United States became heavily involved in the 1960s, with peak US troop levels occurring in 1969. As the Vietnam era slowly concluded, the military expenditure levels again fell but remained above those of the post–Korean War decline.

Figure 13.1. US military expenditures, 1949–2021 (billions of 2020 $)

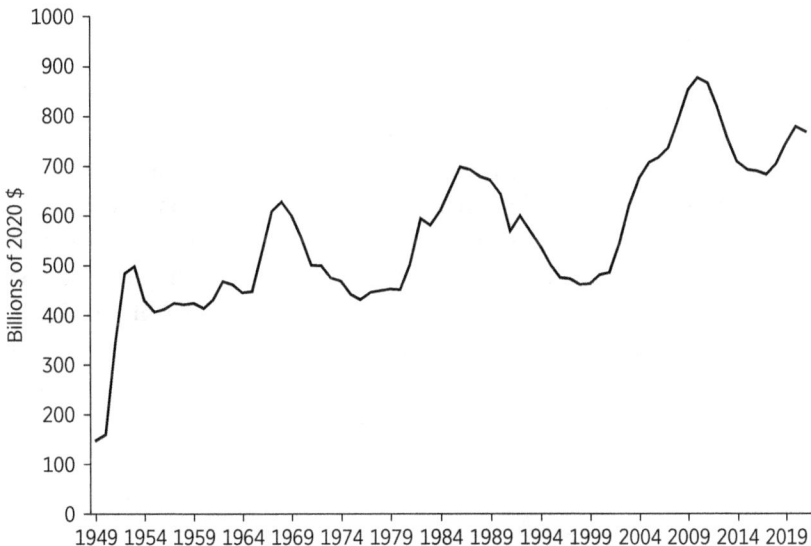

Source: SIPRI Military Expenditure Database 2022, https://www.sipri.org/databases/milex.

Military expenditures again spiked during the 1980s as the United States engaged in the Cold War arms race with the Soviet Union, rising to a peak in 1986. Following the 1986 Reykjavik Summit and the 1987 Intermediate-Range Nuclear Forces Treaty (ACA 2019), expenditures began to decline. As the Soviet Union collapsed in the late 1980s and early 1990s, the decline accelerated, but it did not fall to the level of the trough in the mid-1970s. The early 21st century yielded another increase following the September 11, 2001, terrorist attacks. The events of 9/11 sparked a global war on terror, with major military activities in Afghanistan (2001–21) and Iraq (2003–11). Spending levels once again declined following the end of the Iraq war, but did not reach the lows of the late 1990s. The war in Afghanistan officially ended with the withdrawal of troops on August 31, 2021. Yet as of the time of writing this chapter, the US Congress has passed a bill with a significant increase in defense spending, with the Ukraine-Russia war being seen as a justification for the increase (Shane and Harris 2022; Zengerle 2022).[3] The data illustrate, by any other name, a ratchet effect for military expenditures.

Today's War Economy

In the 20 years between 2001 and 2021, the United States spent an average of $724 billion on military expenditures.[4] For 2021, the United States spent $768 billion, a 10 percent increase over the $698 billion in spending in 1986 at the height of the Cold War. That level of spending amounts to approximately 39 percent of total world military spending. Figure 13.2 provides the percentage spending of the remainder of the world, illustrating the significant proportion that comes from the United States alone, with the closest competitor being the combined spending of Central and Western Europe at 16 percent.

On a per country basis, the United States is not only in the top 10; it also contributes more to spending than the remainder of the top 10 combined. Figure 13.3 provides a comparison of the United States and the next nine countries in terms of military expenditures in 2021, as well as offering a breakdown of those countries' relative expenditures in ascending order. China spent the second-highest amount on its military at $270 billion, but the margin between first and second place is not insignificant, with the United States spending approximately 2.8 times as much.

These military expenditures should not be mistaken as a simple increase due to 21st-century wars. While the wars in Iraq and Afghanistan did, of course, greatly impact the level of defense spending, direct spending on these efforts does not account for the entirety of the defense-related growth. Following the

Figure 13.2. World military expenditures in 2021 (billions of 2020 $)

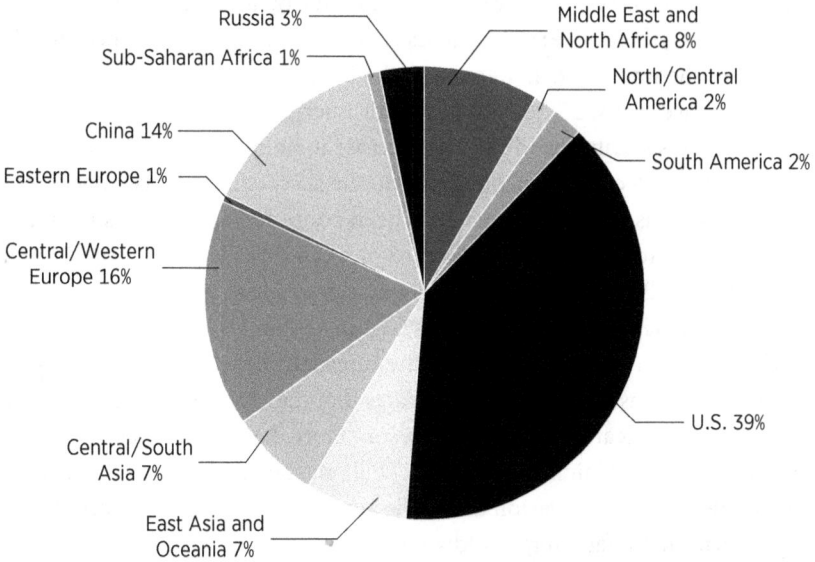

Russia 3%

Sub-Saharan Africa 1%

China 14%

Eastern Europe 1%

Central/Western
Europe 16%

Central/South
Asia 7%

East Asia and
Oceania 7%

Middle East and
North Africa 8%

North/Central
America 2%

South America 2%

U.S. 39%

Source: SIPRI Military Expenditure Database 2022, https://www.sipri.org/databases/milex.

Figure 13.3. Top 10 countries in military expenditures in 2021 (billions of 2020 $)

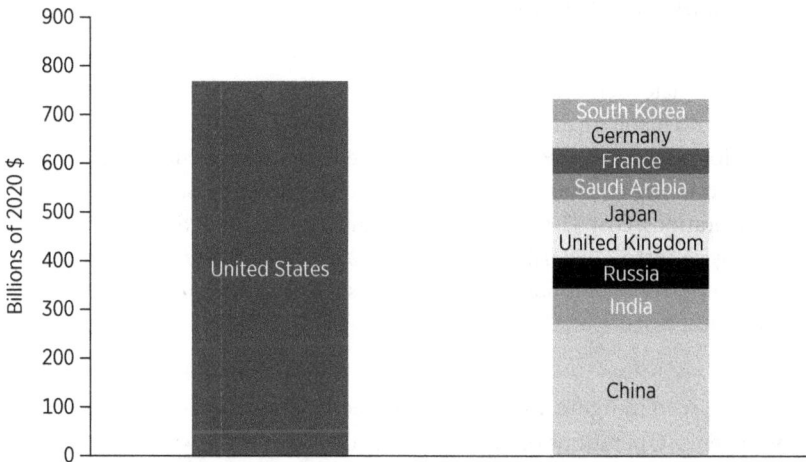

Billions of 2020 $

United States

South Korea
Germany
France
Saudi Arabia
Japan
United Kingdom
Russia
India

China

Source: SIPRI Military Expenditure Database 2022, https://www.sipri.org/databases/milex. See also Peter G. Peterson Foundation, https://www.pgpf.org/sites/default/files/0053_defense_comparison-full.gif.

9/11 attacks there was also substantial growth in spending in the majority of defense and security-related areas. Duncan and Coyne (2013b, 419) show that in 2001–2011, there were significant increases in spending on areas not directly related to the war effort: 43 percent in the Pentagon base budget, 21 percent in nuclear weapons, 27 percent in atomic energy defense, and 240 percent in homeland security spending. The increase in homeland security spending may seem a perfectly rational response to the successful terrorist attacks, but necessity of this level of increase has been contested as an excess response to the actual probability of success then or since (Mueller 2006; Mueller and Stewart 2011, 2015). The increase in nuclear weapons and atomic energy–related activities is even more interesting, as neither Iraq nor Afghanistan is nuclear-weapon capable. Even still, the International Campaign to Abolish Nuclear Weapons (ICAN 2022) estimates that the United States spent $44.2 billion on its nuclear arsenal in 2021, a sum more than three times more than the next country—China spending $11.7 billion. Though this nuclear spending did not deter Russia's invasion of the Ukraine, it did provide significant funding for arms manufacturers worldwide (ICAN 2022).

As part of the Costs of War Project at Brown University, Crawford (2021) offers a more comprehensive breakdown of defense-related spending. Figure 13.4 illustrates one such breakdown.

Crawford (2021, 3) further notes:

> This estimate includes the figures for U.S. wars in the two major war zones and many small war zones. Not including the future obligations to care for veterans through 2050 or estimated homeland security spending, the war in Afghanistan and Pakistan, which is part of the same theater of operations, cost $2.313 trillion through FY2022. The U.S. wars in Iraq and Syria cost $2.058 trillion through FY2022. The post-9/11 wars and counterterror operations in other places, such as Somalia and other parts of Africa, cost about $355 billion.

As can be seen in figure 13.4, there is a specific breakdown for the Overseas Contingency Operations (OCO) spending directly for the wars in Iraq, Syria, and Afghanistan. But there are also separate categories Homeland Security and Domestic Counterterrorism spending, the State Department, and the base budget for the Pentagon.

As noted in the preceding subsection, the US Congress has not let the end of the Afghanistan war slow down the permanent war economy. The Pentagon's $858 billion budget approved by the House and Senate for FY2023 will see

Figure 13.4. Post-9/11 war-related spending, FY2001–22, and obligations for future veterans' care (2021 $)

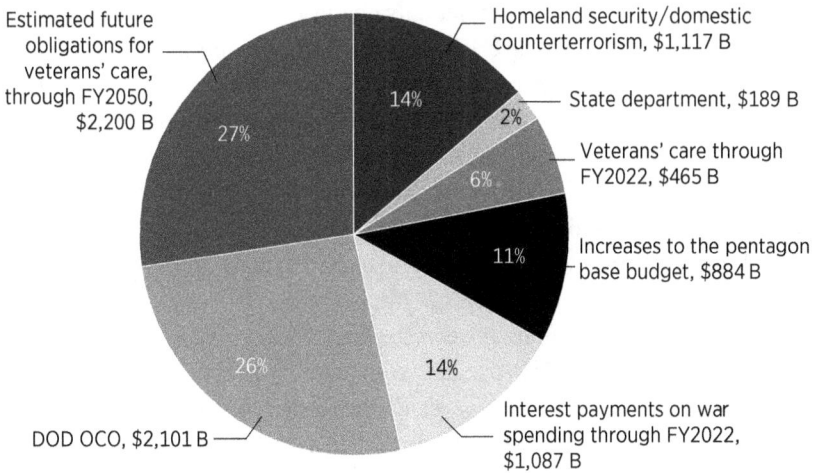

Estimated future obligations for veterans' care, through FY2050, $2,200 B — 27%

14%

Homeland security/domestic counterterrorism, $1,117 B

2% State department, $189 B

6% Veterans' care through FY2022, $465 B

11% Increases to the pentagon base budget, $884 B

26% DOD OCO, $2,101 B

14% Interest payments on war spending through FY2022, $1,087 B

Source: Crawford 2021.

growth "at 4.3 percent per year over the last two years—even after inflation—compared with an average of less than 1 percent a year in real dollars between 2015 and 2021, according to an analysis by Center for Strategic and Budgetary Assessments for The New York Times" (Lipton, Crowley, and Ismay 2022; see also Shane and Harris 2022). Such an increase would see US military spending return to the levels near the peak expenditures realized during the height of the combined Iraq and Afghanistan wars, despite the United States not being actively engaged in the Ukraine-Russia war.

How Did We Get Here? Ratchets, Ratchets Everywhere

Randolph Bourne (1919) once noted that "war is the health of the state." The truth of this oft-used quip is well documented throughout Higgs's work (1987, 2004, 2012a). It should come as no surprise that previous wars and the state are also the health of the permanent war economy. Lessons learned in conflicts are not forgotten, and those lessons apply both militarily and within the industrial sectors that aid in the war efforts. Higgs (2004, 163) argues, "Scholars and laymen alike usually trace the origins of our own Leviathan to the New Deal"; however, "Roosevelt and friends never would—or could—have done what they did in the 1930s without the state-building precedents of World War I." While true, the rise of the permanent war economy can be traced still further back.

The 1898 Spanish-American War cemented the United States as a colonial empire, leading to a more active international role for the United States (Hopkins 2018, 38), and fundamentally changed the nature of the domestic standing army. In his article criticizing the war in its immediate aftermath, William Graham Sumner notes the government's shifting stance toward a standing army and its long-run effects on militarization,[5] writing (1899, 178), "Our politicians will have no trouble to find a war ready for us the next time that they come around to the point where they think that it is time for us to have another. We are told that we must have a big army hereafter." The war and the colonies acquired by its end led to an increased focus on the US Navy and the creation of a naval power (Symonds 2018). Eloranta (2007, 268), using military expenditure data, finds that between the Spanish-American War and World War I, the "UK and the United States seemed to have a complicated, two-way naval 'rivalry' in this period. However, the American navy, of course, was in no way comparable to the British fleet." Though it may not have rivaled the naval power of the British Empire, the focus on maintaining an army and navy in preparation for future wars became a mainstay of American life.

The "Great War" (1914–19) again altered the defense sector in ways that would contribute to the permanent war economy. Beyond the significant growth in general government activities (Higgs 2004; Rockoff 2004), World War I had a lasting impact on the structure of military production in the United States. The war effort established the use of cost-plus contracting for military equipment. This business model would significantly alter the future of the war economy. As Hartung (2011, 35) describes, cost-plus contracts are "an arrangement in which the company had all of its expenses reimbursed and then received an automatic profit on top of that. These generous deals were compounded by a lack of effective oversight and minimal accountability for any malfeasance or misfeasance carried out with taxpayers' money." The deals were generous enough to prompt a backlash after the war, as a strong negative sentiment developed in the United States that held the profits of private business as a major justification for US entry into the war. This view held that businesses[6] with foreign economic interests and the domestic armaments industries used the conflict to boost their own profits. The antibusiness streak that followed in American thinking and politics was sufficient to see the military-industry leaders labeled as "merchants of death" (Engelbrecht and Hanighen 1934[7]; see also Higgs 2005, 7; 2006, 41; Duncan and Coyne 2013a, 231).

The interwar period did see a reduction in military expenditures in part due to the pushback regarding war profiteering. Upon entering office, President Franklin Roosevelt initially proposed a significant cut to the military budget.

However, the army was able to tie itself to the management of the Civilian Conservation Corps—one of the largest employment programs established during the New Deal—to forestall the bulk of the planned cuts (Smith 2007, 314–22). The army found a way to link its budget to the overall employment trend. It was not the only area of the defense sector to do so, however.

The aviation industry, in particular, found success in continuing the cost-plus contract arrangements during the interwar period. While some businesses in this period allowed the War Department to experiment with testing their munitions capabilities (Rutherford 1939, 4), the aviation industry benefited from the unique ability to use government contracts toward production lines that could simultaneously produce outputs for the military and the private sector without a costly conversion. The aviation industry also pioneered lobbying on the grounds of national unemployment in 1934, when Lockheed Aircraft Corporation's funding efforts "debuted the arguments that were to figure so prominently in later debates over government aid to the company—creating jobs and preserving the industrial base" (Hartung 2011, 39–40; Duncan and Coyne 2013a, 230–31).

Though these cases in the interwar period aided in arresting the fall of expenditures, the more obvious period to establish the permanency of the war economy came during World War II and the preparations for it. As noted earlier, it is during this period of military expansion that the term "permanent war economy" entered the lexicon (Oakes 1944). Two significant changes took place during this period to ensure this transition in defense spending. The first is the theoretical linkage between military spending and unemployment, a continuation of Lockheed lobbying strategy. As early as 1939, John Maynard Keynes gave his "Will Re-armament Cure Unemployment?" address on BBC radio, announcing, "The grand experiment has begun. If it works, if expenditure on armaments really does cure unemployment, I predict that we shall never go back all the way to the old state of affairs. . . . Good may come out of evil. We may learn a trick or two, which will come in useful when the day of peace comes" ([1939] 2010, 193). Keynes was not the only one to appeal to this link. A chorus of economists and politicians attached themselves to the idea that the war's end may lead to a collapse back into the depression (Feiler 1942; Hirsch 1944; Slichter 1945; see also Baran and Sweezy 1966; Melman 1970, 1971, 1985; Rosen 2005). These arguments lingered even after the initial drawdown in spending after the war (Hoover 1948, 399; Daugherty 1951, 46; Brady 1952, 43), though the economic collapse did not happen in the period between World War II and the spending increase for the Korean War.

The second significant change stems from the special interests that arose in response to the dramatic expansion of federal spending in the war buildup.

These special interests—the military, organized labor, and war-related private industry—formed a coalition that would reshape the defense sector, and in doing so reshape the US economy (Duncan and Coyne 2013a). Legislative acts in 1940 authorized military branches to negotiate their own cost-plus contracts, returning to the World War I practice in full. This change allowed the branches to offer such contracts to their chosen industries, removing the competitive bidding process in favor of direct negotiation with firms as well as allowing those negotiations to take place with connected firms (Higgs 2006, 49). With the introduction of the direct negotiation procurement process, "deals came to turn not on price, but on technical and scientific capabilities, size, experience, and established reputations as a military supplier—vaguer attributes that are easier to fudge for one's friends" (Higgs 2007, 308; see also Smith [1959] 1991, 311). The influence of the larger corporations often won out over that of the smaller ones (Bean 1994), leading to greater centralization of big business. The result of the increasing centralization ensured that a few large defense industries would come to dominate the sector. By the end of the war, the iron triangle was complete, with "big business, including its powerful friends and representatives . . . and the newly but vastly empowered military establishment together," which "formed a potent political faction" (Higgs 2006, 73; see also Duncan and Coyne 2013b, 2015; Coyne and Duncan 2019).

The political faction was strong enough that as the war ended, "Washington did not dismantle the defense industry it had developed. Instead, the large, diversified industrial conglomerates that had produced defense equipment during the war . . . maintained their defense divisions" (Lynn 2014; see also Higgs 2006). The combination of the wars in Korea and Vietnam further solidified the power of the military-industrial complex, leading to Eisenhower's (1961) warning in his farewell address: "In the councils of government, we must guard against the acquisition of unwarranted influence, whether sought or unsought, by the military-industrial complex. The potential for the disastrous rise of misplaced power exists and will persist." The Cold War era of history saw further centralization of the military-industrial complex beneath the Department of Defense,[8] with political clout becoming the currency of the complex (Melman 1971, 1985). This era also continued the defense sector's favoritism of oligopolistic firms (Kaufman 1972), where a handful of large, well-connected industry leaders spearhead defense production (Higgs 2006, 73; Yarmolinsky 1971, 56–57; Markusen et al. 1991; see also Adams and Adams 1972; Kaufman 1972).

The 21st century has likewise seen a continuation of this trend, with the military-industrial complex working to keep the defense expenditures high throughout the global war on terror (Duncan and Coyne 2013b, 2015; Coyne and Duncan 2019; Coyne and Hall 2014, 2018). The attacks of 9/11 and the subsequent military responses prompted another ratchet for which we are still seeing the effects. Even with the end of the Iraq war and the more recent closure of the Afghanistan war, the war economy maintains its permanency with the planned increases in defense spending. With increases forthcoming, the second of Higgs's major contributions to the permanent war economy literature—that of the costs—remains perpetually relevant.

SEEN AND UNSEEN COSTS OF THE PERMANENT WAR ECONOMY

Much of the literature on defense spending can be broken into two major themes. The first theme centers on national defense as *the* quintessential public good.[9] As a purely public good, defense will presumably be under-provided on the private market. This market failure argument leads to a call for a government provision of defense on efficiency grounds. Generally, the neoclassical model for national defense assumes the government's ability to maximize welfare (Smith 1995, 71) according to "a well defined social welfare function, reflecting some form of social democratic consensus, recognizing some well defined national interest, and threatened by some real or apparent potential enemy" (Dunne 1995, 409). Though this modeling technique allows for simplistic textbook examples and tractable calculations, Higgs (2006, 133) reminds us that in reality, "no one knows the production function for national security," and the optimal level of defense is not a given (see also Coyne 2015).[10]

The second theme, previously mentioned, is that in providing defense, the government will create or increase prosperity more generally (Keynes 1939; Baran and Sweezy 1966; Melman 1970, 1971, 1985; Rosen 2005). Though Melman criticizes the politicizing of the security that takes place within the permanent war economy, he (1985, 15) still subscribes to the claim that World War II allowed for the United States to produce more of both "guns and butter." Higgs (2006, 89) challenges the claim of war prosperity directly, noting that traditional arguments that World War II ended the Great Depression do not "take sufficiently into account the understatement of actual wartime inflation by the official price indexes, the deterioration of quality and disappearance from the market of many consumer goods, the full effect of the nonprice rationing of many widely consumed items, and the additional transaction costs borne and other sacrifices made by consumers to get the goods that were available." If actual consumption data[11] is calculated, it suggests "real consumer well-being during the war . . . declined" (Higgs 2006, 89).

Higgs's response to both themes has continuing relevance for studying the permanent war economy. The continuous state-provided defense spending produces neither efficiency nor prosperity (Coyne 2015). As defense contracts are based on politics rather than price (Higgs 2007, 308), there is little evidence to suggest that spending will align with any social welfare function even if such a function were known. Duncan and Coyne (2015) explore the government failure side of this concept, noting that technical expertise is not the same as expertise. Attempts to provide oversight to the defense sector on efficiency grounds have failed to yield the desired results. If the state provision of defense cannot provide economic efficiency, the corollary is that while the state may increase prosperity for select interests, it lacks the ability to generate prosperity for the economy overall. Rather, defense spending is an exercise in trade-offs and not wealth creation. In his work on World War II, Higgs (1987, 1992, 1993, 2004, 2006) continuously illustrated that the true costs of war preparation and execution are the opportunity costs.

Real Costs Are Opportunity Costs

The notion that wars and war preparation can create a full-employment economy was a "Keynesian illusion" (Higgs 1987, 226). Higgs (1992, 43–44; 2006, 81–82) calculates the employment effects of World War II, illustrating that military employment during the war buildup was not commensurate with civilian employment, particularly not civilian employment in the private sector. Prior to the mobilization, unemployment stood at 9.5 percent, but the wartime effort pulled 22 percent of the prewar labor force into the military (Higgs 1987, 81). While the reorganization of the labor force may have "resolved" the unemployment problem of the Great Depression, "four-tenths of the total labor force was not being used to produce consumer goods or capital capable of yielding consumer goods in the future" (Higgs 1987, 82–83).

These calculations are specific to World War II but are meaningful, as it was this period of history that cemented the idea that prosperity can arise from military spending.[12] The costs in terms of consumption, though, are not a one-time feature of the US economy. Rather, there are significant, continuing opportunity costs of military spending where "diverting workers and resources to a bloated, privileged, anticompetitive procurement complex . . . actually reduced the American capacity to invent, innovate, and enhance productivity along nonmilitary lines" (Higgs 1993, 34).

While not utilizing the 12 million people the armed forces accounted for in the final year of World War II, the permanent war economy does continue to draw from the civilian workforce. In 2021, the official uniformed military personnel from the Department of Defense, the Department of Homeland Security, and the Commissioned Corp combined for 1,454,590 employees. Of those, the Defense Department alone accounted for more than 1.4 million uniformed employees, a number that represents 33 percent of all federal employees, both uniformed and nonuniformed (Congressional Research Service 2022, 6). A 2020 Brookings Institute report estimated that if the military and postal service are excluded, "just over 1% of the U.S. workforce or 0.6% of the total population—are permanently employed by the federal government," with "more than 70% of the federal workforce" serving directly "in defense and security agencies like the Department of Defense, the intelligence community agencies, and NASA" (Hill 2020). Each of these individuals represents a valuable economic resource in the military sector that must be withdrawn from the private sector (Duncan and Coyne 2013b), and they are not the only resources to be reallocated in this manner.

Baker (2007) estimated that excessive military expenditures yield higher interest rates due to government deficits, reducing private-sector borrowing in ways that may result in hundreds of thousands of jobs lost or not created over the long run. The Cost of War Project at Brown University estimated that for "both direct and indirect jobs, the military creates 6.9 jobs per $1 million while the clean energy industry and infrastructure each support 9.8 jobs, healthcare supports 14.403, and education supports 15.2" (Garrett-Peltier 2019).[13] The National Priorities Project calculates the trade-offs to the 2021 defense budget. Table 13.1 provides the estimates[14] of those trade-offs.

Table 13.1. Potential opportunity costs for 2021 military expenditures

Comparable years	Number	Alternative
1	4.29 million	Clean energy jobs
1	6.61 million	Registered nurse
1	8.08 million	Elementary school teachers
1	16.94 million	Jobs at $15 per hour
1	87.97 million	Public housing units
1	257.40 million	Children receiving low-income healthcare
1	1.87 billion	Households with wind power
1	2.11 billion	Households with solar electricity
1	217.65 billion	N95 respirator masks
4	16.97 million	Head Start slots for children
4	19.79 million	Scholarships for university students

Source: National Priorities Project, https://www.nationalpriorities.org/interactive-data/trade-offs/.

Unfortunately, accounting measures of the economy cannot fully realize the foregone alternatives in entrepreneurial activity. The nature of the bureaucratic planning in defense means that the decision makers in the process are unable to adequately evaluate in terms of opportunity costs, which are inherently subjective and, therefore, not acted upon or observable (Buchanan [1969] 1999; Coyne and Hall 2019). Nonetheless, this exercise highlights that there are trade-offs to military spending, which stands in contrast to the view that military spending increases wealth relative to the alternative uses of scarce resources employed. As costly as these one-time trade-offs may be to the non-military economy, it is the continuing presence of a permanent war economy that has distortionary effects on the *processes* of the private economy. These processes can be particularly damaging if they yield wasteful outcomes.

Waste Makes for Bad Trade-Offs

Waste is a prevalent feature of the Department of Defense budget that has been well documented (Fitzgerald 1972; Higgs 1988a, 1988b; McNaugher 1989; Reed 2011; Leo and Ehley 2015; Coyne, Michaluk, and Reese 2016; Reno 2019; Coyne and Duncan 2019). The US Government Accountability Office 2021 report cited the continuing issues of waste and fraud within the Defense Department, noting that the "DOD reported to Congress that from fiscal years 2013 to 2017, over $6.6 billion had been recovered from defense contracting fraud cases" (GAO 2021, 8). By 2020, the Defense Department inspector general was still reporting that "395 of its 1,716 ongoing investigations—or approximately one-in-five—are related to procurement fraud" (GAO 2021, 2). As a specific example, a 2022 analysis by the Project on Government Oversight documented that the military parts supplier TransDigm had overcharged the Pentagon 3,800 percent on routine items (Hartung 2022a; Smithberger 2022). Though individual instances of fraudulent waste may seem small in comparison to overall defense budgets, the volume of such instances sums to a far more wasteful picture in the aggregate (Higgs 1988a).

It is not solely fraudulent behavior that adds to the waste of defense spending. Waste can accrue from overuse and misuse that is considered perfectly legal. The decision-making process of procurement is administratively determined (Duncan and Coyne 2013b, 2015) and quite complex (Coyne and Duncan 2019). Rather than utilizing market mechanisms for determining the allocation of resources, the budgetary process of procurement creates separation between outcomes and "the private sacrifices required for its operation.

Assessing the personal distributions of benefits and costs associated with the various programs is impractical, and likely to remain so" (Brubaker 1997, 355).

Coyne and Duncan (2019) argue that economic waste is not just an error but is a perpetual occurrence due to missing property rights and the lack of residual claimants within the defense sector. The severing of the link between the decision maker and those who bear the cost of the decision leads to a "fiscal commons" (see also Coyne, Michaluk, and Reese 2016). Those operating with the bureaucratic budgeting structure are incentivized to overgraze the fiscal commons (see Wagner 1992, 2002, 2012; Raudla 2010; Lipford and Yandle 2014), so long as they can disburse the costs over the general public and concentrate the benefits among their allies or constituents (see Weingast, Shepsle, and Johnsen 1981, 658; Lipford and Yandle 2014, 468).

Duncan and Coyne (2013b, 426) illustrated this point using Lockheed Martin's F-35 Joint Strike Fighter (JSF). The JSF program was launched in the 1990s and has provided significant profits to the industry. Preble (2009) and Hartung (2011) have both argued against the program's economic viability. Preble (2009, 45) challenged the urgency of need for the next-generation fighter, calling into question the added value of the then-newly created fighter in terms of military capabilities given that such fighters are "facing only a hypothetical enemy in a future war for air supremacy . . . [while] . . . actual foes like the Taliban and al-Qaeda don't have an air force and are not interested in acquiring one" (Preble 2009, 48). As of 2022, the F-35 program continues to highlight the misuse of funds in a weapons program. Hartung (2022a) notes, "The Pentagon is slated to buy more than 2,400 F-35s for the Air Force, Marines, and Navy. The estimated lifetime cost for procuring and operating those planes, a mere $1.7 trillion, would make it the Pentagon's most expensive weapons project ever."

These purchases continue despite a 2016 report from the Project for Government Oversight (Grazier and Smithberger 2016) arguing that the F-35 may never be combat ready, or at least not for the type of combat for which the fighter was originally intended. While the F-35 has flown some missions, the GAO (2022) recently reported that "the F-35 fleet's average mission capable rate—the percentage of time during which the F-35s can fly and perform at least one mission—declined between FY2020 and FY2021. One major reason is that an increasing number of F-35s have not been able to fly because they don't have a working engine." Hartung (2022a) remains critical of the program, noting that even though the fighter is meant to provide air support for troops on the ground, it has proved anything but well-designed to do so.

In fact, that job is already handled far better and more cheaply by the existing A-10 "Warthog" attack aircraft. A 2021 Pentagon assessment of the F-35—and keep in mind that this is the Department of Defense, not some outside expert—found 800 unresolved defects in the plane. The continued overuse and misuse of resources on defense programs is a real problem because the costs are real. These costs are not limited to the monetary ones either.

The Cost Is More Than Spending

The preceding sections offered estimates of the potential trade-offs that come with military spending. While these trade-offs are an important part of the story of the permanent war economy, Higgs (2008) has been quite explicit that his critique goes beyond the issues of scale. The war economy brings about not just changes in federal spending, but changes in the *scope* of federal activity as well (Coyne 2015). In responding to critics of the ratchet effect, Higgs (2008) notes that much of the effect is in the long-run distortions of human action:

> The ratchet effect is a more complex phenomenon . . . where one continually meets path dependencies and contingencies whose resolution is anything but determinate, where real human beings, relying on their attitudes, beliefs, and commitments (shaped by their particular experiences, acquaintances, and loyalties) make genuine—that is, not fully predetermined—choices and thereby set in motion new streams of cause and effect that ripple through time and space.

Throughout his work on the ratchet effect, Higgs illustrates the continuous changes in how the federal government and the citizens view the roles and responsibilities of the federal government. With each crisis, it is not only the level of spending that ratchets up, but the activities in which government is involved as well. Higgs (1987, 2004) details this trend throughout World War I and World War II. Some of the more significant changes in World War I were the introduction of various agencies charged with overseeing or outright controlling economic activity.[15] Some early examples of control came through the nationalization of key industries, the manipulation "of labor-management relations, securities sales, agricultural production and marketing, the distribution of coal and petroleum, international commerce, and the markets for raw materials and manufactured products" Higgs (2004, 164). While many of these changes dissipated after the war, they set a precedent for future activities.

Mayhew (2005) documents other long-lasting policy changes stemming from several US wars, such as (1) the introduction of the Budget and Account

Act of 1921 to create the system of national budgeting, (2) the introduction of extensive national-origins quotas and other immigration restrictions, and (3) the FBI's creation of a General Intelligence Division that would maintain files on private citizens into the Nixon administration. Coyne (2015, 387–88) provides a detailed table including various roles the government took on throughout the two World Wars, the Korean War, and the Vietnam War, including but not limited to: (in WWI) press censorship with the creation of a federal censorship board, censorship through the seizure of telegraphs, curtailing free speech through banning public meetings, and 2,000 arrests under the Sedition Act; (in WWII and the Korean War) human rights violations with the internment of 120,000 Japanese Americans, censorship of battlefield reporting, the suspension of habeas corpus in Hawaii after Pearl Harbor and the use of military tribunals for prosecution of civilians there, and trials before the House Un-American Activities Committee; and (in the Vietnam War) government complicity in attacks on minorities, infiltration and jailing of anti-war press, conspiracy trials of anti-war leaders, CIA mail-opening programs, and 500,000 secret FBI investigations (see also Duncan 2022).

The continuation of the permanent war economy and the global war on terror in the 21st century have yielded new expansions in surveillance of citizens (Greenwald 2013; Kehl 2014), increased influence over the media (Coyne and Hall 2021), and increased militarization of domestic policing (ACLU 2014; Coyne and Hall 2018). Perhaps the best summation of the scope effect remains that from Higgs. Following each of these crises, government takes new roles. Yet by the end of each, such "government actions no longer startled the citizenry; indeed, many Americans, including highly regarded intellectuals and top policymakers, had come to regard them as desirable" (Higgs 2004, 171). Policy changes yield cultural changes, which further alter society in the favor of government and the military.

Not Just Economy but Permanent War

This cultural change may yet be another long-run cost of the permanent war economy. The very existence of the large, well-funded, and influential defense sector has a continuous impact on how the military is viewed in American life. Throughout the 20th and 21st centuries, there has been an increase in cultural militarism (Lutz 2002; Bacevich 2007; ACLU 2014; Coyne and Hall 2018, 2021; Reno 2019, 140–73). The continued use of the vast resources combined with an increased sense of militarism has domestic as well as international implications. Since the end of World War II, the United States has become self-styled as the world's policeman, intent on the continuous projection of power even to the extent of rationalizing "preventative war" (Bacevich 2007, 2010). In 2004 it was pointed out that "the Pentagon currently owns or rents 702 overseas bases in about 130 countries and has another 6,000 bases in the United States and its territories" (Johnson 2004). As of 2021, the number had grown to 750 bases overseas (Deppen 2021). An issue with having such excessive military expenditures as described above—in spending as well as bases held—is the need to justify having it.

Just since the turn of the millennium, the United States and its allies have conducted two significant wars in Iraq (2003–11) and Afghanistan (2001–21), as well as military operations of varying levels in intensity in Yemen (2002, 2011–present), the Philippines (2002), Côte d'Ivoire (2002), Liberia (2003), Georgia (2003, 2008), Djibouti (2003), Haiti (2004), Ethiopia (2004), Kenya (2004), Eritrea (2004), Pakistan (2004–18), Lebanon (2006), Somalia (2007, 2011–present), Libya (2011, 2015–19), Uganda (2011–17), Jordan (2012), Turkey (2012), Chad (2012), Mali (2013), Syria (2014–present), and Iraq again (2014–21). Given the nature of the global war on terror and the lack of standard reporting, it is possible and even likely that this list is not all inclusive. Even so, it provides an estimated 27 conflicts in a 20-year period, more than one conflict per year (see Duncan 2022).

The Cost of War Project estimates that these adventures overseas between 2001 and 2021 have contributed to 897,000–929,00 deaths around the world, noting that this estimate does not include those who died from the indirect effects of the wars, such as water loss, sewage, infrastructure issues, or disease.[16] These post-9/11 wars have not just led to deaths, but have also displaced societies around the world. Vine et al. (2020) "conservatively" estimated that "at least 37 million people have fled their homes in the eight most violent wars the U.S. military has launched or participated in since 2001," an estimate they updated for 2021 to "at least 38 million people have fled their homes—around one million more displaced people than a year earlier" (Vine et al. 2021). The opportunity costs of these overseas activities in terms of human lives lost and displaced are immeasurable but quite obviously significant. Yet so long as the war economy remains permanent, it yields the potential for the costs to continue well into the future.

CONCLUSION

Robert Higgs has had a long, voluminous career. His work on the ratchet effect and his assessment of the defense sector in terms of opportunity costs remain a vitally important research question. The research project into the permanent war economy is far from completed. As Coyne (2015, 391) notes, "Given what is at stake in terms of human well-being, understanding the limits and costs of state-provided defense is just as important as understanding its potential benefits, if not more important." Restraining the growth and distortions from continuing military largesse is not an easy task, as each crisis builds the foundation for further expansions and distortions.

The link between the war economy and threat generation remains a viable area of study, particularly considering the increases in defense expenditures in Europe and Asia. By 2023, the European Defense Agency will see an estimated 16 percent rise in procurement and researching of new weapons over 2020 numbers (EDA 2022). Japan has approved a 26.3 percent increase in defense spending for FY2023 (Kosuke 2022). As other nations ramp up their military expenditures, the possibility of developing their own permanent war economies intensifies. It is unclear, and likely untrue, that these increases will make the world safer (Hartung 2022b). It is a question worth considering.

There are remaining avenues for research into the domestic effects of the permanent war economy. Government surveillance of the citizenry, police militarization, and the general weakening of societal constraints on the domestic use of military applications is a continuing issue. The combined crises of a pandemic and the Ukraine-Russia war may yield further ratchets similar to the historical examples provided above. The long-run effects of these crises are yet to be determined, but the preliminary evidence suggests that an increasing entrenchment of the war economy is on the horizon. With the FY2023 US defense budget primed to elevate military expenditures to or above the levels spent during active engagement in war, Higgs's lessons take on new meaning and continued relevance.

NOTES

1. Even in defining the ratchet, Higgs (1987, 30) notes, "Mere visual inspection, however, may not permit a conclusive judgement." He goes on to suggest that scale as shown by the data are not the full story, a topic that will be discussed at some length below.

2. Federal Reserve Bank of St. Louis, 2020, https://www.stlouisfed.org/on-the-economy/2020 /february/war-highest-defense-spending-measured. Note: The spending numbers by the Federal Reserve are given in 2019 dollars. However, adjusting to 2020 dollars does not change the trillion mark.

3. Data for 2022 and 2023 have not yet been officially released by SIPRI. However, the fiscal 2023 National Defense Authorization Act passed by the House of Representatives and the Senate recommended a record $858 billion (in 2022$), providing $45 billion over the administration's request and containing at least $800 million for security assistance to Ukraine (Shane and Harris 2022; Zengerle 2022).

4. In 2020 constant US$. SIPRI Military Expenditure Database 2022, https://www.sipri.org /databases/milex.

5. Coyne and Hall (2018) document several structural changes to the military during the Spanish-American War, changes abroad that eventually influenced structural changes domestically as well. For example, the military intelligence system developed in the Philippines would set the stage for the eventual rise of the current NSA (Coyne and Hall 2018, 74–83).

6. A similar criticism was given to business for supposedly supporting the Spanish-American War; however, Pratt (1934) shows that businesses were far more reluctant to enter war, as war is rarely truly profitable.

7. The general sentiment is reflected in H. C. Engelbrecht and F. C. Hanighen's book *Merchants of Death* (1934), a study of World War I war profiteering, which became a best-seller the year it was published. Engelbrecht and Hanighen argued that "the profits reported were simply colossal. Du Pont paid a dividend of 100 per cent on its common stock in 1916. The earnings of the United States Steel Corporation for 1917 exceeded by many millions the face value of its common stock, which was largely water. In 1916 this same company reported earnings greater by $70,000,000 than the combined earnings of 1911, 1912, and 1913. Bethlehem Steel paid a stock dividend of 200 per cent in 1917. U.S. Treasury figures show that during the war period 69,000 men made more than $3,000,000,000 over and above their normal income. Almost immediately the cry of profiteering went up" (178).

8. Melman (1971, 1985) attributes much of this centralization to Robert McNamara, who was the US secretary of defense 1961–68.

9. Coyne and Lucas (2016) provide a survey of the most popular economic textbooks, illustrating the prevalence of national defense being the literal textbook example of a public good.

10. Hummel and Lavoie (1990) also illustrate the issues with the idea that national defense is a public good, particularly given the fact that "national defense" has greatly involved adventurism abroad that does not necessarily correlate with defense of the citizens within the United States.

11. Higgs (2006) directly illustrates the opportunity costs of the permanent war economy by constructing calculations of GNP that distinguish between "butter-sacrificing" during military buildup and "butter-enhancing" during a demobilization period. He shows empirically that "changes in the [government military] and [private] shares [of GNP] were almost exactly offsetting. A trade-off equation fitted to the annual changes during 1948–89 has a tight fit ($R2 = 0.814$) and shows that the implicit cost of a one-percentage-point increase in the military share was a reduction of one percentage point in the private share" (Higgs 2006, 132).

12. Higgs (1987, 227) argues that the wartime employment effects came more from the draft than the federal deficits, yet the pervasiveness of the federal-deficit-to-employment idea that came from the war effort led to the 1946 passage of the Employment Act. The Employment Act specifically tasks the federal government with managing industries and "free competitive enterprise" to ensure employment opportunities for citizens.

13. The report goes further to calculate the lost jobs from *just the spending on the active wars* since 2001, estimating that "the $260 billion spent on the war could have produced over 3 million jobs, and thus we lost the opportunity to create 1.4 million jobs on average," and using the largest estimated differential in job creation, "that between defense and primary and secondary education, the lost opportunity is over 3 million jobs" (Garrett-Peltier 2019).

14. In the table, Comparable Years signifies the number of years in which the alternative could be funded for the estimated number. For example, the 2021 military spending could fund 4.29 million clean energy jobs for one year, or 16.97 million Head Start slots for a full four years.

15. Rockoff (2004, 15) argues that the "three most important were (1) the War Industries Board and its autonomous Price Fixing Committee, which dealt with industrial production and prices, (2) The Food Administration, which dealt with agricultural prices and production, and (3) the Fuel Administration, which dealt with fuel prices and production."

16. Cost of War Project, Washington Institute for International & Public Affairs at Brown University, https://watson.brown.edu/costsofwar/figures/2021/WarDeathToll.

REFERENCES

Adams, Walter, and William J. Adams. 1972. "The Military-Industrial Complex: A Market Structure Analysis." *American Economic Review* 62 (1/2): 279–87.

American Civil Liberties Union (ACLU). 2014. "War Comes Home: The Excessive Militarization of American Policing." https://www.aclu.org/report/war-comes-home-excessive-militarization -american-police.

Arms Control Association (ACA). 2019. "The Intermediate-Range Nuclear Forces (INF) Treaty at a Glance." https://www.armscontrol.org/factsheets/INFtreaty.

Bacevich, Andrew. 2007. *The Long War: A New History of U.S. National Security Policy since World War II*. New York: Columbia University Press.

———. 2010. *Washington Rules: America's Path to Permanent War*. New York: Metropolitan Books.

Baker, Dean. 2007. "The Economic Impact of the Iraq War and Higher Military Spending." Center for Economic and Policy Research. https://core.ac.uk/download/pdf/71339692.pdf.

Baran, Paul A., and Paul M. Sweezy. 1966. *Monopoly Capital: An Essay on the American Economic and Social Order*. New York: Monthly Review Press.

Bean, Jonathan J. 1994. "World War II and the 'Crisis' of Small Business: The Smaller War Plants Corporation, 1942–1946." *Journal of Policy History* 6 (3): 215–43.

Bourne, Randolph. 1919. *Untimely Papers*. New York: B. W. Huebsch.

Brady, Robert A. 1952. "Defense Expenditures and the National Economy." *Annals of the American Academy of Political Science and Social Science* 283: 42–54.

Brubaker, Earl R. 1997. "The Tragedy of the Public Budgetary Commons." *Independent Review* 1 (3): 353–70.

Buchanan, James. (1969) 1999. *Cost and Choice: An Inquiry in Economic Theory, Vol. 6 of the Collected Works*. Indianapolis: Liberty Fund.

Congressional Research Service. 2022. "Federal Workforce Statistics Sources: OPM and OMB." CRS Report #R43590.

Coyne, Christopher J. 2015. "Lobotomizing the Defense Brain." *Review of Austrian Economics* 28 (4): 371–96.

Coyne, Christopher J., and Thomas K. Duncan. 2019. "The Unproductive Protective State: The U.S. Defense Sector as a Fiscal Commons." In *James M. Buchanan: A Theorist of Political Economy and Social Philosophy*, edited by Richard E. Wagner, 235–61. Cham, Switzerland: Palgrave Macmillan.

Coyne, Christopher J., and Abigail R. Hall. 2014. "Perfecting Tyranny: Foreign Intervention as Experimentation in Social Control." *Independent Review* 19 (2): 1–25.

———. 2018. *Tyranny Comes Home: The Domestic Fate of U.S. Militarism*. Stanford, CA: Stanford University Press.

———. 2019. "State-Provided Defense as Noncomprehensive Planning." *Journal of Private Enterprise* 34 (1): 75–85.

———. 2021. *Manufacturing Militarism: U.S. Government Propaganda in the War on Terror*. Stanford, CA: Stanford University Press.

Coyne, Christopher J., and David Lucas. 2016. "Economists Have No Defense: A Critical Review of National Defense in Economics Textbooks." *Journal of Private Enterprise* 31 (4): 65–83.

Coyne, Christopher J., Courtney Michaluk, and Rachel Reese. 2016. "Unproductive Entrepreneurship in U.S. Military Contracting." *Journal of Entrepreneurship and Public Policy* 5 (2): 221–39.

Crawford, Neta C. 2021. "The U.S. Budgetary Costs of the Post-9/11 Wars." 20 Years of War: A Cost of War Research Series. https://watson.brown.edu/costsofwar/figures/2021/BudgetaryCosts.

Daugherty, Carroll R. 1951. "Employment Stability and Income Security." *Annals of the American Academy of Political Science and Social Science* 274: 39–46.

Deppen, Patterson. 2021. "The All-American Base World." *TomDispatch*, August 19. https://tomdispatch.com/the-all-american-base-world/.

Duncan, Thomas K. 2022. "The Non-Freedom of Foreign Intervention." SSRN Working Paper. https://papers.ssrn.com/sol3/papers.cfm?abstract_id=4308972.

Duncan, Thomas K., and Christopher J. Coyne. 2013a. "The Origins of the Permanent War Economy." *Independent Review* 18 (2): 219–40.

———. 2013b. "The Overlooked Costs of the Permanent War Economy: A Market Process Approach." *Review of Austrian Economics* 26 (4): 413–31.

———. 2015. "The Revolving Door and the Entrenchment of the Permanent War Economy." *Peace Economics, Peace Science, and Public Policy* 21 (3): 391–413.

Dunne, John P. 1995. "The Defense Industrial Base." In *Handbook of Defense Economics*, vol. 1, edited by Keith Hartley and Todd Sandler, 399–430. New York: Elsevier Science.

Eisenhower, Dwight D. 1961. "Farewell Address to the Nation." January 17. http://www.h-net.org/~hst306/documents/indust.html.

Eloranta, Jari. 2007. "From the Great Illusion to the Great War: Military Spending Behaviour of the Great Powers, 1870–1913." *European Review of Economic History* 11 (2): 255–83.

Engelbrecht, H. C., and F. C. Hanighen. 1934. *Merchants of Death: A Study of the International Armament Industry*. New York: Dodd, Mead.

European Defence Agency (EDA). 2022. "European Defence Spending Surpasses €200 Billion for First Time." December 8. https://eda.europa.eu/news-and-events/news/2022/12/08/european-defence-spending-surpasses-200-billion-for-first-time-driven-by-record-defence-investments-in-2021.

Feiler, Arthur. 1942. "Full Employment of Resources and War Economy." *Social Research* 9 (1): 141–45.

Fitzgerald, A. Earnest. 1972. *The High Priests of Waste*. New York: W. W. Norton.

Garrett-Peltier, Heidi. 2019. "War Spending and Lost Opportunities." Cost of War Project, Washington Institute for International & Public Affairs at Brown University. https://watson.brown.edu/costsofwar/costs/economic/economy/employment.

Grazier, Dan, and Mandy Smithberger. 2016. "F-35 May Never Be Ready for Combat." Project on Government Oversight, September 9. https://www.pogo.org/investigation/2016/09/f-35-may-never-be-ready-for-combat.

Greenwald, Glenn. 2013. *No Place to Hide: Edward Snowden, the NSA, and the U.S.* New York: Picador.

Hartung, William D. 2011. *Prophets of War: Lockheed Martin and the Making of the Military-Industrial Complex*. New York: Nation Books.

———. 2022a. "What a Waste: $778 Billion for the Pentagon and Still Counting." Quincy Institute for Responsible Statecraft, February 3. https://quincyinst.org/2022/02/03/what-a-waste-778-billion-for-the-pentagon-and-still-counting/.

———. 2022b. "Russia's Invasion of Ukraine Is No Reason to Increase the Pentagon Budget." *Forbes*, September 22. https://www.forbes.com/sites/williamhartung/2022/09/22/russias-invasion-of-ukraine-is-no-reason-to-increase-the-pentagon-budget/.

Higgs, Robert. 1985. "Crisis, Bigger Government, and Ideological Change: Two Hypotheses on the Ratchet Phenomenon." *Explorations in Economic History* 22 (1): 1–28.

———. 1987. *Crisis and Leviathan: Critical Episodes in the Growth of American Government*. New York: Oxford University Press.

———. 1988a. "Hard Coals Make Bad Laws: Congressional Parochialism versus National Defense." *Cato Journal* 8 (1): 79–106.

———. 1988b. "U.S. Military Spending in the Cold War Era: Opportunity Costs, Foreign Crises, and Domestic Constraints." *Cato Policy Analysis No. 114*. Washington, DC: Cato Institute.

———. 1992. "Wartime Prosperity? A Reassessment of the U.S. Economy in the 1940s." *Journal of Economic History* 52 (1): 41–60.

———. 1993. "How Military Mobilization Hurts the Economy." In *Second Thoughts: Myths and Morals of U.S. Economic History*, edited by D. N. McCloskey, 34–44. New York: Oxford University Press.

———. 1994. "The Cold War Economy: Opportunity Costs, Ideology, and the Politics of Crisis." *Explorations in Economic History* 31: 283–312.

———. 1997. "Regime Uncertainty: Why the Great Depression Lasted So Long and Why Prosperity Resumed after the War." *Independent Review* 1 (4): 561–90.

———. 1999. "From Central Planning to the Market: The American Transition, 1945–1947." *Journal of Economic History* 59 (3): 600–623.

———. 2001. "The Cold War Is Over, But U.S. Preparation for It Continues." *Independent Review* 6 (2): 287–305.

———. 2004. *Against Leviathan: Government Power and a Free Society*. Oakland, CA: Independent Institute.

———. 2005. "Government and the Economy: The World Wars." Working Paper no. 59. Oakland, CA: Independent Institute.

———. 2006. *Depression, War, and Cold War: Studies in Political Economy*. New York: Oxford University Press.

———. 2007. "Military-Economic Fascism: How Business Corrupts Government, and Vice Versa." *Independent Review* 12 (2): 299–316.

———. 2008. "Underappreciated Aspects of the Ratchet Effect." *The Beacon*, December 16. https://blog.independent.org/2008/12/16/underappreciated-aspects-of-the-ratchet-effect/.

———. 2011. "To Fight or Not to Fight: War's Payoffs to U.S. Leaders and to the American People." *Independent Review* 16 (1): 141–50.

———. 2012a. *Resurgence of the Warfare State: The Crisis since 9/11*. Oakland, CA: Independent Institute.

———. 2012b. *Delusions of Power: New Explorations of the State, War, and the Economy*. Oakland, CA: Independent Institute.

———. 2019. *Economic and Political Change after Crisis: Prospects for Government, Liberty, and the Rule of Law*. New York: Routledge.

Hill, Fiona. 2020. "Public Service and the Federal Government." Brookings Institute Policy, May 27. https://www.brookings.edu/policy2020/votervital/public-service-and-the-federal-government/.

Hirsch, Julius. 1944. "Facts and Fantasies Concerning Full Employment." *American Economic Review* 34 (1): 118–27.

Hooks, Gregory. 1991. *Forging the Military-Industrial Complex: World War II's Battle of the Potomac*. Chicago: University of Illinois Press.

Hoover, Calvin B. 1948. "Keynes and the Economic System." *Journal of Political Economy* 56 (5): 392–402.

Hopkins, A. G. 2018. *American Empire: A Global History*. Princeton, NJ: Princeton University Press.

Hummel, Jeffrey Rogers, and Don Lavoie. 1990. "National Defense and the Public-Goods Problem." In *Arms, Politics, and the Economy*, edited by Robert Higgs, 37–60. Oakland, CA: Independent Institute.

ICAN. 2022. *Squandered: 2021 Global Nuclear Weapons Spending*. International Campaign to Abolish Nuclear Weapons, June. https://www.icanw.org/squandered_2021_global_nuclear_weapons_spending_report.

Johnson, Chalmers. 2004. "America's Empire of Bases." *TomDispatch*, January 15. https://tomdispatch.com/chalmers-johnson-on-garrisoning-the-planet/.

———. 2008. "Bankrupting the American Republic: The Permanent War Economy and Soaring Deficits." *Asia-Pacific Journal* 6 (1): 1–7.

Kaufman, Richard F. 1972. "MIR Ving the Boondoggle: Contracts, Subsidy, and Welfare in the Aerospace Industry." *American Economic Review* 62 (1/2): 288–95.

Kehl, Danielle. 2014. "Surveillance Costs: The NSA's Impact on the Economy, Internet Freedom, and Cybersecurity." *New America's Open Technology Institute Policy Paper*.

Keynes, John Maynard. (1939) 2010. "Will Re-armament Cure Unemployment?" In *Keynes on the Wire: John Maynard Keynes*, edited by Donald E. Moggridge, 187–93. New York: Palgrave MacMillan.

Kosuke, Takahashi. 2022. "Japan Approves 26.3% Increase in Defense Spending for Fiscal Year 2023." *The Diplomat*, December 24. https://thediplomat.com/2022/12/japan-approves-26-3-increase-in-defense-spending-for-fiscal-year-2023/.

Leo, Jacqueline, and Brianna Ehley. 2015. "With $8.5 Trillion Unaccounted for, Why Should Congress Increase the Defense Budget?" *The Fiscal Times*, March 19. http://www.thefiscaltimes.com/2015/03/19/85-Trillion-Unaccounted-Should-Congress-Increase-Defense-Budget.

Lipford, Jody W., and Bruce Yandle. 2014. "Grazing the State and Local Fiscal Commons: Do Different Tax Prices Lead to More or Less Grazing?" *Public Finance Review* 42 (4): 466–86.

Lipton, Eric, Michael Crowley, and John Ismay. 2022. "Military Spending Surges, Creating New Boom for Arms Makers." *New York Times*, December 18. https://www.nytimes.com/2022/12/18/us/politics/defense-contractors-ukraine-russia.html.

Lutz, Catherine. 2002. "Making War at Home in the United States: Militarization and the Current Crisis." *American Anthropologist* 104 (3): 723–35.

Lynn III, William J. 2014. "The End of the Military-Industrial Complex: How the Pentagon Is Adapting to Globalization." *Foreign Affairs* 93 (6). http://www.foreignaffairs.com/articles/142199/william-j-lynn-iii/the-end-of-the-military-industrialcomplex.

Markusen, Ann, Peter Hall, Scott Campbell, and Sabina Deitrick. 1991. *The Rise of the Gunbelt: The Military Remapping of Industrial America*. New York: Oxford University Press.

Mayhew, David R. 2005. "Wars and American Politics." *Perspectives in Politics* 3 (3): 473–93.

McNaugher, Thomas L. 1989. *New Weapons, Old Politics: America's Military Procurement Muddle*. Washington, DC: Brookings Institution Press.

Melman, Seymour. 1970. *Pentagon Capitalism: The Political Economy of War*. New York: McGraw-Hill.

———, ed. 1971. *The War Economy of the United States: Readings in Military History and Economy*. New York: St. Martin's Press.

———. 1985. *The Permanent War Economy: American Capitalism in Decline*. New York: Simon and Schuster.

Mueller, John. 2006. *Overblown: How Politicians and the Terrorism Industry Inflate National Security Threats, and Why We Believe Them*. New York: Free Press.

Mueller, John, and Mark G. Stewart. 2011. *Terror, Security, and Money: Balancing the Risks, Benefits, and Costs of Homeland Security*. Oxford: Oxford University Press.

———. 2015. *Chasing Ghosts: The Policing of Terrorism*. Oxford: Oxford University Press.

Oakes, Walter J. 1944. "Towards a Permanent War Economy?" *Politics* 1 (1): 11–17.

Pratt, Julius W., 1934. "American Business and the Spanish-American War." *Hispanic American Historical Review* 14 (2): 163–201.

Preble, Christopher A. 2009. *The Power Problem: How American Military Dominance Makes Us Less Safe, Less Prosperous, and Less Free.* Ithaca, NY: Cornell University Press.

Raudla, Ringa. 2010. "Governing Budgetary Commons: What Can We Learn from Elinor Ostrom?" *European Journal of Law and Economics* 30: 201–21.

Raymond, Jack. 1964. *Power at the Pentagon.* New York: Harper and Row.

Reed, John. 2011. "$46 Billion Worth of Cancelled Programs." Military.com, July 19. https://www .military.com/defensetech/2011/07/19/46-billion-worth-of-cancelled-programs.

Reno, Joshua O. 2019. *Military Waste: The Unexpected Consequences of Permanent War Readiness.* Oakland, CA: University of California Press.

Rockoff, Hugh. 2004. "Until It's Over, Over There: The U.S. Economy in World War I." NBER Working Paper 10580. http://www.nber.org/papers/w10580.

Rosen, Elliot A. 2005. *Roosevelt, the Great Depression, and the Economics of Recovery.* Charlottesville: University of Virginia Press.

Rutherford, Harry K. 1939. "Mobilizing Industry for War." *Harvard Business Review* 18 (1): 1–10.

Shane, Leo, and Bryant Harris. 2022. "Congress Reveals Plan to Increase Defense Budget by 8%." *DefenseNews*, December 7. https://www.defensenews.com/congress/budget/2022/12/07 /congress-reveals-plan-to-increase-defense-budget-by-8/.

Slichter, Sumner H. 1945. "How to Stimulate Postwar Employment." *Annals of the American Academy of Political and Social Sciences* 238: 158–66.

Smith, Jean Edward. 2007. *FDR.* New York: Random House.

Smith, R. Elberton. (1959) 1991. *The Army and Economic Mobilization.* Washington, DC: Center for Military History, United States Army.

Smith, Ron. 1995. "The Demand for Military Expenditures." In *Handbook of Defense Economics*, vol. 1, edited by Keith Hartley and Todd Sandler, 69–88. New York: Elsevier Science.

Smithberger, Mandy. 2022. "Spare Parts Contractor Profits from Broken System." Project on Government Oversight, January 12. https://www.pogo.org/analysis/2022/01/spare-parts -contractor-profits-from-broken-system.

Sumner, William G. 1899. "The Conquest of the United States by Spain." *Yale Law Journal* 8 (4): 168–93.

Symonds, Craig L. 2018. *American Naval History: A Very Short Introduction.* New York: Oxford University Press.

Trevino, Ruben, and Robert Higgs. 1992. "Profits of U.S. Defense Contractors." *Defense Economics* 3: 211–18.

US Government Accountability Office (GAO). 2021. "DOD Fraud Risk Management: Actions Needed to Enhance Department-Wide Approach, Focusing on Procurement Fraud Risks." Report to Congressional Requestors, GAO-21-309.

———. 2022. "F-35 Sustainment: Uncertainties and Has Not Met Key Objectives." Testimony Before the Subcommittee on Readiness, Committee on Armed Services, House of Representatives, GAO-22-105995.

Vance, T. N. 1951a. "The Permanent War Economy Part I: Its Basic Characteristics." *New International* 17 (1): 29–44.

———. 1951b. "The Permanent War Economy Part II: Declining Standards of Living." *New International* 17 (2): 67–92.

———. 1951c. "The Permanent War Economy Part III: Increasing State Intervention." *New International* 17 (3): 131–59.

———. 1951d. "The Permanent War Economy Part IV: Military-Economic Imperialism." *New International* 17 (4): 232–48.

———. 1951e. "The Permanent War Economy Part V: Some Significant Trends." *New International* 17 (5): 251–66.

———. 1951f. "The Permanent War Economy Part VI: Taxation and Class Struggle." *New International* 17 (6): 251–66.

Vatter, Harold G. 1985. *The U.S. Economy in World War II*. New York: Columbia University Press.

Vine, David, Cala Coffman, Katalina Khoury, Madison Lovasz, Helen Bush, Rachael Leduc, and Jennifer Walkup. 2020. "Creating Refugees: Displacement Caused by the United States' Post 9/11 Wars." Cost of War Project, Washington Institute for International & Public Affairs at Brown University. https://watson.brown.edu/costsofwar/files/cow/imce/papers/2020 /Displacement_Vine%20et%20al_Costs%20of%20War%202020%2009%2008.pdf.

———. 2021. "Creating Refugees: Displacement Caused by the United States' Post-9/11 Wars." Cost of War Project, Washington Institute for International & Public Affairs at Brown University. https://watson.brown.edu/costsofwar/costs/human/refugees.

Wagner, Richard E. 1992. "Grazing the Federal Budget Commons: The Rational Politics of Budgetary Irresponsibility." *Journal of Law and Politics* 9: 105–19.

———. 2002. "Property, Taxation, and the Budgetary Commons." In *Property, Taxation, and the Rule of Law*, edited by Donald P. Racheter and Richard E. Wagner, 33–47. Norwell, MA: Kluwer Academic.

———. 2012. *Deficits, Debt, and Democracy: Wrestling with Tragedy on the Fiscal Commons*. Cheltenham, UK: Edward Elgar.

Weingast, Barry R., Kenneth A. Shepsle, and Christopher Johnsen. 1981. "The Political Economy of Benefits and Costs: A Neoclassical Approach to Distributive Politics." *Journal of Political Economy* 89 (4): 642–64.

Woods, Thomas E. 2010. "The Neglected Costs of the Warfare State: An Austrian Tribute to Seymour Melman." *Journal of Libertarian Studies* 22: 103–25.

Yarmolinsky, Adam. 1971. *The Military Establishment: Its Impacts on American Society*. New York: Harper and Row.

Zengerle, Patricia. 2022. "U.S. Senate Passes Record $858 Billion Defense Act, Sending Bill to Biden." *Reuters*, December 15. https://www.reuters.com/world/us/us-senate-backs-record -858-billion-defense-bill-voting-continues-2022-12-16/.

Chapter 14

What About the Healthcare State?

Robert Higgs's Contributions to Health Economics

Raymond J. March

conomist and historian Robert Higgs is best recognized for his extensive and important work in economic history and political economy.
His significant historical scholarship examines how the US economy
prospered during the Gilded Age and the economic advancement of Blacks
after the Civil War, among other insightful topics (Higgs 1971, 1973, 1977, 1982).
Higgs's masterful contributions to political economy examine the determi-
nants of the growth of government, the prevalence of ratchet effects following
crisis periods when governments expand, and the erosion of constitutional
constraints on government power through the expansions of the welfare and
warfare states (Higgs 1987, 2006, 2007). In addition to his numerous scholarly
contributions, Higgs is a prolific and lucid writer for public audiences. A collection of his shorter writings published in his book *Taking a Stand: Reflections on
Life, Liberty, and the Economy* won the Independent Publisher's Independent
Voice Award in 2016.

While widely cited and recognized for these accomplishments, Higgs receives
significantly less recognition and praise for his scholarly work in health economics.[1] It is unclear why. While less numerous than his works in other areas,
Higgs addresses a considerable range of vitally important topics within the field
of health economics and the US healthcare system. Through edited volumes,
journal articles, and policy briefs, Higgs provides commentary on the role of
decision-making under uncertainty by healthcare consumers, comparative institutional structures of healthcare sectors, regulatory standards for medical device
quality, and growth of federal health agencies (Higgs 1994a; 1995a, 1995b).

Unsurprisingly, given his research interest in the mechanisms by which governments expand in power and scope, much of Higgs's work in health economics

I would like to thank Veeshan Rayamajhee and Christopher Coyne for their comments and suggestions in improving this chapter. I would also like to thank Robert Higgs, who visited Texas Tech
University while I was a graduate student and encouraged me to continue writing about the FDA and
healthcare economics. I did, and he is a big reason why.

examines the growth and impact of the Food and Drug Administration (FDA). Specifically, Higgs analyzes the political exchanges that allowed the FDA to expand since the late 1930s, the effects of regulation within the US medical device market, public choice explanations for the FDA's approval process, and the role of crises and fear in the expanding regulatory scope and influence of the FDA.

Much of Higgs's work in health economics was written in the mid-1990s. However, his findings and insights are vital to health economics research and for developing policy for contemporary healthcare issues. Efforts to protect consumers from potentially harmful products, determining the most effective regulatory apparatus and stringency for the FDA, analyzing the effectiveness of markets in the provision of healthcare goods, and other topics addressed by Higgs in the mid-1990s remain among the most active research questions in health economics today.

This chapter argues that Higgs's insights are undeservingly underappreciated and remain relevant for both contemporary scholarship and policy. To this end, I review Higgs's works on the role of markets in promoting consumer welfare within a health economics framework, his analysis of the FDA using a political economy framework, and his analysis of the growth of the FDA. I focus on these aspects of Higgs's works because they form his most significant contributions to the health economics academic field while providing the most useful insights into improving the US healthcare system in the future.

The next section reviews Higgs's insights into the role of markets and consumer welfare in healthcare, followed by a review of Higgs's contributions examining the political economy of the FDA. A fourth section traces Higgs's research on the growth of the FDA over time through the mechanisms of crisis response and fear. Following that, the chapter reviews contemporary research providing insight into the potential for healthcare reform and the effectiveness of markets in addressing several of health economics' most examined research questions before concluding.

CONSUMER WELFARE, MARKET FAILURE, AND MARKETS

The study of economics generally begins with scarcity, eventually building into the analysis of exchange and markets. The subfield of health economics generally begins by assuming that exchanges of healthcare goods involve difficulties and guide healthcare markets toward inefficiency. Many of these perceived market failures theoretically harm or prevent consumers from making optimal choices. Mushkin (1958) explicitly outlines diseconomies, pricing issues, and a lack of professional standards within the medical discipline as reasons "preferences [of consumers] are not a wholly reliable guide to allocate healthcare resources" (790). Arrow (1963) argues in "Uncertainty and the Welfare Economics of Medical Care," which some health economists consider to be the foundational paper in health economics (Jakovljevic and Ogura 2016), that asymmetric information between patients and physicians prevents healthcare markets from maximizing total welfare. From this conclusion, Arrow recommends "nonmarket social institutions" to correct for inherent market failures and to protect consumer welfare (947).

Devising "nonmarket social institutions" has arguably become the primary goal of much health economics research and the target of many health policy efforts. Writing nearly 40 years after the publication of Arrow's paper, Savedoff (2004) characterizes health economics research as "efforts to develop a new set of nonmarket institutions adequate to manage this rapidly changing industry" (140). By "adequate management," the author means governmental regulations and controls to protect consumers by regulating which medical goods and services become available and what regulatory standards they must meet to reach the market.

This approach to addressing the perceived pervasiveness of market failure in healthcare markets results in a considerably high degree of regulation for the US healthcare industry (Ampaabeng, Nelson, and Amez-Droz 2020). In addition to numerous (and often complex) regulations, economists commonly recommend "nudging" consumers into "healthier" choices through carefully adjusting choice architectures (Thaler and Sunstein 2008; Volpp and Asch 2017; Ammerman, Hartman, and DeMarco 2017). Consequently, much of the US healthcare system's regulatory structure and governmental influence exists (in theory) to assist comparatively disadvantaged consumers in making optimal choices by limiting exposure to risky and/or potentially harmful goods.

In contrast, Higgs's analysis of healthcare begins with standard rational choice theory. Consumers choose goods they believe will most benefit them. However, Higgs (1994a) notes that risk elements are inescapable in any consumer choice. Medical goods (including treatments, medical devices, procedures, etc.) are often risky, offering potential user benefits while also containing some chance of failing to improve consumer well-being or making their condition worse. Consequently, he writes, "No amount of premarket testing can eliminate all such uncertainties. . . . Evidence that a particular system of quality assurance has or might have flaws carries little weight in itself" (Higgs 1994a, 59). The implication, he argues, is that justifying regulations that limit access to certain medical goods on the grounds of market failure is inadequate.

Higgs is also skeptical of the aggregate cost-benefit analysis approach to justify preventing or removing risky medical products from the market because they require making interpersonal utility comparisons (Higgs 1994a). Instead, he argues that "banning a risky product *cannot* [italics mine] improve consumer welfare, properly understood" (3). He further explains, "The utility that consumers maximize by their choices is prospective and subjective utility, not ex-post utility and utility as gauged by someone else in possession of different information" (6). Other parties, such as drug producers or perhaps regulators, might possess different or comparatively more information about risky products. However, assuming these parties have "perfect information" is "an irrelevant and misleading standard of reference" (Higgs 1994a, 6–7) to determine a suitable regulatory standard.

Rather than supporting a system of regulations to address risky products or correct inefficiencies stemming from market failures, Higgs (2004) argues that a *market* provides the best option to provide assurance for medical goods. Consumers hope to improve their health, but they understand that many goods that can improve their health can have varying outcomes. Their willingness to consume these goods and to accept the risks of using them heavily depends on their current state of health. Consumers in comparatively poorer health may be more willing to use goods with lower chances of successful treatment and a higher likelihood of harm to mitigate their condition (Higgs 1994a).

Higgs is one of the few economists to forcefully argue that the market is the best institutional arrangement to provide assurance for medical goods and allow consumers with varying states of health and wiliness to accept risk (Higgs 1993, 1994a). In his words:

> Just as market exchange of existing goods can improve the subjective wellbeing of consumers with different preferences, the opportunity to trade in the risk dimension of goods can improve the subjective wellbeing of consumers otherwise stuck in some fixed distribution of risk bearing. (Higgs 1994a, 5)

He further elaborates:

> A free market in risky goods, on the other hand, permits the flexibility for individuals to adjust their choices to the differences in their conditions and preferences. Some consumers desire to become very well informed before taking the risk of using a new drug or device; others are willing to assume the risk quicker. (Higgs 1994a, 9).

Higgs's insights into the reliability of the market to assess and distribute inherently risky goods and his methodological criticism of market-failure justifications to curb market transactions for these goods are critical aspects of his research in health economics. However, his primary reason to favor the market process over governmental regulation comes from a comparative institutional analysis framework. As he stresses, "The critical question is whether another [way to distribute medical goods] works better" (Higgs 2004, 59). Here, he refers explicitly to comparing the FDA, the nation's most influential federal regulatory agency, to alternative methods to regulate medical goods.[2] His primary concerns with the effectiveness of the FDA rest on elementary insights from public choice analysis.

THE POLITICAL ECONOMY OF THE FDA

The mission statement for the FDA indicates the agency is "responsible for protecting the public health by ensuring the safety, efficacy, and security of human and veterinary drugs, biological products, and medical devices; and by ensuring the safety of our nation's food supply, cosmetics, and products that emit radiation" (FDA 2018c, 1). Although seemingly narrow, this regulatory scope encompasses a vast number of goods. Philipson et al. (2008) estimate that the agency regulates some aspects of goods that compose approximately 20 percent of all consumer spending.[3] The regulatory scope of the FDA also permeates much of the US healthcare industry, which comprises a considerable amount of the US economy. Hartman et al. (2024) estimate that healthcare spending comprises 20 percent of the US's GDP. US healthcare spending per capita is also ranked first among developed nations. Consequently, understanding the FDA's processes to approve, not approve, and monitor countless consumer products is vital to understanding health economics and the broader US economy.

However, understanding how the FDA makes decisions and creates its decision-making processes requires understanding the organization's incentives, resources, and constraints. Higgs begins his assessment of the FDA lucidly—"putting aside what the FDA is supposed to achieve, and considering instead what it clearly does in actuality, we can see that *its major activity is banning existing products from the market*" [italics original] (Higgs 2004, 60). As the monopoly provider of regulatory standards for the goods it regulates, Higgs (2004) notes that "like other forms of central planning, it cannot solve the problems of information and incentives inherent in its way of dealing with the issues within its jurisdiction" (61).

Higgs utilizes three fundamental insights of political economy to analyze the "central planners" incentives—methodological individualism, rational choice, and political exchange—to determine policy and regulatory outcomes (Buchanan 2003). Rather than speaking of the agency's decisions as a singular entity, Higgs focuses on the incentive structure of individual reviewers within the organization who receive and review clinical trial results and other information that drug developers submit to the FDA to have their products approved. Because reviewers face potential backlash from politicians and the public by approving a potentially unsafe or ineffective product, Higgs argues that reviewers have a strong incentive to avoid allowing comparatively risky products to reach the market (often referred to as a Type II error). As he explains, "FDA reviewers do not want to make any kind of error, but the reviewer's incentives lead them to systematically try much harder to avoid a Type II error (possible only when a product is approved) than to avoid a Type I error (possible only when a product is not approved)" (Higgs 2004b, 61). More recent assessments of the FDA's decision to approve products reach similar conclusions (Isakov, Lo, and Montazerhodjat 2019).

Similar incentives to avoid taking risks pervade much of the FDA. Although reviewers, superiors, and others perform different tasks and have separate responsibilities within the agency, their incentives follow the predictions of the economic analysis of bureaucracy (Tullock [1965] 2005). As Higgs (1995b) describes, "Like any normal government bureaucracy, the FDA prefers more power to less, larger budgets to smaller, more employees to fewer" (3). To satisfy these goals, the FDA has strong incentives to request additional tests, raise standards, and expand its approval procedure to reduce Type II errors. Due to these incentives, the FDA approval process features prolonged approval periods and comparatively higher costs to complete (Tabarrok 2000). Both factors negatively impact the profitability of some new treatments, devices, and other goods in the US market. Longer and more expensive approval processes also negatively impact innovation within the healthcare field (Higgs 1994b).

Numerous studies across several decades find that the cost of having a drug approved by the FDA had increased substantially, with little evidence of improvements to product safety (Grabowski, Vernon, and Thomas 1978; Grabowski, Vernon, and DeMasi 2002; Grabowski and Wang 2008). Further, because many treatments are withheld from the market due to the cost of these regulatory barriers, many patients endure prolonged suffering and die before potentially life-saving or life-improving treatments are approved for patient use (Higgs 1994b, 1995b). Olsen (2015) estimates that in the United States approximately 25,000 cancer patients die annually while waiting for treatment the FDA later approved.

While the FDA's incentive structure and its impact on approving new drugs is widely acknowledged by economists today, Higgs remains one of the first to recognize these dynamics and to fully incorporate them into his analyses. This is most apparent in his work examining the impact of FDA regulation on the medical device market.[4] The FDA originally gained oversight of the medical device market in the late 1930s. However, its authority greatly expanded in the late 1970s with congressional approval of the Medical Device Amendments of 1976. As part of the amendments, the FDA was tasked with sorting all medical devices (including new applicants and previous devices grandfathered into the new system) into three categories. Class I and Class II devices are largely regulated through good manufacturing practices and general controls (as determined by the FDA). Class III devices are regulated through good manufacturing practices, general controls, and a formal premarket approval process.[5] The FDA determined what class new medical devices or older medical devices grandfathered into the new system.

Higgs (1995b) examines the allocation of medical devices into Class I and II (containing less risk) and Class III (comparatively riskier) categorizations following the Medical Device Amendments and finds that the FDA decided that unless new medical devices were "substantially equivalent" to a "premarket device," new devices were automatically classified as Class III, undergoing premarket authorization and a formal approval process (58).[6] Consequently, 98 percent of new medical devices were categorized as Class III (Higgs 1995b). His analysis strongly suggests that the agency is most influenced by its incentive to increase regulatory scrutiny, which allows it to expand its use of resources while remaining conservative in its approval of medical devices. Higgs (1995b) also finds that only 9 percent of all medical devices grandfathered in after the amendments were required to submit premarket applications (to begin the approval process), indicating that additional oversight from the FDA was likely unnecessary.

The FDA's ability to increase its regulatory scope and political influence to regulate medical devices, pharmaceuticals, or other goods is seldom achievable without political exchange. Higgs (1995b) is aware of this, noting that "in jockeying to enhance its power and resources . . . the agency [FDA] works with members of Congress, especially the chairmen and ranking minority members of pertinent committees and their staff; with lobbyists and representatives of organized interest groups" (2). In this system of political exchange, the FDA petitions Congress or subcommittees for additional resources or the power to increase regulatory stringency and scope because of a perceived public health concern. Political actors seek public approval and expand their influence, allowing the FDA "broad new statutory authority" to obtain more influence and resources (Higgs 1995c, 4). Lobbyists and interest groups give the FDA public recognition for increasing their stringency, broadening their oversight and providing financial and other support to political figures to endorse favorable legislation. In these political exchange relationships, each party benefits while the public bears the cost through reduced innovation and competition among healthcare goods producers (Higgs 1995c).

Exchanges between the FDA, Congress, and special-interest groups within the healthcare industry are rampant, financially lucrative, and long-standing. Chu (2008) finds that total campaign contributions from pharmaceutical producers increased from approximately $72 million in 1998 to approximately $148 million in 2006 (in 2000 dollars). More recently, Fox (2022) finds that healthcare companies spent approximately $690 million lobbying the federal government in 2021, constituting the largest amount spent for any US industry.

The well-established "revolving door" between the FDA and the pharmaceutical industry provides further evidence of political exchange. Ruwart (2018) finds that only approximately 10 percent of FDA employees left for the pharmaceutical industry from 1958 to 1963. However, after Congress passed the Kefauver-Harris Drug Amendments in 1962, which granted the FDA authority to regulate pharmaceuticals for safety and efficacy, this figure increased to 73 percent by 1969.

Last, Higgs's recognition of the knowledge problem faced by the FDA when centrally planning acceptable degrees of safety and efficacy for medical-goods markets leads him to conclude that the agency is not up for the task (Higgs 1994a). Because the FDA's regulatory standards and requirements impose static restraints on the dynamic process of innovating new healthcare goods, they will strongly distort the market for adapting to time and place circumstances (Hayek 1945; Higgs 1994a). For example, Tabarrok (2017) argues that the FDA approval process is too antiquated to determine safety and efficacy standards for genomic (gene-based) medication. March, Martin, and Redford (2016) note that the FDA's inability to regulate products using synthetic human hormones delayed the approval of human insulin in the US healthcare market.

The knowledge problem faced by the FDA also limits its effectiveness in determining reliable standards to determine which products are safe and effective. Referencing deaths from previously approved prescription drugs, Higgs (1994b) alarmingly notes, "Fatal reactions to *FDA-approved* [italics original] drugs amount to the fourth leading cause of death in the United States, after heart disease, cancer, and stroke" (65). He further elaborates:

> These deaths, not to mention the estimated 2.2 million serious injuries to hospitalized patients and the unknowing but most likely large number of deaths and injuries to non-hospitalized patients from the same cause, adverse reactions to approved drugs, are precisely the sort of harm from which the FDA's vast apparatus of regulation is supposed to be protecting the American public. (Higgs 2004, 65)

Higgs's use of political economy insights to analyze the FDA strongly indicates that incentive and knowledge problem concerns result in considerable public harm through unintended consequences of the agency's decisions. Despite the shortcomings and damages caused by the FDA, the agency is often viewed favorably by the public (Gaffney 2014). Reconciling these considerations, in addition to the FDA's expanded role in regulating medical goods since its conception, requires further explanation. Higgs provides one by incorporating his insights regarding the roles of crises and public fear in expanding the size of government, including its regulatory agencies (Higgs 1987, 2007).

CRISIS AND THE GROWTH OF THE FDA

Until the early 1900s, medical goods regulation was a professional and state-level concern in the United States (Burnham 2015). Quality standards and treatment effectiveness were discussed primarily in professional journals and medical almanacs (Burnham 2015). States only began regulating educational and professional requirements for physicians to practice medicine in the late 1870s and early 1880s (Hamowy 1979; Geloso and March 2021). The original FDA began in 1906 with the passing of the Pure Food and Drug Act (FDA 2018b). The modern FDA, tasked with deciding the safety and efficacy of many goods, began after Congress passed the 1962 Kefauver-Harris Drug Amendments, providing the agency with this regulatory authority.

Economists began examining the impact of the FDA in the early 1970s. Peltzman (1973) published the first cost-benefit analysis of the agency, where he concludes that the adoption of the 1962 Kefauver-Harris Amendments slowed drug approval times, increased the cost required to develop a new drug, and prevented new drugs from entering the market. He also found minimal effect on improving the number of safe and effective drugs to enter the market. Later analyses largely confirmed Peltzman's findings (Grabowski, Vernon, and Thomas 1978; Wiggins 1981; Grabowski, Vernon, and DeMasi 2002). Consistent and pervasive empirical findings of unintended consequences from the FDA motivated widespread criticism from the economics profession (Klein 2000, 2008).

Higgs's contribution to this scholarship was to analyze and explain why the agency expanded over time. Following a similar framework developed in his research analyzing the growth of government during crises, Higgs attributes much of the FDA's expansion to public fear and state-led opportunism. As he notes, "Over the ages, governments refined their appeals to popular fears, fostering an ideology that emphasizes the people's vulnerability to a variety of internal and external dangers from which their governors . . . are represented to be their protectors" (Higgs 2007, 7). In the case of the FDA, Higgs argued that public fears arise from not knowing the potential dangers of using medical goods created by supposed devious business practices. As Higgs (1995b) elaborates, "People who know little or nothing about the pertinent facts fill the gaps with ideological assumptions. Many people assume that businesses try to profit from the sale of dangerous products and therefore must be strictly regulated by government" (9). Higgs (1995a) also notes that the FDA and Congress depend heavily on the public's ignorance to bolster their own reputations and influence.

The public's preconceived notions of malicious producers selling harmful goods are reinforced when news of a potentially dangerous medical product emerges. Media coverage combined with political promises to solve the problem with more regulation garners public approval, allowing the FDA's authority and scope to expand. Higgs (1995b) finds that the FDA's emergence following the Pure Food and Drug Act of 1906 largely stemmed from descriptions of unsanitary meat packing plants in Upton Sinclair's novel *The Jungle*.[7] He also attributes passing the Food, Drug, and Cosmetic Act of 1938 to the Elixor Sulfanilamide tragedy, and the Kefauver-Harris Drug Amendments in 1962 to public outcry following the thalidomide baby scandal.[8] Returning to his work on medical device regulation, Higgs (1995b) began his analysis of FDA expansion in the 1970s with reported faulty intrauterine contraceptive devices and malfunctioning pacemakers. Both prompted the quick adoption of the Medical Device Amendments in 1976. He further links the passage of the Safe Medical Devices Act of 1990 with reports of fractured Bjork-Shiley convexo-concave heart valves. He then argues that Congress approved granting additional resources for the FDA to better enforce previously existing regulations of medical devices following reports of leaking silicone breast impacts resulting in injuries and disease in patients.

While failed medical devices and faulty products did harm consumers, Higgs maintains that the threat to the public in each instance was oversold and that the corresponding increase in FDA authority was not proportionate. Higgs (1995b) notes that an estimated 86,000 patients received a Bjork-Shiley heart valve, with a reported 450 deaths from product failure—indicating a device failure rate of approximately 0.05 percent.[9] Despite reports of faulty breast implants resulting in disease and other health concerns, studies conducted by the University of Michigan, University of Maryland, Harvard Medical School, and the Mayo Clinic found no evidence between developing lupus, rheumatoid arthritis, sclerosis, scleroderma, and other conditions allegedly linked to faulty breast implants (Higgs 1995b, 65). These considerations led Higgs (1995b) to conclude that "the FDA acted hastily on the basis of anecdotal and unsystematic evidence" (65).

The cost of "hastily" increasing the FDA's regulatory authority came at the expense of considerable medical device innovation. From 1983 to 1990 the FDA approved approximately 45 new medical devices a year. From 1991 until 1994, following the Safe Medical Devices Act of 1990, the FDA approved an average of approximately 23 new medical devices annually (Higgs 1995b). Average approval times for a new medical device application increased largely over the same period—approximately 150 days in the late 1980s and approximately 690 days from 1991 to 1994 (Higgs 1995c). As of 2021, the average time required to approve a medical device ranges from 7 to 280 days, depending on various factors (Hetrick 2021).

With few exceptions, the FDA continues to expand its regulatory scope through the same mechanism illustrated by Higgs's research. Most recently, the FDA began regulating tobacco and vaping products over public fears that these products were negatively impacting younger users (FDA 2022a, 2022b).[10] One challenge to curtailing the growth of regulatory agencies is that once expansive powers are granted through government legislation, the mechanism used to expand regulatory stringency or scope remains long after (Higgs 1987, 2007). As Higgs (1995a) elaborates, "The underlying problem remains that Congress has given the agency enormously broad and discretionary powers, and the people who control the exertion of those powers . . . remain embedded in the same political process" (97).

CONTEMPORARY HEALTHCARE, HIGGS'S LESSONS, AND PROSPECTS FOR REFORM

Higgs's work in health economics and his analysis of the FDA stresses the limitations and negative effects of state intervention in healthcare markets. Contemporary research and recent events further suggest that Higgs's insights into the effectiveness of markets and severe limitations of state intervention within the healthcare market are correct. His research, although much of it was written decades earlier, also provides valuable insights into improving the current healthcare system.

The FDA and other regulatory agencies heavily regulate nearly all aspects of the US healthcare market. However, contemporary research analyzing comparatively less regulated aspects of the US healthcare market largely indicates that less regulatory control and more reliance on market mechanisms provide benefits to patients without sacrificing considerable safety or efficacy. Consider the example of off-label drug prescriptions, where medical professionals prescribe drugs for conditions other than what the FDA approved for them. Tabarrok (2000) and March (2017a) find that drug producers, pharmacies, and physicians effectively find off-label uses of pharmaceuticals and other treatments absent the FDA's regulatory process.

Prescribing drugs for ailments other than their approved use is extremely common. Ruwart (2018) estimates that 60 percent of prescriptions are for off-label uses. While the FDA approves drugs prescribed off-label, its widespread use strongly indicates that markets are highly effective in determining drug efficacy. Higgs's insights that markets can effectively mitigate the risks of some treatments more effectively than government regulation is also supported by contemporary research. Analyzing the private and public regulation of the acne medication isotretinoin, March (2017b) concludes that physicians and drug providers can provide more effective governance in preventing serious side effects of some medications than government programs.[11]

While much of Higgs's research analyzes what mechanisms or exogenous shocks lead to governmental expansion, he also argues that extreme hardships can pressure government agencies to relinquish long-standing regulatory authority (Higgs 2007). He specifically chronicles several instances of FDA deregulation stemming from public pressures:

> The FDA's having to fend off powerful critics in the mid-1990s reminds us that from time to time the victims of government regulation do rise up against it, and occasionally they succeed in slaying a dragon. The most notable counterattack occurred in the late 1970s and early 1980s, when a slew of deregulatory reforms gained enactment. The upshot was the reduction or elimination of several forms of economic regulation that had been in place since the 1930s or longer. (163)

Numerous public protests and pressures after the early 1980s provide further evidence of Higgs's hypothesis. In 1987, pressure from physicians and patients prompted the FDA to allow access to experimental medication to treat AIDS and HIV outside of clinical trials (Darrow, Avorn, and Kesselheim 2014). The agency allowing access to treatment allowed for a market for assurance for these treatments to emerge and for patients to assess their willingness to weigh costs and benefits with the guidance of medical professionals. Greater access to experimental medication was later provided through the agency's Expanded Access Program and, most recently, federal right-to-try legislation. Both programs began as grassroots efforts (Jarow et al. 2017; Tedeschi 2017). Public and political pressure also worked to amend the FDA's formal drug approval process to some extent. In 2012, the FDA began providing an accelerated approval process for generic medications under the Food and Drug Administration Safety and Innovation Act. Consequently, the backlog of generic drugs in the agency's approval process decreased from approximately 2,800 to 100 from 2011 to 2018 (March 2019).

Deregulatory actions taken by the FDA during the COVID-19 pandemic provide especially fruitful insight for Higgs's hypothesis because they occurred during a public health crisis—suggesting there can be a crisis *without* leviathan. Facing a shortage of COVID-19 tests during the first several months of the pandemic, March (2021a) finds the FDA's use of Emergency Use Authorization (EUA) allowed the United States to increase testing capacity with minimal loss to testing quality rapidly. March (2021b) finds that the EUA for the experimental COVID-19 treatment remdesivir was similarly successful. March (2021b) and Mello, Greene, and Sharfstein (2020) also note that protests and other public displays of frustration with access to medical goods played an influential role in the FDA's use of the EUA.

CONCLUSION

While Higgs is best known for his work in economic history, governmental growth, and the political economy of crises, his work in health economics is equally valuable to the field. Unfortunately, these works are still considerably less examined and appreciated.

Unlike the standard market-failure-based arguments for government regulation in the healthcare industry, Higgs argues that pervasive risk in healthcare choices requires a market to effectively allocate risky medical goods to consumers with varying risk tolerance levels. He casts considerable doubt on the ability of the government, specifically the FDA, to provide effective regulation for medical goods due to elementary public choice considerations. He also remains one of few economists to address the question of how the FDA became one of the most powerful regulatory agencies. His work on the FDA's regulation of medical devices strongly bolsters his arguments for the agency's ineffectiveness and harmfulness while offering insight into the primary way it obtains more resources and influence regardless. Recent research on the effectiveness of off-label drug prescription, private management of comparatively risky treatments, and the effectiveness of EUAs during the COVID-19 pandemic all strongly support Higgs's insights.

Higgs's work in health economics will hopefully be given greater attention and consideration by academics and policymakers. However, the greater challenge Higgs's work in health economics and other areas remains how to decrease the size of government and prevent its seemingly inevitable progress toward leviathan. While comparatively rarer than regulatory expansion in healthcare markets, deregulation is possible when public outcry is sufficient. Federal programs allowing patients to use experimental medications and the common use of EUAs during the COVID-19 pandemic stemming from public pressure and grassroots movements provide several examples.

Although this chapter provided several contemporary examples of deregulation, US healthcare remains one of the economy's most regulated, politically connected, and impactful industries. Institutional changes required to prevent and reverse this trend foremost require ideological shifts away from favoring government involvement and toward entrusting markets and free exchanges within healthcare markets. Perhaps the first step in this endeavor is understanding the value and merit of markets and the shortcomings and harms created by government control in healthcare markets. Few scholars have made a more complete and compelling case to this end than Robert Higgs.

NOTES

1. For example, as of December 6, 2022, Google Scholar finds Higgs's edited volume *Hazardous to Our Health: FDA Regulation of Healthcare Products* has been cited 30 times since it was published in 1995. His most cited journal article in the field of health economics according to the same source is "Banning a Risky Product Cannot Improve Any Consumer's Welfare (Properly Understood), with Applications to FDA Testing Requirements," which received 102 citations since it was published in 1994. In comparison, his journal article "Regime Uncertainty: Why the Great Depression Lasted So Long and Why Prosperity Resumed after the War" is cited 419 times and was published in 1997. Higgs also personally alludes to his work in health economics and analysis of the FDA being less appreciated than his other work. During an interview conducted with the Mises Institute in 2011, Higgs was asked by the interviewer, "What do you think is an area you've worked on that you don't want to be forgotten about [or] which you wish more attention [would] be paid to?" He responds, "I would hope . . . the Food and Drug Administration would someday arouse many more people" (https://www.youtube.com/watch?v=67eelZustMk).

2. One potential way to examine whether the US approach to regulating medical goods "works better" is to compare it to regulatory standards and processes found in other nations. While

some of Higgs's work engages in comparative systems analysis of healthcare markets in other countries (Higgs 1993), this is a comparatively smaller area of his research, and much of it is dated. I therefore do not focus on these comparisons in this chapter.

3. Estimating the scope and degree of FDA regulatory authority varies. Although consumer healthcare spending increased considerably since 2008, the current estimate is likely higher. Writing 13 years before Philipson et al. (2008), Higgs (1995b) estimated that 25 percent of all consumer goods are at least partially regulated by the FDA.

4. Higgs's focus on medical device regulation can easily be considered a contribution to the FDA and health regulation literature given considerably more analysis dedicated to pharmaceutical regulation (Peltzman 1973; Philipson et al. 2008; Tabarrok 2017).

5. The FDA's approval process for medical devices is largely similar to its process of approving pharmaceuticals (Hansen 1995).

6. Whether the devices were sufficiently similar was determined by the FDA.

7. Francis (2020) finds that many readers of *The Jungle* failed to realize the book is fictional.

8. The FDA never approved thalidomide, and it only underwent two clinical trials in the United States (Bernstein and Sullivan 2015). Reported birth defects from thalidomide were significantly more common in Europe than in the United States because the drug was available over the counter in Europe. These considerations suggest the FDA did not require additional regulatory authority to prevent future similar events.

9. Higgs (1995b) further elaborates that as late as 1992, nearly 20 years after many of the devices were implanted, approximately 51,000 patients were still alive. It is also important to consider that replacing a heart valve is a life-saving and life-prolonging procedure.

10. Curiously, March (2018) finds that high school vaping rates began decreasing in 2011, indicating that changes in teenage use cannot fully be attributed to the FDA's regulatory actions.

11. Isotretinoin can be very harmful to fetal development if a patient becomes pregnant while receiving treatment.

REFERENCES

Ammerman, Alice S., Terry Hartman, and Molly DeMarco. 2017. "Behavioral Economics and the Supplemental Nutrition Assistance Program: Making the Healthy Choice the Easy Choice." *American Journal of Preventive Medicine* 52 (2): S145–50.

Ampaabeng, Kofi, Jonathan Nelson, and Elise Amez-Droz. 2020. "Healthcare RegData: Quantifying the Volume of Healthcare Regulations." Mercatus Center at George Mason University.

Arrow, Kenneth J. 1963. "Uncertainty and the Welfare Economics of Medical Care." *American Economic Review* 53 (5): 941–73.

Bernstein, Adam, and Patricia Sullivan. 2015. "Frances Oldham Kelsey, FDA Scientist Who Kept Thalidomide Off U.S. Market, Dies at 101." *Washington Post*, August 7. https://www.washingtonpost.com/national/health-science/frances-oldham-kelsey-heroine-of-thalidomide-tragedy-dies-at-101/2015/08/07/ae57335e-c5da-11df-94e1-c5afa35a9e59_story.html.

Buchanan, James M. 2003. "Public Choice: Politics without Romance." *Policy: A Journal of Public Policy and Ideas* 19 (3): 13–18.

Burnham, John C. 2015. *Health Care in America: A History.* Baltimore: Johns Hopkins University Press.

Chu, Alvin. C. 2008. "Special Interest Politics and Intellectual Property Rights: An Economic Analysis of Strengthening Patent Protection in the Pharmaceutical Industry." *Economics and Politics* 20 (2): 185–215.

Darrow, Jonathan J., Jerry Avorn, and Aaron S. Kesselheim. 2014. "New FDA Breakthrough-Drug Category—Implications for Patients." *New England Journal of Medicine* 370 (13): 1252–58.

Food and Drug Administration (FDA). 2018a. "Part II: 1938, Food, Drug, Cosmetic Act." https://www.fda.gov/about-fda/changes-science-law-and-regulatory-authorities/part-ii-1938-food-drug-cosmeticact#:~:text=FDR%20signed%20the%20Food%2C%20Drug,adequate%20directions%20for%20saf.e%20use.

———. 2018b. "When and Why Was FDA Formed?" https://www.fda.gov/about-fda/fda-basics/when-and-why-was-fda-formed#:~:text=Though%20FDA%20can%20trace%20its,Pure%20Food%20and%20Drugs%20Act.

———. 2018c. "What We Do." https://www.fda.gov/about-fda/what-we-do.

———. 2022a. "Tobacco Products: FDA's Center for Tobacco Products (CTP) Works to Ensure a Healthier Life for Every Family." https://www.fda.gov/tobacco-products#:~:text=A%20new%20federal%20law%20gives,FDA%20cannot%20be%20legally%20marketed.

———. 2022b. "E-Cigarettes, Vapes, and Other Electronic Nicotine Delivery Systems (ENDS)." https://www.fda.gov/tobacco-products/products-ingredients-components/e-cigarettes-vapes-and-other-electronic-nicotine-delivery-systems-ends.

Fox, Brooke. 2022. "Healthcare Companies Spent More on Lobbying Than Any Other Industry Last Year." *Stigler Center for the Study of Economy and State*, June 29. https://www.promarket.org/2022/06/29/healthcare-companies-spent-more-on-lobbying-than-any-other-industry-last-year/.

Francis, Meredith. 2020. "How Upton Sinclair's 'The Jungle' Unintentionally Spurred Food Safety Laws." *Window to the World*, January 23. https://interactive.wttw.com/playlist/2020/01/23/the-jungle-food-safety.

Gaffney, Alexander. 2014. "Public View of FDA Continues to Improve in New Poll." *Regulatory News*, October 2. https://www.raps.org/regulatory-focus%E2%84%A2/news-articles/2014/10/public-view-of-fda-continues-to-improve-in-new-poll.

Geloso, Vincent J., and Raymond J. March. 2021. "Rent-Seeking for Madness: The Political Economy of Mental Asylums in the United States, 1870 to 1910." *Public Choice* 189 (3): 375–404.

Grabowski, Henry G., John M. Vernon, and Joseph A. DeMasi. 2002. "Returns on Research and Development for 1990s New Drug Introductions." *PharmacoEconomics* 20: 11–29.

Grabowski, Henry G., John M. Vernon, and Lacy Glenn Thomas. 1978. "Estimating the Effects of Regulation on Innovation: An International Comparative Analysis of the Pharmaceutical Industry." *Journal of Law and Economics* 21: 133–63.

Grabowski, Henry G., and Y. Richard Wang. 2008. "Do Faster Drug Administration Drug Reviews Adversely Affect Patient Safety? An Analysis of the 1992 Prescription Drug User Fee Act." *Journal of Law and Economics* 51: 377–405.

Hamowy, Ronald. 1979. "The Early Development of Medical Licensing Laws in the United States." *Journal of Libertarian Studies* 3 (1): 73–119.

Hansen, Ronald W. 1995. "FDA Regulation of the Pharmaceutical Industry." In *Hazardous to Our Health? FDA Regulation of Healthcare Products*. Edited by Robert Higgs. Oakland, CA: Independent Institute.

Hartman, M., A. B. Martin, L. Whittle, A. Catlin, and National Health Expenditure Accounts Team. 2024. "National Health Care Spending in 2022: Growth Similar to Prepandemic Rates." *Health Affairs* 43 (1): 6–17.

Hayek, Fredrick A. 1945. "The Use of Knowledge in Society." *American Economic Review* 35 (4): 519–30.

Hetrick, Carrie. 2021. "How Long Does It Take the FDA to Approve a Medical Device?" Sterling Medical Devices, September 1. https://sterlingmedicaldevices.com/thought-leadership/medical-device-design-industry-blog/how-long-does-it-take-the-fda-to-approve-a-medical-device/.

Higgs, Robert. 1971. "Race, Skills, and Earnings: American Immigrants in 1909." *Journal of Economic History* 31 (2): 420–28.

———. 1973. "Race, Tenure, and Resource Allocation in Southern Agriculture, 1910." *Journal of Economic History* 33 (1): 149–69.

———. 1977. *Competition and Coercion: Blacks in the American Economy, 1865–1914.* Chicago: University of Chicago Press.

———. 1982. "Accumulation of Property by Southern Blacks before World War I." *American Economic Review* 72 (4): 725–37.

———. 1987. *Crisis and Leviathan.* New York: Oxford University Press.

———. 1993. "Allocation of Risks Associated with Medical Goods: Government Regulation versus Market Processes." *Journal of Private Enterprise* 9: 59–69.

———. 1994a. "Banning a Risky Product Cannot Improve Any Consumer's Welfare (Properly Understood), with Applications to FDA Testing Requirements." *Review of Austrian Economics* 7 (2): 3–20.

———. 1994b. "Should the Government Kill People to Protect Their Health?" *Foundation for Economic Education*, January 1. https://fee.org/articles/should-the-government-kill-people-to-protect-their-health/.

———. 1995a. "How FDA Is Causing a Technological Exodus: A Comparative Analysis of Medical Device Regulation—United States, Europe, Canada, and Japan." Competitive Enterprise Institute.

———. 1995b. "FDA Regulation of Medical Devices." In *Hazardous to Our Health? FDA Regulation of Healthcare Products.* Edited by Robert Higgs. Oakland, CA: Independent Institute.

———. 1995c. "Wrecking Ball: FDA Regulation of Medical Devices." Cato Institute Policy Analysis No. 235 (August 7th). Cato Institute, Washington, DC.

———. 2004. *Against Leviathan: Government Power and a Free Society.* Oakland, Calif.: The Independent Institute.

———. 2006. *Depression, War, and Cold War: Studies in Political Economy.* New York: Oxford University Press.

———. 2007. *Neither Liberty nor Safety: Fear, Ideology, and the Growth of Government.* Oakland, CA: Independent Institute.

———. 2011. "Against Leviathan: Robert Higgs." Interview by Jeffery Tucker. *Mises media.* Audio, 14:40. https://www.youtube.com/watch?v=67eelZustMk.

Independent Publisher. 2016. "Announcing the 2016 Outstanding Books of the Year." https://www.independentpublisher.com/article.php?page=2047.

Isakov, Leah, Andrew W. Lo, and Vahid Montazerhodjat. 2019. "Is the FDA too Conservative or too Aggressive?: A Bayesian Decision Analysis of Clinical Trial Design." *Journal of Econometrics* 211 (1): 119–36.

Jakovljevic, Mihajlo, and Seiritsu Ogura. 2016. "Health Economics at the Crossroads of Centuries—From the Past to the Future." *Public Health* 4: 1–5.

Jarow, Jonathan P., Peter Lurie, Sarah Crowley Ikenberry, and Steven Lemery. 2017. "Overview of FDA's Expanded Access Program for Investigational Drugs." *Therapeutic Innovation and Regulatory Science* 51 (2): 177–79.

Klein, Daniel B. 2000. "Economists against the FDA." *Ideas on Liberty* 50: 18–21.

———. 2008. "Colleagues, Where Is the Market Failure? Economists on the FDA." *Econ Journal Watch* 5 (3): 316.

March, Raymond J. 2017a. "Entrepreneurship in Off-Label Drug Prescription: Just What the Doctor Ordered!" *Journal of Private Enterprise* 32 (3): 75.

———. 2017b. "Skin in the Game: Comparing the Private and Public Regulation of Isotretinoin." *Journal of Institutional Economics* 13 (3): 649–72.

———. 2018. "FDA Still Hooked on Meddling in Nicotine Markets." *The Beacon*, October 8. https://blog.independent.org/2018/10/08/fda-still-hooked-on-meddling-in-nicotine-markets/.

———. 2019. "FDA Approves Record Number of Generic Drugs in 2018." *Foundation for Economic Education*, January 10. https://fee.org/articles/fda-approved-record-number-of-generic-drugs-in-2018/.

———. 2021a. "Flatten the Bureaucracy: Deregulation and COVID-19 Testing." *Independent Review* 25 (4): 521–36.

———. 2021b. "The FDA and the COVID-19: A Political Economy Perspective." *Southern Economic Journal* 87 (4): 1210–28.

March, Raymond J., Adam G. Martin, and Audrey Redford. 2016. "The Substance of Entrepreneurship and the Entrepreneurship of Substances." *Journal of Entrepreneurship and Public Policy* 5 (2).

Mello, Michelle M., Jeremy A. Greene, and Joshua M. Sharfstein. 2020. "Attacks on Public Health Officials during COVID-19." *Journal of the American Medical Association* 324: 741–42.

Mushkin, Selma J. 1958. "Toward a Definition of Health Economics." *Public Health Reports* 73 (9): 785.

Olsen, Darcy. 2015. *The Right to Try: How the Federal Government Prevents Americans from Getting the Life-Saving Treatments They Need*. New York: HarperCollins.

Peltzman, Sam. 1973. "An Evaluation of Consumer Protection Legislation: The 1962 Drug Amendments." *Journal of Political Economy* 81 (5): 1049–91.

Philipson, Tomas J., Ernst R. Berndt, Adrian H. B. Gottschalk, and Eric Sun. 2008. "Cost-Benefit Analysis of the FDA: The Case of the Prescription Drug User Fee Acts. *Journal of Public Economics* 92 (5–6): 1306–25.

Ruwart, Mary J. 2018. *Death by Regulation: How We Were Robbed of a Golden Age of Health and How We Can Reclaim It*. San Francisco: Sunstar.

Savedoff, William D. 2004. "Kenneth Arrow and the Birth of Health Economics." *Bulletin of the World Health Organization* 82: 139–40.

Tabarrok, Alexander T. 2000. "Assessing the FDA via the Anomaly of Off-Label Drug Prescribing." *Independent Review* 5 (1): 25–53.

———. 2017. "Discussion: The FDA Is Unprepared for Personalized Medicine." *Biostatistics* 18: 403–4.

Tedeschi, Bob. 2017. "With Patients Demanding Experimental Drugs, 'Right to Try' Is Becoming the Law of the Land. *Statnews*, March 3. https://www.statnews.com/2017/03/23/right-to-try/.

Thaler, Richard H., and Cass R. Sunstein. 2008. *Nudge*. New York: Penguin.

Tullock, Gordon. (1965) 2005. "The Politics of Bureaucracy." In *The Selected Works of Gordon Tullock: Vol. 6, Bureaucracy*. Indianapolis: Liberty Fund.

Volpp, K. G., and D. A. Asch. 2017. "Make the Healthy Choice the Easy Choice: Using Behavioral Economics to Advance a Culture of Health." *QJM: An International Journal of Medicine* 110 (5): 271–75.

Wiggins, Steven N. 1981. "Product Quality Regulation and New Drug Introductions: Some New Evidence from the 1970s." *Review of Economics and Statistics* 63 (4): 615–19.

Chapter 15

If Angels Were to Govern Men

Tate Fegley

I n his essay "If Men Were Angels: The Basic Analytics of the State versus Self-Government," Robert Higgs (2007a) extends and improves upon the insights of James Madison as expressed in the Federalist No. 51. Madison discusses the paradox of government—how to empower the state to govern but also to constrain it lest it become tyrannical. If sinful man needs civil government because he is sinful, giving power to another sinful man, or group of sinful men, to reign over him presents difficulties. Madison famously states, "If men were angels, no government would be necessary. If angels were to govern men, neither external nor internal controls on government would be necessary" (Madison [1788] 2001, 331). Further, for Madison, the idea of not having a state is inconceivable, and all parties in a state of nature, for the sake of security, would choose to submit to the authority of a state. Table 15.1 illustrates how Higgs summarizes Madison's model.

Higgs notes that in light of the expansive theoretical and empirical research on stateless societies, they are, in fact, conceivable. Further, in societies with or without a state there are irredeemably vicious people, but in the latter type of society they will tend to gain control of the state and thereby have the capacity to inflict much more harm than otherwise. As such, Higgs proposes the model shown in table 15.2 as more realistic.

Although Madison is joined by many other classical liberal thinkers in considering it obvious that having a state is preferable to anarchy, given that men are indeed not angels, Higgs argues that the burden of proof is on the statists to show that the immense harms that states perpetrate daily is preferable to the largely imagined horrors of statelessness. If states killed an estimated 262 million *of their own citizens* in the 20th century (Rummel n.d.), vastly dwarfing all nonstate threats to life, liberty, and property, is it a foregone conclusion that anarchy is worse? And speaking of those nonstate threats, Higgs (2007a, 61) notes,

> In the United States, for example, a country brimming with official "protectors" of every imaginable stripe, the populace suffered in 2004, according to figures the government itself endorses, approximately

16,000 murders, 95,000 forcible rapes, 401,000 robberies, 855,000 aggravated assaults, 2,143,000 burglaries, 6,948,000 larcenies and thefts, and 1,237,000 motor vehicle thefts. (US Census Bureau 2007, 191)

To which Higgs asks, "where's the protective *quid pro quo*? They broke the egg of our liberties, without a doubt, but where's the bloody omelet of personal protection and social order?" (2007a, 61).

Ultimately, the criticisms of anarchy apply at least as much, if not more so, to the state. For example, Olson (2000, 63–65) argues that some portion of labor in a stateless society will be allocated to stealing rather than production, the corresponding theft-resistant forms of production will make society less productive, and thus anarchy not only involves the loss of life but also increases the incentives to engage in theft and defense against theft. By concluding that, therefore, no population would ever choose anarchy, Olson commits the Nirvana Fallacy (Demsetz 1969) in immediately declaring a state-dominated arrangement to be preferable to anarchy. Higgs convincingly argues that, compared to actual existing states, all of Olson's propositions are backward.

While Higgs's essay focused on the bottom row of the previous two tables, what I wish to do here is analyze the top row with the slight modification of considering a society in which sinful men are governed by angels. In doing so I will argue in favor of table 15.3's description of statelessness as preferable to an angelic state.[1]

Although this may seem like a pointless exercise—after all, there currently are no societies on earth in which men are governed by angels—one of the fruits of engaging in it is isolating those problems of statist governance in which man's lack of moral perfection is at fault from those in which it is

Table 15.1. Madison's model

	No State	State
Men are angels	OK	OK
Men are not angels	Not conceivable	Best conceivable

Source: Higgs 2007a, 56.

Table 15.2. Higgs's more realistic model

	No State	State
Men are angels	OK	OK
Men are not angels	Bad situation	Worse situation

Source: Higgs 2007a, 58.

Table 15.3. What if men are governed by angels?

	No State	State
Men are governed by angels	Best situation	OK
Men are not angels	Bad situation	Worse situation

not. In this sense, I aim to extend the insights of the Austrian school's foremost contribution to political economy, which is the concept of economic calculation (Boettke 1998). This chapter is a near mirror-image of Powell and Coyne (2003): whereas they showed that pessimistic assumptions about human behavior do not justify state power, my goal is to show that idealistic assumptions about the behavior of individuals in government do not imply that the monopoly provision by a "protective state"—internal security, contract enforcement, and defense against external threats (Buchanan [1975] 2000)—is preferable to statelessness.

I proceed as follows: In the next section, "angels" are defined for the purposes of this chapter. After that, I consider what implications an angelic government has for the ideal role of a state dedicated to preserving the core rights of citizens from a classical liberal perspective. I then analyze the trade-offs an angelic state faces in how best to provide security and in using force to do so. Finally, I consider whether an angelic government can fully prevent the cronyism present in the protective state.

DEFINING "ANGELS"

For the purposes of this chapter, we can understand an angel to be someone who, as a government actor, faithfully pursues the goal of limited, liberal governance, and seeks to avoid public choice problems.[2] In other words, there is no concern about principle-agent problems, no shirking, no (intended) cronyism, and no opportunism. To the extent that an angel can truly represent the interests of his constituents (setting aside the issue of whether a congressional district of 600,000 constituents can actually have unified interests to be meaningfully represented) and these interests are possible to identify, an angelic representative will seek to satisfy them at the lowest cost. Likewise, as a bureaucrat, the angel will seek to satisfy the public-spirited mission of the bureaucracy at the lowest cost. The public choice insights regarding the conflicts between the self-interests of bureaucrats and the public interest, such as the fact that bureaucrats seek to maximize their budgets, do not apply when angels man the bureaucracy. When angels are in control of personnel, the "best" get on top. Importantly, however, angels do not have any greater epistemological abilities than men.

WHAT ROLE SHOULD AN ANGELIC STATE HAVE?

Even if angels were to govern men, one question that must be answered is what the role of the angelic state ought to be. Given that angels are not omniscient, an angelic state could not centrally plan an economy. Indeed, a primary takeaway of Mises's ([1920] 1990) argument concerning the impossibility of economic calculation under socialism is that it is not an issue of central planners or workers being insufficiently motivated to do a good job. Even if man became a new socialist man under socialism, the calculation problem would remain.

As such, there must be some limits on the scope of government, even if angels are at the helm. But what are the proper limits of an angelic state? If one considers consumer welfare to be an important consideration, economic calculation is indispensable in answering this question. Among those who care about human liberty and appreciate the difficulties the American Framers were attempting to address, there have been various answers. The Framers themselves, as expressed in the US Constitution, could be described as agnostic on this question, having defined limits on the central government while leaving the states to perform most governing functions. Classical liberal economists such as James Buchanan ([1975] 2000, 89) see a proper role for the protective state, which protects the rights of citizens as determined at the constitutional stage, and a productive state, which is "that agency through which individuals provide themselves with 'public goods.'" Others consider only the protective state to be just or desirable (Mises [1927] 1985; Nozick 1974; Rand 1967).

The defining feature of a bureaucracy is that the decision-making process within such an organization is not according to profit-and-loss accounting (Mises [1944] 2007). In other words, the realm of public administration begins where economic calculation ends (Aligica, Boettke, and Tarko 2019; Boettke 2018). However, the choice of where public administration begins is precisely that: a choice. It is not a fact of nature. Economists, despite their sincere beliefs to the contrary, are not able to determine *a priori* what sectors of the economy are most amenable to bureaucratic administration. A common argument is that free-rider problems render voluntary action unable to provide certain goods or provide them in the optimal amount.

Lawson and Clark (2017), for instance, argue that stargazers in a city face a free-rider problem in that though they may collectively be willing to pay non-stargazers a sufficient amount to convince them to turn off their lights, one would rather get the benefit without himself paying. If a sufficient number of stargazers attempt to free ride in the hope that other stargazers will pay the cost, then the good may not be provided at all. As such, the state can improve consumer welfare by taxing the stargazers at or below their maximum willingness to pay and then pay the non-stargazers to turn off their lights, thereby preventing free riding and ensuring that the good is provided. However, in the real world we do not know consumers' willingness to pay outside of the market process (Rothbard 1956).

Further, even if we observed in the real world that stargazers did not collectively raise sufficient money to pay off the non-stargazers, we cannot conclude that therefore a free-rider problem prevented the good from being provided (Rothbard 2009, 1029–41). That is, there is no observable difference between transaction costs "preventing" transactions from taking place and consumers demonstrating their preference to abstain from buying a particular good because the cost is deemed to be too high. Therefore, an outside observer cannot claim that a state apparatus improves welfare by forcing people to make transactions they otherwise would not have chosen for themselves, for it is only through the market process that it can be determined what consumers truly want, given the range of feasible options.

In light of this reality, if part of the angelic state's goal is to maximize the attainment of citizens' ends given the resources available, the proper economic role of the state is not given. Rather, in order to determine the optimal arrangements through which various goods are provided, the particular arrangements themselves must be subject to a market test. Contrary to the assumption that a state is necessary for the definition of property rights,[3] the private creation and enforcement of law is historically documented (see Anderson and Hill [1979] 2017; Benson 1990; Ellickson 1991; Friedman 1979).

Boudreaux and Holcombe (1989) elaborate a framework in which constitutions are created by entrepreneurs trying to attract tenants to their developments, in contrast to the framework of unanimous constitutional convention *a la* Buchanan and Tullock (1962). In a similar vein, Leeson (2011) explains how a system of clubs offering contracts to satisfy differentiated governance demands for both protection- and nonprotection-related public goods leads to self-enforcing constitutional contracts. Murphy (2010) also provides a robust theoretical defense of the stability of private property anarchism. When governance services are provided through a system of private property and voluntary exchange, they can be subject to economic calculation, ameliorating the problems identified in this chapter.

This leads to the question: if governance can be subject to a competitive market process, what advantage would a monopoly government, even if fully staffed by angels, provide? For if those same angels lived in a stateless society populated by the same people, presumably they would voluntarily be chosen by consumers and outcompete any potential competitors.[4] To make this point is no more profound than stating the obvious fact that imposing a monopoly will reduce welfare compared to allowing competition.

THE TRADE-OFF BETWEEN SECURITY, CONVENIENCE, PRIVACY, AND DIGNITY

A decision that a security provider must make is over the security measures in place in various contexts. One arm of the federal security apparatus with which Americans deal every day is the Transportation Security Administration (TSA), a function of which is to monopolize airline security. Although the moral failings of TSA agents are well documented (McDonald 2020), replacing those agents with angels would not solve all problems.

One of those problems that would not be solved is the trade-off between making the airport and airplanes as secure as possible and in maximizing the convenience of travelers in complying with security requirements. Without a market process in which consumers are offered different options and enabled to demonstrate their preferences, the optimal point (or points, depending on the consumer and the range of options that are viable to offer) along this trade-off cannot be known. The party best situated to make decisions about security is the airlines themselves, given the billions in capital they have invested and their desire to attract customers. They neither want to be so lax in security procedures that their capital, employees, or passengers are put at unnecessary risk, nor wish to be so onerous in security that customers are alienated and choose a competitor.[5]

It should also be emphasized that convenience is not the only value presenting a trade-off against security. There are also values of privacy and dignity. The TSA offers Precheck, which allows travelers to trade privacy and a fee in order to obtain more convenience. Assuming they are not just for theater, body scanners improve security at the expense of dignity. Finding the optimal trade-off among these competing values is an entrepreneurial decision that can only be deemed successful from a consumer desire perspective when there is free entry and consumers are able to voluntarily choose between service providers. Having angels staff state bureaucracies does not obviate this crucial role for entrepreneurs in developing market prices that allow for profit-and-loss calculation.

These trade-offs are also present in other security contexts. Consider the controversial "stop-and-frisk" practices of the New York Police Department, in which officers will stop, question, and pat down individuals whom they have reasonable, articulable suspicion are engaged in illegal activity. In the original case in which the US Supreme Court considered this practice, *Terry v. Ohio* (1968), the Court's justification for allowing officers to engage in "Terry stops" was for their own safety—to determine through a limited search whether the suspect was armed.

However, like the expansions of state power documented by Higgs (1987), there has been a ratchet effect in terms of the ability of police to legally engage in searches and seizures. Terry stops later expanded to include not just the ability to engage in a limited search for weapons for the purpose of officer safety, but also to pat down suspects for contraband.[6] Pretextual traffic stops, where the police stop a vehicle for a minor traffic violation for the ulterior purpose of investigating some other type of crime such as drug possession, are also legal,[7] as is engaging in a full search of a car[8] or a piece of luggage[9] should a trained dog alert on it. Thus, the history of the US Supreme Court in interpreting the constitutional limitations of domestic law enforcement parallels the Court's history of interpreting the limitations of the emergency powers of the federal government in times of war (see Coyne 2011, 2018; Higgs 1987, 2004, 2007b). Whether the goal of public policy is to eradicate drugs or win wars, if civil liberties stand in the way the Supreme Court has typically been accommodating to the other branches of government.

While supporters of stop-and-frisk claim that it has the benefit of reducing violent crime by empowering police to detect firearms being carried illegally, detractors point to unacceptably high rates of fruitless frisks concentrated among racial minorities (Bellin 2014; Bratton and Kelling 2015; MacDonald 2016). For angelic police, both ensuring public safety and avoiding subjecting citizens to unnecessary indignities are valued. What are they to do? A major issue in this case is that the bundle of services provided in the physical form of the streets, sidewalks, and public areas of New York City are government property and therefore not subject to economic profit-and-loss accounting. Without the institutions that allow economic calculation, angelic police would be in the dark about how best to provide security as evaluated by the service recipients.

Analogous dilemmas exist in fully private contexts, with the major difference being that the entrepreneurs making decisions over security procedures have access to market feedback from the customers being subject to those procedures in terms of whether they purchase or abstain from purchasing. This trade-off is particularly salient for businesses operating in higher crime areas and who by necessity have to make additional efforts in protecting themselves from crime. Many of these efforts consist of "target-hardening" in the form of erecting physical barriers to prevent theft and other crime.

An example of this is a grocery store in the Atlanta metro area that installed interior walls with a single entrance and exit around aisles of the store that contain more expensive, theft-prone items (Kennedy and Wilkerson 2019). This comes at the cost of potentially alienating some customers who perceive they are being treated like criminals or otherwise making the shopping experience less pleasant while generating the benefit of preventing some theft that would have otherwise occurred. Comparing monetary revenues and costs before and after implementing the security measures, business owners are able to determine whether they are closer to or further away from the optimal trade-off between preventing theft and creating a pleasant environment for consumers.

What these examples demonstrate is that although the provision of security may seem like something amenable to bureaucratic administration in the Misesian sense (Mises [1944] 2007)—that is, subject to strict regimentation by rules that enable a bureaucrat to algorithmically respond to any particular situation according to relevant criteria—there are several competing values being pursued in complex situations, making a large degree of discretion necessary (Lipsky 1983). Police officers enforcing statutes on the street is unlike the situation faced by the employees at the Department of Motor Vehicles in deciding who may legally operate a semitrailer on government roads, wherein the outcome is a result of whether the applicant meets all the criteria specified to qualify for this particular license. The limitless potential of relevant variations in criteria that could affect officer decision-making cannot be laid out in advance, and therefore a large degree of discretion is necessary. Making the optimal decision from the standpoint of consumer welfare is not only a matter of choosing the moral good—which is something an angel is well qualified to do—but also a matter of entrepreneurial judgment.

FINDING THE OPTIMAL USE OF FORCE

Would having angelic police solve all of the problems now associated with that supposedly essential government role of ensuring domestic tranquility? No. Not all of the problems in policing, considering the modern American context, are issues stemming from the morally dubious behavior of law enforcement agents.

Consider an example. In 2018, the Philadelphia Police Department was called by the manager of a Starbucks location due to two men loitering in the café, refusing to either purchase something or leave. The police arrested the two men. This event became well-publicized, creating negative press for Starbucks. In response, the Starbucks CEO personally met and apologized to the men and closed thousands of Starbucks locations for a day of training (Siegel and Horton 2018).

In this case, the officers involved acted by the book. Acting on behalf of Starbucks, the location manager was fully within her rights to have the men ejected from the café. The officers successfully kept the peace and took the men into custody without causing physical injury. Was this not a success? In this case, we see that the Starbucks manager made an entrepreneurial error in having these men ejected, as it created significant negative press and Starbucks spent a considerable sum of money on damage control. Although the men imposed costs on Starbucks by taking up physical space that could have been used by paying customers and Starbucks was within its legal rights to have them physically removed, the costs of removal ended up being greater than the costs of tolerating them. And so even though angelic cops could not have done better in terms of carrying out the enforcement, it is only because the policing provided in this situation is bundled with services subject to a profit-and-loss test that we are able to determine that this use of police resources was suboptimal.

We could imagine a similar situation outside a profit-and-loss context that would render it impossible to determine whether enforcing certain rules is optimal. Many public parks face a "loitering" problem where homeless individuals choose to camp in the park and sleep on park benches, and where some people play their music more loudly than others would like or otherwise behave in ways that make the park less valuable to others. However, the individuals engaging in these activities demonstrate that their use of public parks in this way is more valuable to them than alternative uses. Without rules specifying otherwise (or, more precisely, rules specifying otherwise that police are willing and able to enforce), alternative conflicting uses become part of the public domain. Without property rights over these spaces, it cannot be determined whether they are being allocated to their most highly valued uses. Therefore, unlike the Starbucks case, when policing is not tied to a context where economic calculation is possible, the extent to which loitering ought to be tolerated (if satisfying individuals' highest ranked ends is the goal) cannot be known.

It should also be emphasized that there can be too much toleration of loitering from the standpoint of profit-seeking enterprises in their attempts to satisfy consumers. A separate experience of Starbucks is a testament to this. In July 2022, Starbucks announced that it was closing locations in several major cities due to concerns of staff and customer safety. In some of these locations, individuals were using the store restrooms to use drugs. Interestingly, in a statement to the press, the Starbucks CEO placed at least partial blame on the cities' police forces for failing to keep violent or otherwise undesirable individuals off the streets (and, by extension, out of Starbucks' cafés).[10] This strongly suggests that Starbucks overcorrected in terms of its policies regarding what conduct to tolerate at its locations. The losses attributed to safety issues became so great that it decided to close, thus demonstrating how profit and loss reveal whether rules regarding the use of force are optimal.

To reiterate, the government faces the same problem in "public," unowned spaces. Making decisions over their use via political means does not guarantee that those resources will be allocated to more highly valued uses (and indeed precludes the ability to determine whether such a thing has occurred). Voters may express their dissatisfaction with the rules enforced over public spaces, as was arguably the case with the recall of progressive San Francisco district attorney Chesa Boudin in 2022. Furthermore, "public interest" litigants may successfully override the wishes of voters, to the extent local ordinances reflect such wishes, when they get federal courts to declare rules regarding camping in public spaces unconstitutional, as occurred in the Ninth Circuit Court over ordinances in Boise, Idaho.[11] But neither of these methods results in resources being allocated in ways that maximize the satisfaction of consumer preferences.

CAN ANGELS PREVENT CRONYISM?

Dwight D. Eisenhower delivered one of the most well-known presidential farewell addresses, in which he warned about the growing threat of the military-industrial complex. Since then, that complex has grown massively, and changes in rules governing defense contracting have allowed it to become more entrenched (Higgs 2006, 36–40). Coyne and Hall (2019a) argue that cronyism is an inevitable feature of government-provided national defense. Would a government of angels lead to a different outcome?

Coyne and Hall (2019a) list a number of ways in which cronyism can manifest itself: rent-seeking and rent extraction, the revolving door, and local politics versus the "national interest." Regarding the first of these, angelic politicians would avoid engaging in rent extraction, which refers to the use of discretionary political power to extract rents from those wishing to avoid political disfavor. The reason is that this would not be in the best interest of their constituents, who wish to acquire a certain amount of defense at the lowest cost. Instead of showing favoritism to particular private defense contractors who lobby (i.e., rent seek), an angelic politician would choose the contractor who offers the lowest bid price to fulfill the contract. In other words, an angelic representative would faithfully pursue the interests of whom he represents and not use it as an opportunity to transfer wealth for his own benefit.

However, a major problem becomes immediately apparent—what contracts the representative should seek to fulfill is not at all obvious. It is an entrepreneurial question that politicians, even angelic ones, cannot answer absent competition and the market process. As noted by Coyne and Hall (2019b), this entrepreneurial problem exists on two dimensions. The first is identifying the best means of allocating resources to produce a given output. The second is determining which outputs are value-added from an economic perspective. While competition between contractors can conceivably help on the first dimension, the latter cannot be determined in a system of taxpayer-funded monopoly provision of national defense. Therefore, although angelic politicians may be able to avoid the most blatant abuses of cronyism, such as procuring obsolete equipment that everyone knows will not be used on the battlefield, there is still the high likelihood of entrepreneurial error and the lack of a mechanism to identify it despite their best intentions.

A similar analysis applies to the issue of the "revolving door," which refers to the movement back and forth between actors in the government and in the private sector (Duncan and Coyne 2015, 391). The movement of personnel between these sectors *per se* is not, in itself, a problem. Rather, the problem is the rents extracted from taxpayers, by narrowly opportunistic private and public actors, to either overpay for defense or for goods and services that are unnecessary. As above, angelic politicians would avoid this opportunistic behavior, but the calculation and knowledge problems remain.

When we consider an angelic politician acting in a context where there is an apparent conflict between local politics and the "national interest," we can imagine a potential resolution to this problem. That is, a Congress full of angels could credibly commit to cooperation in order to avoid the prisoner's dilemma of pork-barrel spending. The nation as a whole would be better off if there were no wealth transfers between districts for the purpose of "bringing home the bacon" for local constituents. However, any single member of Congress unilaterally rejecting pork-barrel spending for his or her own district would be a "sucker." Thus, when all members of Congress agree to eliminate all pork-barrel spending and privileges, there is no conflict between the local and the national interest.

In attempting to isolate the cronyism problems that plague national defense by imagining alternative outcomes if government consisted entirely of angels, we see that the calculation and knowledge problems are inseparable from public choice problems, if not necessary inputs. That is, if the optimal amounts and types of defense goods and services were known, then there would be little room for cronyism, as no discretion would be necessary. The defense procurement process could be run by a computer algorithm.

We also see that the problem goes beyond what Hayek ([1944] 1994, 82–83) identified in terms of the inability of government planning authorities to tie themselves "down in advance to general and formal rules which prevent arbitrariness" because of "circumstances which cannot be foreseen in detail." With angels, there is no issue of having to be tied down, so developing "general and formal rules" to prevent arbitrariness is unnecessary. However, the lack of ability to separate the economically viable from all the options that are technically feasible necessarily renders any decision arbitrary. Further, even if the future circumstances Hayek refers to *could* be foreseen in detail, such that appropriate general and formal rules could be implemented, this still would not solve the calculation problem.

While it is certainly the case that the open-ended nature of national defense allows great amounts of room for arbitrariness (especially when activities such as maintaining an empire can be categorized as "defense"), there are still many technically feasible ways in which resources can be allocated even if the obviously economically efficient activities are eliminated. Therefore, even if the issue of how to constitutionally constrain government actors were solved by putting angels in charge, the serious economic problem of what national defense goods and services to produce remains.

DOES A GOVERNMENT OF ANGELS FULLY SOLVE ALL PUBLIC CHOICE PROBLEMS?

Even if angels were available to be elected to office, it is not clear that a morally imperfect electorate would choose them. This is a direct implication of their rejection of cronyism. The funds received by politicians from rent-seeking special interests do not simply supplement politicians' wealth but are used to help them win elections.[12] Although it is quite likely that most voters, if polled, would report preferring politicians who are independent of the influence of special interests, this does not mean that such politicians are the ones who actually win political office.

Political institutions, even democratic ones, necessarily give power to some over others. Those who capture control over such institutions will be those who value it most highly (Brennan and Buchanan [1985] 2000), which will be those who can best wield it to transfer wealth and power to themselves and their allies. This issue is inherent to the political means of acquiring wealth— having institutions that allow the legalized involuntary transfer of wealth will attract people who seek to transfer the wealth to themselves in spite of the best intentions of the designers of such institutions. The tendency for even a minimal, protective state is to grow in size and scope (Coyne 2018). Indeed, a limited government designed by individuals explicitly opposed to standing armies and empire is capable of becoming an empire itself (Coyne 2022).

Even if angelic office-seekers were motivated to acquire office in order to prevent such cronyism, there are a number of public choice reasons to expect that they will be unsuccessful, such as the fact that political wealth transfers benefit concentrated interests whereas the benefits sought by angels are dispersed. Perhaps a nondemocratic constitutional system for bestowing power would better ensure that angels acquire and maintain power, but even nondemocratic systems eventually have transfers in power from some individuals to others. As such, there would still be an incentive to expend resources in order to capture rents. Ultimately, a government of lifetime-appointed, infinitely lived angels with the goal of defending the public from political expropriation could not do better than a stateless society where expropriating political institutions did not exist.

CONCLUSION

There is a tendency among classical liberal thinkers to minimize, if not entirely disregard, the entrepreneurial problems involved in providing the governance services associated with the protective state. The practical tasks of law enforcement, public safety, adjudication, and protection from external threats involve the allocation of scarce resources among various ends, the optimal solution to which is not given. One of the primary concerns for James Madison and other Framers of the US Constitution was how to empower the state to perform these functions while checking its ability to undermine liberty. For Madison, if the government could consist of angels, all problems of governance would be solved.

Contra Madison, having angels in charge of monopoly government would not solve all problems. Without private property in the means of production and voluntary exchange of capital and consumer goods, angels will have no nonarbitrary way of solving the problem of how to decide among various technologically feasible combinations of factors of production when it comes to producing governance. It is the open-endedness of these economic problems that is a necessary condition for the cronyism inherent in a protective state. Further, while having a government of angels would mitigate cronyism, the wealth-extracting institutions of the state remain an attractive target for non-angels who seek to enrich themselves via political means.

Therefore, when we compare a stateless society of angelic entrepreneurs competitively providing governance services to a monopoly government of angels, the former is preferable, as it allows for a greater degree of economic calculation in the realm of providing governance services, as well as eliminates the danger of the state apparatus being commandeered to do what states typically do: plunder and kill on an industrial scale. The state, even one consisting of angels, is, in the words of Robert Higgs, "too dangerous to tolerate" (Misesmedia 2013).

NOTES

1. One may wonder what it means for men to be governed by angels in a stateless society. The assumption being made here is that however many angels are necessary to man the state apparatus in a situation with a state, those same angels would also populate the stateless society. In other words, this is an exercise in comparing the outcomes of the very same population living under statelessness versus one being governed by an angelic state. The same functions provided by the protective state would be provided competitively by entrepreneurs, who may or may not be angels depending on what lines of production angelic labor has a comparative advantage.

2. But see below on how, even with angels governing men, some public choice problems may persist.

3. See, for example, Buchanan (1974, 915), which criticizes Friedman (1973) and other "property rights anarchists" for overlooking the issues involved in defining a baseline set of rights from which to negotiate governance contracts. Leeson (2011, 302) notes that Buchanan's approach to establishing constitutional government faces the same problem regarding the initial definition of rights. However, both Leeson and Friedman (1996) argue that a strong party attempting to violently appropriate all rights is prohibitively costly, so there will exist some undefined baseline of rights under statelessness from which to negotiate, which may affect the associated distribution of income but not its economic efficiency.

4. It is also not unreasonable to imagine that angels' comparative advantage may be in something other than what we may categorize as "governance," but we wouldn't know absent the free movement of angelic labor.

5. Worth noting is the fact that Delta Airlines spent $5 million on investments to improve the efficiency of security screening at the Hartsfield-Jackson Atlanta International Airport, which benefited passengers of all airlines (Tucker 2017). Because of profit-and-loss accounting, Delta was able to determine whether such investments in improving security efficiency (even if the airline was not able to capture all the benefits) were worth undertaking.

6. *Minnesota v. Dickerson* (1993).

7. *Whren v. United States* (1996).

8. *Rodriguez v. United States* (2015).

9. *United States v. Place* (1983).

10. This suggests an additional dilemma for Starbucks: in these situations, the company still has the option of ejecting these individuals, but obviously wants to avoid a repeat of the incident in Philadelphia. The CEO's statement suggests he would like the enforcement without it being associated with Starbucks itself. This represents a challenge for businesses that cater to a clientele that desires to think of itself as living consistently with progressive beliefs about supporting the disadvantaged and only supporting businesses that share those values, yet also desires not having to interact with the disadvantaged.

11. *Martin v. Boise* (2018).

12. The resources expended by rent seekers are not limited to helping favored candidates win political office but also include, among other things, capturing the media in order to promote narratives in support of expanding relevant government spending (Coyne and Hall 2023).

REFERENCES

Aligica, Paul Dragos, Peter J. Boettke, and Vlad Tarko. 2019. *Public Governance and the Classical-Liberal Perspective: Political Economy Foundations*. Oxford: Oxford University Press.

Anderson, Terry L., and Peter Jensen Hill. (1979) 2017. "An American Experiment in Anarcho-Capitalism: The Not so Wild, Wild West." *Journal of Libertarian Studies* 3: 9–29.

Bellin, Jeffrey. 2014. "The Inverse Relationship between the Constitutionality and Effectiveness of New York City Stop and Frisk." *Boston University Law Review* 94: 1495.

Benson, Bruce L. 1990. *The Enterprise of Law: Justice without the State*. San Francisco: Pacific Research Institute for Public Policy.

Boettke, Peter J. 1998. "Economic Calculation: The Austrian Contribution to Political Economy." In *Advances in Austrian Economics*, vol. 5, edited by Peter J. Boettke and Sanford Ikeda, 131–58. Greenwich, CT: JAI Press.

———. 2018. "Economics and Public Administration." *Southern Economic Journal* 84 (4): 938–59. https://doi.org/10.1002/soej.12265.

Boudreaux, Donald J., and Randall G. Holcombe. 1989. "Government by Contract." *Public Finance Review* 17 (3): 264–80.

Bratton, William J., and George L. Kelling. 2015. "Why We Need Broken Windows Policing." *City Journal*, 1–14.

Brennan, Geoffrey, and James M. Buchanan. (1985) 2000. *The Reason of Rules: Constitutional Political Economy*, vol. 10 of *The Collected Works of James M. Buchanan*. Indianapolis: Liberty Fund.

Buchanan, James M. 1974. "Review of *The Machinery of Freedom: Guide to a Radical Capitalism*, by David Friedman." *Journal of Economic Literature* 12 (3): 914–15.

Buchanan, James M., and Gordon Tullock. 1962. *The Calculus of Consent: Logical Foundations of Constitutional Democracy*. Ann Arbor: University of Michigan Press.

———. (1975) 2000. *The Limits of Liberty: Between Anarchy and Leviathan*, vol. 7 of *The Collected Works of James M. Buchanan*. Indianapolis: Liberty Fund.

Coyne, Christopher J. 2011. "Constitutions and Crisis." *Journal of Economic Behavior and Organization* 80 (2): 351–57.

———. 2018. "The Protective State: A Grave Threat to Liberty." In *Buchanan's Tensions: Reexamining the Political Economy and Philosophy of James M. Buchanan*, edited by Peter J. Boettke and Solomon Stein, 147–69. Arlington, VA: Mercatus Center at George Mason University.

———. 2022. *In Search of Monsters to Destroy: The Folly of American Empire and the Paths to Peace*. Oakland, CA: Independent Institute.

Coyne, Christopher J., and Abigail R. Hall. 2019a. "Cronyism: Necessary for the Minimal, Protective State." *Independent Review* 23 (3): 399–410.

———. 2019b. "State-Provided Defense as Noncomprehensive Planning." *Journal of Private Enterprise* 34 (1): 75–85.

———. 2023. "How to Run Wars: A Confidential Playbook for the National Security Elite." *Independent Review* 27 (4): 613–25.

Demsetz, Harold. 1969. "Information and Efficiency: Another Viewpoint." *Journal of Law and Economics* 12 (1): 1–22.

Duncan, Thomas K., and Christopher J. Coyne. 2015. "The Revolving Door and the Entrenchment of the Permanent War Economy." *Peace Economics, Peace Science, and Public Policy* 21 (3): 391–413.

Ellickson, Robert C. 1991. *Order without Law: How Neighbors Settle Disputes*. Cambridge, MA: Harvard University Press.

Friedman, David. 1973. *The Machinery of Freedom*. New York: Harper Colophon.

———. 1979. "Private Creation and Enforcement of Law: A Historical Case." *Journal of Legal Studies* 8 (2): 399–415.

———. 1996. "Anarchy and Efficient Law." In *For and against the State: New Philosophical Readings*, edited by John T. Sanders and Jan Narveson, 235–54. Lanham, MD: Rowman and Littlefield.

Hayek, F. A. (1944) 1994. *The Road to Serfdom*. Chicago: University of Chicago Press.

Higgs, Robert. 1987. *Crisis and Leviathan: Critical Episodes in the Growth of American Government*. New York: Oxford University Press.

———. 2004. *Against Leviathan: Government Power and a Free Society*. Oakland, CA: Independent Institute.

———. 2006. *Depression, War, and Cold War: Studies in Political Economy*. Oxford: Oxford University Press.

———. 2007a. "If Men Were Angels: The Basic Analytics of the State versus Self-Government." *Journal of Libertarian Studies* 21 (4): 55–68.

———. 2007b. *Neither Liberty nor Safety: Fear, Ideology, and the Growth of Government*. Oakland, CA: Independent Institute.

Kennedy, Jamie, and Daniel Wilkerson. 2019. "Enclosed Aisles of Goods at Kroger Angers Metro Atlanta Customers." CBS46 News Atlanta, September 25. https://www.cbs46.com/news /enclosed-aisles-of-goods-at-kroger-angers-metro-atlanta-customers/article_5f826642-e009 -11e9-97e5-33bd60a8bbe3.html.

Lawson, Robert A., and J. R. Clark. 2017. "Taxation in the Liberal Tradition." *Review of Austrian Economics* 32: 1–7.

Leeson, Peter T. 2011. "Government, Clubs, and Constitutions." *Journal of Economic Behavior and Organization* 80 (2): 301–8.

Lipsky, Michael. 1983. *Street Level Bureaucracy: Dilemmas of the Individual in Public Services*. New York: Russell Sage Foundation.

MacDonald, Heather. 2016. *The War on Cops: How the New Attack on Law and Order Makes Everyone Less Safe*. New York: Encounter Books.

Madison, James. (1788) 2001. "Federalist No. 51." In *The Federalist*, edited by Robert Scigliano, 330–35. New York: Modern Library.

McDonald, Jennifer. 2020. "Jetway Robbery? Homeland Security and Cash Seizures at Airports." Washington, DC: Institute for Justice.

Mises, Ludwig von. (1920) 1990. *Economic Calculation in the Socialist Commonwealth*. Auburn, AL: Ludwig von Mises Institute.

———. (1927) 1985. *Liberalism: In the Classical Tradition*, 3rd ed. San Francisco: Cobden Press.

———. (1944) 2007. *Bureaucracy*. Indianapolis: Liberty Fund.

Misesmedia. 2013. "The State Is Too Dangerous to Tolerate | Robert Higgs." July 29. https://www .youtube.com/watch?v=RILDjo4EXV8.

Murphy, Robert P. 2010. *Chaos Theory: Two Essays on Market Anarchy*, 2nd ed. Auburn, AL: Ludwig von Mises Institute.

Nozick, Robert. 1974. *Anarchy, State, and Utopia*. New York: Basic Books.

Olson, Mancur. 2000. *Power and Prosperity: Outgrowing Communist and Capitalist Dictatorships.* New York: Basic Books.

Powell, Benjamin, and Christopher J. Coyne. 2003. "Do Pessimistic Assumptions about Human Behavior Justify Government?" *Journal of Libertarian Studies* 17 (4): 17–37.

Rand, Ayn. 1967. *Capitalism: The Unknown Ideal.* New York: Signet.

Rothbard, Murray N. 1956. "Toward a Reconstruction of Utility and Welfare Economics." In *On Freedom and Free Enterprise: Essays in Honor of Ludwig von Mises,* edited by Mary Sennholz, 224–62. Princeton, NJ: D. Van Nostrand.

——. 2009. *Man, Economy, and State with Power and Market,* 2nd ed. Auburn, AL: Ludwig von Mises Institute.

Rummel, R. J. n.d. "20th Century Democide." http://www.hawaii.edu/powerkills/20TH.HTM.

Siegel, Rachel, and Alex Horton. 2018. "Starbucks to Close 8,000 Stores for Racial-Bias Education on May 29 after Arrest of Two Black Men." *Washington Post,* April 17. https://www.washington post.com/news/business/wp/2018/04/17/starbucks-to-close-8000-stores-for-racial-bias -education-on-may-29-after-arrest-of-two-black-men/.

Tucker, Jeffrey A. 2017. "Delta Paid for Its Own Security Upgrade and Fixed Everything." FEE.org, February 24. https://fee.org/articles/delta-paid-for-its-own-security-upgrade-and-fixed -everything/.

US Census Bureau. 2007. "Statistical Abstract of the United States: 2007." Washington, DC: US Government Printing Office.

Chapter 16

Two Paths toward Anarcho-pacifism

Lessons from Christianity and Modern Economics

Edward P. Stringham and Spencer D. Brown

The most common view about the necessity and desirability of government is presented in the first three sentences of Robert Higgs's (1987, 3) *Crisis and Leviathan*: "We must have government. Only government can perform certain tasks successfully. Without government to defend us from external aggression, preserve domestic order, define and enforce private property rights, few of us could achieve much."[1] A few writers, however, including Higgs later in his career, question this belief. When a set of thinkers come to a conclusion at odds with the commonly held perspective, one can usually trace their uncommon perspective to a particular source. (For example, the thinkers who first advocated global free trade, criticized price controls, or advocated pure laissez-faire more broadly were probably economists who read common authors such as Adam Smith and were talking with each other.) Rarely, however, do two groups of thinkers who have disparate assumptions and worldviews and are not influenced by one another come to similar analytical claims and normative conclusions.

One such occurrence, which is the focus of this chapter, is how certain 19th-century Christian writers such as Leo Tolstoy and 20th- and 21st-century laissez-faire economists such as Murray Rothbard and Robert Higgs came to question the necessity and desirability of the state. These authors can be considered anarchists and pacifists. Fiala (2021) describes the varying degrees of pacifism from opposition to all war to opposition to use of force even in self-defense, but we focus on the broad definition of "pacifism [as] a commitment to peace and opposition to war." Fiala notes that "the word 'pacifism' is derived from the word 'pacific,' which means 'peace making," and Harper (1951), Coyne (2014), and Coyne and Crockett (2023) use the term "peace monger" as someone committed to peace. We use the noun "anarchist" in its first Oxford dictionary definition: "a person who believes that laws and gov-

We thank Carol Any, Christopher Coyne, and Harry David for helpful comments and suggestions.

ernments are not necessary" (Oxford 2023). (This is quite different from the definition of the term as a supporter of lawlessness.) Or, to use a phrase associated with William Lloyd Garrison, we refer to it as "no-governmentalism" and respect for the universal human rights of all.

Other 19th-century Christian anarcho-pacificists include William Lloyd Garrison, Adin Ballou, Barton Stone, and David Lipscomb, and other 20- and 21st-century economics-influenced anarcho-pacifists include F. A. Harper, Robert Lefevre, Christopher Coyne, and Abigail Hall.[2] Nineteenth-century Christians certainly were not influenced by modern economists, and few modern economists seem to explicitly base their arguments on the foundation presented by Tolstoy. But the two sets of thinkers defend very similar normative positions.

This chapter highlights how despite the two groups' different influences, values, and times, Christian social reformers such as Leo Tolstoy and modern laissez-faire economists such as Robert Higgs reach similar conclusions about the nature and desirability of the state. Tolstoy and Higgs perceive the condition of the world they live in as precarious, largely because of people's mindset of reliance on and submission to the state. They view the state not as a protector but as an oppressor. They share many overlapping perspectives on individualism (albeit in different forms) and consensual organization of society. They uphold similar values for humanity: to be free, safe, and able to live as a person should. The two believe that through individual action, one can be a catalyst of freedom from the state's oppression and lead others to freedom as well.

THE KINGDOM OF GOD IS WITHIN YOU, AND ECONOMIC ARGUMENTS FOR PACIFISM

Let us consider some overlapping arguments of these two seemingly unrelated groups of authors. Tolstoy is best known for the epic novels *War and Peace* ([1869] 2006) and *Anna Karenina* ([1887] 2008) and others including *The Cossacks* ([1862] 2006), *The Death of Ivan Ilyich* ([1886] 1981), *Kreutzer Sonata* ([1889] 2003), and *Resurrection* ([1899] 2009). He achieved massive fame during his lifetime and was praised not only by the Academy of Sciences ("There is no other person whose death could have in equal measure shaken the entire world"; Nickell 2010[3]) but also by Vladimir Lenin ([1910] 1973), who describes "[Tolstoy's] universal significance as an Artist and his universal fame as a thinker and preacher." Tolstoy released the moral and social commentary *What I Believe* in 1884 and expanded it into *The Kingdom of God Is within You* a decade later. Viewing them as dangerous, the government banned both (Tolstoy [1894] 2010, vi).[4]

The censorship, "a quick and devastating" Anthony-Fauci-and-Francis-Collins-style "take down," if you will, likely decreased the readership and influence of these works. According to Google Scholar, *The Kingdom of God Is within You* has around 500 academic citations total, or fewer than four citations per year since publication. To compare it to a more recent economics book in the anarcho-pacifist tradition, our friend Coyne's (2008) *After War* has approximately 360 academic citations total, or 25 citations per year since publication. Considering that Tolstoy is considered the most famous author in the world during his lifetime and is one of the most famous novelists in history, *The Kingdom of God Is within You* received much less acclaim relative to his other work.

Although Tolstoy's *The Kingdom of God Is within You* is not a household title, it had a profound influence on some of the most important social reformers in history. Mahatma Gandhi stated that the book overwhelmed him. Four decades younger than Tolstoy (1828–1910), Gandhi (1869–1948) corresponded with Tolstoy the year before the Russian author's death. In their correspondence, Gandhi (1909–10) refers to himself as "a humble follower of yours" and "your obedient servant"; he later listed Tolstoy as one of his three most important influences. Martin Luther King Jr. was also heavily influenced both directly and indirectly by Tolstoy: his study of Gandhi's methods of peaceful resistance led him to the Tolstoian origins of the practice (Potter 2022). Catholic Worker Movement founder Dorothy Day (1938, 40) states that along with Dostoevsky, "Tolstoi made me cling to a faith in God" and states (1938, 68) that when she was 18 she "wavered between Socialism, Syndicalism (the I.W.W.s), and Anarchism. When I read Tolstoi I was an anarchist."[5]

In contrast to the economic writers whom we address below, Tolstoy takes a religious, theological, or spiritual outlook. He makes the case that even when change is required to solve urgent social issues, the government and other institutions are driven by self-interest and resist such change. *The Kingdom of God Is within You* analyzes government, anarchism, and individual liberty. Among other points, Tolstoy concludes:

a. The state is not created to advance morality and instead corrupts it.

b. The state actively works to unsettle the public so it can exercise more control.

c. The public must wise up and passively resist violence and the state.

We can see that these conclusions differ from many teachings associated with the Orthodox Church or other established churches. Tolstoy was able to come to different conclusions because he believed the Church had become corrupted and distorted Christ's teachings. After he publicly renounced the Church, he was excommunicated in 1901, which was likely not something Church officials had hoped for given Tolstoy's fame.

Now let us consider the parallel arguments and normative conclusions of 20th- and 21st-century laissez-faire economists. Higgs comments that he came to his conclusions about power, anarchism, and pacifism through his study of economics and history. But later, Higgs read Tolstoy and noticed many similarities between their ideas. In a 2014 presentation ("The Anarcho-pacifism of Leo Tolstoy"), Higgs states, "I perceive several parallels between the preceding analysis and my own analyses of the nature and functioning of the state."[6]

Similarly to Tolstoy, Higgs realizes the detriment of centralized power to society. Some of Higgs's main arguments that mirror Tolstoy's include the following:

a. The state is not created to advance economic well-being and instead corrupts it.

b. The state actively works to create crises so it can expand power.

c. The public must wise up and passively resist violence and the state.

As we can see, Higgs's judgments about the nature of the state and how to deal with the state are very similar to Tolstoy's. Both authors conclude that the state was created and exists for the benefit of those who control the state, not the average person, and that it seeks to expand its power at the expense of the public. Continuously using crises and propagandist nationalist narratives to garner and preserve public support, the state is able to preserve and extend its power. This allows the state to control the public for its own preservation. The state expands into former private societal roles, but the control seldom subsides.

Not only do their judgments about the nature of the state sound similar, but the authors also propose similar ways to diminish state oppression. Both support learning, educating others, and, if possible, minimizing one's interaction with the state. That modern American economists came to similar positive assessments and normative conclusions before studying Tolstoy indicates something timeless and important about these ideas. Now let us consider some of their parallel arguments in detail.

THE STATE IS NOT CREATED TO ADVANCE MORALITY OR TO PROTECT THE PUBLIC

Tolstoy's normative perspective centers on Jesus's teachings in the Sermon on the Mount and the importance of turning the other cheek. Tolstoy views as the source of morality the individual, not the state, which he considers a manifestation of force and at odds with Jesus's teachings. Tolstoy ([1894] 2010, 200) writes, "Christianity in its true significance abolishes the state, annihilates all governments." Such a perspective is quite in line with that of Higgs, who rejects the idea that government is the source of order and exists to protect you. Higgs (2007a) writes, "The beginning of political wisdom is the realization that despite everything you've always been taught, the government is not really on your side; indeed it is out to get you."

The main appeal of the state lies in its argument that the state is necessary for stability and peace. Tolstoy and Higgs view this perspective as false. Indeed, in his article "If Men Were Angels," Higgs (2007b, 62) argues that the opposite is true: "Under state domination, social disorder tends to increase." Higgs (58) contends that "the outcome in a society under a state will be worse, indeed, much worse, because first, the most vicious people in society will tend to gain control of the state, and second, by virtue of this control over the state's powerful engines of death and destruction they will wreak vastly more harm than they ever could have caused outside the state." Tolstoy makes a similar argument about those wanting to get in power and the outcomes associated with power. Tolstoy ([1894] 2010, 242) writes, "But ruling means using force, and using force means doing to him to whom force is used, what he does not like and what he who uses the force would certainly not like done to himself. Consequently, ruling means doing to others what we would not they should do unto us, that is, doing wrong." Tolstoy ([1894] 2010, 242) also writes, "The good cannot seize power, nor retain it; to do this—men must love power. And love of power is inconsistent with goodness; but quite consistent with the very opposite qualities—pride, cunning, cruelty. Without the aggrandizement of self and the abasement of others, without hypocrisies and deceptions, without prisons, fortresses, executions, and murders, no power can come into existence or be maintained."

From an economic lens, Higgs looks down upon government control of markets and individual choices. Providing the opportunity for some individuals to control others inevitably leads to abuse of power. The state itself is corrupt because it is a platform for those inclined to enact control over society; assuming that the state is created, let alone incentivized, to protect the life and liberty of the people it governs is wishful thinking. States are nothing more than the source of disorder both within borders through internal conflict and outside their borders through war.

In chapter 12 of *The Kingdom of God Is within You*, Tolstoy compares private criminals with the state and argues that government actors are worse.

Tolstoy ([1894] 2010, 280) writes, "Undisguised criminals and malefactors do less harm than those who live by legalized violence, disguised by hypocrisy," drawing an important comparison between private entities' and governments' abilities to cause harm to others.[7] Through observing history, it becomes clear that the potential for catastrophic violence against a population is much greater in the hands of a government than a private organization. When a state decides to use violence, there is no method of preventing the suffering of those targeted by the state, regardless of the immorality of the violence.[8] This is because the laws and constitutions of the state are written and enforced by the state and allow such violence but back it with the full force of the state.

Mirroring Tolstoy, Higgs states, "With regard to large-scale death and destruction, no person, group, or private organization can even begin to compare to the state, which is easily the greatest instrument of destruction known to man. All nonstate threats to life, liberty, and property appear to be relatively petty, and therefore can be dealt with. Only states can pose truly massive threats, and sooner or later the horrors with which they menace mankind invariably come to pass" (Higgs 2007b, 60).

Particularly in the case of militarily strong nations such as the United States, China, or even North Korea, governments time and time again demonstrate their reliance on force, whether at their borders, overseas, or domestically, to retain power. The crux of violence allows a state to remain a state through instilling fear. But by instilling in citizens the ideas of nationalism, the greater good, and national security, a state dissipates its ability to discern whether its own actions are morally right or wrong and exerts even greater control over them.

THE STATE WORKS TO UNSETTLE THE PUBLIC SO IT CAN EXPAND ITS POWER

The state garners support from its subjects in many ways; one of the most important ones is instilling fear. Once subjects both fear and support their state, they can be mobilized for many projects, including committing violence against foreigners or even their fellow citizens. Tolstoy refers to the state's "hypnotizing process," which allows the state to fluidly encroach upon the rights of its subjects, who are sometimes eager for it to do so:

> This hypnotizing process is organized at the present in the most complex manner, and starting from their earliest childhood, continues to act on men till the day of their death. It begins in their earliest years in the compulsory schools. . . . In republican states they teach them the savage

superstition of patriotism and the same pretended obedience to the governing authorities. . . . The patriotic superstition is encouraged by the creation, with money taken from the people, of national fêtes, spectacles, monuments, and festivals to dispose men to attach importance to their own nation, and to the aggrandizement of the state and its rulers, and to feel antagonism and even hatred for other nations. . . . Under every government without exception everything is kept back that might emancipate and everything encouraged that tends to corrupt the people. (Tolstoy [1894] 2010, 194)

Like Tolstoy, Higgs views government propaganda as designed to support the state's claimed right to rule the masses and drown out opposing voices. In Higgs's 2014 lecture about Tolstoy, he uses the above quote to portray the striking similarity in their viewpoints on patriotism. What Tolstoy refers to as hypnosis, Higgs refers to as ideological learning. Higgs (2014) explains:

As for why we submit to the state's outrages, the most persuasive answers have to do with fear of the state (and nowadays, for many, fear of self-responsibility as well), with apprehension about sticking one's neck out when other victims may fail to join forces with those who resist first and, probably most important, with the ideological "hypnosis" (as Leo Tolstoy characterized it) that keeps most people from being able to imagine life without the state or to understand why the state's claim to intrinsic immunity from the morality that binds all other human beings is the purest bunk.

In *Crisis and Leviathan*, Higgs (1987) writes how the expansion of a government is supported through propaganda: "The barrage of propaganda always hits some targets, if only the unsophisticated or devoutly patriotic—possibly a huge throng. Conceivably, then, ideological learning makes a discrete leap as a result of social crisis and the attendant expansion toward Big Government. This could be the way in which, as Sumner put it, 'the experiment enters into the life of the society and never can be got out again'"(188).

When people undergo ideological learning, that is, hypnotization, they become tools of the state, even though it acts against their interests.[9] This allows the state to grow and enlist citizens to do its duties. Enlisting the individuals to be part of military efforts is among the most long-standing examples, but a more recent example is governments' enlisting during COVID-19 a private unpaid army of scolds who helped government lock down schools, churches, gyms, restaurants, bars, and all "nonessential" businesses: "Where's your mask?!"

Coined by Higgs, the ratchet effect is a framework for understanding the expansion of government power and concomitant loss of individual liberties. Higgs (1987, 98) writes, "Conventional measures of the size of government indicate a 'ratchet' during the twentieth century: after each major crisis the size of government, though smaller than during the crisis, remained larger than it would have been had the precrisis rate of growth persisted during the interval occupied by the crisis." The ratchet effect framework helps explain why government power and control grow over time. Once a government program or policy is established, it acquires a constituency of vested interests who will fight tenaciously to preserve it, regardless of its original purpose or current utility.

In the ratcheting process, crises are the reason for state expansion and invasion of personal liberty. Some examples are the World Wars, the New Deal, and the war on drugs. These repeated expansions distend the scale and scope of the state and its control of citizens. Even after the crisis is gone, the expansions, which were justified as temporary measures, become entrenched. States preserve the expansions to benefit themselves. After the crises, the state works to shift public ideology to normalize the loss of individual liberty. That includes getting the public to forget how things were in the past.

The ratchet effect can be seen in countless areas of public policy including taxation, spending, and regulation. For example, once taxes are increased, they rarely decrease. Consider the following quote that Tolstoy provides from a contemporary, Count Komarovsky, who sounds quite like 21st-century Higgs: "New taxes and duties are being devised everywhere, and the financial oppression of the nations knows no limits. If we glance at the budgets of the states of Europe for the last hundred years, what strikes us most of all is their rapid and continually growing increase" (quoted in Tolstoy [1894] 2010, 125).

Tolstoian insights about the state's efforts to monopolize the establishment of culture and the dissemination of information mirror Higgs's analysis of ratcheting government. Among the factors that contribute to the ratchet effect is mass fearmongering, used to manufacture crises and convey to the people that expansion is a necessary response. The state induces its subjects to support new government powers, however drastic they may be. Tolstoy emphasizes the hypocrisy of those with power:

> Still there are people who believe in this, busy themselves over peace
> congresses, read addresses, and write books. And governments, we may
> be quite sure, express their sympathy and make a show of encouraging
> them. In the same way they pretend to support temperance societies,
> while they are living principally on the drunkenness of the people; and

> pretend to encourage education, when their whole strength is based on
> ignorance; and to support constitutional freedom, when their strength
> rests on the absence of freedom; and to be anxious for the improve-
> ment of the condition of the working classes, when their very existence
> depends on their oppression; and to support Christianity, when Chris-
> tianity destroys all government. (Tolstoy [1894] 2010, 148)

Tolstoy says that the government claims to be on the side of good when the opposite is true. He argues that the state devises new institutions or co-opts existing institutions to offer false promises of hope and protection: "To be able to do this they have long ago elaborated methods encouraging temperance, which cannot suppress drunkenness; methods of supporting education, which not only fail to prevent ignorance, but even increase it; methods of aiming at freedom and constitutionalism, which are no hindrance to despotism; meth-ods of protecting the working classes, which will not free them from slavery; and a Christianity, too, they have elaborated, which does not destroy, but supports governments" (Tolstoy [1894] 2010, 148). Tolstoy notes that the increasing corruption of different facets of life, from education to religion to public wel-fare, is rooted in state interventionism and the pretense of aid.

As a state continues to intervene, it strips individuals not just of their free-dom but also of their ability to live in a consistently moral way. Tolstoy ([1894] 2010) writes, "All men of the modern world exist in a state of continual and flagrant antagonism between their conscience and their way of life. This antag-onism is apparent in economic as well as political life. But most striking of all is the contradiction between the Christian law of the Brotherhood of men existing in the conscience and the necessity under which all men are placed by compulsory military service of being prepared for hatred and murder—of being at the same time a Christian and a gladiator" (116). By undermining basic moral-ity, the state confuses individuals and helps shift public ideology in its favor. It leads to greater and greater public indifference about or support for further state intervention.

THE PUBLIC MUST WISE UP AND PASSIVELY RESIST VIOLENCE AND THE STATE

Tolstoy and Higgs have a dim view of the state and recognize how pervasive the state is. But neither is a nihilist who would say, "If you can't beat them, join them." Both authors argue that individuals must take a peaceful stand against the state. Tolstoy ([1894] 2010, 230–31) writes, "All state obligations are against the conscience of a Christian—the oath of allegiance, taxes, law proceedings, and military service. And the whole power of the government rests on these very obligations. Revolutionary enemies attack the government from without. Christianity does not attack it at all, but, from within, it destroys all the foundations on which government rests." With Tolstoy's doctrine of nonviolence comes his belief that one should live one's life according to Christ. He says that if one wishes for the world to change, one must start with oneself. Tolstoy (195) writes, "Yet the fact that the freedom of all men will be brought about only through the freedom of individual persons, becomes more and more clear as time goes on." He believes that individuals' pursuit and achievement of freedom can inspire others to do the same and escape the shackles of obedience.

Tolstoy expounds the idea with an allegory of a bee flying away from a bee-covered tree branch and inspiring thousands of her six-legged cohorts to do the same. The bee's wings represent the faculty of entering the Christian conception of life: enabling one to follow proper Christian teachings and live for God:

> If every bee who could fly, did not try to fly, the others, too, would never be stirred, and the swarm would never change its position. And if the man who has mastered the Christian conception of life would not, without waiting for other people, begin to live in accordance with this conception, mankind would never change its position. But only let one bee spread her wings, start off, and fly away, and after her another, and another, and the clinging, inert cluster would become a freely flying swarm of bees. Just in the same way, only let one man look at life as Christianity teaches him to look at it, and after him let another and another do the same, and the enchanted circle of existence in the state conception of life, from which there seemed no escape, will be broken through. (Tolstoy [1894] 2010, 214)

In line with the methodological individualism of modern political economists such as Higgs, Tolstoy proclaims that individual decision-making determines outcomes in society. He calls upon individuals to lead the life they know is most fulfilling by liberating themselves from the muddled ideology of the masses and pursuing their destiny as a mind and soul free from the state's violence. The widespread choice to reject the teachings of the state would be the ultimate catalyst for its demise (183).

Tolstoy's and Higgs's solutions share a focus on education and awareness. Although Higgs supports peaceful anarchy, most of the time he is more pessimistic than Tolstoy about the prospects for standing up to and diminishing the power of government. Nevertheless, the titles of a few of Higgs's many books and articles are instructive about how Higgs believed that one should spend time educating people about the importance of standing up to government: *Against Leviathan* (2004), "Fear: The Foundation of Every Government's Power" (2006), *Opposing the Crusader State: Alternatives to Global Interventionism* (Higgs and Close 2007), *Neither Liberty nor Safety: Fear, Ideology, and the Growth of Government* (Higgs 2007c), "If Men Were Angels: The Basic Analytics of the State versus Self-Government" (2007b), "The Complex Course of Ideological Change" (2008a), and "Peace and Pacifism" (2008b). As someone who believes that the strength of the state ultimately rests on the ideological views of the public, Higgs has spent his career working to undermine the belief that government is our savior. He has dedicated a large portion of his life to education—teaching, speaking to the public, and writing for a variety of audiences—and understands it as key to challenging the oppression. The less that people believe that the state is a benevolent force, the less reliant and supportive of government they will be. Higgs also pondered the idea that individuals take action and remove themselves as much as possible from state control, including by emigrating from countries with more state power.[10] We might even think about this proposal in light of Tolstoy's allegory of the bee.

Whereas Higgs appeals to people's self-interest for avoiding the state or opting out of the state's control, Tolstoy makes a moral case. He argues that the ultimate abolition of the state will come when people follow their religious conscience:

> But no considerations as to how far the state is useful or beneficial to the men who help to support it by serving in the army, nor the advantages or disadvantages for the individual of compliance or non-compliance with the state demands, will decide the question of the continued existence or the abolition of government. This question will be finally decided beyond appeal by the religious consciousness or conscience of every man who is forced, whether he will or no, through universal conscription, to face the question whether the state is to continue to exist or not. ([1894] 2010, 162)

To Tolstoy, the fate of the state is ultimately determined by all of us. Tolstoy believes that peaceful resistance through individual action under an oppressive regime can create meaningful change.

CONCLUSION

Despite different backgrounds and worldviews, some 19th-century Christian authors and 21st-century laissez-faire economists come to very similar conclusions regarding the nature and desirability of the state. Tolstoy and Higgs share the belief that the state is oppressive rather than protective and that it is responsible for moral and economic decay. They argue that an organization that relies on coercion attracts those who want to exercise violence and coercion, and only creates more conflict and exacerbates problems. But an alternative to the state and its war making exists. Private civil society is capable of organizing itself in a manner far more equitable and fairer than is possible under centralized state power. Some people, according to Tolstoy ([1894] 2010, 355), "do not notice" the narrow limits of freedom provided by a state, and others "consider this amount so trifling that they do not recognize it at all." But a third division of people are "champions of complete free will—keep[ing] their eyes fixed on their hypothetical free will and neglect[ing] this which seemed to [others] such a trivial degree of freedom."[11] Humanity will be better off organizing society based on consensual interaction. The state only detracts from the more natural and moral motivators of society: peaceful cooperation and love for one another.

NOTES

1. Other prominent modern political economists to hold such a position range from James Buchanan (1975) to Robert Nozick (1973). For an overview of perspectives on the classical liberal state, see Smith (2013), Butler (2015), and Boettke and Leeson (2015).

2. For an overview of the non-economics-influenced literature on pacifism, see Fiala (2020), Holmes (2013), and Stringham's college professor Cicovacki (2017). For an overview of the economics-influenced literature on pacifism, see Coyne (2020).

3. This quote originates from *Journal des Débats* and was then adopted by the Academy of Sciences. For a discussion about the international reception of Tolstoy's death, see Nickell (2010).

4. Our colleague Carol Any reports to us that the book was first published in Russia in 1906. For a fascinating and terrifying account of later censorship of Russian literature, see Any (2020). The book focuses on subordination and suppression under Stalin, but it is highly relevant in America today.

5. For an excellent overview of Tolstoy's embrace of Christ's Sermon on the Mount, anarchism, and pacifism, and an overview of the thinkers whom Tolstoy influenced, see Christoyannopoulos (2020). For an overview of Christianity and anarchism more broadly, see Christoyannopoulos (2011).

6. Higgs (2014) notes that he had just recently come across Tolstoy's writings on the topic: "You can generally expect that your teachers will really have a lot of expertise in the topics they select to teach you; for this session that's not the case. In fact, this is a talk I've never given before, and in many ways, it's an area that I know practically nothing about, so this is as new to me as it may or may not be to you, but nonetheless there is a reason why I decided to present a session on Tolstoy's anarchism and his pacifism."

7. Tolstoy did not deny the existence of private privation and spends much time in his nonfiction and novels through the characters moralizing against wronging others even if an action did not involve violence. One of the main themes of *Resurrection* (Tolstoy [1900] 2009) involves a character attempting to atone for abandoning his paramour.

8. Tolstoy ([1894] 2010, 267) states, "All violence rests, we know, on those who do the beating, the handcuffing, the imprisoning, and the killing with their own hands. If there were no soldiers or armed policemen, ready to kill or outrage anyone as they are ordered, not one of those people who sign sentences of death, imprisonment, or galley-slavery for life would make up his mind to hang, imprison, or torture a thousandth part of those whom, quietly sitting in his study, he now orders to be tortured in all kinds of ways, simply because he does not see it nor do it himself, but only gets it done at a distance by these servile tools."

9. Tolstoy ([1894] 2010, 288) notes the time required to hypnotize a population and distinguishes between ideological hypnotization by a state and traditional hypnotization by a hypnotizer or scientist: "The difference between those hypnotized by scientific men and those under the influence of state hypnotism, is that an imaginary position is suggested to the former suddenly by one person in a very brief space of time, and so the hypnotized state appears to us in a striking and surprising form, while the imaginary position suggested by the state influence is induced slowly, little by little, imperceptibly from childhood, sometimes during years, or even generations, and not in one person alone but in a whole society."

10. Higgs (2013) suggests that Americans should consider moving to countries with less powerful governments: "Not because I think any other country is a paradise, by the way, but because I think no other country has the means that the government of this country has to carry out these horrifying surveillance programs and other measures of State tyranny. . . . Many other countries in the world are perfectly awful from the standpoint of the kinds of governments they have, but thank goodness those governments are poorer."

11. At the end of *The Kingdom of God Is Within You*, Tolstoy ([1894] 2010, 368) concludes that true power not held by external organizational forces but by oneself and that humans are meant to serve humanity, not governments. He states, "That is why Power cannot require of us what is irrational and impossible: the organization of our temporary external life, the life of society or of the state that Power demands of us only what is reasonable, certain, and possible: to serve the kingdom of God that is, to contribute to the establishment of the greatest possibly Union between all things—a union Possible only in the truth; and to recognize him to profess the revealed truth, which is always in our power. . . . The sole meaning of life is to serve Humanity by contributing to the establishment of the kingdom of god, which can only be done by the recognition and profession of the truth by every man."

REFERENCES

Any, Carol. 2020. *The Soviet Writers' Union and Its Leaders: Identity and Authority under Stalin.* Evanston, IL: Northwestern University Press.

Boettke, Peter, and Peter Leeson. 2015. *The Economic Role of the State.* Cheltenham, UK: Edward Elgar.

Buchanan, James. 1975. *The Limits of Liberty: Between Anarchy and Leviathan.* Chicago: University of Chicago Press.

Butler, Eamonn. 2015. *Classic Liberalism—A Primer.* London: Institute of Economic Affairs.

Christoyannopoulos, Alexandre. 2011. *Christian Anarchism: A Political Commentary on the Gospel.* Exeter, UK: Imprint Academic.

———. 2020. *Tolstoy's Political Thought: Christian Anarcho-pacifist Iconoclasm Then and Now.* London: Routledge.

Cicovacki, Predrag. 2017. *Gandhi's Footprints.* Oxfordshire, UK: Routledge.

Coyne, Christopher J. 2008. *After War.* Palo Alto, CA: Stanford University Press.

———. 2014. "Foreign Intervention: A Case for Humility." George Mason University Working Paper in Economics No. 15–19.

———. 2020. *Defense, Peace, and War Economics.* Cambridge: Cambridge University Press.

Coyne, Christopher J., and Amy Crockett. 2023. "A Conflict of Peace Visions: The Peacemonger Mentality vs. the Warmonger Mentality." *Journal of Private Enterprise* 38 (3): 1–24.

Day, Dorothy. 1938. *From Union Square to Rome.* Silver Spring, MD: Preservation of the Faith Press.

Fiala, Andrew. 2020. *The Routledge Handbook of Pacifism and Nonviolence.* Oxfordshire, UK: Routledge.

———. 2021. "Pacifism." In *The Stanford Encyclopedia of Philosophy.* Edited by Edward N. Zalta. Palo Alto, CA: Stanford University Press.

Harper, F. A. 1951. *In Search of Peace.* Irvington-on-Hudson, NY: Foundation for Economic Education.

Higgs, Robert. 1987. *Crisis and Leviathan.* Oxford: Oxford University Press.

———. 2004. *Against Leviathan.* Oakland, CA: Independent Institute.

———. 2006. "Fear: The Foundation of Every Government's Power." *Independent Review* 10: 447–66.

———. 2007a. "Four Types of Government Operatives: Bullies, Muggers, Sneak Thieves, and Con Men." *Independent Institute Commentary.* Oakland, CA: Independent Institute.

———. 2007b. "If Men Were Angels: The Basic Analytics of the State versus Self-Government." *Journal of Libertarian Studies* 21 (4): 55–68.

———. 2007c. *Neither Liberty nor Safety: Fear, Ideology, and the Growth of Government.* Oakland, CA: Independent Institute.

———. 2008a. "The Complex Course of Ideological Change." *American Journal of Economics and Sociology* 67 (4): 547–66.

———. 2008b. "Peace and Pacifism." In *Encyclopedia of Libertarianism.* Edited by Ronald Hamowy. Los Angeles, CA: Sage.

———. 2013. "The State Is Too Dangerous to Tolerate." Lecture. Mises Institute, Auburn, AL.

———. 2014. "The Anarcho-Pacifism of Leo Tolstoy." Lecture. Mises Institute, Auburn, AL.

Higgs, Robert, and Carl P. Close (eds.). 2007. *Opposing the Crusader State: Alternatives to Global Interventionism.* Oakland, CA: Independent Institute.

Holmes, Robert. 2013. *The Ethics of Nonviolence: Essays by Robert L. Holmes.* London: Bloomsbury Academics.

Lenin, Vladimir. (1910) 1973. "Leo Tolstoy as the Mirror of the Russian Revolution." In *Lenin Collected Works,* vol. 15, 202–9. Moscow: Progress Publishers.

Nickell, William. 2010. "The Great Writer of All the Lands—Russia Reads the International Reception of Tolstoj's Death" *Revue des Études Slaves* 81 (1): 33–46.

Nozick, Robert. 1973. *Anarchy, State, and Utopia.* New York: Basic Books.

Oxford. 2023. *Oxford Learners Dictionary.* Oxford: Oxford University Press.

Potter, Bill. 2022. "Death of Leo Tolstoy." *Landmark Events History Highlights,* November 20.

Smith, George. 2013. *The System of Liberty: Themes in the History of Classical Liberalism.* Cambridge: Cambridge University Press.

Tolstoy, Leo. (1862) 2006. *The Cossacks.* Translated by Peter Constantine. New York: Random House.

———. (1869) 2006. *War and Peace.* Translated by Constance Garnett. New York: Barnes and Noble Classics.

———. (1886) 1981. *The Death of Ivan Ilyich.* Translated by Lynn Solotaroff. New York: Bantom Classics.

———. (1887) 2008. *Anna Karenina*. Translated by Louise Maude and Aylmer Maude. Oxford: Oxford University Press.

———. (1894) 2010. *The Kingdom of God Is within You*. Translated by Constance Garnett. New York: Cassell.

———. (1889) 2003. *The Kreutzer Sonata*. Translated by Isai Karmen. New York: Random House.

———. (1899) 2009. *Resurrection*. Translated by Louise Maude. Oxford: Oxford University Press.

Appendix: Select Publications by Robert Higgs

Publications are listed in chronological order.

BOOKS

"Location Theory and the Growth of Cities in the Western Prairie Region, 1870–1900." Unpublished PhD diss., Johns Hopkins University, 1968.

The Transformation of the American Economy, 1865–1914: An Essay in Interpretation. New York: John Wiley and Sons, 1971. Reprint edition paperback with a new preface, Auburn, AL: Ludwig von Mises Institute, 2011.

Competition and Coercion: Blacks in the American Economy, 1865–1914. New York: Cambridge University Press, 1977. Paperback edition with a new preface, Chicago: University of Chicago Press, 1980. Paperback reissue edition, New York: Cambridge University Press, 2008.

Emergence of the Modern Political Economy. Edited with an introduction by Robert Higgs. Greenwich, CT: JAI Press, 1985.

Crisis and Leviathan: Critical Episodes in the Growth of American Government. New York: Oxford University Press, 1987. Paperback edition, 1989; 25th anniversary edition, with a new preface, Oakland, CA: Independent Institute, 2012. Russian translation, *Кризис и Левиафан. Поворотные моменты роста американского правительства*. Moscow: IRISEN, 2010. Spanish translation, *Crisis y Leviatan*. Madrid: Deusto-Instituto Juan de Mariana-Value School, 2021.

[With Charlotte Twight] "Congressional Parochialism versus National Defense." Unpublished book ms., 1989.

Arms, Politics, and the Economy: Historical and Contemporary Perspectives. Edited with an introduction by Robert Higgs. New York: Holmes and Meier, 1990.

Hazardous to Our Health? FDA Regulation of Health Care Products. Edited with an introduction, a chapter, and a conclusion by Robert Higgs. Oakland, CA: Independent Institute, 1995.

Against Leviathan: Government Power and a Free Society. Oakland, CA: Independent Institute, 2004.

Re-Thinking Green: Alternatives to Environmental Bureaucracy. Edited with an introduction by Robert Higgs and Carl P. Close. Oakland, CA: Independent Institute, 2005.

Resurgence of the Warfare State: The Crisis since 9/11. Oakland, CA: Independent Institute, 2005.

The Challenge of Liberty: Classical Liberalism Today. Edited with an introduction by Robert Higgs and Carl P. Close. Oakland, CA: Independent Institute, 2006.

Politická ekonomie strachu [The Political Economy of Fear]. Prague: Alfa Publishing a Liberální Institut, 2006.

Depression, War, and Cold War: Studies in Political Economy. New York: Oxford University Press, 2006. Paperback edition published under the title *Depression, War, and Cold War: Challenging the Myths of Conflict and Prosperity*. Oakland, CA: Independent Institute, 2009. Croatian translation, *Depresija, rat i strah*. Zagreb: Politička kultura, 2008.

[With 15 coauthors] *Government and the American Economy: A New History*. Chicago: University of Chicago Press, 2007.

Neither Liberty nor Safety: Fear, Ideology, and the Growth of Government. Oakland, CA: Independent Institute, 2007.

Opposing the Crusader State: Alternatives to Global Interventionism. Edited with an introduction by Robert Higgs and Carl P. Close. Oakland, CA: Independent Institute, 2007.

Delusions of Power: New Explorations of the State, War, and Economy. Oakland, CA: Independent Institute, 2012.

Taking a Stand: Reflections on Life, Liberty, and the Economy. Oakland, CA: Independent Institute, 2015.

ARTICLES IN PEER-REVIEWED PROFESSIONAL JOURNALS

"The Growth of Cities in a Midwestern Region, 1870–1900." *Journal of Regional Science* 9 (December 1969): 369–75.

[With H. Louis Stettler III] "Colonial New England Demography: A Sampling Approach." *William and Mary Quarterly* 27 (April 1970): 282–94. Reprinted in the Bobbs-Merrill Reprint Series in American History, No. H-413.

"Railroad Rates and the Populist Uprising." *Agricultural History* 44 (July 1970): 291–97. Reprinted in *Historical Analysis: Contemporary Approaches to Clio's Craft*, edited by Richard E. Beringer. New York: John Wiley and Sons, 1978, 313–17. Also reprinted in *Issues in American Economic History*, 3rd ed., edited by Gerald D. Nash, 217–23. Lexington, MA: D.C. Heath, 1980. Part of this article is reproduced in Susan Previant Lee and Peter Passell, *A New View of American Economic History*, 299. New York: Norton, 1979. Part also reproduced in Jeremy Atack and Peter Passell, *A New Economic View of American History from Colonial Times to 1940*, 421. New York: Norton, 1994.

"Central Place Theory and Regional Urban Hierarchies: An Empirical Note." *Journal of Regional Science* 10 (August 1970): 253–55.

"Williamson and Swanson on City Growth: A Critique." *Explorations in Economic History* 8 (Winter 1971): 203–11.

"Regional Specialization and the Supply of Wheat in the United States, 1867–1914: A Comment." *Review of Economics and Statistics* 53 (February 1971): 101–2.

"American Inventiveness, 1870–1920." *Journal of Political Economy* 79 (May–June 1971): 661–67.

"Race, Skills, and Earnings: American Immigrants in 1909," *Journal of Economic History* 31 (June 1971): 420–28. Reprinted in *Issues in American Economic History*, 3rd ed., edited by Gerald D. Nash, 262–69. Lexington, MA: D.C. Heath, 1980.

"Did Southern Farmers Discriminate?" *Agricultural History* 46 (April 1972): 325–28.

"Property Rights and Resource Allocation under Alternative Land Tenure Forms: A Comment." *Oxford Economic Papers* 24 (November 1972): 428–31.

"Race, Tenure, and Resource Allocation in Southern Agriculture, 1910." *Journal of Economic History* 33 (March 1973): 149–69. [See the Editor's Notes, *Journal of Economic History* 33 (September 1973): 668 for correction of a substantive printer's error in this article.]

"Mortality in Rural America, 1870–1920: Estimates and Conjectures." *Explorations in Economic History* 10 (Winter 1973): 177–95.

"Patterns of Farm Rental in the Georgia Cotton Belt, 1880–1900." *Journal of Economic History* 34 (June 1974): 468–82.

"Tractors or Horses: Some Basic Economics in the Pacific Northwest and Elsewhere." *Agricultural History* 49 (January 1975): 281–83. Reprinted in *Agriculture in the Development of the Far West*, edited by James H. Shideler, 281–83. Washington, DC: Agricultural History Society, 1975.

"Did Southern Farmers Discriminate? Interpretive Problems and Further Evidence." *Agricultural History* 49 (April 1975): 445–47.

"The Boll Weevil, the Cotton Economy, and Black Migration, 1910–1930." *Agricultural History* 50 (April 1976): 335–50. Reprinted in an anthology prepared by Linda Heywood and published by Ginn Press, 1987, for use at Howard University.

"Participation of Blacks and Immigrants in the American Merchant Class, 1890–1910: Some Demographic Relations." *Explorations in Economic History* 13 (April 1976): 153–64.

"Firm-Specific Evidence on Racial Wage Differentials and Workforce Segregation." *American Economic Review* 67 (March 1977): 236–45.

[With Robert McGuire] "Cotton, Corn and Risk in the Nineteenth Century: Another View." *Explorations in Economic History* 14 (April 1977): 167–82.

"Landless by Law: Japanese Immigrants in California Agriculture to 1941." *Journal of Economic History* 38 (March 1978): 205–25. Reprinted in *American Immigration and Ethnicity: Vol. 4, Immigrants on the Land: Agriculture, Rural Life, and Small Towns*, edited by George E. Pozzetta, 59–79. New York: Garland, 1991. Also reprinted in *Japanese Immigrants and American Law: The Alien Land Laws and Other Issues*. Edited by Charles McClain. New York: Garland, 1994.

"Racial Wage Differentials in Agriculture: Evidence from North Carolina in 1887." *Agricultural History* 52 (April 1978): 308–11.

"The Wealth of Japanese Tenant Farmers in California, 1909." *Agricultural History* 53 (April 1979): 488–93.

"Comments" [on "Class Structure and Economic Development in the American South, 1865–1955," by Jonathan M. Wiener]. *American Historical Review* 84 (October 1979): 993–97.

"Cycles and Trends of Mortality in 18 Large American Cities, 1871–1900." *Explorations in Economic History* 16 (October 1979): 381–408.

[With David Booth] "Mortality Differentials within Large American Cities in 1890." *Human Ecology* 7 (December 1979): 353–70. An abstract of a preliminary version of this paper was published in *Population Index* 44 (July 1978): 405.

"Urbanization and Invention in the Process of Economic Growth: Simultaneous-Equations Estimates for the United States, 1880–1920." *Research in Population Economics* 2 (1980): 3–20.

"Discussion" [of "Regulation, Property Rights, and Definition of 'the Market': Law and the American Economy," by Harry N. Scheiber]. *Journal of Economic History* 41 (March 1981): 110–11.

"Edward Franklin Meeker (1943–1980)." *Explorations in Economic History* 18 (April 1981): 209–10. A shorter version of this memorial appears in the *Journal of Economic History* 41 (March 1981): 202.

"Legally Induced Technical Regress in the Washington Salmon Fishery." *Research in Economic History* 7 (1982): 55–86. Reprinted in *Empirical Studies in Institutional Change*, edited by Lee J. Alston, Thrainn Eggertsson, and Douglass C. North, 247–79. New York: Cambridge University Press, 1996.

[With Lee J. Alston] "Contractual Mix in Southern Agriculture since the Civil War: Facts, Hypotheses, and Tests." *Journal of Economic History* 42 (June 1982): 327–53.

"Accumulation of Property by Southern Blacks before World War I." *American Economic Review* 72 (September 1982): 725–37.

"The Business Cycle, Mortality—and Ideology: A Reply to Chernomas." *International Journal of Health Services* 14 (1984): 135–40.

"Accumulation of Property by Southern Blacks before World War I: Reply." *American Economic Review* 74 (September 1984): 777–81.

[With Andrew Rutten] "Graphic Tests of Easterlin's Hypothesis: Science or Art?" *Research in Population Economics* 5 (1984): 201–12.

"Crisis, Bigger Government, and Ideological Change: Two Hypotheses on the Ratchet Phenomenon." *Explorations in Economic History* 22 (January 1985): 1–28. Parts of this article were reprinted in Jeremy Atack and Peter Passell, *A New Economic View of American History from Colonial Times to 1940*, 654–55. New York: Norton, 1994.

[With Charlotte Twight] "National Emergency and Private Property Rights: Historical Relations and Present Conditions." *Journal of Private Enterprise* 2 (Fall 1986): 122–26. A summary version appeared under various headlines in various newspapers, e.g., *St. Louis Post-Dispatch*, Sept. 25, 1986; *Easton Express*, Oct. 26, 1986; *Houston Post*, Oct. 3, 1986; *Norfolk Ledger-Star*, Nov. 6, 1986; *Orange County Register*, Nov. 12, 1986; *Oakland Tribune*, Dec. 8, 1986.

[With Charlotte Twight] "National Emergency and the Erosion of Private Property Rights." *Cato Journal* 6 (Winter 1987): 747–73. Reprinted without footnotes and references in *Toward Liberty: The Idea That Is Changing the World*, edited by David Boaz, 353–69. Washington, DC: Cato Institute, 2002.

"Identity and Cooperation: A Comment on Sen's Alternative Program." *Journal of Law, Economics, and Organization* 3 (Spring 1987): 140–42.

[With Charlotte Twight] "Economic Warfare and Private Property Rights: Recent Episodes and Their Constitutionality." *Journal of Private Enterprise* 3 (Fall 1987): 9–14.

"Hard Coals Make Bad Law: Congressional Parochialism versus National Defense." *Cato Journal* 8 (Spring/Summer 1988): 79–106.

"Organization, Ideology and the Free Rider Problem: Comment." *Journal of Institutional and Theoretical Economics* 145 (March 1989): 232–37.

"Do Legislators' Votes Reflect Constituency Preference? A Simple Way to Evaluate the Senate." *Public Choice* 63 (November 1989): 175–81.

"Eighteen Problematic Propositions in the Analysis of the Growth of Government." *Review of Austrian Economics* 5 (1991): 3–40.

"Wartime Prosperity? A Reassessment of the U.S. Economy in the 1940s." *Journal of Economic History* 52 (March 1992): 41–60. Excerpted in "Recommendations for Further Reading," *Journal of Economic Perspectives* 6 (Fall 1992): 202. Reprinted in *War Finance, Vol. III: War in the Twentieth Century*, ed. Larry Neal, 261–80. Cheltenham, UK: Edward Elgar, 1994.

[With Ruben Trevino] "Profits of U.S. Defense Contractors," *Defence Economics* 3 (1992): 211–18. Reprinted in *The Economics of Defence*, edited by Keith Hartley and Todd Sandler. Cheltenham, UK: Edward Elgar, 2001.

"Federalism, State Action, and 'Critical Episodes' in the Growth of American Government: Reply to Ballard Campbell." *Social Science History* 16 (Winter 1992): 579–82.

"Allocation of Risks Associated with Medical Goods: Government Regulation versus Market Process." *Journal of Private Enterprise* 9 (Summer 1993): 59–69.

[With Anthony Kilduff] "Public Opinion: A Powerful Predictor of U.S. Defense Spending." *Defence Economics* 4 (1993): 227–38.

"The Cold War Economy: Opportunity Costs, Ideology, and the Politics of Crisis." *Explorations in Economic History* 31 (July 1994): 283–312.

"Banning a Risky Product Cannot Improve Any Consumer's Welfare (Properly Understood), with Applications to FDA Testing Requirements." *Review of Austrian Economics* 7 (1994): 3–20.

"Public Opinion: A Powerful Predictor of U.S. Defense Spending? [Reply to Comment]." *Defence and Peace Economics* 5 (1994): 255–58.

"From Central Planning to the Market: The American Transition, 1945–1947." *Journal of Economic History* 59 (September 1999): 600–23.

"On Ackerman's Justification of Irregular Constitutional Change: Is Any Vice You Get Away with a Virtue?" *Constitutional Political Economy* 10 (November 1999): 375–83.

"Wartime Socialization of Investment: A Reassessment of U.S. Capital Formation in the 1940s." *Journal of Economic History* 64 (June 2004): 500–520.

"Coasian Contracts in the Coeur d'Alene Mining District." *Cato Journal* 25 (Spring/Summer 2005): 407–22. A revised version appears in *Independent Review* 17 (Fall 2012): 239–52.

"The Ongoing Growth of Government in the Economically Advanced Countries." *Advances in Austrian Economics* 8 (2005): 279–300.

"If Men Were Angels: The Basic Analytics of the State versus Self-government." *Journal of Libertarian Studies* 21 (Winter 2007): 55–68. Reprinted by Liberty

Activism in pamphlet form, available at http://libertyactivism.info/uploads /7/7f/If_Men_Were_Angels_-_Robert_Higgs.pdf.

"The Complex Course of Ideological Change," *American Journal of Economics and Sociology* 67 (October 2008): 547–65.

"A Revealing Window on the U.S. Economy in Depression and War: Hours Worked, 1929–1950." *Libertarian Papers* 1, 4 (2009). Available only online, at http://www.libertarianpapers.org/articles/2009/lp-1-4.doc.

"Two Ideological Ships Passing in the Night." [A contribution to the symposium "Economists on the Welfare State and the Regulatory State: Why Don't Any Argue in Favor of One and Against the Other?"] *Econ Journal Watch* 12 (January 2015): 36–41.

ORIGINAL CHAPTERS IN BOOKS

"Cities and Yankee Ingenuity, 1870–1920." In *Cities in American History*, ed. Kenneth T. Jackson and Stanley K. Schultz, 16–22. New York: Knopf, 1972.

"Urbanization and Inventiveness in the United States, 1870–1920." In *The New Urban History: Quantitative Explorations by American Historians*, edited by Leo F. Schnore, 247–59. Princeton, NJ: Princeton University Press, 1975.

"Race and Economy in the South, 1890–1950." In *The Age of Segregation: Race Relations in the South, 1890–1945*, edited by Robert Haws, 89–116. Jackson: University Press of Mississippi, 1978.

"Introduction." In *Emergence of the Modern Political Economy*, edited by Robert Higgs, ix–xvii. Greenwich, CT: JAI Press, 1985.

"Can the Constitution Protect Private Rights during National Emergencies?" In *Public Choice and Constitutional Economics*, edited by James Gwartney and Richard Wagner, 369–86. Greenwich, CT: JAI Press and Cato Institute, 1988.

"Black Progress and the Persistence of Racial Economic Inequalities, 1865– 1940." In *The Question of Discrimination: Racial Inequality in the U.S. Labor Market*, edited by Steven Shulman and William Darity Jr., 9–31. Middletown, CT: Wesleyan University Press, 1989.

"Introduction: Fifty Years of Arms, Politics, and the Economy." In *Arms, Politics, and the Economy: Historical and Contemporary Perspectives*, edited by Robert Higgs, xv–xxxii. New York: Holmes and Meier, 1990.

"How Military Mobilization Hurts the Economy." In *Second Thoughts: Myths and Morals of U.S. Economic History*, edited by Donald N. McCloskey, 34–41. New York: Oxford University Press, 1993.

"Private Profit, Public Risk: Institutional Antecedents of the Modern Military Procurement System in the Rearmament Program of 1940–1941." In *The Sinews of War: Essays on the Economic History of World War II*, edited by Geofrey T. Mills and Hugh Rockoff, 166–98. Ames: Iowa State University Press, 1993.

"In a National Emergency, Government Must Control the Economy," and "For Safety's Sake, Government Must Regulate the Markets for Medical Products." In *Clichés of Politics*, edited by Mark Spangler, 75–79, 206–9. Irvington-on-Hudson, NY: Foundation for Economic Education, 1994.

"Introduction," "FDA Regulation of Medical Devices," and "Diminishing the Harm." In *Hazardous to Our Health? FDA Regulation of Health Care Products*, edited by Robert Higgs, 1–11, 55–96, and 97–101. Oakland, CA: Independent Institute, 1995.

[With Robert A. Margo] "Black Americans: Income and Standard of Living from the Days of Slavery to the Present." In *The State of Humanity*, edited by Julian L. Simon, 178–84. Oxford: Blackwell, 1995.

"War and Leviathan in Twentieth-Century America: Conscription as the Keystone." In *The Costs of War: America's Pyrrhic Victories*, edited by John V. Denson, 309–22. New Brunswick, NJ: Transaction, 1997.

[With Carl P. Close] "Introduction." In *Re-Thinking Green: Alternatives to Environmental Bureaucracy*, edited by Robert Higgs and Carl Close, 1–20. Oakland, CA: Independent Institute, 2005.

[With Carl Close] "Introduction." In *The Challenge of Liberty: Classical Liberalism Today*, edited by Robert Higgs and Carl Close, ix–xxiii. Oakland, CA: Independent Institute, 2006.

"Banca Libre vs. Responsabilidad Fiscal." [Spanish translation of a conference address delivered in English.] In *100 años de Dolarización, o un siglo sin Banca Central: El caso de Panamá*, 75–81. Panamá: Fundación Libertad, 2006.

"The World Wars." In Price V. Fishback and [15] others, *The Government and the American Economy: A New History*, 431–55. Chicago: University of Chicago Press, 2007.

[With Carl Close] "Introduction." In *Opposing the Crusader State: Alternatives to Global Interventionism*, edited by Robert Higgs and Carl Close, ix–xxv. Oakland, CA: Independent Institute, 2007.

"Government Growth." In *The Concise Encyclopedia of Economics*, 2nd ed., edited by David R. Henderson, 227–30. Indianapolis: Liberty Fund, 2008.

"Peace and Pacifism" and "War." In *The Encyclopedia of Libertarianism*, edited by Ronald Hamowy, 373–76 and 529–31. Thousand Oaks, CA: Sage, 2008.

"Foreword. In Arthur A. Ekirch Jr., *The Decline of American Liberalism*, reprint ed.; xv–xix. Oakland, CA: Independent Institute, 2009.

"Democracy and *Faits Accomplis*." In *Property, Freedom, and Society: Essays in Honor of Hans-Hermann Hoppe*, edited by Jörg Guido Hülsmann and Stephan Kinsella, 249–62. Auburn, AL: Ludwig von Mises Institute, 2009.

"Foreword." In Ralph Raico, *Great Wars and Great Leaders: A Libertarian Rebuttal*, iii–v. Auburn, AL: Ludwig von Mises Institute, 2010.

"War Is Horrible, but . . ." In *Why Peace*, edited by Marc Guttman, 288–98. East Lyme, CT: Marx Guttman, 2012.

"The Economics of the Great Society: Theories, Policies, and Consequences." In *The Great Society*, edited by Gary Wolfram, 27–42. Hillsdale, MI: Hillsdale College Press, 2012.

"World War II." In *Routledge Handbook of Major Events in Economic History*, edited by Randall E. Parker and Robert Whaples, 191–200. New York: Routledge, 2013.

"Crisis without Leviathan?" In *Economic and Political Change after Crisis: Prospects for Government, Liberty, and the Rule of Law*, edited by Stephen H. Balch and Benjamin Powell, 13–35. London: Routledge, 2019.

BOOK REVIEWS, REVIEW ARTICLES, BOOK NOTES, AND RELATED LETTERS

[With R. M. Hartwell] "Good Old Economic History." [A review article on *The Unbound Prometheus*, by David S. Landes.] *American Historical Review* 76 (April 1971): 467–74.

[With R. M. Hartwell] Letter to the Editor. *American Historical Review* 77 (February 1972): 237–39.

Review of *Economic History and the Social Sciences: Problems of Methodology*, by Elias H. Tuma. *Economic History Review* 25 (August 1972): 535–37.

Review of *Science, Technology, and Economic Growth in the Eighteenth Century*. Edited with an introduction by A. E. Musson. *Economic History Review* 25 (August 1972): 518–20.

Review of *The Study of Economic History: Collected Inaugural Lectures, 1893–1970*. Edited with an introduction by N. B. Harte. *Economic History Review* 25 (August 1972): 508–9.

Review of *Railroads and the Granger Laws*, by George H. Miller. *Agricultural History* 46 (October 1972): 522–23.

Letter to the Editor. *Business History Review* 47 (Summer 1973): 278.

Review of *The Dimensions of Quantitative Research in History*. Edited with an introduction by William O. Aydelotte, Allan G. Bogue, and Robert W. Fogel. *Business History Review* 47 (Autumn 1973): 375–76.

Review of *The Populist Context: Rural versus Urban Power on a Great Plains Frontier*, by Stanley B. Parsons. *Agricultural History* 48 (January 1974): 231–32.

Review of *Black Business in the New South: A Social History of the North Carolina Mutual Life Insurance Company*, by Walter B. Weare. *American Historical Review* 79 (February 1974): 240.

Review of *Late Nineteenth-Century American Development: A General Equilibrium History*, by Jeffrey G. Williamson. *Agricultural History* 49 (October 1975): 690–92.

Review of *The American Economy between the World Wars*, by Jim Potter. *American Historical Review* 81 (June 1976): 685–86.

Review of *Survey of Afro-American Experience in the U.S. Economy*, by Martin O. Ijere. *Agricultural History* 53 (January 1979): 418.

Review of *The Political Economy of the Cotton South: Households, Markets, and Wealth in the Nineteenth Century*, by Gavin Wright. *Journal of American History* 66 (June 1979): 153.

Review of *Agriculture in the Postbellum South: The Economics of Production and Supply*, by Stephen J. DeCanio. *Journal of Economic History* 39 (June 1979): 588–89.

Review of *The Economic History of World Population*, by Carlo M. Cipolla. *Southern Economic Journal* 46 (October 1979): 664–65.

Review of *Farmers without Farms: Agricultural Tenancy in 19th-Century Iowa*, by Donald L. Winters. *American Historical Review* 84 (October 1979): 1169.

Review of *Wealth and Poverty*, by George Gilder. *Journal of Economic History* 41 (December 1981): 957–59.

Review of *Affluence, Altruism, and Atrophy: The Decline of Welfare States*, by Morris Silver. *Journal of Economic History* 41 (December 1981): 957–59.

Review of *The Harder We Run: Black Workers since the Civil War*, by William H. Harris. *Journal of Economic History* 42 (June 1982): 475–76.

Review of *The United States and the Problem of Recovery after 1893*, by Gerald T. White. *Agricultural History* 56 (July 1982): 603–4.

Review of *Market Institutions and Economic Progress in the New South, 1865–1900*. Edited by Gary M. Walton and James F. Shepherd. *Journal of Economic History* 43 (December 1982): 957–58.

Review of *Good and Faithful Labor: From Slavery to Sharecropping in the Natchez District, 1860–1890*, by Ronald L. F. Davis. *Journal of American History* 69 (March 1983): 986–87.

Letter to the Editor. *Journal of American History* 70 (December 1983): 750–51.

"When Ideological Worlds Collide: Reflections on Kraditor's *Radical Persuasion*." [A review article on *The Radical Persuasion, 1890–1917: Aspects of the Intellectual History and the Historiography of Three American Radical Organizations*, by Aileen S. Kraditor.] *Continuity: A Journal of History* (Fall 1983): 99–112.

"Capitalism and the Environment." [A letter to the editor.] *New York Times Book Review* (June 17, 1984): 31.

Review of *Branches without Roots: Genesis of the Black Working Class in the American South, 1862–1882*, by Gerald David Jaynes. *Journal of Economic History* 46 (September 1986): 866–68.

Review of *The Control Revolution: Technological and Economic Origins of the Information Society*, by James R. Beniger. *Journal of Economic History* 47 (March 1987): 281–82.

"The Rise of Big Business in America." [A review article on *Entrepreneurs vs. The State: A New Look at the Rise of Big Business in America, 1840–1920,* by Burton W. Folsom Jr.] *The World & I,* 3 (March 1988): 404–9.

"The Good War's Bad Legacy." [A review of *Washington Goes to War,* by David Brinkley.] *Reason* 20 (November 1988): 50–52.

Review of *Balanced Budgets and American Politics,* by James D. Savage. *Journal of Economic History* 48 (December 1988): 965–66.

"*Crisis and Leviathan:* Higgs Response to Reviewers." *Continuity: A Journal of History* (Spring/Fall 1989): 92–105.

Review of *Markets in History: Economic Studies of the Past.* Edited by David W. Galenson. *Business History Review* 64 (Spring 1990): 187–89.

"Of Smokestacks and Rhinos." [A review of *Economics and the Environment: A Reconciliation,* edited by Walter Block.] *Liberty* 3 (May 1990): 57–59.

Review of *Taxation by Political Inertia: Financing the Growth of Government in Britain,* by Richard Rose and Terence Karran. *Public Choice* 65 (June 1990): 298–99.

"Rational Man and All the Rest." [A review article on *Nuts and Bolts for the Social Sciences,* by Jon Elster.] *Liberty* 4 (November 1990): 73–76.

Review of *Miles of Smiles, Years of Struggle: Stories of Black Pullman Porters,* by Jack Santino. *Labor History* 32 (Winter 1991): 151–52.

Review of *The Machinery of Freedom: Guide to a Radical Capitalism,* 2nd ed., by David Friedman. *Public Choice* 69, 1 (February 1991): 115–16.

Review of *Economic Analysis of Property Rights,* by Yoram Barzel. *Journal of Economic Literature* 29 (March 1991): 88–90.

Review of *The Capacity to Budget,* by Allen Schick. *Journal of Economic History* 51 (June 1991): 523–24.

"Leviathan at Bay?" [A review article on *Quicksilver Capital: How the Rapid Movement of Wealth Has Changed the World,* by Richard B. McKenzie and Dwight R. Lee.] *Liberty* 5 (November 1991): 64–70.

"Origins of the Corporate Liberal State." [A review article on *The Corporate Reconstruction of American Capitalism, 1890–1916: The Market, the Law, and Politics,* by Martin J. Sklar.] *Critical Review* 5 (Fall 1991): 475–95.

Review of *Historical Economics: Art or Science?*, by Charles P. Kindleberger. *Journal of Interdisciplinary History* 23 (1992): 138–39.

Review of *Race and Schooling in the South, 1880–1950: An Economic History*, by Robert A. Margo. *Journal of Economic Literature* 30 (March 1992): 220–21.

Review of *The United States as a Developing Country: Studies in U.S. History in the Progressive Era and the 1920s*, by Martin J. Sklar. *Journal of Economic History* 53 (March 1993): 194–95.

"Know Thy Enemy." [A book note on *The Foundations of Economic Analysis*, by Paul A. Samuelson.] *Reason* 25 (December 1993): 38.

Review of *I Dissent: The Legacy of Chief Justice James Clark McReynolds*, by James E. Bond. *Pacific Northwest Quarterly* 85 (January 1994): 45.

"Stifled Words Can Kill You." [A book note on *Bad Prescription for the First Amendment*, edited by Richard T. Kaplar.] *Liberty* 7 (May 1994): 64.

"An Economist, Among Other Things." [A book note on *Opening Doors: The Life and Work of Joseph Schumpeter*, by Robert Loring Allen.] *Liberty* 7 (May 1994): 65–66.

"Let's Hear It for Democracy." [A book note on *A Democracy at War: America's Fight at Home and Abroad in World War II*, by William L. O'Neill.] *Liberty* 7 (May 1994): 63–64.

"An FDA Fable." [A review of *The FDA Follies*, by Herbert Burkholz.] *Reason* 26 (October 1994): 70–73.

"Renaissance Economist." [A book note on *Knowledge and Persuasion in Economics*, by Donald N. McCloskey.] *Liberty* 8 (January 1995): 65.

"Mr. Higgs Replies (to a Comment on My Review of Burkholz)." *Reason* 26 (February 1995): 9–10.

Review of *The Economic Foundations of Government*, by Randall G. Holcombe. *Public Choice* 83 (April 1995): 195–97.

Review of *Economic without Time: A Science Blind to the Forces of Historical Change*, by Graeme Donald Snooks. *Southern Economic Journal* 61 (April 1995): 1240–41.

"Coercion Is Not a Societal Constant: Reply to Samuels." *Critical Review* 9 (Summer 1995): 431–36.

Review of *Leviathan at War*, ed. Edmund A. Opitz. *The Freeman* 45 (December 1995): 792–94.

Review of *The State as a Monster: Gustav Cassel and Eli Heckscher on the Role and Growth of the State*, by Benny Carlson. *Journal of the History of Economic Thought* 17 (1995): 338–40.

Review of *Social Policy in the United States: Future Possibilities in Historical Perspective*, by Theda Skocpol. *Journal of Economic History* 56 (March 1996): 270–71.

"The Bloody Hinge of American History." [A review article on *Emancipating Slaves, Enslaving Free Men: A History of the American Civil War*, by Jeffrey Rogers Hummel.] *Liberty* 10 (May 1997): 51–57.

Review of *The American Century: The Rise and Decline of the United States as a World Power*, by Donald W. White. *Journal of Economic History* 57 (December 1997): 970–72.

Review of *The Road from Serfdom: The Economic and Political Consequences of the End of Communism*, by Robert Skidelsky. *Journal of Economic History* 58 (March 1998): 293–95.

Review of *Socialism and War: Essays, Documents, Reviews. Collected Works of F. A. Hayek, Vol. 10*, edited by Bruce Caldwell. *Quarterly Journal of Austrian Economics* 1 (Spring 1998): 81–84.

Review of *The Rise of Big Government in the United States*, by John F. Walker and Harold G. Vatter. *Journal of Economic History* 58 (September 1998): 902–3.

Review of *Beating Plowshares into Swords: The Political Economy of American Warfare, 1606–1865*, by Paul A. C. Koistinen. *Business History Review* 72 (Winter 1998): 627–29.

Review of *From Wealth to Power: The Unusual Origins of America's World Role*, by Fareed Zakaria. *The Freeman* 49 (April 1999): 57–58.

Review of *Planning War, Pursuing Peace: The Political Economy of American Warfare, 1920–1939*, by Paul A. C. Koistinen. *Journal of Economic History* 59 (September 1999): 845–46.

Review of *In Restraint of Trade: The Business Campaign against Competition, 1918–1938*, by Butler D. Shaffer. *Quarterly Journal of Austrian Economics* 3 (Winter 2000): 91–94.

"Sherman and the Ethics of War." [A letter to the editor.] *New York Times Book Review*, August 19, 2001, 4.

Review of *Power and Prosperity: Outgrowing Communist and Capitalist Dictatorships*, by Mancur Olson. *Review of Austrian Economics* 14 (December 2001): 355–62.

Review of *The Future of U.S. Capitalism*, by Frederic L. Pryor. Economic History Services (online), October 24, 2002, http://www.eh.net/bookreviews/library/0554.shtml.

Review of *Is War Necessary for Economic Growth? Military Procurement and Technology Development*, by Vernon W. Ruttan. Economic History Services (online), June 21, 2006.

Review of *The Pearl Harbor Myth: Rethinking the Unthinkable*, by George Victor. *The Freeman* 58 (May 2008): 43–44.

"An Economic Analysis of National Reconstruction at Gunpoint: Review Essay on *After War: The Political Economy of Exporting Democracy*, by Christopher J. Coyne (Stanford University Press, 2007)." *Review of Austrian Economics* 21, no. 4 (2008): 341–47.

Review of *Churchill, Hitler, and "The Unnecessary War": How Britain Lost Its Empire and the West Lost the World*, by Patrick J. Buchanan. *The Freeman* 59 (July/August 2009): 42–43.

Review of *New Deal or Raw Deal? How FDR's Economic Legacy Has Damaged America*, by Burton Folsom Jr. *The Freeman* 59 (September 2009): 50–51.

"Derek Leebaert's 'Magic and Mayhem,'" *The Beacon*, March 6, 2011.

"Sheldon Pollacks's Interpretation of War, Taxation, and the U.S. State." [A review essay on *War, Revenue, and State Building: Financing the Development of the American State*, by Sheldon D. Pollack.] *Journal of Policy History* 23 (2011): 267–72.

Review of *Unwarranted Influence: Dwight D. Eisenhower and the Military-Industrial Complex*, by James Ledbetter. *Journal of Cold War Studies* 14 (Spring 2012): 181–83.

Review of *FDR Goes to War: How Expanded Executive Power, Spiraling National Debt, and Restricted Civil Liberties Shaped Wartime America*, by Burton W. Folsom Jr., and Anita Folsom. *The Freeman* (October 2012): 42–43.

"State-Led Humanitarian Aid: Another Case of 'Government Failure.'"
[A review of Christopher J. Coyne, *Doing Bad by Doing Good:
Why Humanitarian Action Fails.*] *Review of Austrian Economics* 26
(December 2013): 493–96.

Review of *Interpreting American History: The New Deal and the Great
Depression.* Edited by Aaron D. Purcell. *History: Reviews of New Books* 44,
2 (April 2016): 43.

ARTICLES IN *THE INDEPENDENT REVIEW*

"Editor's Welcome" and "Etceteras." *Independent Review* 1 (Spring 1996): 5–7
and 151.

"Etceteras." *Independent Review* 1 (Fall 1996): 309–10.

"Etceteras: Public Choice and Political Leadership." *Independent Review* 1
(Winter 1997): 465–67.

"Regime Uncertainty: Why the Great Depression Lasted So Long and Why
Prosperity Resumed after the War." *Independent Review* 1 (Spring 1997):
561–90.

"Etceteras: Fifty Years of the Mont Pèlerin Society." *Independent Review* 1
(Spring 1997): 623–25.

"Etceteras: Bolingbroke, Nixon, and the Rest of Them." *Independent Review* 2
(Summer 1997): 155–58.

"Etceteras: Death and Taxes." *Independent Review* 2 (Fall 1997): 325–28.

"Etceteras: Puritanism, Paternalism, and Power." *Independent Review* 2 (Winter
1998): 469–44.

"Etceteras: A Tale of Two Labor Markets." *Independent Review* 2 (Spring 1998):
625–30.

"Etceteras: Official Economic Statistics: The Emperor's Clothes Are Dirty."
Independent Review 3 (Summer 1998): 147–53.

"Etceteras: What Professor Stiglitz Learned in Washington." *Independent Review*
3 (Fall 1998): 301–2.

"A Carnival of Taxation." *Independent Review* 3 (Winter 1999): 433–38.

"Etceteras: We're All Sick, and Government Must Heal Us." *Independent Review* 3 (Spring 1999): 623–27.

"Etceteras: Escaping Leviathan?" *Independent Review* 4 (Summer 1999): 153–58.

"Etceteras: Lock 'em Up!" *Independent Review* 4 (Fall 1999): 309–13.

"Etceteras: Regulatory Harmonization: A Sweet-Sounding, Dangerous Development." *Independent Review* 4 (Winter 2000): 467–74.

"Etceteras: The So-called Third Way." *Independent Review* 4 (Spring 2000): 625–30.

"Etceteras: Results of a Fifty-Year Experiment in Political Economy." *Independent Review* 5 (Summer 2000): 153.

"In Memoriam: Paul Heyne, 1931–2000." *Independent Review* 5 (Summer 2000): 155–56 [see correction in *Independent Review* 5 (Fall 2000): 315].

"Etceteras: Unmitigated Mercantilism." *Independent Review* 5 (Winter 2001): 469–72.

"Etceteras: Results of Another Fifty-Year Experiment in Political Economy." *Independent Review* 5 (Spring 2001): 625.

"Etceteras: The Cold War Is Over, but U.S. Preparation for It Continues." *Independent Review* 6 (Fall 2001): 287–305.

"Etceteras: Pity the Poor Japanese." *Independent Review* 7 (Summer 2002): 149–51.

"Etceteras: Government Protects Us?" *Independent Review* 7 (Fall 2002): 309–13.

"Etceteras: Lies, Damn Lies, and Conventional Measures of the Growth of Government." *Independent Review* 9 (Summer 2004): 147–53.

"Etceteras: Benefits and Costs of the U.S. Government's War Making." *Independent Review* 9 (Spring 2005): 623–27.

"Etceteras: 'Not Merely Perfidious but Ungrateful': The U.S. Takeover of West Florida." *Independent Review* 10 (Fall 2005): 303–10.

"Etceteras: Fear: The Foundation of Every Government's Power." *Independent Review* 10 (Winter 2006): 447–66.

"Etceteras: On 'Winning the War.'" *Independent Review* 11 (Summer 2006): 155–60.

"Etceteras: Results of Still Another Fifty-Year Experiment in Political Economy." *Independent Review* 12 (Summer 2007): 151–52.

"Etceteras: Military-Economic Fascism: How Business Corrupts Government and Vice Versa." *Independent Review* 12 (Fall 2007): 299–316.

"Etceteras: Military Spending / Gross Domestic Product = Nonsense for Budget Policy Making." *Independent Review* 13 (Summer 2008): 147–49.

"Etceteras: Caging the Dogs of War: How Major U.S. Neoimperialistic Wars End." *Independent Review* 13 (Fall 2008): 299–312.

"Etceteras: Who Was Edward M. House?" *Independent Review* 13 (Winter 2009): 455–62.

"Etceteras: A Revealing Window on the U.S. Economy in Depression and War: Hours Worked, 1929–1950." *Independent Review* 14 (Summer 2009): 151–60.

"Etceteras: Recession and Recovery: Six Fundamental Errors of the Current Orthodoxy." *Independent Review* 14 (Winter 2010): 465–72.

"Etceteras: The Dangers of Samuelson's Economic Method." *Independent Review* 15 (Winter 2011): 471–76.

"Etceteras: To Fight or Not to Fight: War's Payoffs to U.S. Leaders and to the American People." *Independent Review* 16 (Summer 2011): 141–50.

"Etceteras: Are Questions of War and Peace Merely One Issue among Many for Libertarians?" *Independent Review* 16 (Fall 2011): 307–12.

"Etceteras: War Is Horrible, but . . ." *Independent Review* 17 (Fall 2012): 305–16.

"Etceteras: Truth and Freedom in Economic Analysis and Economic Policy Making." *Independent Review* 17 (Winter 2013): 467–72.

"Etceteras: Real Gross Domestic Private Product, 2000–2012." *Independent Review* 18 (Summer 2013): 157–60.

"Etceteras: The Sluggish Recovery of Real Net Domestic Private Business Investment." *Independent Review* 18 (Fall 2013): 313–15.

"Etceteras: Worrisome Changes in U.S. Labor Force and Employment since 2007." *Independent Review* 18 (Winter 2014): 471–77.

"Etceteras: The Salmon Trap: An Analogy for People's Entrapment by the State." *Independent Review* 18 (Spring 2014): 625–27.

"Etceteras: The Fed's Immiseration of People Who Live on Interest Earnings." *Independent Review* 19 (Summer 2014): 151–55.

"Etceteras: Ronald Coase, Anomalous Superstar of the Economics Profession." *Independent Review* 19 (Fall 2014): 309–12.

"Etceteras: Tolstoy's Manifesto on the State, Christian Anarchy, and Pacifism." *Independent Review* 19 (Winter 2015): 471–79.

[With Elizabeth Bernard Higgs] "Etceteras: Compassion—a Critical Factor for Attaining and Maintaining a Free Society." *Independent Review* 19 (Spring 2015): 627–30.

"Etceteras: Gross Domestic Product—an Index of Economic Welfare or a Meaningless Metric?" *Independent Review* 20 (Summer 2015): 153–57.

"Etceteras: How Big Is Government in the United States?" *Independent Review* 20 (Fall 2015): 317–19.

"Etceteras: Ludwig von Mises and Dietrich von Hildebrand: Some Remarkable Parallels." *Independent Review* 20 (Winter 2016): 473–76.

"Etceteras: Douglass C. North: Trailblazer." *Independent Review* 21 (Summer 2016): 139–42.

"Etceteras: Can the State Enforce Virtuous Behavior?" *Independent Review* 21 (Fall 2016): 311–13.

"Etceteras: First, Do No Harm." *Independent Review* 21 (Winter 3017): 477–78.

"Etceteras: Moderation in Response to Provocation Is No Vice." *Independent Review* 22 (Summer 2017): 159–60.

"Etceteras: Freedom of Movement—the Sine Qua Non of Economic Prosperity and Progress." *Independent Review* 22 (Fall 2017): 317–20.

"Etceteras: Principal-Agent Theory and Representative Government." *Independent Review* 22 (Winter 2018): 479–80.

"Etceteras: Ideology and Political Divisiveness." *Independent Review* 22 (Spring 2018): 638–40.

"Etceteras: Feedback and Correction in Government and the Market." *Independent Review* 23 (Summer 2018): 157–59.

"Etceteras: Against the Whole Concept and Construction of the Balance of International Payments." *Independent Review* 23 (Fall 2018): 319–20.

"Etceteras: Two Worlds: Politics and Everything Else." *Independent Review* 23 (Winter 2019): 477–79.

"Etceteras: Pressure-Release Valves in Participatory Fascism." *Independent Review* 24 (Fall 2019): 319–20.

About the Contributors

Donald J. Boudreaux, professor of economics, George Mason University; senior fellow, F. A. Hayek Program for Advanced Study in Philosophy, Politics, and Economics, Mercatus Center at George Mason University

Spencer D. Brown, alumnus, Trinity College

Sarah Burns, associate professor of political science, Rochester Institute of Technology

Laurie Calhoun, senior fellow, Libertarian Institute, and research fellow, Independent Institute

Art Carden, professor of economics, Samford University

Christopher J. Coyne, professor of economics, George Mason University; associate director, F. A. Hayek Program for Advanced Study in Philosophy, Politics, and Economics, Mercatus Center at George Mason University

Thomas K. Duncan, associate professor of economics, Radford University

Tate Fegley, assistant professor and chair of business and economics, Montreat College

Vincent Geloso, assistant professor of economics, George Mason University

Nathan P. Goodman, senior fellow, F. A. Hayek Program for Advanced Study in Philosophy, Politics, and Economics, Mercatus Center at George Mason University

Anthony Gregory, Hoover Fellow, Hoover Institution on War, Revolution, and Peace at Stanford University

Abigail R. Hall, associate professor of economics, University of Tampa

Jayme S. Lemke, senior fellow, F. A. Hayek Program for Advanced Study in Philosophy, Politics, and Economics, Mercatus Center at George Mason University

Raymond J. March, assistant professor of economics, Angleo State University, Free Market Institute

Jonathan Newman, Henry Hazlitt Research Fellow, Mises Institute

Edward P. Stringham, Shelby Cullom Davis Professor of American Business and Economic Enterprise, Trinity College

Robert Whaples, professor of economics, Wake Forest University

Yuliya Yatsyshina, associate program director for Academic & Student Programs at the Mercatus Center at George Mason University

Index

Note: Bold indicates an overarching discussion. An italic *t* after a page number refers to a table and an italic *f* refers to a figure.